Children's Illustrated Thesaurus

How to use this book

The *Children's Illustrated Thesaurus* is easy to use when you want to find a synonym to improve your writing. Synonyms are words that can have the same meaning as other words—see page 6 for more information.

Related words
Words that relate to the entry to expand your vocabulary even further come at the end.

Entry
This is the word you want to find a synonym for.

Guideword
The word on the top left shows you the first entry on the page.

>> **ab**andon

Synonym
Alternative words you can use instead of the entry word are shown in **bold**.

Definition
What the word means.

Example sentence
Helping you find the right word by putting it in context.

abandon 1
verb to leave someone or something » *The child abandoned its toy.*
desert, jilt, leave, leave behind, forsake, leave in the lurch

The child abandoned its toy.

abandon 2
noun lack of restraint » *Raj began to laugh with abandon.*
recklessness, wildness
antonym: **control**

abate
verb to become less » *The four-day flood abated and the road became visible.*
decrease, diminish, ebb, lessen, subside, wane

ability
noun the skill needed to do something » *Sheila has the ability to get along with others.*
capability, competence, expertise, skill, talent, aptitude, dexterity, proficiency
antonym: **inability**

able
adjective good at doing something » *Luca proved himself to be an able teacher when all his pupils passed the exam.*
accomplished, capable, efficient, expert, first-rate, skilled, talented, competent, proficient

abolish
verb to get rid of something » *The children wanted to abolish the school's homework policy.*
annul, do away with, overturn, put an end to, quash, rescind, revoke

about 1
preposition relating to or concerning » *Laura was happy about her excellent exam results.*
concerning, on, regarding, relating to

about 2
adverb not exactly » *I think the movie lasts about one hour.*
almost, approximately, around, nearly, roughly

above 1
preposition over or higher than something » *The bird flew above the clouds.*
higher than, over
antonym: **below**
• related words: prefixes **super-, supra-, sur-**

The bird flew above the clouds.

above 2
preposition greater than a certain level or amount » *The number of visitors will rise above the 100 mark.*
beyond, exceeding

abrupt 1
adjective sudden or unexpected » *They were surprised at the teacher's abrupt departure.*
sudden, unexpected, unforeseen, precipitate, unanticipated

abrupt 2
adjective unfriendly and impolite » *He was taken aback by her abrupt manner.*
curt, rude, short, terse, brusque, uncceremonious
antonym: **polite**

absent
adjective not present » *Hugo was absent from school yesterday and missed the mock test.*
away, elsewhere, gone, missing
antonym: **present**

absent-minded
adjective forgetful or not paying attention » *Nora's absent-minded father left the camera under the seat.*
distracted, forgetful, inattentive, out to lunch (informal)

absolute 1
adjective total and complete » *I can't understand him—he is talking absolute nonsense.*
complete, downright, pure, sheer, thorough, total, utter, unmitigated, unqualified

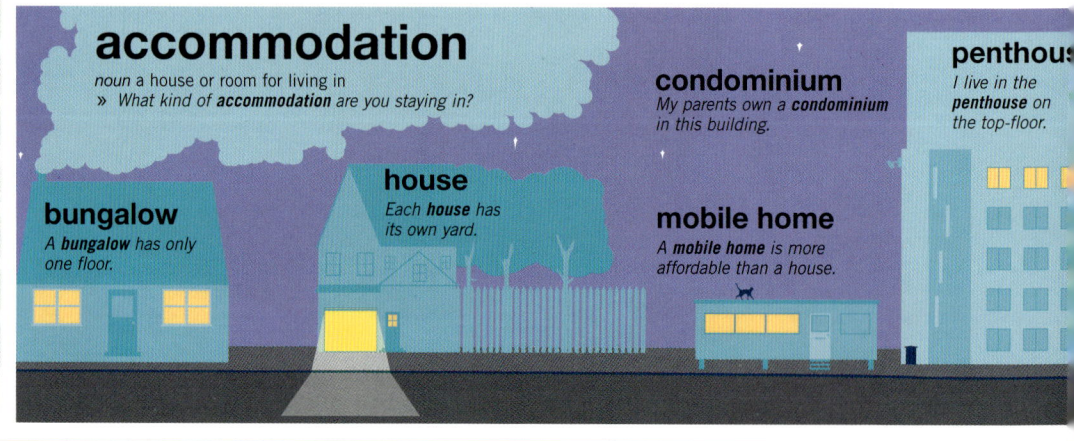

Entry number
If there is more than one sense of the word, each one has a separate entry.

Part of speech
For example, noun, verb, or adjective. See page 7 for more about parts of speech.

More synonyms
Shown in grey, these are slightly more complicated or advanced synonyms.

Shades of
Instead of a definition, colour entries have a list of shades.

yellow
noun or adjective
• Shades of yellow:
amber, canary yellow, citrus yellow, daffodil, gold, lemon, mustard, primrose, saffron, sand, straw, topaz

Guideword
The word on the top right shows you the last entry on the page.

accompany »

absolute 2
adjective having total power » Louis XIV of France was an absolute monarch and had complete authority on all state matters.
dictatorial, supreme, tyrannical

absorb
verb to soak up or take in something » A sponge can absorb a lot of water.
digest, soak up, take in

abstain
verb to choose not to do something » Vegetarians abstain from eating meat.
avoid, deny yourself, forgo, give up, refrain, desist, forbear, renounce

absurd
adjective ridiculous or nonsensical » The movie's plot was absurd; I couldn't make sense of it.
crazy (informal), illogical, ludicrous, nonsensical, ridiculous, incongruous, preposterous

abundance
noun a great amount of something » There is an abundance of wildlife in the rainforest.
affluence, bounty, plenty, cornucopia, plethora
antonym: shortage

There was an **abundant** supply of cakes at the party.

abundant
adjective present in large quantities » There was an abundant supply of cakes at the party.
ample, copious, full, plentiful
antonym: scarce

abuse 1
noun cruel treatment of someone » Animal abuse is rightly illegal.
exploitation, harm, hurt, ill-treatment, oppression

abuse 2
noun unkind remarks directed towards someone » The cyclist shouted abuse at the man driving dangerously.
censure, derision, insults, invective

abuse 3
verb to speak insultingly to someone » The fans verbally abused the rival hockey team.
curse, insult, scold

abusive
adjective rude and unkind » Don't use abusive language when speaking to people, because it will offend them.
disparaging, insulting, offensive, rude, scathing, censorious, vituperative

abyss
noun a very deep hole » He peered over the edge of the abyss.
chasm, fissure, gorge, pit, void

He peered over the edge of the **abyss**.

accelerate
verb to go faster » The car accelerated to reach the higher speed limit.
hurry, quicken, speed up
antonym: decelerate

accept
verb to receive or agree to something » Lucas accepted the party invitation.
acknowledge, agree to, concur with, consent to, take
antonym: refuse

acceptable
adjective good enough to be accepted » His messy handwriting was not acceptable.
adequate, all right, fair, good enough, passable, satisfactory, tolerable

accidental
adjective happening by chance » The fire was accidental.
casual, chance, inadvertent, random
antonym: deliberate

accommodate
verb to provide someone with a place to stay » A hotel was built to accommodate guests for weddings.
house, put up, shelter

accommodating
adjective willing to help » The waiter was very accommodating and found us a new table.
considerate, helpful, hospitable, kind, obliging

accommodation
noun a house or room for living in
▼ SEE BELOW

accompany 1
verb to go somewhere with someone » Children must be accompanied by an adult.
conduct (formal), escort, go with, usher

Alphabet bars
The highlighted letter shows you which section you're in.

Antonym
A word that means the opposite to the entry.

▼, ▲, ◀◀, ▶▶
See below/above/ left/right: Look at the big illustration for this entry.

Usage
Shows when and how some synonyms are used.

Example sentence
These show each synonym in a sentence.

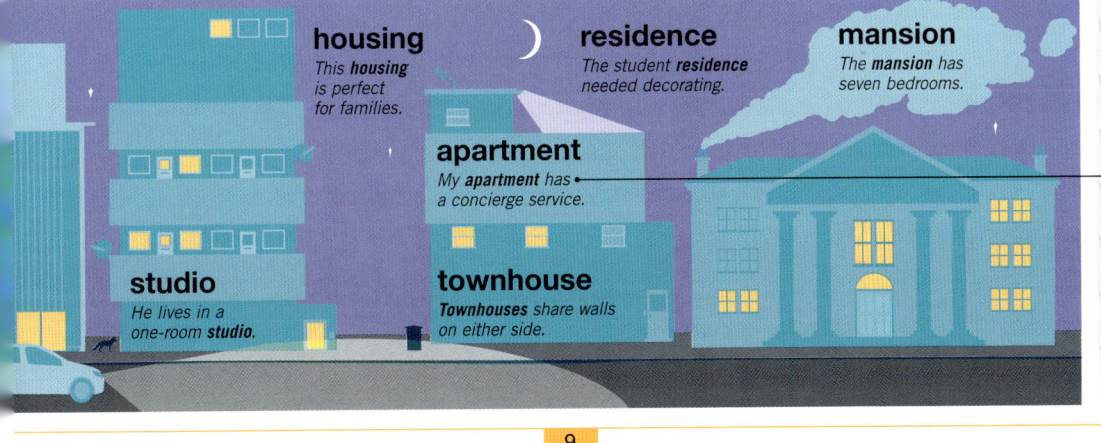

housing This **housing** is perfect for families.

residence The student **residence** needed decorating.

mansion The **mansion** has seven bedrooms.

apartment My **apartment** has a concierge service.

studio He lives in a one-room **studio**.

townhouse **Townhouses** share walls on either side.

9

5

Why use a thesaurus?

The main reason for using a thesaurus is to find synonyms, or alternative words, to help you with your writing. In addition, this thesaurus will identify what kind of word (part of speech) it is and provide helpful definitions and examples. It will also give antonyms, or words that mean the opposite to the one you look up, wherever possible.

What is a synonym?

A synonym is a word that means the same—or almost the same—as another word: for example, "little" and "small." Most of the time, there is no such thing as a true synonym. If two words mean exactly the same thing, then why bother having both? Rather, a synonym can or could mean the same thing as another word depending on how you use it. Usually, however, synonyms have little differences in meaning that make one word more suitable to use than another. For example, "little girl" usually means a young girl, but a "small girl" suggests she is not big in size.

*This puppy could be described as **little** or **small**.*

*The **little** girl is the young girl on the right.*

*The **small** girl is the short girl on the left.*

Improve your vocabulary

Synonyms can help you improve your writing by using more interesting words. For example, instead of putting "she said" in a story, using "she shouted" can tell the reader that she might be angry or in a noisy room. It is also much more interesting to use and read a variety of words than writing "she said" all the time!

What is an antonym?

An antonym is a word that means the opposite of another word: for example, "big" is an antonym of "small."

*A **small** frog*

*A **big** elephant*

Parts of speech

To help you find the right entry in the thesaurus, it can help to know the type of word (or "part of speech") you're looking up. Some words can be used in different ways, such as "bend"—this can be a verb (to bend over) or a noun (a bend in the river). Here are the main parts of speech and how they fit together.

Grace **bent** over to pick a flower.

The river has many **bends**.

Noun
An object, person, or place. A noun doesn't have to be a visible thing—"fact" and "history" are also nouns. Things with a name (such as a country or a person) are known as proper nouns.

Adjective
A describing word, such as green, big, or old. Adjectives are used to describe nouns.

The fairground has **bright** lights and fun rides.

Alicia wrinkled her nose when she tasted the **bitter** lemon.

Verb
An action (or "doing word"). These include any sort of action—such as run, breathe, and sleep—and also "helping" verbs, which may be used with other verbs to show how possible or necessary an action is. These include: have, will, be, must, may, and do. For example, he must run to catch the bus; she will come to the party.

John **ran** to catch the bus.

Adverb
A word that gives more information about a verb, adjective, or another adverb. These often end in "ly," such as quietly and helpfully, but don't have to—today, very, and forwards are all adverbs.

Pat arrived at **exactly** 5 o'clock.

The dog leaped **high** in the air.

Preposition
A word that shows how one noun (person or thing) relates to another, such as "in," "with," and "in spite of."

Interjection
A word that can be used on its own without a full sentence, such as "ouch" and "hello."

Sentence formation
This is how the parts of speech fit together in a sentence.

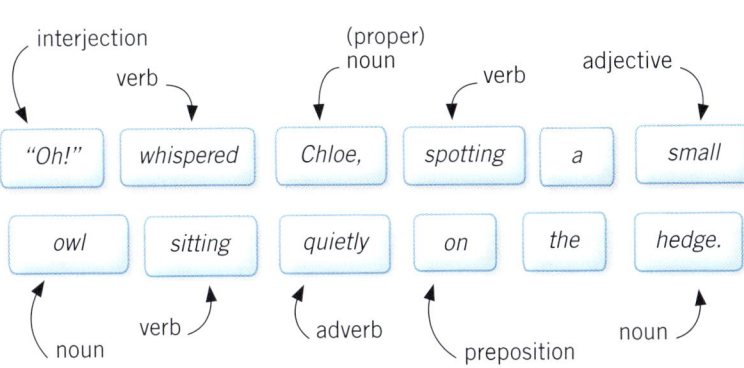

» abandon

abandon [1]
verb to leave someone or something » *The child abandoned its toy.*
desert, jilt, leave, leave behind, forsake, leave in the lurch

*The child **abandoned** its toy.*

abandon [2]
noun lack of restraint » *Raj began to laugh with abandon.*
recklessness, wildness
antonym: control

abate
verb to become less » *The four-day flood abated and the road became visible.*
decrease, diminish, ebb, lessen, subside, wane

ability
noun the skill needed to do something » *Sheila has the ability to get along with others.*
capability, competence, expertise, skill, talent, aptitude, dexterity, proficiency
antonym: inability

able
adjective good at doing something » *Luca proved himself to be an able teacher when all his pupils passed the exam.*
accomplished, capable, efficient, expert, first-rate, skilled, talented, competent, proficient

abolish
verb to get rid of something » *The children wanted to abolish the school's homework policy.*
annul, do away with, overturn, put an end to, quash, rescind, revoke

about [1]
preposition relating to or concerning » *Laura was happy about her excellent exam results.*
concerning, on, regarding, relating to

about [2]
adverb not exactly » *I think the movie lasts about one hour.*
almost, approximately, around, nearly, roughly

above [1]
preposition over or higher than something » *The bird flew above the clouds.*
higher than, over
antonym: below
related words: prefixes super-, supra-, sur-

*The bird flew **above** the clouds.*

above [2]
preposition greater than a certain level or amount » *The number of visitors will rise above the 100 mark.*
beyond, exceeding

abrupt [1]
adjective sudden or unexpected » *They were surprised at the teacher's abrupt departure.*
sudden, unexpected, unforeseen, precipitate, unanticipated

abrupt [2]
adjective unfriendly and impolite » *He was taken aback by her abrupt manner.*
curt, rude, short, terse, brusque, uncermonious
antonym: polite

absent
adjective not present » *Hugo was absent from school yesterday and missed the mock test.*
away, elsewhere, gone, missing
antonym: present

absent-minded
adjective forgetful or not paying attention » *Nora's absent-minded father left the camera under the seat.*
distracted, forgetful, inattentive, out to lunch (informal)

absolute [1]
adjective total and complete » *I can't understand him— he is talking absolute nonsense.*
complete, downright, pure, sheer, thorough, total, utter, unmitigated, unqualified

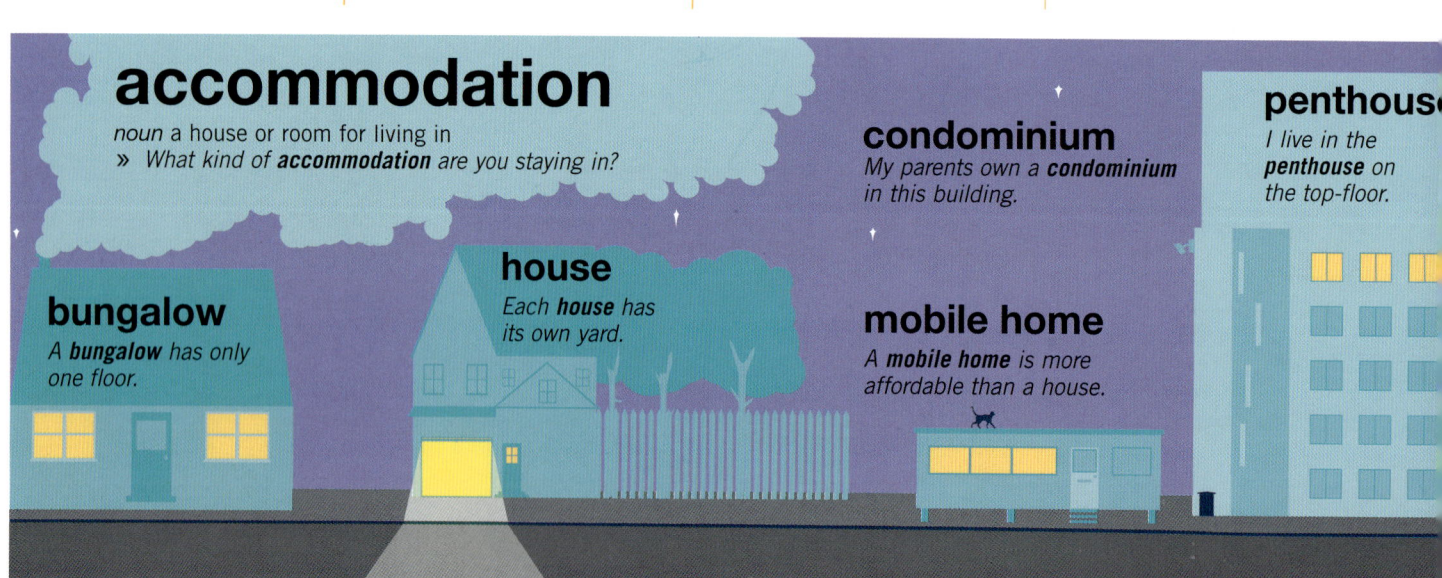

accommodation
noun a house or room for living in » *What kind of **accommodation** are you staying in?*

bungalow — *A **bungalow** has only one floor.*

house — *Each **house** has its own yard.*

condominium — *My parents own a **condominium** in this building.*

mobile home — *A **mobile home** is more affordable than a house.*

penthouse — *I live in the **penthouse** on the top-floor.*

accompany »

absolute [2]
adjective having total power » *Louis XIV of France was an absolute monarch and had complete authority on all state matters.*
dictatorial, supreme, tyrannical

absorb
verb to soak up or take in something » *A sponge can absorb a lot of water.*
digest, soak up, take in

abstain
verb to choose not to do something » *Vegetarians abstain from eating meat.*
avoid, deny yourself, forgo, give up, refrain, desist, forbear, renounce

absurd
adjective ridiculous or nonsensical » *The movie's plot was absurd; I couldn't make sense of it.*
crazy (informal)**, illogical, ludicrous, nonsensical, ridiculous,** incongruous, preposterous

abundance
noun a great amount of something » *There is an abundance of wildlife in the rainforest.*
affluence, bounty, plenty, cornucopia, plethora
antonym: **shortage**

*There was an **abundant** supply of cakes at the party.*

abundant
adjective present in large quantities » *There was an abundant supply of cakes at the party.*
ample, copious, full, plentiful
antonym: **scarce**

abuse [1]
noun cruel treatment of someone » *Animal abuse is rightly illegal.*
exploitation, harm, hurt, ill-treatment, oppression

abuse [2]
noun unkind remarks directed towards someone » *The cyclist shouted abuse at the man driving dangerously.*
censure, derision, insults, invective

abuse [3]
verb to speak insultingly to someone » *The fans verbally abused the rival hockey team.*
curse, insult, scold

abusive
adjective rude and unkind » *Don't use abusive language when speaking to people, because it will offend them.*
disparaging, insulting, offensive, rude, scathing, censorious, vituperative

abyss
noun a very deep hole » *He peered over the edge of the abyss.*
chasm, fissure, gorge, pit, void

*He peered over the edge of the **abyss**.*

accelerate
verb to go faster » *The car accelerated to reach the higher speed limit.*
hurry, quicken, speed up
antonym: **decelerate**

accept
verb to receive or agree to something » *Lucas accepted the party invitation.*
acknowledge, agree to, concur with, consent to, take
antonym: **refuse**

acceptable
adjective good enough to be accepted » *His messy handwriting was not acceptable.*
adequate, all right, fair, good enough, passable, satisfactory, tolerable

accidental
adjective happening by chance » *The fire was accidental.*
casual, chance, inadvertent, random
antonym: **deliberate**

accommodate
verb to provide someone with a place to stay » *A hotel was built to accommodate guests for weddings.*
house, put up, shelter

accommodating
adjective willing to help » *The waiter was very accommodating and found us a new table.*
considerate, helpful, hospitable, kind, obliging

accommodation
noun a house or room for living in
▼ SEE BELOW

accompany [1]
verb to go somewhere with someone » *Children must be accompanied by an adult.*
conduct (formal)**, escort, go with, usher**

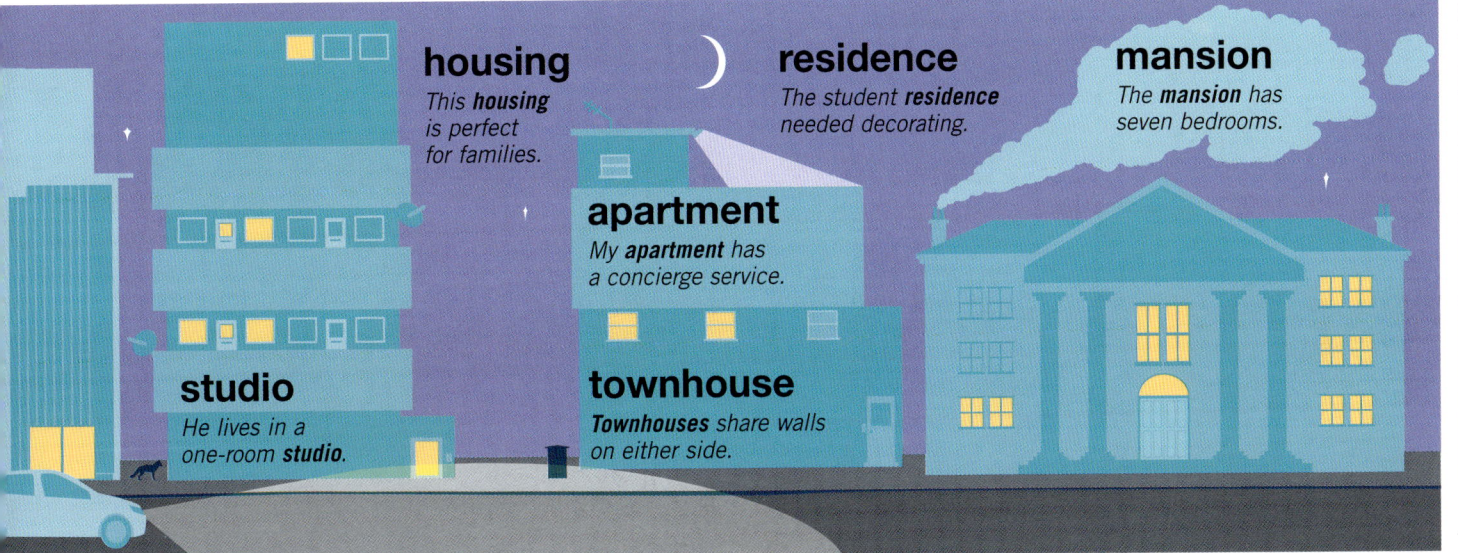

housing
This **housing** is perfect for families.

studio
He lives in a one-room **studio**.

apartment
My **apartment** has a concierge service.

townhouse
Townhouses share walls on either side.

residence
The student **residence** needed decorating.

mansion
The **mansion** has seven bedrooms.

9

» accompany

A B C D E F G H I J K L M N O P Q R S T U V W X Y Z

act
2 verb to perform in a play or movie

Get ready to start **acting!**

I shall **act out** the part of the king!

But I want to **perform** that role!

accompany 2
verb to occur with something » A cold is often accompanied by a cough.
come with, go together with

accomplish
verb to manage to do something » The whole team worked together to accomplish their goal.
achieve, bring about, complete, do, fulfill, manage, effect, execute, realize

accurate
adjective correct to a detailed level » Use a ruler to make the drawing more accurate.
correct, exact, faithful, precise, right, strict, true
antonym: inaccurate

accuse
verb to charge someone with doing something wrong » Jack was accused of losing the office keys again.
blame, censure, charge, cite, denounce, impeach, incriminate, indict

Jack was **accused** of losing the office keys again.

accustomed
adjective used to something » Pupils become accustomed to early morning starts for school.
adapted, familiar, used
antonym: unaccustomed

achieve
verb to gain by hard work or ability » She achieved the highest marks in the competition.
accomplish, carry out, complete, do, fulfill, perform

She **achieved** the highest marks in the competition.

achievement
noun something that someone has succeeded in doing » Finishing a marathon is a huge achievement.
accomplishment, deed, exploit, feat

acquire
verb to get something » I have recently acquired a digital camera.
attain, gain, get, obtain, pick up, procure, secure

act 1
verb to do something » The referee acted correctly in giving a penalty to the player.
function, operate, perform, work

act 2
verb to perform in a play or movie
▲ SEE ABOVE

act 3
noun a single thing someone does » Adopting the stray dog was an act of kindness.
accomplishment, achievement, deed, feat, undertaking

action 1
noun the process of doing something » This letter requires immediate action—please do not ignore it.
activity, operation, process

action 2
noun something that is done » He did not like his actions questioned.
accomplishment, achievement, deed, exploit, feat

active 1
adjective full of energy » Andrea was always so active and fun to be around.
energetic, lively, restless, sprightly, vivacious, dynamic, indefatigable

active 2
adjective busy and hardworking » Parents were very active in the school community.
busy, engaged, enthusiastic, hardworking, industrious, involved, occupied

activity 1
noun a situation in which lots of things are happening » There is an extraordinary amount of activity in the school.
action, bustle, energy, liveliness

activity 2
noun something you do for pleasure » The gym offers sporting activities such as running on the treadmill.
hobby, interest, pastime, pursuit

The gym offers sporting **activities** such as running on the treadmill.

actual
adjective real, rather than imaginary or guessed at » That is the estimate: the actual figure is much higher.
authentic, genuine, realistic, true, verified

advance

*I don't like the way you **play** him.*

*You're too young to **characterize** her well.*

*I'm perfect to **portray** the lady.*

*I'd like to **play the part of** the queen.*

*You're old enough to **personify** her grandmother.*

acute 1
adjective severe or intense
» *He suddenly had an acute pain in his back.*
critical, extreme, grave, great, intense, serious, severe

He suddenly had an **acute** pain in his back.

acute 2
adjective very intelligent
» *She has an acute mind and was always the best at problem-solving.*
alert, astute, bright, keen, perceptive, quick, sharp, shrewd, discriminating, discerning, perspicacious

adapt
verb to alter for a new use
» *The offices were adapted for use as a library.*
adjust, alter, change, convert, modify

add 1
verb to put something with something else » *She added more pages to the book.*
attach, augment, supplement, adjoin, affix, append

add 2
verb to combine numbers or quantities » *Add all the items together to find out how much you have bought.*
add up, count up, total
antonym: **subtract**

Add all the items together to find out how much you have bought.

addition
noun something that has been added to something else
» *The showroom revealed recent additions to their range of cars.*
increase, supplement, addendum, adjunct, appendage

adequate
adjective enough in amount or quality for a purpose
» *Adequate protein is part of a balanced diet.*
acceptable, ample, enough, satisfactory, sufficient
antonym: **insufficient**

administer 1
verb to be responsible for managing something
» *It must be hard work to administer a large company.*
be in charge of, command, control, direct, manage, run, supervise

administer 2
verb to inflict or impose something on someone
» *He administered strict curfews on the boys.*
carry out, deal, dispense, execute, impose, inflict, perform, mete out

admiration
noun a feeling of great liking and respect » *I have always had the greatest admiration for her.*
appreciation, approval, esteem, regard, respect

admire
verb to like and respect someone or something
» *They admired him for his work.*
appreciate, look up to, respect, value, esteem, venerate
antonym: **scorn**

admit 1
verb to agree that something is true » *The driver admitted that he was lost.*
accept, acknowledge, grant
antonym: **deny**

admit 2
verb to allow to enter
» *Pablo was admitted to the university.*
accept, let in, receive, take in
antonym: **exclude**

adult
noun a grown-up person
» *A family ticket covers two adults and three children.*
grown-up, man, woman
antonym: **child**

A family ticket covers two **adults** and three children.

advance 1
verb to move forward or develop » *The forces advanced on the battlefield.*
make inroads, press on, proceed, progress

advance 2
noun progress in something
» *Scientific advances help us explore the Solar System in ever greater detail.*
breakthrough, development, gain, progress, step

11

advantage

advantage
noun a more favourable position or state
» Sara had the advantage of knowing his favourite hiding place.
ascendancy, benefit, dominance, superiority
antonym: disadvantage

advertise
verb to present something to the public in order to sell it » Printed bags are a good way to advertise a store.
plug (informal), promote, publicize, push, blazon, promulgate

advertisement
noun a public announcement to sell or publicize something » Mia placed an advertisement in the local newspaper.
ad (informal), banner ad, commercial, notice, plug (informal)

Mia placed an **advertisement** in the local newspaper.

advice
noun a suggestion as to what to do » Take my advice and don't order the fish pie.
counsel (formal), guidance, opinion, suggestion

advise 1
verb to offer advice to someone » His friend advised him to leave as soon as possible.
caution, counsel, recommend, suggest, urge, commend, prescribe

advise 2
verb to notify someone » I would like to advise you of my decision to change courses.
inform, make known, notify

adviser
noun a person whose job is to give advice » My mother spent the day in meetings with her advisers.
aide, consultant, guru, mentor, tutor

advocate
verb to publicly support a plan or course of action » Tom advocates Mr. Johnson to be the new governor.
back, champion, endorse, favour, promote, recommend, support, uphold

affair
noun an event or series of events » The wedding was a large affair.
business, event, issue, matter, question, situation, subject

affect
verb to influence something or someone » More than 7 million people have been affected by the drought.
act on, alter, change, impinge on

affection
noun a feeling of fondness for someone or something » She thought of him with affection.
attachment, fondness, liking, love, warmth
antonym: dislike

affectionate
adjective full of fondness for someone or something » Elsa gave her dog an affectionate pat.
caring, fond, loving, tender
antonym: cold

Elsa gave her dog an **affectionate** pat.

afraid
adjective scared of something unpleasant happening
▶▶ SEE RIGHT

after
adverb at a later time
» After the main course, you can choose a dessert.
afterwards, following, later, subsequently
antonym: before
related word: prefix post-

again
adverb happening one more time » When he didn't get a reply, Carlos texted his best friend again.
afresh, anew, once more

against 1
preposition in opposition to » We are against the increase in student fees.
averse to, hostile to, in opposition to, versus
related words: prefixes anti-, contra-, counter-

We are **against** the increase in student fees.

against 2
preposition in preparation for or in case of something » When you go out, dress well to protect yourselves against the cold.
in anticipation of, in expectation of, in preparation for

aggressive
adjective full of hostility and violence » Hungry sharks can be very aggressive.
hostile, quarrelsome, belligerent, pugnacious
antonym: peaceful

agile
adjective able to move quickly and easily » He is as agile as a cat.
lithe, nimble, sprightly, supple, limber, lissom, lissome
antonym: clumsy

agitate 1
verb to campaign energetically for something » The workers had begun to agitate for better conditions in the office.
campaign, demonstrate, protest, push

agitate 2
verb to worry or distress someone » Everything she said agitated me.
bother, distress, disturb, trouble, upset, worry, discompose, faze, perturb

agree 1
verb to have the same opinion as someone » They all agreed to go bowling.
assent, be of the same opinion, concur, see eye to eye
antonym: disagree

agree 2
verb to match or be the same as something » His statement agrees with the facts given by other witnesses.
accord, conform, match, square, tally

agreeable 1
adjective pleasant or enjoyable » I've just had the most agreeable vacation—I want to go back!
delightful, enjoyable, lovely, nice, pleasant, pleasurable
antonym: disagreeable

» **agreeable**

alike

① *adjective* similar in some way
» The snakes look so **alike**.

close
A king snake is **close** in appearance to a coral snake.

similar
These snakes have **similar** patterns.

the same
All snakes have **the same** body shape.

identical
Their colours are **identical**, just in a different order.

indistinguishable
The two snakes are almost **indistinguishable** from each other.

antonym: **different**
The butterflies are **different** in colour and shape.

agreeable ②
adjective willing to allow or do something » Alison said she was agreeable to this plan.
game, happy, prepared, ready, willing,
amenable, compliant

agreement
noun a decision reached by two or more people » The two countries have signed agreements on fishing and oil rights.
arrangement, contract, deal (informal), **pact, settlement, treaty,**
compact, covenant

aim ①
verb to plan to do something » The school aims to recruit three new teachers next year.
aspire, attempt, intend, plan, propose, strive

aim ②
noun what someone intends to achieve » My main aim is to be captain of the hockey team.
ambition, goal, intention, objective, plan, target

alarm ①
noun a feeling of fear » The cat sprang back in alarm.
anxiety, apprehension, fright, nervousness, panic, scare,
consternation, trepidation
antonym: **calm**

The cat sprang back in **alarm**.

amount

alarm [2]
noun a device used to warn people of something
» *The burglar alarm woke up the whole street.*
distress signal, siren, warning

alarm [3]
verb to fill with fear
» *We could not see what had alarmed him.*
distress, frighten, panic, scare, startle, unnerve
antonym: **calm**

alert [1]
adjective paying full attention
» *The alert guard caught the shoplifter red-handed.*
attentive, observant, on guard, vigilant, wary
antonym: **unaware**

alert [2]
verb to warn of danger
» *The swimmers alerted the passer-by that they needed help.*
forewarn, inform, notify, warn

The swimmers alerted the passer-by that they needed help.

alike [1]
adjective similar in some way
◀◀ SEE LEFT

alike [2]
adverb in a similar way
» *All the children taking part in the parade were dressed alike—it was hard to tell them apart.*
equally, in the same way, similarly, uniformly

alive [1]
adjective having life
» *Doctors worked around the clock to keep the patient alive.*
animate, breathing, living
antonym: **dead**

alive [2]
adjective lively and active
» *After jogging up the hill, Liam felt alive with energy.*
active, alert, animated, energetic, full of life, lively, vivacious
antonym: **dull**

After jogging up the hill, Liam felt alive with energy.

all
pronoun the whole of something
» *Did you eat all the cookies?*
each, every one, everything, the whole amount, the (whole) lot
related words:
prefixes **pan-, panto-**

allow [1]
verb to permit someone to do something
» *Jane's mother allowed her to go to the party.*
approve, authorize, let, permit, stand for, tolerate,
give leave, sanction
antonym: **forbid**

allow [2]
verb to set aside for a particular purpose
» *Allow four hours for the paint to dry.*
allocate, allot, assign, grant, set aside

all right
adjective acceptable » *It was all right but nothing special.*
acceptable, adequate, average, fair, okay or **OK** (informal)

almost
adverb very nearly
» *The number of children in a class has almost doubled in less than a decade.*
about, approximately, close to, nearly, not quite, practically

alone
adjective not with other people or things » *He was all alone in the middle of the hall.*
detached, isolated, separate, single

aloud
adverb out loud
» *Our father read aloud to us.*
audibly, out loud

also
adverb in addition
» *Carlos is also an excellent basketball player.*
as well, besides, furthermore, into the bargain, moreover, too

always
adverb all the time or forever
» *Zoe's always singing— she never stops!*
constantly, continually, every time, forever, invariably, perpetually

amaze
verb to surprise greatly
» *Noah amazed us with his knowledge of local history.*
astonish, astound, shock, stagger, stun, surprise,
dumbfound, flabbergast, stupefy

amazement
noun complete surprise
» *Much to my amazement, Yasmin arrived on time.*
astonishment, shock, surprise, wonder,
perplexity, stupefaction

Kirsten surfed the most amazing wave.

amazing
adjective very surprising or remarkable » *Kirsten surfed the most amazing wave.*
astonishing, astounding, staggering, startling, stunning, surprising

among [1]
preposition surrounded by
» *The broken bike lay among piles of chains and pedals.*
amid, in the middle of, in the thick of, surrounded by

The broken bike lay among piles of chains and pedals.

among [2]
preposition between more than two » *The donations will be divided among seven charities.*
between, to each of

amount
noun how much there is of something
» *I get a huge amount of homework every weekend.*
expanse, quantity, volume

15

ample

*There was **ample** space in the tent for both children and the dog.*

ample
adjective of an amount: more than enough » *There was ample space in the tent for both children and the dog.*
abundant, enough, plenty of, sufficient

ancestor
noun a person from whom someone is descended » *Leon could trace his ancestors back 100 years.*
forebear, forefather, precursor, progenitor

anger [1]
noun extreme annoyance » *She vented her anger at the umpire.*
fury, outrage, rage, wrath, choler, ire, pique, spleen, vexation

anger [2]
verb to make someone angry » *The politician's remarks angered his critics.*
enrage, infuriate, outrage
antonym: **calm**

angry
adjective very annoyed
▶▶ SEE RIGHT

animal
noun a living creature » *Dogs and cats are the nation's favourite animals.*
beast, creature
related word: prefix **zoo-**

animosity
noun a feeling of strong dislike towards someone » *There is no animosity between the two players—they get on well.*
antagonism, antipathy, dislike, hatred, hostility, ill will, malice, resentment

announce
verb to make known something publicly » *He announced the winner of the competition live on the radio.*
advertise, make known, proclaim, reveal, tell, tweet, promulgate, propound

*He **announced** the winner of the competition live on the radio.*

announcement
noun a statement giving information about something » *There has been no formal announcement about the school trip.*
advertisement, broadcast, bulletin, declaration, report, statement

annoy
verb to irritate or displease someone » *Try making a note of the things that annoy you.*
bother, displease, get on someone's nerves (informal), **hassle** (informal), **irritate, plague, vex**

annoyance [1]
noun a feeling of irritation » *Isaac made no secret of his annoyance at bad grammar.*
displeasure, irritation

annoyance [2]
noun something that causes irritation » *Snoring can be more than an annoyance.*
bore, drag (informal), **nuisance, pain** (informal), **pain in the neck** (informal), **pest**

answer [1]
verb to reply to someone » *I waited all day for him to answer my question.*
reply, respond, retort
antonym: **ask**

answer [2]
noun a reply given to someone » *He walked away without waiting for an answer.*
reply, response, retort, rejoinder, riposte
antonym: **question**

anxiety
noun nervousness or worry » *It's natural to have some anxiety before starting a new school.*
apprehension, concern, fear, misgiving, nervousness, unease, worry, perturbation, trepidation

anxious
adjective nervous or worried » *Nicole was very anxious before starting the exam.*
apprehensive, bothered, concerned, fearful, nervous, troubled, uneasy, worried

*Nicole was very **anxious** before starting the exam.*

apathetic
adjective not interested in anything » *He was apathetic about politics.*
cool, indifferent, passive, uninterested
antonym: **enthusiastic**

apologize
verb to say sorry for something » *I apologize for being late.*
ask forgiveness, beg someone's pardon, express regret, say sorry

*Lily **appealed** for people to sign her petition.*

appeal [1]
verb to make an urgent request for something » *Lily appealed for people to sign her petition.*
beg, call upon, plead, request, entreat, implore, pray

appeal [2]
verb to attract or interest » *The idea of getting a sports car appealed to him.*
attract, fascinate, interest, please

appeal [3]
noun a formal request for something » *The speaker made an appeal for quiet.*
petition, plea, request, entreaty, supplication

appear [1]
verb to become visible or present » *A woman appeared at the far end of the street.*
come into view, crop up (informal), **emerge, show up** (informal), **surface, turn up**
antonym: **disappear**

appear [2]
verb to begin to exist » *Small white flowers appear in the spring.*
become available, be invented, come into being, come into existence, come out

appearance [1]
noun the time when something begins to exist » *We were surprised but pleased at the new girl's appearance in our class.*
advent, arrival, coming, debut, emergence, introduction

16

appreciate »

Sofia really cares about her appearance.

appearance 2
noun the way that a person looks » *Sofia really cares about her appearance.*
bearing, image, look, looks, demeanour, mien

application
noun a computer program designed for a particular purpose » *This application runs on all tablets.*
app, software

appointment 1
noun an arrangement to meet someone » *Valeria has an appointment with the dentist.*
date, interview, meeting, rendezvous

appointment 2
noun the choosing of a person to do a job » *Roy was pleased with his appointment as the new class president.*
election, naming, nomination, selection

appointment 3
noun a job » *He applied for an appointment in Alberta.*
assignment, job, place, position, post

appreciate 1
verb to value something highly » *Joe appreciates good movies.*
admire, prize, rate highly, respect, treasure, value
antonym: **scorn**

appreciate 2
verb to understand a situation or problem » *I didn't appreciate the seriousness of it at the time.*
be aware of, perceive, realize, recognize, understand

angry

adjective very annoyed » *The **angry** bull charged across the field.*

annoyed

cross

enraged

fuming

furious

indignant

irate

livid

mad (informal)

raging

17

» appropriate

*Jeans are not **appropriate** clothes for a formal occasion.*

appropriate
adjective suitable or acceptable for a given situation
» *Jeans are not appropriate clothes for a formal occasion.*
apt, correct, fitting, proper, suitable, apposite, congruous, germane
antonym: **inappropriate**

approval 1
noun agreement given to something » *The idea will require approval from teachers and parents.*
agreement, authorization, blessing, endorsement, permission, sanction, assent, imprimatur, mandate, ratification

approval 2
noun liking and admiration of a person or thing
» *He wanted to gain his father's approval.*
admiration, esteem, favour, praise, respect
antonym: **disapproval**

approve 1
verb to think something or someone is good
» *Not everyone approved of the choice of players.*
admire, favour, praise, respect, think highly of
antonym: **disapprove**

approve 2
verb to agree formally to something » *They approved the plan for a new playground.*
authorize, consent to, endorse, permit, sanction
antonym: **veto**

approximate
adjective close but not exact
» *The approximate time the concert ends is 10 p.m.*
estimated, inexact, loose, rough
antonym: **exact**

ardent
adjective full of enthusiasm and passion » *Stefan was an ardent performer.*
avid, devoted, enthusiastic, fervent, intense, keen, passionate, zealous
antonym: **apathetic**

*Stefan was an **ardent** performer.*

area 1
noun a particular part of a place » *Elena lived in an exclusive area of the city.*
district, locality, neighbourhood, region, zone

area 2
noun the size of a two-dimensional surface
» *The islands cover a total area of 625 square kilometres.*
expanse, extent, range, size

argue 1
verb to disagree with someone in an angry way » *They argued over the cost of the taxi fare.*
bicker, disagree, fall out (informal), **feud, fight, quarrel, squabble, wrangle**

argue 2
verb to try to prove
» *Lena argued that the dog could not have scratched the table.*
assert, claim, debate, maintain, reason, controvert, expostulate, remonstrate

argument 1
noun an angry disagreement
» *He got into an argument with one of the protesters.*
altercation, clash, disagreement, dispute, feud, fight, quarrel, row, squabble, wrangle (informal)

argument 2
noun a set of reasons presented for something
» *There's a strong argument for going home now.*
case, grounds, logic, reasoning

arrange 1
verb to make plans to do something » *Why don't you arrange to meet him later?*
fix up, organize, plan, schedule

arrange 2
verb to set things out in a particular order
» *Lucy's sister arranged the books on the shelves.*
classify, group, order, organize, sort, array, systematize

*Lucy's sister **arranged** the books on the shelves.*

arrest 1
verb to take someone into custody » *Police arrested five men.*
apprehend, capture, collar (slang), **seize, take prisoner**

arrest 2
noun the act of arresting someone » *The police made two arrests.*
apprehension, capture, seizure

article 1
noun a piece of writing in a newspaper or magazine
» *There's an article about the new park in today's paper.*
feature, item, piece, story

article 2
noun a particular item
» *How many articles are on the table?*
item, object, thing

ashamed
adjective feeling embarrassed or guilty » *He was not ashamed of what he had done.*
embarrassed, guilty, humiliated, sheepish, sorry, chagrined, mortified
antonym: **proud**

ask 1
verb to put a question to someone » *Erin asked me if I'd enjoyed my dinner.*
inquire, interrogate, query, question, quiz
antonym: **answer**

ask 2
verb to make a request to someone » *We had to ask him to leave.*
appeal, beg, demand, implore, plead, seek, beseech, entreat

ask 3
verb to invite someone
» *Everybody in the class had been asked to the party.*
bid (literary), **invite**

aspect
noun a feature of something
» *Exam results are only one aspect of a school's success.*
consideration, element, factor, feature, part, point, side

assemble 1
verb to fit the parts of something together
» *The children were assembling model planes.*
build, construct, erect, make, put together

attack »

*The tourists **assembled** in a line next to the bus.*

assemble [2]
verb to gather together in a group » *The tourists assembled in a line next to the bus.*
collect, come together, congregate, convene, gather, mass

assistant
noun a person who helps someone » *The assistant took notes as his boss spoke about his plans for the week.*
aide, ally, colleague, helper, right-hand man

associate [1]
verb to connect one thing with another » *Dark clouds are associated with rain.*
connect, couple, identify, link

associate [2]
verb to spend time with a person » *I began associating with different groups of people.*
hang out (informal)**, mingle, mix, run around** (informal)**, socialize,** consort, fraternize

associate [3]
noun a person known through work » *After arriving late, she joined her business associates at the meeting.*
colleague, co-worker, workmate

association [1]
noun an organization » *Many schools have a parents' association.*
body, club, company, confederation, group, institution, league, society, syndicate, fraternity

association [2]
noun a connection or involvement with a person or group » *Did you know about his association with the band?*
affiliation, attachment, bond, connection, relationship, tie, affinity, liaison

assume [1]
verb to accept that something is true » *Lewis assumed that Jon knew what he was doing.*
believe, guess (informal)**, imagine, suppose, think**

assume [2]
verb to take responsibility for something » *I will assume the role of team leader.*
accept, shoulder, take on, undertake

astute
adjective very intelligent or perceptive » *Amy's an astute judge of character.*
alert, clever, keen, perceptive, quick, sharp, shrewd, smart, discerning

attach
verb to join or fasten things together » *The gadget can be attached to any surface.*
affix, connect, couple, fasten, join, link, tie
antonym: **separate**

attachment [1]
noun a feeling of love and affection » *A mother and child form a close attachment.*
affection, bond, fondness, liking, love

attachment [2]
noun a part that connects to something else » *The drill comes with a wide range of attachments.*
accessory, component, fitting, fixture, part, unit

attack [1]
verb to use violence against someone or something
▼ SEE BELOW

---

attack
[1] verb to use violence against someone or something » *William's army attacked King Harold's knights.*

- I really didn't want to be involved in this **raid**.
- What if they decide to **invade** Normandy?
- I've always wanted to **storm** England.
- Your **assault** will go down in history.
- Forward, men, and **set upon** the cavalry.
- **Charge!**

19

attack

attack [2]
verb to criticize someone strongly » *She attacked the minister's views on education.*
bawl out (informal), **blast, censure, criticize, put down** (informal), **vilify** (formal), **berate, dress down, lambaste, revile**

attack [3]
noun violent physical action against someone or something » *It was an unprovoked attack on the surprised man.*
assault, charge, invasion, offensive, onslaught, raid

attempt [1]
verb to try to do something » *They attempted to escape.*
endeavour, seek, strive, try, try your hand at

attempt [2]
noun an act of trying to do something » *It was Ryan's third attempt at the pole vault.*
bid, crack (informal), **go** (informal), **shot** (informal), **stab** (informal), **try**

It was Ryan's third attempt at the pole vault.

attitude
noun someone's way of thinking and behaving » *Having a positive attitude helps you achieve your dreams.*
outlook, perspective, point of view, position, stance

attract
verb to appeal to or interest » *The trial races have attracted many leading riders.*
appeal to, draw, entice, lure, pull (informal), **tempt**
antonym: **repel**

The leading star is very attractive.

attractive
adjective pleasant, especially to look at » *The leading star is very attractive.*
appealing, charming, fetching, handsome, lovely, pretty, comely, prepossessing, winsome
antonym: **unattractive**

attribute
noun a quality or feature » *Anna's main attribute is her unfailing generosity.*
characteristic, feature, property, quality, trait, idiosyncrasy, peculiarity

augment
verb to add something to something else » *Sally augmented her allowance money by dogsitting for the neighbours when they went out for the day.*
add to, boost, complement, increase, reinforce, supplement, top up

authentic
adjective real and genuine » *The cake was made from an authentic French recipe.*
bona fide, genuine, real, true
antonym: **fake**

automatic [1]
adjective operating mechanically by itself » *Modern trains have automatic doors.*
automated, mechanical, robot, self-propelled

automatic [2]
adjective without conscious thought » *Breathing is an automatic physical function.*
instinctive, involuntary, natural, reflex

automobile
noun a vehicle for carrying a few people » *After thinking about it, Ali decided to buy an expensive automobile.*
car, vehicle

After thinking about it, Ali decided to buy an expensive automobile.

available
adjective ready for use » *There are three apartments available for rent in the building.*
accessible, at hand, at someone's disposal, free, handy, to hand
antonym: **unavailable**

average [1]
adjective standard or normal » *I get up at 7 a.m. on an average weekday, but tomorrow is a holiday so I'll sleep longer.*
normal, regular, standard, typical, usual

average [2] : **on average**
adverb for the most part » *Men are, on average, taller than women.*
as a rule, generally, normally, typically, usually

avoid [1]
verb to keep away from someone or something » *She thought he was trying to avoid her.*
dodge, elude, eschew (formal), **evade, shun, sidestep, steer clear of**

avoid [2]
verb to make an effort not to do something » *Liam avoided going out by pretending to be ill.*
dodge, duck out of (informal), **get out of, refrain from, shirk, circumvent, give a wide berth to**

aware [1] : **aware of**
adjective conscious of something » *Ava was acutely aware of the noise of the city.*
acquainted with, conscious of, familiar with, mindful of
antonym: **unaware**

aware [2]
adjective knowing about something » *Keep me aware of any developments.*
informed, in the picture, knowledgeable, in the loop

awful
adjective very unpleasant or very bad » *The weather this morning is awful.*
appalling, dreadful, frightful, ghastly, horrendous, terrible, abysmal, deplorable

The weather this morning is awful.

Bb

babble
verb to talk in an excited way
» *Tim babbled on and on about how much fun he'd had at the party.*
burble, chatter, gabble, prattle

baby
noun a very young child
» *Jia enjoyed playing with her baby brother.*
babe, bambino (informal)**, child, infant, newborn**

Jia enjoyed playing with her baby brother.

back 1
noun the part that is behind the front » *Write a message on the back of a postcard.*
end, rear, reverse, stern
antonym: **front**

Write a message on the back of a postcard.

back 2
verb to support a person or organization
» *Mina's friends backed her campaign for student president.*
advocate, encourage, endorse, favour, promote, support, champion, second
antonym: **oppose**

background
noun where you come from; your class, education, training, or experience » *Marianne came from a rich background.*
culture, environment, history, upbringing

bad 1
adjective harmful, unpleasant, or upsetting » *I have bad news—the vacation is cancelled.*
damaging, destructive, detrimental, distressing, disturbing, grim, harmful, painful, traumatic, unhealthy, unpleasant, unsettling, upsetting
antonym: **good**

bad 2
adjective of poor quality
» *The roads were bad and full of potholes.*
defective, deficient, faulty, imperfect, inadequate, inferior, pathetic, poor, sorry, unsatisfactory
antonym: **satisfactory**

bad 3
adjective evil in character
» *Superheroes always win over the bad guys.*
corrupt, criminal, depraved, evil, immoral, sinful, villainous, wicked, wrong
antonym: **good**

badly 1
adverb in an inferior way
» *This essay is badly written, with poor grammar.*
inadequately, ineptly, poorly, shoddily, unsatisfactorily
antonym: **well**

badly 2
adverb seriously
» *Ben was badly hurt in a fall.*
deeply, desperately, gravely, seriously
antonym: **slightly**

badly 3
adverb in a cruel manner
» *Jim would never treat his dog badly—he adores it.*
brutally, callously, cruelly, savagely, viciously
antonym: **well**

bait
noun something used to catch someone or something
» *Charles used worms as bait to catch fish.*
bribe, decoy, inducement, lure, temptation

balance 1
verb to make or remain steady
» *The gymnast balanced gracefully on one leg.*
level, stabilize, steady

The gymnast balanced gracefully on one leg.

balance 2
noun a stable relationship between things » *There must be a balance between study and play time.*
equilibrium, equity, equivalence, parity

The dog loved playing with the ball.

ball
noun a round object
» *The dog loved playing with the ball.*
drop, globe, pellet, sphere, globule, orb, spheroid

ban 1
verb to disallow something
» *Adults are banned from taking part in the kids' race.*
bar, disqualify, exclude, forbid, outlaw, prohibit, banish, proscribe, suppress
antonym: **permit**

ban 2
noun a rule disallowing something » *There is a ban on chewing gum in school.*
disqualification, embargo, prohibition, suppression
antonym: **permit**

band 1
noun a group of musicians who play together
» *Luiz was a singer in a rock-and-roll band.*
group, orchestra, combo, ensemble

band 2
noun a group of people who share a common purpose
» *The protest was led by a band of angry students.*
bunch, company, crowd, gang, party, troupe

The protest was led by a band of angry students.

» bang

hammer — Mike **hammered** on the door to be let in.

knock — I **knocked** on the window, but they didn't hear me.

pound — We **pounded** on the walls.

hit — The ball **hit** the post.

thump — The children cheered and **thumped** on their desks.

beat — The group sat in a circle, **beating** small drums.

slam — I **slammed** down the phone.

bang

1 *verb* to hit or put something down hard, with a loud noise
» Charlie **banged** the drums so loudly, my ears hurt.

22

bay

bang 1
verb to hit or put something down hard, with a loud noise
◀◀ SEE LEFT

bang 2
noun a sudden, short, loud noise » *The microwave exploded with a bang.*
blast, boom, crack, detonation, explosion, thump

bang 3
noun a hard or painful bump against something » *I got a nasty bang on the elbow.*
blow, clout (informal), **knock, thump, whack**

banish 1
verb to exile someone » *Aliyah banished Doug from the house until he took off his muddy shoes.*
deport, eject, evict, exile, expel, transport

banish 2
verb to get rid of something or someone » *The kids finally banished their boredom with a game of hide and seek.*
discard, dismiss, dispel, eliminate, eradicate, remove

bank 1
noun the edge of a river or lake » *Ed stood for ages fishing on the river bank.*
brink, edge, shore, side

Ed stood for ages fishing on the river bank.

bank 2
noun a store of something » *Supplies are running low at the blood bank.*
fund, hoard, reserve, stock, store, reservoir, stockpile

bar 1
noun a piece of metal » *The prison cell had bars across the window.*
pole, rail, rod, shaft

bar 2
verb to stop someone » *Bryan's bodyguards barred the way as his fans rushed towards him.*
obstruct, prevent

Bryan's bodyguards barred the way as his fans rushed towards him.

bare 1
adjective not covered » *Stella wore shorts to the beach, and she burned her bare legs in the sun.*
exposed, uncovered
antonym: **covered**

bare 2
adjective with nothing on top or inside » *Len forgot to buy groceries, so the cupboard was bare.*
empty, open, spartan, vacant

barely
adverb only just » *It's too early in the morning for Lisa to join us for a walk; she'll be barely awake.*
almost, hardly, just, scarcely

The Sahara is a barren desert.

barren
adjective with nothing growing on it » *The Sahara is a barren desert.*
arid, desert, desolate, dry, empty, waste, unfruitful, unproductive
antonym: **fertile**

barrier 1
noun something preventing entry » *There were barriers to prevent the audience from getting onto the stage.*
barricade, fence, obstruction, wall, fortification, obstacle, rampart

barrier 2
noun something that prevents progress » *A lack of funds is the biggest barrier preventing me from travelling to South Africa in the summer.*
handicap, hindrance, hurdle, impediment, obstacle

barter
verb to exchange goods or services without money » *I bartered my comic book for Wayne's baseball.*
exchange, give in exchange, swap, trade, trade off, bargain

base 1
noun the lowest part of something » *They played at the base of the cliffs.*
bed, bottom, foot, foundation, pedestal, stand
antonym: **top**

base 2
noun the place you work from » *He lived at the military base.*
camp, centre, headquarters, post, station

base 3
verb to use as a foundation » *The movie is based on a true story.*
build, derive, found, ground, hinge

basic
adjective most necessary » *A basic first aid kit includes bandages.*
elementary, essential, fundamental, key, necessary, vital, central, indispensable, primary

basis
noun the main principle of something » *An old fairy tale forms the basis of the new fantasy movie.*
core, fundamental, heart, premise, principle

bay 1
noun a curve or inlet in a coastline » *The Bay of Fundy has the highest tides on Earth.*
cove, gulf, inlet, sound

bay 2
verb to make a howling noise » *The wolf bayed in the moonlight.*
bark, cry, howl, yelp

The wolf bayed in the moonlight.

23

beach

beach
noun a sandy shore by a body of water
▼ SEE BELOW

bear 1
verb to carry something
» The ice wasn't thick enough to bear their weight.
carry, convey, shoulder, support, take

bear 2
verb to have or show something
» The room bore the signs of a lively party.
exhibit, harbour, have

The room bore the signs of a lively party.

bear 3
verb to accept something
» Jim can't bear the sound of cutlery scraping on a plate.
abide, endure, stomach, suffer, tolerate

beat 1
verb to hit someone or something hard
» Sheila beat the drum.
batter, buffet, hit, pound, strike, thrash

beat 2
verb to defeat
» Ethan is a slow runner and was easily beaten in the race.
defeat, outdo, outstrip, overcome, overwhelm, vanquish, conquer, master, surpass

beat 3
noun a rhythm » Rock music has a thumping beat.
cadence, metre, rhythm, stress, time

beautiful
adjective attractive or pleasing
» A beautiful picture can brighten up a room.
attractive, delightful, fine, gorgeous, lovely, pleasing, exquisite, fair
antonym: ugly

The coast is an area of outstanding natural beauty.

beauty 1
noun the quality of being beautiful » The coast is an area of outstanding natural beauty.
attractiveness, charm, elegance, loveliness
antonym: ugliness

beauty 2
noun a good-looking person
» She was a dark-eyed beauty.
hunk (male; informal), looker, stunner (informal)

beauty 3
noun an attractive feature
» The beauty of the plan is its simplicity.
advantage, asset, attraction, benefit

because
conjunction for the reason that
» I didn't go to the restaurant because I was tired.
as, since, in that, on account of, owing to

before
adverb at a previous time
» Have you ever been to Greece before?
earlier, formerly, in advance, previously, sooner
antonym: after
related words: prefixes ante-, fore-, pre-

beg
verb to ask anxiously for something
» The girl begged her dad for another ice cream.
beseech, implore, petition, plead, entreat, importune

The girl begged her dad for another ice cream.

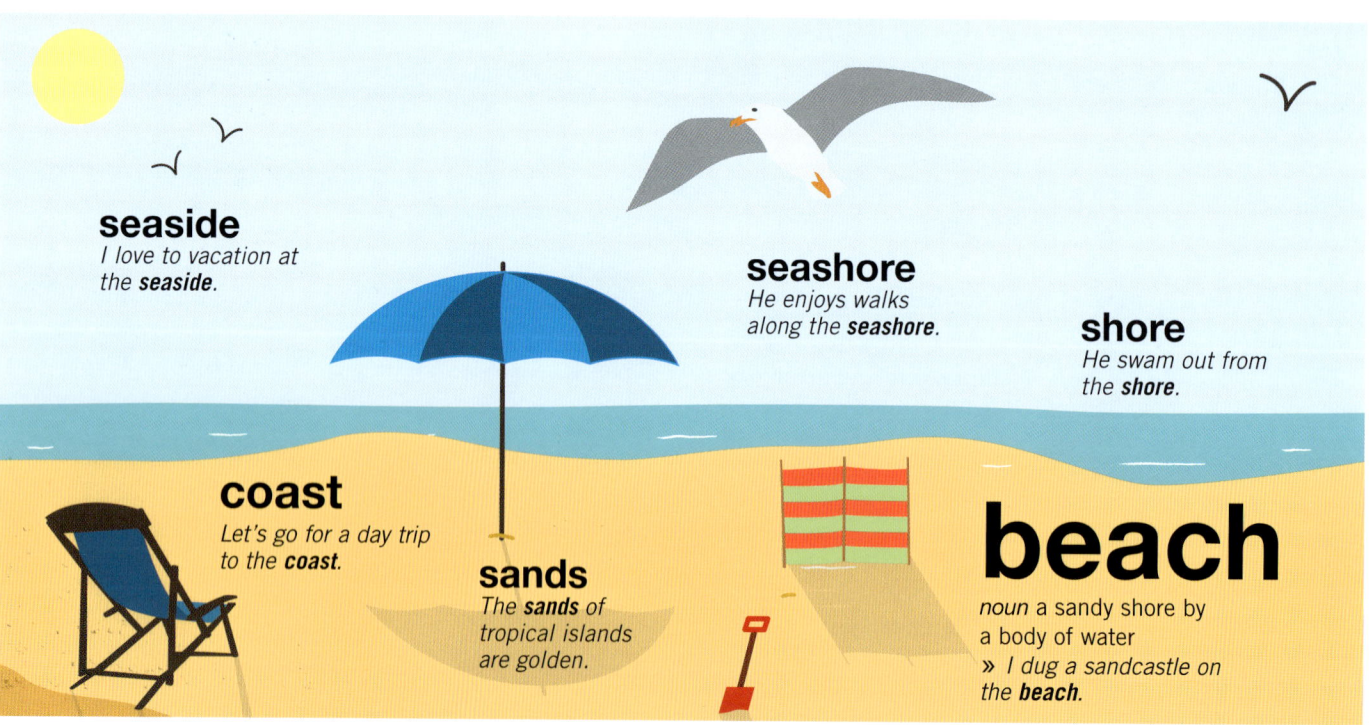

seaside
I love to vacation at the seaside.

seashore
He enjoys walks along the seashore.

shore
He swam out from the shore.

coast
Let's go for a day trip to the coast.

sands
The sands of tropical islands are golden.

beach
noun a sandy shore by a body of water
» I dug a sandcastle on the beach.

begin
verb to start or cause to start » *When did the show begin?*
commence (formal), **initiate, originate, set about, start,** inaugurate, instigate, institute
antonym: **end**

beginner
noun someone learning to do something » *Ali joined the "French for beginners" class.*
apprentice, learner, novice, starter, trainee
antonym: **expert**

beginning
noun where something starts » *The audience quieted down at the beginning of the play.*
birth, commencement (formal), **opening, origin, outset, start,** inauguration, initiation, onset
antonym: **end**

behave
verb to act in a certain way » *If you don't behave nicely, we'll have to leave the party.*
act, function, operate, work

belief 1
noun the certainty something is true » *Miriam's belief that it was going to be a fine summer turned out to be right.*
confidence, conviction, judgment, opinion, trust, view

belief 2
noun a principle of a religion or system » *His religion gave him a strong set of beliefs.*
creed, doctrine, dogma, faith, ideology, principle, tenet

believable
adjective possible or likely to be the case » *The book is full of believable characters that I can relate to.*
credible, imaginable, likely, plausible, possible, probable
antonym: **unbelievable**

believe
verb to accept something is true » *Don't believe everything you read in the papers.*
accept, assume, presume, swallow (informal), **trust**
antonym: **doubt**

belittle
verb to make someone or something seem less important » *Ted always belittles me in front of my friends—it really shakes my confidence.*
deride, detract from, downgrade, scorn, undervalue, denigrate, disparage, minimize
antonym: **praise**

beloved
adjective dearly loved » *Anthony proposed to his beloved girlfriend.*
adored, cherished, darling, dearest, precious, treasured
antonym: **despised**

Anthony proposed to his beloved girlfriend.

below
preposition or adverb lower down » *The basement is below the ground floor.*
beneath, down, lower, under, underneath
antonym: **above**

bend 1
verb to make or become curved » *Bend the bar into a horseshoe.*
buckle, curve, turn, twist, warp

bend 2
verb to curve the body downwards » *I bent over and kissed her cheek.*
arch, bow, crouch, incline, lean, stoop

bend 3
noun a curve in something » *Watch out for the sharp bend in the road.*
arc, corner, curve, loop, turn, angle, arch, twist

beneficial
adjective giving some benefit » *Eating fruit is beneficial to your health.*
advantageous, good for you, healthy, helpful, useful, wholesome

benefit 1
noun an advantage » *Meeting interesting people is one of the benefits of joining a club.*
advantage, asset, boon, gain, good, help, profit, use
antonym: **disadvantage**

benefit 2
verb to help in something » *The experience will benefit you when you take the test.*
aid, assist, enhance, further, help, profit
antonym: **harm**

benevolent
adjective kind and helpful » *Arthur was a benevolent king who cared about his people.*
benign, charitable, compassionate, humane, kind, altruistic, beneficent, philanthropic

beside
preposition next to » *We sat beside each other watching TV.*
adjacent to, alongside, close to, near, next to

We sat beside each other watching TV.

best 1
adjective of the highest standard » *That was the best movie I have seen in a long time.*
finest, first-rate, foremost, greatest, leading, outstanding, pre-eminent, principal, superlative, supreme, top
antonym: **worst**

best 2
adjective most desirable » *Offering to pay for the broken window was the best thing to do.*
correct, most fitting, right
antonym: **worst**

best 3
noun the preferred thing » *Of all my presents, this looks the best—can I open it first?*
cream, elite, finest, pick
antonym: **worst**

Of all my presents, this looks the best—can I open it first?

betray 1
verb to break someone's trust » *I was betrayed by someone I thought was a friend.*
break your promise, double-cross (informal), **inform on**

betray 2
verb to show feelings » *Jeremy's voice betrayed little emotion over the phone.*
expose, manifest, reveal, show

» be**tter**

large great significant enormous huge immense

big

[1] *adjective* of a large size
» The diplodocus was a **big** dinosaur...

better [1]
adjective of more worth than another » *The weather today was better than yesterday.*
finer, grander, greater, higher-quality, nicer, preferable, superior, surpassing, worthier
antonym: **inferior**

better [2]
adjective well after being ill » *I hope you feel better soon.*
cured, fully recovered, healthier, improving, on the mend (informal)**, recovering, stonger, well**
antonym: **worse**

beware
verb to be cautious » *The sign warned us to beware of the dog.*
be careful, be cautious, be wary, guard against, look out, watch out

The sign warned us to **beware** of the dog.

bias
noun prejudice for or against a person, group, or idea » *The café had a bias for hiring staff who speak Spanish.*
bigotry, favouritism, prejudice

biased
adjective showing prejudice » *The basketball team were biased against short players.*
one-sided, partial, partisan, prejudiced, slanted, weighted
antonym: **neutral**

big [1]
adjective of a large size
▲ SEE ABOVE

big [2]
adjective someone of great importance » *My cousin met some big Hollywood stars at the film festival.*
eminent, important, influential, leading, major, powerful, principal, prominent, significant
antonym: **unimportant**

big [3]
adjective an important issue or problem » *Moving to a new town was a big decision.*
critical, grave, momentous, serious, urgent, weighty
antonym: **minor**

bill
noun a statement of how much is owed » *The party of 20 ran up a huge bill in the restaurant.*
account, charges, check, invoice, statement

bit
noun a small amount » *A bit of muffin fell on the floor while Stan was eating it.*
crumb, fragment, grain, part, piece, scrap, iota, jot, speck

bite
verb to cut into something with your teeth » *Rachel's cat bit me.*
chew, gnaw, nibble, nip

Matt and Joe had a **bitter** argument over the accident.

bitter [1]
adjective angry and resentful » *Matt and Joe had a bitter argument over the accident.*
acrimonious, begrudging, embittered, rancorous, resentful, sour

bitter [2]
adjective tasting or smelling sharp » *Something in the pie had a bitter taste.*
acid, acrid, astringent, sharp, sour, tart
antonym: **sweet**

block »

gigantic massive colossal **vast**

antonym:
little
...but compsognathus was a **little** beast!

bizarre
adjective very strange or eccentric » *Chang has some bizarre ideas about what to do on vacation.*
curious, eccentric, extraordinary, odd, outlandish, peculiar, strange, weird
antonym: **ordinary**

black
noun or *adjective*
Shades of black:
coal-black, ebony, inky, jet, jet-black, pitch-black, raven, sable, sooty

blame 1
verb to believe someone caused something » *Don't blame me for losing the gift.*
accuse, charge, hold responsible

blame 2
noun the responsibility for something bad » *I'm not going to take the blame for forgetting the tickets!*
accountability, fault, guilt, liability, rap (slang), **responsibility,** culpability, incrimination

blank 1
adjective with nothing on it » *Use a blank sheet of paper.*
bare, clean, clear, empty, plain, unmarked

blank 2
adjective showing no feeling » *John just looked blank upon hearing the news.*
deadpan, dull, empty, impassive, vacant

blend 1
verb to mix things so as to form a single item or substance » *Jill used a mixer to blend the ingredients.*
combine, merge, mingle, mix
antonym: **separate**

*Jill used a mixer to **blend** the ingredients.*

blend 2
verb to combine in a pleasing way » *The colours blend in with the rest of the decor.*
complement, coordinate, go well, harmonize, match, suit

blend 3
noun a mixture or combination of things » *The menu was a blend of French and Chinese flavours.*
alloy, amalgamation, combination, compound, fusion, mix, mixture

bless
verb to hope for care, protection, and goodwill » *The mayor blessed the new ship by breaking a bottle of champagne on its bow.*
anoint, consecrate, dedicate, hallow
antonym: **curse**

blessing 1
noun something good » *Good health is a blessing.*
benefit, boon, gift, godsend, help
antonym: **disadvantage**

blessing 2
noun approval or permission to do something » *Fiona got married with her parents' blessing.*
approval, backing, consent, leave, permission, support, approbation, sanction
antonym: **disapproval**

blob
noun a small amount of a thick or sticky substance » *The artist squeezed out a blob of pink paint.*
bead, dab, drop, droplet

*The artist squeezed out a **blob** of pink paint.*

block 1
noun a large piece » *A block of wood fell near his foot.*
bar, brick, chunk, ingot, lump, piece

27

block

block [2]
verb to close by putting something across
» *Rubble blocked the river.*
choke, clog, obstruct, plug
antonym: **unblock**

block [3]
verb to prevent something happening » *The neighbours blocked his plan to build a high fence.*
bar, check, halt, obstruct, stop, thwart

blockage
noun a thing that clogs something » *There was a blockage in the pipe.*
block, obstruction, stoppage

blog
noun a journal written on the internet » *Have you seen Mindy's new fashion blog?*
microblog, vlog, weblog

blow [1]
verb to move or cause to move in the wind » *The wind blew Gary's papers away.*
buffet, drive, flutter, sweep, waft, whirl

blow [2]
noun a hit from something » *Danny gave the punching bag a mighty blow.*
bang, knock, smack, punch, thump, whack

Danny gave the punching bag a mighty blow.

blow [3]
noun something disappointing or upsetting » *Losing the match was a terrible blow.*
bombshell, disappointment, misfortune, setback, shock, upset, calamity, catastrophe, jolt

blue
noun or adjective
Shades of blue:
aqua, aquamarine, azure, baby blue, cerulean, cobalt, cyan, duck-egg, electric blue, gentian, indigo, lapis lazuli, midnight blue, navy, Nile blue, peacock blue, periwinkle, powder blue, robin's egg blue, royal blue, sapphire, sky blue, teal, turquoise, ultramarine

blunt [1]
adjective having rounded edges » *Blunt scissors can't cut through cardboard.*
dull, rounded, unsharpened
antonym: **sharp**

blunt [2]
adjective saying what you think » *Steve's speech was blunt and to the point.*
bluff, brusque, forthright, frank, outspoken, straightforward, explicit, tactless, trenchant
antonym: **tactful**

blush [1]
verb to go red in the face » *Fatima blushed when her name was called out to receive an award.*
colour, go crimson, flush, go red, turn red, turn scarlet

blush [2]
noun a red colour » *Ann took the gift with a blush.*
colour, flush, glow

boast
verb to talk proudly » *Carol boasted about her expensive costume.*
brag, crow

boastful
adjective tending to brag about things » *The boastful liar told us he was a millionaire.*
bragging, cocky, conceited, crowing, egotistical, swaggering
antonym: **modest**

Exercise is good for your body and mind.

body [1]
noun all your physical parts » *Exercise is good for your body and mind.*
build, figure, form, frame, physique, shape
related words: adjectives
corporal, physical

body [2]
noun a dead body » *The body of the former president lay in state.*
carcass, corpse, dead body, remains

body [3]
noun an organized group of people » *Local bodies worked together to put on a successful summer fair.*
association, band, company, confederation, organization, society, bloc, collection, corporation

boil [1]
verb to bubble » *The water is boiling in the pan.*
bubble, fizz, foam, froth, effervesce

boil [2]
noun a swelling on the skin » *Ted had a boil on his neck.*
blister, swelling, tumour, carbuncle, pustule

bold [1]
adjective confident and not shy » *It was a bold move to invite the entire school to her party.*
brash, brazen, cheeky, confident, forward, impudent, barefaced
antonym: **shy**

bold [2]
adjective unafraid of risk or danger » *The crew made a bold attempt at rescuing the boat.*
adventurous, brave, courageous, daring, fearless, intrepid, audacious, heroic, valiant
antonym: **cowardly**

bold [3]
adjective clear and noticeable » *Emily and Cathy's outfits were a riot of bold colours.*
bright, flashy, loud, striking, strong, vivid, conspicuous, prominent, pronounced
antonym: **dull**

Emily and Cathy's outfits were a riot of bold colours.

bolt
verb to escape or run away » *The horse bolted from the stable after Claude left the door open.*
dash, escape, flee, fly, run away, run off, rush

bomb [1]
noun an explosive device » *Luckily, the bomb failed to detonate, so no one was hurt.*
device, explosive, missile, rocket, shell, torpedo, grenade, mine, projectile

bomb [2]
verb to attack with bombs » *The old factory was bombed during the war.*
attack, blow up, bombard, destroy, shell, torpedo

bond [1]
noun a close relationship » *There is a special bond between parent and child.*
attachment, connection, link, relation, tie, union, affiliation, affinity

28

bounce »

bond 2
noun a pledge or promise made between people » *Marriage is a solemn bond between two people who love one another.*
agreement, contract, obligation, pledge, promise, word, compact, covenant, guarantee

bond 3
verb to attach separate things » *The strips of wood are bonded together to form a stronger, solid block.*
bind, fasten, fuse, glue, paste

book 1
noun a number of pages in a cover » *I'm reading a great book just now.*
eBook, publication, textbook, volume, work
▼ SEE BELOW

book 2
verb to arrange to have or use » *The theatre tickets are booked for Tuesday evening.*
charter, engage, organize, reserve, schedule

border 1
noun a dividing line between things or places » *There were long lines of traffic waiting to cross the border between the two countries.*
borderline, boundary, frontier, line

border 2
noun an edge of something » *Draw a border around your picture.*
bounds, edge, limits, margin, rim

border 3
verb to form an edge » *Tall trees bordered the fields.*
edge, fringe, hem, rim, trim

bored
adjective impatient and not interested in something » *I am bored with this subject.*
fed up, tired, uninterested, wearied
antonym: **interested**

I am bored with this subject.

boredom
noun a lack of interest » *Boredom can set in on long car journeys.*
apathy, dullness, flatness, monotony, tedium, weariness
antonym: **interest**

boring
adjective dull and uninteresting » *Garth couldn't wait for the boring movie to end.*
dull, flat, humdrum, monotonous, tedious, tiresome, insipid, repetitious, stale
antonym: **interesting**

boss
noun a person in charge of employees » *The boss had to make some difficult decisions.*
chief, director, employer, head, leader, manager

bossy
adjective telling people what to do » *Sophia is a rather bossy little girl.*
arrogant, authoritarian, dictatorial, domineering, imperious, overbearing

botch
verb to do something badly » *Dad botched decorating the cake, so we had to get one from the bakery.*
bungle, mar, mess up

bother 1
verb to annoy or intrude on someone » *Stop bothering your mother when she's busy working!*
annoy, concern, disturb, get on someone's nerves (informal), **trouble, worry,** harass, inconvenience

bother 2
noun trouble and difficulty » *Getting dried off after swimming is such a bother.*
annoyance, difficulty, inconvenience, irritation, pain (informal), **trouble, worry,** nuisance, strain

bottom 1
noun the lowest part of something » *The dog sat at the bottom of the stairs.*
base, bed, depths, floor, foot
antonym: **top**

The dog sat at the bottom of the stairs.

bottom 2
adjective in the lowest place or position » *I keep my socks in the bottom drawer.*
base, basement, ground, lowest
antonym: **highest**

bounce 1
verb to spring back » *The ball bounced against the wall.*
bump, ricochet, rebound, recoil

book
1 types of books

anthology · atlas · autobiography · biography · dictionary · directory · encyclopedia · glossary · guidebook · journal · manual · novel · phrasebook · thesaurus

» **bounce**

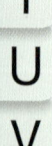

A B C D E F G H I J K L M N O P Q R S T U V W X Y Z

Sue **bounced** across the field.

bounce 2
verb to move up and down » *Sue bounced across the field.*
bob, bound, jump

box
noun a container with a firm base and sides » *Sara's things were packed in boxes, ready to move.*
carton, case, chest, container, trunk

boy
noun a male child » *I knew Adam when he was a boy.*
fellow, lad, schoolboy, youngster, youth

boycott
verb to refuse to do or buy something » *They boycotted the company due to its policies.*
blacklist, embargo, exclude, reject, spurn, proscribe, refrain from

brag
verb to boast about something » *People who brag about their achievements are really annoying.*
boast, crow

braggart
noun a person who boasts » *David was a braggart, telling everyone about his new sports car.*
bigmouth (slang), **boaster, bragger, show-off**

brave 1
adjective willing to do dangerous things » *Rescuing the girl from the water was a brave act.*
bold, courageous, fearless, heroic, plucky, valiant, daring, intrepid, valorous
antonym: **cowardly**

brave 2
verb to face something without fear » *Fans braved the rain to hear the star sing.*
face, stand up to

bravery
noun the quality of being courageous » *The knight was rewarded for his bravery.*
boldness, courage, fortitude, heroism, pluck, valour, fearlessness, gallantry, mettle
antonym: **cowardice**

breach 1
noun a breaking of a law or agreement » *Coming into work late is a breach of contract.*
infringement, offence, trespass, violation, contravention, transgression

breach 2
noun a gap in something » *The dog stuck his head through a breach in the fence.*
crack, gap, hole, opening, rift, split, chasm, fissure, rupture

The dog stuck his head through a **breach** in the fence.

break 1
verb to separate into pieces
▶▶ SEE RIGHT

break 2
verb to fail to keep a rule or promise » *Sal broke his promise to attend the party.*
breach, contravene, infringe, violate

break 3
noun a short period of rest or change » *I took a five-minute break from writing.*
interlude, interval, pause, recess, respite, rest

breed 1
noun a type of animal » *The farm specialized in rare breeds of cattle.*
kind, species, stock, strain, type, variety

breed 2
verb to reproduce and take care of » *Daniel breeds dogs for the police.*
cultivate, develop, keep, nurture, raise, rear

breed 3
verb to produce offspring » *Chickens can breed throughout the year.*
multiply, produce, propagate, reproduce, engender, procreate

Chickens can **breed** throughout the year.

brief 1
adjective lasting for a short time » *Ethan made a brief appearance on television*
fleeting, momentary, quick, short, swift, ephemeral, temporary, transitory
antonym: **long**

brief 2
verb to give necessary information » *The teacher briefed the class on the project.*
advise, fill in (informal), **inform, instruct, prepare, prime**

bright 1
adjective strong and startling » *Lighthouses emit a bright light that is visible from a distance.*
brilliant, dazzling, glowing, luminous, radiant, vivid, blazing, illuminated, resplendent
antonym: **dull**

Lighthouses emit a **bright** light that is visible from a distance.

bright 2
adjective clever and alert » *You are a bright student; you always get good grades.*
brainy (informal), **brilliant, clever, ingenious, intelligent, smart,** acute, astute, sharp
antonym: **dim**

bright 3
adjective cheerful and lively » *Lily always has a bright smile on her face.*
cheerful, happy, jolly, light-hearted, lively, merry

brilliant 1
adjective very bright » *The diamond reflected a brilliant light.*
bright, dazzling, gleaming, glowing, luminous, radiant, sparkling, vivid
antonym: **dull**

30

break

1 verb to separate into pieces
» He **broke** the ice with a hammer

crack
The wall **cracked** from top to bottom.

disintegrate
Tissue paper **disintegrates** in water.

crumble
Crumble the stock cube into the water.

demolish
The derelict house needed **demolishing**.

fragment
The picture **fragmented** into tiny pieces.

fracture
She **fractured** her arm.

shatter
The dropped plate **shattered**.

splinter
The wood **splintered** as he cut it.

smash
The ball **smashed** the window.

snap
The pencil **snapped** in half.

split
Split the apple to share it.

wreck
The iceberg **wrecked** the ship's hull.

brilliant »

brilliant

brilliant [2]
adjective very clever
» *Ed is a brilliant pupil, and grasps complex ideas easily.*
acute, brainy (informal), **bright, clever, intelligent, perceptive, sharp, smart**
antonym: **stupid**

brilliant [3]
adjective wonderful or superb
» *It's a brilliant movie.*
first-class, great, magnificent, marvellous, outstanding, superb, tremendous, wonderful
antonym: **terrible**

bring [1]
verb to take somewhere
» *Can you please bring the laundry downstairs?*
bear, carry, convey, lead, take, transport

*Can you please **bring** the laundry downstairs?*

bring [2]
verb to cause to happen
» *The new factory will bring more jobs to the city.*
cause, create, inflict, produce, result in, wreak, effect, occasion

bring about
verb to cause something to happen » *It was Donald's arrogance that brought about his downfall.*
cause, create, generate, make happen, produce, provoke

broad [1]
adjective large, especially from side to side » *The bodybuilder had broad shoulders.*
expansive, extensive, large, thick, vast, wide, ample, spacious
antonym: **narrow**

broad [2]
adjective including or affecting many different things or people
» *We discussed a broad range of issues.*
comprehensive, extensive, general, sweeping, universal, wide, wide-ranging

broad [3]
adjective general rather than detailed » *The documents provided a broad outline of the plan.*
approximate, general, non-specific, rough, sweeping, vague

broadcast [1]
noun a program on radio or television » *The news broadcast starts at 6 p.m.*
podcast, program, show, transmission, webcast

broadcast [2]
verb to send out so that it can be seen or heard » *You can hear the concert broadcast live on the radio.*
air, show, stream, transmit

broadcast [3]
verb to make known publicly
» *You don't need to broadcast your feelings to the entire world.*
advertise, announce, make public, proclaim, tweet

broken [1]
adjective in pieces
» *Jo called the police when she saw the broken window.*
burst, demolished, fractured, fragmented, shattered, smashed

*Jo called the police when she saw the **broken** window.*

broken [2]
adjective not kept
» *Frank had heard so many broken promises, he no longer believed what Sally said.*
infringed, violated, disobeyed, transgressed

brown
noun or adjective
Shades of brown:
auburn, bay, beige, bronze, brunette, buff, burnt sienna, burnt umber, café au lait, camel, chestnut, chocolate, cinnamon, coffee, dun, fawn, ginger, hazel, khaki, mahogany, mocha, oatmeal, ochre, putty, russet, rust, sandy, sepia, tan, taupe, tawny, terracotta, umber

build [1]
verb to make something
» *Simon used brick and mortar to build a new garden wall.*
assemble, construct, erect, fabricate, form, make
antonym: **dismantle**

*Simon used brick and mortar to **build** a new garden wall.*

build [2]
verb to develop gradually
» *I want to build a relationship with the new neighbours.*
develop, extend, increase, intensify, strengthen, augment, enlarge, escalate

build [3]
noun the size of a body
» *Pedro is of medium build.*
body, figure, form, frame, physique, shape

building
noun a structure with walls
» *The office building had 14 floors.*
edifice, structure

bulge [1]
verb to swell out » *The frog's vocal sac bulges as it sings to attract a mate.*
expand, protrude, stick out, swell

*The frog's vocal sac **bulges** as it sings to attract a mate.*

bulge [2]
noun a lump in something
» *My wallet made a bulge in my pocket.*
bump, hump, lump, protrusion, swelling

bully [1]
noun someone who deliberately frightens or hurts others
» *No one likes the class bully.*
oppressor, persecutor

bully [2]
verb to frighten or hurt someone deliberately and repeatedly » *I wasn't going to let him bully me.*
intimidate, oppress, persecute, pick on, tease, torment

bully [3]
verb to make someone do something by using force
» *Chloe used to bully me into doing her homework.*
force, intimidate, pressurize, coerce, dragoon

buy

bump 1
verb to hit something » *Ted bumped his elbow on the wall.*
bang, collide, hit, jolt, knock, strike

bump 2
noun a dull noise » *Layla heard a bump outside.*
bang, knock, thud, thump

bump 3
noun a raised part of something » *Look out for the bump in the road.*
bulge, hump, knob, lump, swelling, contusion, node, protuberance

bunch 1
noun a group of people » *The volunteers are a great bunch of people.*
band, crowd, gaggle, gang, group, lot, multitude

bunch 2
noun several cut flowers held together » *Wyatt had left a bunch of flowers in her hotel room.*
bouquet, posy, spray

*Wyatt had left a **bunch** of flowers in her hotel room.*

bunch 3
noun a group of things » *George took out a bunch of keys and found the right one for the lock.*
batch, bundle, cluster, heap, load, pile, set

burden 1
noun a load that is carried » *My shopping bags turned out to be a real burden.*
load, weight

burden 2
noun something that worries you » *Betty had the added burden of looking after a sick pet.*
anxiety, care, strain, stress, trouble, worry, affliction, millstone, trial
related word:
adjective **onerous**

bureaucracy
noun complex rules and procedures » *Is there too much bureaucracy in government?*
administration, officialdom, red tape (informal), **regulations**

burn 1
verb to be on fire » *A fire burned in the fireplace.*
be ablaze, be on fire, blaze, flame, flare, flicker

*A fire **burned** in the fireplace.*

burn 2
verb to destroy with fire » *The rioters burned the house down.*
char, incinerate, scorch, singe

burst 1
verb to split apart » *Bella blew too much air into the balloon and it burst.*
break, crack, explode, puncture, rupture, split

burst 2
verb to happen or appear suddenly » *Marco burst into the room with important news.*
barge, break, erupt, rush

burst 3
noun a short period of something » *After a burst of energy, the dog fell asleep.*
fit, outbreak, rush, spate, surge, torrent

business 1
noun the buying and selling of goods or services » *Leah made a career in business.*
commerce, dealings, industry, trade, trading, transaction

business 2
noun an organization selling goods or services » *Monica wanted to work for the family business.*
company, corporation, enterprise, establishment, firm, organization, concern, conglomerate, venture

business 3
noun any event or situation » *This business has upset me.*
affair, issue, matter, problem, question, subject

bustle 1
verb to move hurriedly » *My mother bustled about the room putting things in place.*
dash, fuss, hurry, rush, scurry, scuttle

bustle 2
noun busy and noisy activity » *The city is full of the bustle of modern life.*
activity, commotion, excitement, flurry, fuss, hurry
antonym: **peace**

*The city is full of the **bustle** of modern life.*

busy 1
adjective doing something » *I can't go out tonight, I'm busy.*
active, employed, engaged, engrossed, occupied, working
antonym: **idle**

busy 2
adjective full of activity » *The station was busy with commuters.*
active, full, hectic, lively, restless

*The station was **busy** with commuters.*

busy 3
verb to occupy or keep busy » *Kathryn busied herself in the kitchen.*
absorb, employ, engage, immerse, occupy

but 1
conjunction although » *Heat the water until it is very hot but not boiling.*
although, though, while, yet

but 2
preposition with the exception of » *I packed everything but my hairdryer for my vacation.*
except, except for, other than, save

buy
verb to obtain with money » *I'd like to buy that bag.*
acquire, invest in, obtain, pay for, procure, purchase
antonym: **sell**

a b c d e f g h i j k l m n o p q r s t u v w x y z

33

» calculate

Cc

calculate
verb to work out a number or amount » *Cathy wanted to calculate the cost of the trip.*
compute, count, determine, work out

Cathy wanted to calculate the cost of the trip.

calculated
adjective deliberately planned » *Although it was winter, Anthony took a calculated risk and took the road through the mountains.*
aimed, designed, intended, planned
antonym: **unplanned**

call 1
verb to give a name » *He was called Jeff.*
christen, designate, dub, name

call 2
verb to telephone » *Ruby called my phone.*
contact, phone, ring, telephone

call 3
verb to say loudly » *I heard someone calling my name.*
announce, cry, cry out, shout, yell

call 4
noun an instance of someone shouting out » *There was a call for volunteers.*
cry, shout, yell

callous
adjective not concerned about other people » *He was mean and had a callous disregard for other people.*
cold, heartless, indifferent, insensitive, hard-bitten, hardhearted, unsympathetic
antonym: **caring**

calm 1
adjective not worried or excited » *Mia found that practising yoga helped her to keep calm.*
collected, composed, cool, impassive, relaxed, imperturbable, unemotional, unruffled
antonym: **worried**

Mia found that practising yoga helped her to keep calm.

calm 2
adjective still because there is no wind » *Tuesday was a fine, clear, and calm day.*
still, tranquil
antonym: **rough, windy**

calm 3
noun the state of being peaceful » *In the calm of the night, the bats emerged from the cave.*
calmness, peace, peacefulness, quiet, serenity, stillness

calm 4
verb to make less upset or excited » *He tried to calm the baby when it cried.*
quieten, relax, soothe, mollify, placate

campaign
noun actions planned to get a certain result » *She went on a campaign, seeking votes to be elected president.*
crusade, movement, operation, push

She went on a campaign, seeking votes to be elected president.

cancel 1
verb to stop something from happening » *We're going to have to cancel our picnic because it's raining.*
abandon, call off

cancel 2
verb to stop something from being valid » *Peter needed to cancel his lost credit card.*
annul, quash, repeal, revoke, abrogate, countermand, rescind

candid
adjective honest and frank » *She gave a candid interview and revealed many secrets.*
blunt, frank, honest, open, straightforward, truthful

candidate
noun a person being considered for a position » *Hugh was the best candidate for the job.*
applicant, competitor, contender, nominee, possibility, runner

capable
adjective able to do something well » *Miguel was a capable leader and brought out the best in his team.*
able, accomplished, adept, competent, efficient, proficient, skilful
antonym: **incompetent**

capacity 1
noun the maximum amount that something holds or produces » *What is the capacity of the glass?*
dimensions, room, size, space, volume

capacity 2
noun a person's power or ability to do something » *Her capacity to help was limited by being so far away.*
ability, capability, facility, gift, potential, power

capture 1
verb to take prisoner » *Sharon's knight captured Ian's king on the chessboard.*
apprehend, arrest, catch, seize, take
antonym: **release**

capture 2
noun the act of capturing » *The fish couldn't evade its capture by the bear.*
arrest, seizure, taking, trapping

The fish couldn't evade its capture by the bear.

car
noun a vehicle for carrying a few people » *Dad drove the car to the station to pick us up.*
auto, **automobile** (formal), **vehicle**, **wheels** (slang)

care 1
verb to be concerned about something » *I care about the environment.*
be bothered, **be concerned**, **be interested**, **mind**

care 2
noun something that causes you to worry » *Luke didn't have a care in the world.*
anxiety, **concern**, **stress**, **trouble**, **woe**, **worry**, **tribulation**, **vexation**

care 3
noun close attention when doing something » *We took great care to make him feel at home.*
attention, **caution**, **pains**, **circumspection**, **forethought**

careful 1
adjective acting with care » *Be careful with that vase.*
cautious, **prudent**, **chary**, **circumspect**, **punctilious**
antonym: **careless**

careful 2
adjective complete and well done » *The experiment needs careful planning.*
meticulous, **painstaking**, **precise**, **thorough**
antonym: **careless**

careless 1
adjective not taking enough care » *Heather had careless and messy handwriting.*
irresponsible, **neglectful**, **sloppy** (informal), **cavalier**, **lackadaisical**, **slapdash**, **slipshod**
antonym: **careful**

careless 2
adjective relaxed and unconcerned » *Sal shrugged and gave a careless laugh.*
casual, **nonchalant**, **offhand**

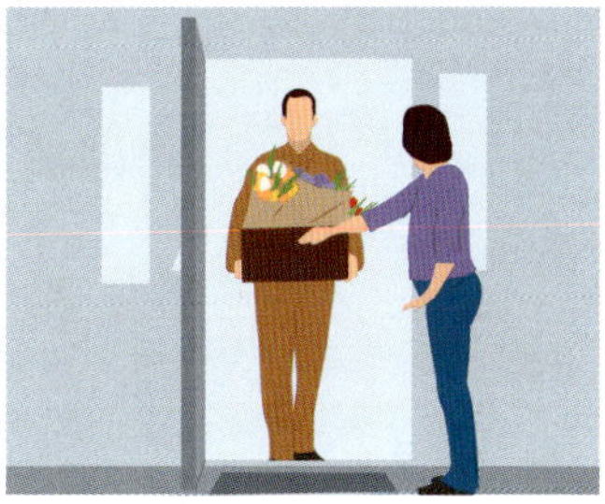

He carried the heavy box.

carry
verb to hold and take something somewhere » *He carried the heavy box.*
bear, **convey** (formal), **lug**, **take**, **transport**

carry out
verb to do and complete something » *The surgeon carried out the operation.*
accomplish, **achieve**, **fulfill**, **perform**, **execute**, **implement**

carve
verb to make something by cutting
▼ SEE BELOW

case 1
noun a particular situation or example » *There have been six cases of chickenpox in my class this year.*
example, **illustration**, **instance**, **occasion**, **occurrence**

case 2
noun a container for holding something » *Kay kept her glasses in a red case.*
box, **container**, **holder**, **receptacle**

Kay kept her glasses in a red case.

case 3
noun a trial or inquiry » *The court case was heard behind closed doors.*
action, **lawsuit**, **proceedings**, **trial**

hew
He had hewn the original block that the lion was carved from.

sculpt
It was his first time sculpting a large statue.

engrave
He intended to engrave the title into the block.

inscribe
He finished by inscribing his name on the sculpture.

chisel
He chiselled the details into the lion's face.

carve
verb to make something by cutting
» *He carved the lion out of a block of stone.*

cut
He cut the excess stone from the tail.

whittle
He preferred to whittle wood than to carve stone.

» **ca**sual

celebration
noun an event in honour of a special occasion
» *The family dinner was a birthday **celebration**.*

festival
*They went to church for the religious **festival**.*

gala
*The sporting contest finished with a **gala**.*

festivity
*The wedding **festivities** went on for a week.*

party
*Would you like to come to my **party**?*

revelry
*She joined in the **revelry** with lots of enthusiasm.*

---

casual 1
adjective happening by chance » *The casual meeting led to a great friendship.*
accidental, chance, incidental, fortuitous, serendipitous, unintentional, unpremeditated
antonym: **deliberate**

casual 2
adjective showing no concern or interest » *Mick gave a casual glance over his shoulder.*
careless, cursory, nonchalant, offhand, relaxed, blasé, insouciant, lackadaisical, perfunctory
antonym: **concerned**

cat
noun a small animal kept as a pet » *Fiona had three cats.*
feline, kitty, puss or **pussy** or **pussycat** (informal)
related words:
adjective **feline**; *male* **tom**; *female* **queen**; *young* **kitten**

Fiona had three **cats**.

catch 1
verb to capture an animal or fish » *Dad went fishing to catch some trout for dinner.*
capture, snare, trap

catch 2
verb to capture a person » *The police planned a way to catch the suspects.*
apprehend, arrest

catch 3
noun a device that fastens something » *The windows were fitted with safety catches.*
bolt, clasp, clip, latch

catch 4
noun a hidden difficulty » *The catch is that it will take a month to arrive.*
disadvantage, drawback, snag, fly in the ointment, stumbling block

category
noun a set of things with something in common » *The items were organized into six different categories.*
class, classification, group, set, sort, type

cause 1
noun what makes something happen » *The cause of the fire was unknown.*
origin, root, source

36

cause [2]
noun an aim supported by a group » *Sarah took up the cause to save the old theatre.*
aim, ideal, movement

cause [3]
noun the reason for something » *The boys gave us cause to believe the story was true.*
basis, grounds, justification, motivation, motive, reason

cause [4]
verb to make something happen » *The broken-down train caused delays.*
bring about, create, generate, produce, provoke, effect, engender, lead to, result in

caution [1]
noun great care taken in order to avoid danger » *Use caution when skating.*
care, prudence, forethought, circumspection

*Use **caution** when skating.*

caution [2]
verb to scold or warn someone against doing something » *The policeman cautioned that riding a bike without a helmet is dangerous.*
alert, reprimand, warn

cautious
adjective acting very carefully to avoid danger » *The zookeeper was cautious in the crocodile enclosure.*
careful, guarded, tentative, wary, prudent
antonym: **daring**

cease [1]
verb to stop happening » *The noise ceased and peace was restored.*
be over, come to an end, die away, end, finish, stop
antonym: **begin**

cease [2]
verb to stop doing something » *He ceased talking when the teacher called for quiet.*
desist from, discontinue, finish, give up, stop, suspend
antonym: **start**

celebrate
verb to do something special to mark an event » *It's my birthday—let's celebrate!*
commemorate, party, rejoice
antonym: **mourn**

celebration
noun an event in honour of a special occasion
◀◀ SEE LEFT

celebrity
noun a famous person » *The presenter interviewed the celebrity on the red carpet.*
big name, name, personality, star, superstar, VIP

*The presenter interviewed the **celebrity** on the red carpet.*

censure [1]
noun strong disapproval » *His bad behaviour led to censure from his parents.*
blame, condemnation, criticism, disapproval, reproach

censure [2]
verb to criticize severely » *The school censured Mike for his graffiti.*
condemn, criticize, denounce, reproach, berate, castigate

centre [1]
noun the mid-point of a circle or activity » *We headed for the city centre.*
core, focus, heart, hub, middle
antonym: **edge**

centre [2]
verb to have as the main subject » *The argument centred on the school's uniform policy.*
concentrate, focus, revolve

ceremony [1]
noun formal actions done for a special occasion » *They had a traditional wedding ceremony.*
observance, pomp, rite, ritual, service, tradition

*They had a traditional wedding **ceremony**.*

ceremony [2]
noun formal and polite behaviour » *The mayor was welcomed with great ceremony.*
decorum, etiquette, formality, niceties, protocol

certain [1]
adjective definite or reliable » *It is certain to rain.*
definite, established, guaranteed, inevitable, known, sure, undeniable
antonym: **uncertain**

certain [2]
adjective having no doubt in your mind » *Lily's certain that she will succeed.*
clear, confident, convinced, definite, positive, satisfied, sure
antonym: **uncertain**

certainly
adverb without any doubt » *I'll certainly do all I can to help.*
definitely, undeniably, undoubtedly, unquestionably, without doubt

challenge [1]
noun a suggestion to try something » *The coach set the team a series of challenges.*
dare, face-off (informal)

challenge [2]
verb to give someone a challenge » *Sue challenged me to a game of tennis.*
dare, defy

challenge [3]
verb to question the truth or value of something » *I challenged Jeff's story about where he had been.*
dispute, question

champion [1]
noun a person who wins a competition » *She won the contest to become the regional judo champion.*
hero, title holder, victor, winner

*She won the contest to become the regional judo **champion**.*

champion »

» champion

champion 2
noun someone who supports a group, cause, or principle » *Judith became a champion for animal rights.*
advocate, defender, guardian, protector

champion 3
verb to support a group, cause, or principle » *We championed his request for new sports equipment.*
defend, fight for, promote, stick up for (informal), support, uphold, advocate, espouse

chance 1
noun a possibility of something happening » *Lucy had a good chance of success.*
likelihood, odds, possibility, probability, prospect

chance 2
noun an opportunity to do something » *Please give me a chance to explain why I'm late.*
occasion, opening, opportunity, time

chance 3
noun the way things happen without being planned » *We met up by chance.*
accident, coincidence, fortune, luck
related word:
adjective fortuitous

change 1
noun an alteration in something » *There was a change in her attitude from sulky to helpful.*
alteration, difference, modification, transformation, metamorphosis, mutation, transition, transmutation

change 2
verb to make or become different » *We changed the garage into a TV room.*
alter, convert, moderate, modify, reform, transform, metamorphose, mutate, transmute

change 3
verb to exchange one thing for another » *Can I change the red T-shirt for a black one?*
barter, exchange, interchange, replace, substitute, swap, trade

Can I **change** the red T-shirt for a black one?

changeable
adjective likely to change all the time » *The weather was changeable—hot one minute and cold the next.*
erratic, fickle, irregular, unpredictable, unstable, variable, volatile, mercurial, mutable, protean
antonym: constant

character 1
noun the qualities of a person » *She has a sunny character.*
nature, personality, temperament, disposition, makeup, quality, temper

character 2
noun an honourable nature » *Mark showed great character in handling a tricky situation.*
honour, integrity, strength

characteristic 1
noun a typical quality » *Mark's chief characteristic is honesty.*
attribute, feature, property, quality, trait, idiosyncrasy, peculiarity, quirk

characteristic 2
adjective typical of a person or thing » *Jack responded with characteristic generosity.*
distinctive, distinguishing, typical, idiosyncratic, peculiar, singular, symptomatic
antonym: uncharacteristic

charge 1
verb to ask someone for money as a payment » *The store charged me a fair price.*
ask (for), bill, demand, levy

charge 2
noun the price you have to pay for something » *There was an additional charge for a bag.*
cost, fee, payment, price

charge 3
verb to rush forward, often to attack someone » *The rhino charged towards us.*
dash, rush, stampede, storm

The rhino **charged** towards us.

charm 1
noun an attractive quality » *The house has real charm.*
allure, appeal, attraction, magnetism, fascination

charm 2
verb to use charm to please someone » *He charmed the audience with his smile.*
bewitch, captivate, delight, entrance, beguile, enchant, enrapture

child
noun a young person » *She was their fourth child.*

 newborn

 baby

 infant

 tot

 toddler

 kid   juvenile

chase 1
verb to try to catch someone or something » *My sister chased me until I gave up.*
hunt, pursue

chase 2
verb to force to go somewhere » *The dog chased the postman out of the gate.*
drive, hound, expel, put to flight

chat 1
noun a friendly talk » *Eloise came over and joined us for a chat.*
conversation, gossip, natter (informal), **talk**

chat 2
verb to talk in a friendly way » *Dan chatted to his father.*
gossip, natter (informal), **talk**

cheap 1
adjective costing very little » *Cheap flights are available.*
bargain, economical, inexpensive, reasonable, cut-price, low-cost, low-priced
antonym: **expensive**

cheap 2
adjective inexpensive but of poor quality » *His cheap trousers ripped when he sat down.*
inferior, second-rate, tawdry

He cheated in the exam.

cheat
verb to get something from someone dishonestly » *He cheated in the exam.*
con (informal), **deceive, defraud, dupe, fleece, rip off** (slang), **swindle,** hoodwink

check 1
verb to examine something » *Please check all the details before signing.*
check out (informal), **examine, inspect, test,** inquire into, look over, scrutinize

check 2
verb to reduce or stop something » *Hand washing will check the spread of germs.*
control, curb, halt, inhibit, restrain, stop

check 3
noun an examination » *The technician performed a thorough check of the equipment.*
examination, inspection, test

cheek
noun speech or behaviour that is rude or disrespectful » *I'm amazed they had the cheek to ask in the first place.*
audacity, gall, impudence, insolence, nerve, rudeness, effrontery, temerity

cheeky
adjective rude and disrespectful » *The children were cheeky to their mom.*
impertinent, impudent, insolent, rude
antonym: **polite**

cheerful
adjective in a happy mood » *Eliza was feeling cheerful, despite the rain.*
bright, buoyant, cheery, happy, jaunty, jolly, light-hearted, merry
antonym: **miserable**

Eliza was feeling cheerful, despite the rain.

cheery
adjective happy and cheerful » *Jill sounded very cheery on the phone.*
cheerful, chirpy, good-humoured, happy, jolly, sunny, upbeat, genial, jovial
antonym: **gloomy**

chew
verb to break food up with the teeth » *My mom always told me to eat slowly and chew properly with my mouth closed.*
crunch, gnaw, munch, champ, chomp, masticate

chief 1
noun the leader of a group or organization » *He was the new chief of police.*
boss, chieftain, director, governor, head, leader, manager

chief 2
adjective most important » *The job went to one of his chief rivals.*
foremost, key, main, prevailing, primary, prime, principal, pre-eminent, premier

child
noun a young person
▼ SEE BELOW

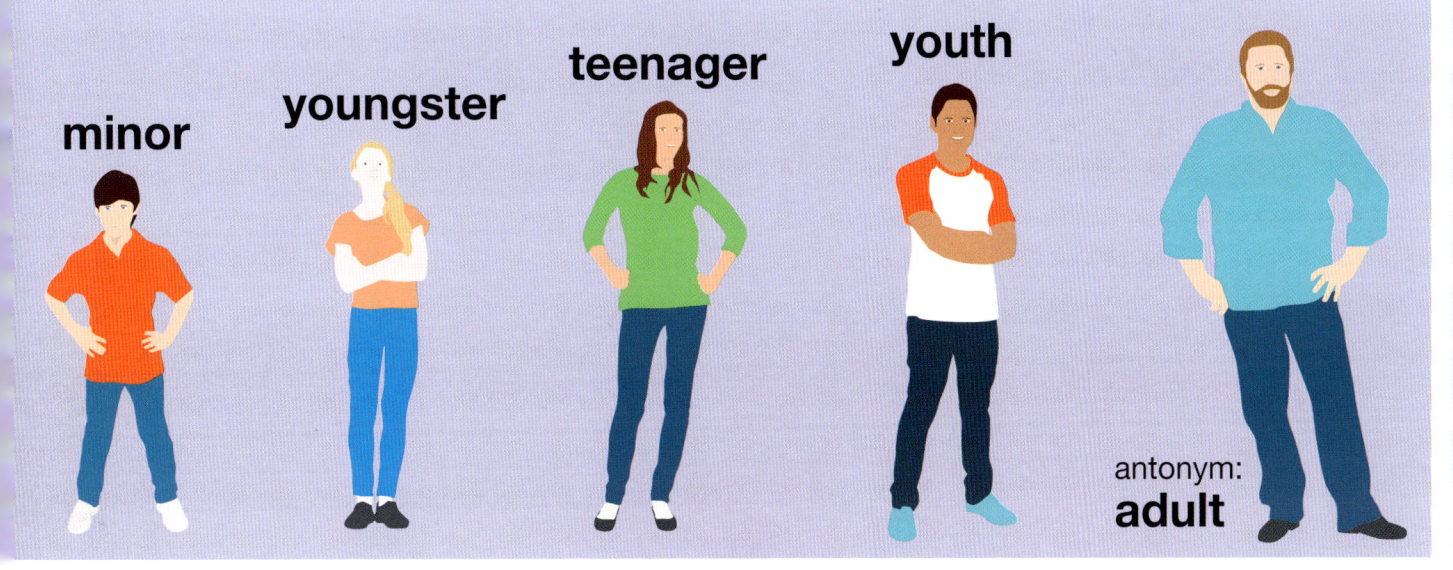

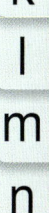

---

child »

minor   youngster   teenager   youth

antonym: **adult**

» **childish**

childish
adjective immature and foolish
» *Sulking and stamping your feet when you don't get your own way is childish behaviour.*
immature, infantile, juvenile, puerile
antonym: **mature**

choice 1
noun a range of things to choose from » *The hat is available in a choice of colours and sizes.*
range, selection, variety

choice 2
noun the power to choose
» *Paul was given a choice about what to eat.*
alternative, option, say

choose
verb to decide to have or do something » *There were so many flavours of ice cream to choose from.*
opt for, pick, select, take, elect, settle on

chop
verb to cut down or into pieces
» *I saw him chopping wood with an axe.*
cut, fell, hack, lop, cleave, hew

I saw him chopping wood with an axe.

circulate
verb to pass around
» *Grandpa's birthday card was circulated around the family for everyone to sign.*
distribute, propagate, spread, disseminate, promulgate

The city was built on the banks of a river.

city
noun a large town
» *The city was built on the banks of a river.*
metropolis, town, municipality
related word: *adjective* **civic**

civilized
adjective having an advanced society » *We live in a civilized country.*
cultured, enlightened

claim 1
verb to say something is the case » *Mr. Brown claims to have lived here all his life.*
allege, assert, hold, insist, maintain, profess

claim 2
noun a statement that something is the case
» *Emma admitted that the claims about her were true.*
allegation, assertion, pretension, protestation

clash 1
verb to fight or argue with another person » *My brother and sister constantly clash, but they always make up.*
battle, fight, quarrel, wrangle

clash 2
verb of two things: to be so different that they do not go together » *David's plan to stay in the playground clashed with the teacher's demand that he come into the classroom.*
conflict, contradict, differ, disagree, go against, jar

clash 3
noun a fight or argument
» *The latest clash between the two teams ended in players being given penalties.*
battle, conflict, confrontation, fight, skirmish (informal), **squabble, struggle**

clasp 1
verb to hold something tightly
» *Helena clasped her locket in her hands.*
clutch, embrace, grip, hold, hug, press, squeeze

clasp 2
noun a fastening such as a hook or catch » *Miriam undid the clasp on her coat.*
buckle, catch, clip, fastener, fastening

class 1
noun a group of a particular type » *Animals are grouped into classes including mammals, birds, fish, reptiles, and amphibians.*
category, genre, grade, group, kind, set, sort, type

class 2
verb to regard as being in a particular group
» *The children were classed into different team colours.*
categorize, classify, designate, grade, rank, rate

The children were classed into different team colours.

classify
verb to arrange similar things in groups » *We can classify the books into fiction and non-fiction.*
arrange, categorize, grade, rank, sort, pigeonhole, systematize, tabulate

clean 1
adjective free from dirt or marks » *Patrick's clothes are always very clean.*
immaculate, impeccable, laundered, spotless, washed
antonym: **dirty**

clean 2
adjective free from germs or infection » *There was a source of clean drinking water.*
antiseptic, hygienic, purified, sterilized, uncontaminated, unpolluted
antonym: **contaminated**

clean 3
verb to remove dirt from
▶▶ SEE RIGHT

clear 1
adjective easy to see or understand » *It was clear from her tearful voice that she was upset.*
apparent, blatant, conspicuous, definite, evident, explicit, obvious, plain, incontrovertible, manifest, palpable, patent, unequivocal

clear 2
adjective easy to see through » *The liquid inside the glass beaker was clear.*
crystalline, glassy, translucent, transparent, limpid, pellucid, see-through
antonym: **cloudy**

The liquid inside the glass beaker was clear.

close »

clear [3]
verb to prove someone is not guilty » *Bea was cleared of having any part in the incident.*
absolve, acquit
antonym: **convict**

clever
adjective very intelligent » *Luis was clever and always scored high marks in exams.*
brainy (informal)**, bright, intelligent, shrewd, smart, astute, quick-witted, sagacious**
antonym: **stupid**

climb
verb to move upwards over something » *We climbed the mountain in a day.*
ascend, clamber, mount, scale

close [1]
verb to shut something » *Claire closed the gate behind her when she left.*
secure, shut
antonym: **open**

Claire closed the gate behind her when she left.

close [2]
verb to block so that nothing can pass » *All the roads out of town are closed.*
bar, block, obstruct, seal

close [3]
adjective near to something » *We went to a restaurant close to our home.*
adjacent, adjoining, at hand, handy, near, nearby, neighbouring
antonym: **distant**

cleanse
There are lotions to **cleanse** the skin.

dust
I vacuumed, **dusted**, and polished the living room.

scour
He **scoured** the sink.

sponge
Sponge down the surfaces.

scrub
I started to **scrub** off the dirt.

swab
The sailor **swabbed** the deck.

wipe
She **wiped** the windows with a dry cloth.

wash
He **washed** dishes in a restaurant.

clean
[3] verb to remove dirt from » *She cleaned the house from top to bottom.*

antonym: **soil**
Using a dirty mop can soil the floor.

41

» close

apparel
She often chose bright **apparel** in the summer.

clothing
We are collecting food and **clothing** for the homeless.

attire (formal)
The T-shirt was not suitable **attire** for work.

dress
She liked to wear her party **dress**.

wear
She didn't have much winter **wear**.

outfit
The red shirt was an essential part of her **outfit**.

gear (informal)
She had some sports **gear** including a tennis dress.

wardrobe
She planned to buy herself a whole new **wardrobe** in the Fall.

costume
Her favourite **costume** came from her sister.

garments
There were too many **garments** in her closet.

garb
She preferred colourful **garb**.

clothes

plural noun the things people wear
» Alicia spends all her money on **clothes**.

close [4]
adjective friendly and loving
» We became close friends.
attached, dear, devoted, familiar, friendly, intimate, loving
antonym: **distant**

cloth
noun woven or knitted fabric
» The sofa was covered in bright red cloth.
fabric, material, textile

clothes
plural noun the things people wear
▲ SEE ABOVE

cloud [1]
noun a mass of vapour or smoke » The sky was dark with clouds.
billow, fog, haze, mist, vapour

cloud [2]
verb to make something confusing » Anger has clouded his judgment.
confuse, distort, muddle

cloudy [1]
adjective full of clouds
» It's a very cloudy sky today.
dull, gloomy, leaden, overcast
antonym: **clear**

cloudy [2]
adjective difficult to see through » The liquid in the glass was cloudy.
muddy, murky, opaque
antonym: **clear**

club [1]
noun an organization for people with a special interest
» We joined the swimming club today.
association, circle, group, guild, society, union

club [2]
noun a heavy stick » *Andy dressed up as a caveman and carried a club to the costume party.*
bat, stick, truncheon

clue
noun something that helps to solve a problem or mystery » *The police looked for clues to solve the crime.*
hint, indication, lead

clumsiness
noun awkwardness of movement » *Meg's usual clumsiness was made worse by her high-heeled shoes.*
awkwardness, ungainliness

Meg's usual clumsiness was made worse by her high-heeled shoes.

clumsy
adjective moving awkwardly » *Rob is big and clumsy in his movements.*
awkward, gauche, lumbering, uncoordinated, ungainly, accident-prone, bumbling, gawky, maladroit
antonym: **graceful**

coast
noun the land next to the sea » *We vacationed on the coast this year.*
beach, border, coastline, seaside, shore

coat [1]
noun an animal's fur or hair » *Anna gave the dog's coat a brush.*
fleece, fur, hair, hide, pelt, skin, wool

coat [2]
noun a warm piece of outerwear clothing » *You'll need a coat; it's cold outside.*
jacket, overcoat, parka, raincoat

coating
noun a layer of something » *The lake had a thin coating of ice.*
coat, covering, layer

The lake had a thin coating of ice.

coax
verb to persuade gently » *We coaxed her into coming to the shopping mall with us.*
cajole, persuade, talk into, inveigle, prevail upon, wheedle

coil
verb to wind in loops » *The snake coiled its body around the tree.*
curl, loop, spiral, twine, twist, wind

cold [1]
adjective having a low temperature » *The spring weather felt so cold that it felt more like midwinter.*
arctic, biting, bitter, bleak, chilly, freezing, icy, raw, wintry
antonym: **hot**

cold [2]
adjective not showing affection » *Aunt Maud was a cold, unfeeling person who loved her cats more than people.*
aloof, distant, frigid, lukewarm, reserved, stony, standoffish, undemonstrative
antonym: **warm**

collapse [1]
verb to fall down » *Stand clear—the old building looks like it could collapse at any minute.*
fall down, give way

collapse [2]
verb to fail » *The business collapsed due to a lack of money.*
fail, fold, founder

collapse [3]
noun the failure of something » *The collapse of the project was caused by a disagreement in the team.*
downfall, failure

colleague
noun a person someone works with » *My colleagues all worked extremely hard on the latest project.*
associate, fellow worker, partner, workmate

collect
verb to gather together » *My brother Sebastian collects stamps that come from all over the world.*
accumulate, assemble, gather, raise, aggregate, amass
antonym: **scatter**

My brother Sebastian collects stamps that come from all over the world.

We visited the collection of paintings in the gallery.

collection
noun a group of things collected together » *We visited the collection of paintings in the gallery.*
assortment, group, store

colloquial
adjective used in everyday conversation » *Martin used colloquial expressions like: "He's gone nuts."*
conversational, everyday, informal, demotic, idiomatic, vernacular

colony [1]
noun a country controlled by another country » *Canada used to be made up of French and English colonies.*
dependency, dominion, territory

colony [2]
noun a group of settlers in a place » *A colony of Scots settled in Australia.*
community, outpost, settlement

colossal
adjective very large indeed » *The statue was colossal.*
enormous, gigantic, huge, immense, mammoth, massive, vast
antonym: **tiny**

colour [1]
verb to give something a colour » *Jules used hair dye to colour his hair.*
dye, paint, stain, tint

colour

colour [2]
verb to affect the way you think
» *The rainy weather coloured her opinion of the trip.*
bias, distort, prejudice, slant

colour [3]
noun a shade or hue
» *Annette's favourite colour is blue.*
hue, pigmentation, shade, tint
▶▶ SEE RIGHT

colour [4]
noun a substance used to give colour » *She added a few drops of red food colour to the icing.*
dye, paint, pigment

colourful [1]
adjective full of colour
» *The parrots have such colourful feathers.*
bright, brilliant, intense, jazzy (informal)**, rich, vibrant, vivid, kaleidoscopic, multicoloured, psychedelic**
antonym: **dull**

colourful [2]
adjective interesting or exciting
» *The girl gave a colourful account of her journey to the farm.*
graphic, interesting, lively, rich, vivid
antonym: **dull**

combination
noun a mixture of things
» *Green is a combination of yellow and blue.*
amalgamation, blend, mix, mixture, amalgam, composite, meld

Green is a combination of yellow and blue.

combine
verb to join or mix together
» *The performer combined magic and dance in his act.*
amalgamate, blend, fuse, integrate, merge, mix, unite, meld, synthesize
antonym: **separate**

come [1]
verb to move or arrive somewhere » *The teacher came into the room.*
appear, arrive, enter, materialize, show up (informal)**, turn up** (informal)

come [2]
verb to happen or take place
» *The opportunity to audition comes only twice a year.*
happen, occur, take place

comfort [1]
noun a state of ease
» *The seating in the airy living room was designed for comfort.*
ease, luxury, wellbeing

The seating in the airy living room was designed for comfort.

comfort [2]
noun relief from worry or unhappiness » *Jan's words gave him some comfort.*
consolation, help, relief, satisfaction, support

comfort [3]
verb to give someone comfort
» *The woman tried to comfort her screaming baby.*
cheer, console, reassure, soothe

Trish made herself comfortable and read a book.

comfortable [1]
adjective physically relaxing
» *Trish made herself comfortable and read a book.*
cosy, easy, homely, relaxing, restful
antonym: **uncomfortable**

comfortable [2]
adjective feeling at ease
» *The couple sat together in comfortable silence.*
at ease, at home, contented, happy, relaxed
antonym: **uneasy**

command [1]
verb to order someone to do something » *The soccer coach commanded the team to run around the field.*
bid, demand, direct, order, charge

command [2]
verb to be in charge of
» *The politician asked to meet the general who had commanded the rescue mission.*
control, head, lead, manage, supervise

command [3]
noun an order to do something
» *Everyone in the class jumped up and down at the teacher's command.*
bidding, decree, directive, injunction, instruction, order, behest, edict

command [4]
noun knowledge and ability
» *Ned had a good command of several languages.*
grasp, knowledge, mastery

commemorate
verb to do something in memory of » *A concert was held to commemorate the anniversary of the victory.*
celebrate, honour, memorialize, pay tribute to

comment [1]
verb to make a remark
» *She was asked to comment on the situation.*
mention, note, observe, point out, remark, say, interpose, opine

She was asked to comment on the situation.

comment [2]
noun something you say
» *Mary made a nice comment about my new hairstyle.*
observation, remark, statement

commit
verb to do something
» *It appears that a crime has been committed.*
carry out, do, perform, perpetrate

common [1]
adjective of many people
» *The statue was a common stop for tourists.*
general, popular, prevailing, prevalent, universal, widespread
antonym: **rare**

co**mmon** »

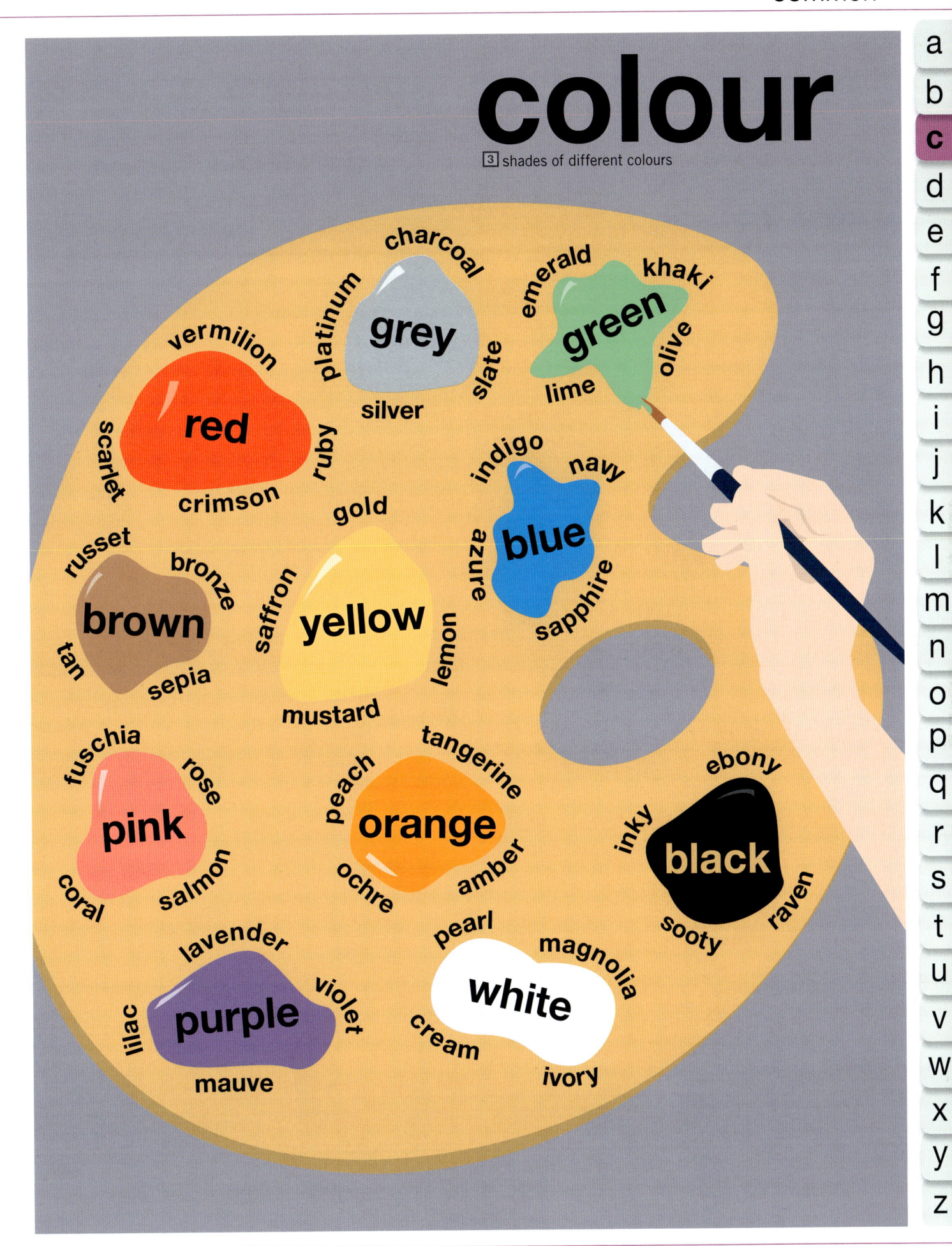

colour

3 shades of different colours

- **red**: vermilion, scarlet, ruby, crimson
- **grey**: charcoal, platinum, silver, slate
- **green**: emerald, khaki, olive, lime
- **brown**: russet, bronze, tan, sepia
- **yellow**: saffron, gold, lemon, mustard
- **blue**: indigo, navy, azure, sapphire
- **pink**: fuschia, rose, coral, salmon
- **orange**: peach, tangerine, ochre, amber
- **black**: ebony, inky, sooty, raven
- **purple**: lavender, violet, lilac, mauve
- **white**: pearl, magnolia, cream, ivory

45

competitor

noun a person who competes for something
» He was one of seven **competitors** in the quiz.

adversary, competition, opponent, rival, challenger, contestant, opposition

common [2]
adjective not special
» Sparrows are common birds.
average, commonplace, everyday, ordinary, plain, standard, usual, run-of-the-mill
antonym: **special**

common [3]
adjective having bad taste or manners » Harry was common and rude.
coarse, rude, vulgar
antonym: **refined**

common sense
noun good judgment in practical matters » Use your common sense to find the clue.
good sense, judgment, level-headedness, prudence, wit

communicate [1]
verb to be in touch with someone » We communicate mainly by text message.
be in contact, be in touch, correspond

communicate [2]
verb to pass on information » The results will be communicated by post.
convey, impart, inform, pass on, retweet, spread, transmit, tweet, disseminate, make known

companion
noun someone you travel with or spend time with » Matt has been her constant companion for the last six years.
comrade, crony (old-fashioned), friend, pal (informal), partner

company [1]
noun a business » The store was run by a large company.
business, corporation, establishment, firm, house

company [2]
noun a group of people » A company of actors performed a play.
assembly, band, circle, community, crowd, ensemble, group, party, troupe, concourse, coterie

company [3]
noun the act of spending time with someone » I really enjoy your company.
companionship, presence

compare
verb to look at things for similarities or differences » Compare the two pictures and spot the differences.
contrast, juxtapose, weigh

compartment [1]
noun one of the separate parts of an object » The fridge has a freezer compartment at the top.
bay, chamber, division, section

The passengers in the compartment waited for the train to move.

compartment [2]
noun a section of a railway carriage » The passengers in the compartment waited for the train to move.
carriage

compassionate
adjective feeling or showing sympathy and pity for others » The compassionate man adopted the stray dog.
caring, humane, kind, kind-hearted, merciful, sympathetic, tender, benevolent, humanitarian

The fridge has a freezer compartment at the top.

conceit »

compensate [1]
verb to repay someone for loss or damage » *The company offered to compensate the customer for the broken laptop plus the inconvenience.*
atone, refund, repay, reward, make amends, make restitution, recompense, reimburse, remunerate

compensate [2]
verb to cancel out » *Theo's enthusiasm compensated for his lack of skill at knitting.*
balance, cancel out, counteract, make up for, offset, counterbalance, redress

compensation
noun something that makes up for loss or damage » *She received compensation for the damage to her property.*
amends, atonement, damages, payment, recompense, reimbursement, remuneration, reparation, restitution

compete
verb to try to win » *The teams competed for the title in the final game of the season.*
contend, contest, fight, vie

The teams competed for the title in the final game of the season.

competition [1]
noun an attempt to win » *There's a lot of competition for places on the team.*
contention, contest, opposition, rivalry, struggle

competition [2]
noun a contest to find the winner in something » *Jemima won the surfing competition.*
championship, contest, event, tournament

competitor
noun a person who competes for something
◀◀ SEE LEFT

complain
verb to express dissatisfaction » *Poppy complained to the teacher that John had taken her pencil.*
carp, find fault, grouse, grumble, kick up a fuss (informal), **moan, whine,** bemoan, bewail

Poppy complained to the teacher that John had taken her pencil.

complaint
noun an instance of complaining about something » *There have been a number of complaints about the noise from the construction site.*
criticism, grievance, grumble, objection, protest

complete [1]
adjective to the greatest degree possible » *The garden had undergone a complete transformation.*
absolute, consummate, outright, perfect, thorough, total, utter

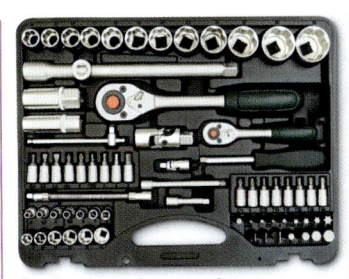

Lesley owned a complete set of tools with all the attachments.

complete [2]
adjective with nothing missing » *Lesley owned a complete set of tools with all the attachments.*
entire, full, intact, undivided, whole
antonym: **incomplete**

complete [3]
verb to finish » *Tim has just completed his first fun run.*
conclude, end, finish

complex [1]
adjective having many different parts » *The complex puzzle took a long time to solve.*
complicated, difficult, intricate, involved, tangled, convoluted, tortuous
antonym: **simple**

complex [2]
noun an emotional problem » *Vincent has a complex about being accident prone.*
fixation, obsession, phobia, preoccupation, problem, thing (informal)

complicated
adjective complex and difficult » *The questions in the test were so complicated that he couldn't understand them.*
complex, convoluted, elaborate, intricate, involved, labyrinthine, perplexing
antonym: **simple**

compose
verb to create or write » *Stephen has composed a song.*
create, devise, invent, produce, write

comprehend
verb to understand or appreciate something » *It took me a moment to comprehend what Lewis was saying.*
appreciate, fathom, grasp, see, take in, understand, work out

compulsory
adjective required by law » *School attendance is compulsory.*
mandatory, obligatory, required, requisite
antonym: **voluntary**

computer
noun an electronic machine that stores and processes data » *Ana used a computer to work out the company's profits.*
laptop, PC, tablet

Ana used a computer to work out the company's profits.

con [1]
verb to trick someone into doing or believing something » *Joshua conned me into buying his broken bike.*
cheat, deceive, mislead, swindle, trick, defraud, dupe

con [2]
noun a trick intended to mislead or disadvantage someone » *The packaging is a con—it makes the contents look twice as big as they are.*
bluff, deception, fraud, swindle, trick

conceit
noun excessive pride » *The singer made so many demands; his conceit was insufferable.*
egotism, pride, self-importance, vanity, narcissism, vainglory

conceited

adjective too proud » *She was conceited—so full of herself.*
cocky, egotistical, self-important, vain, narcissistic, swollen-headed, vainglorious
antonym: **modest**

concentrate 1

verb to give something all your attention » *Hannah was trying hard to concentrate on her studies.*
be engrossed in, focus your attention on, give your attention to, put your mind to

Hannah was trying hard to concentrate on her studies.

concentrate 2

verb to be found in one place » *The guitar shops are concentrated in one street.*
accumulate, collect, gather

concern 1

noun a feeling of worry » *Martin's timing was a concern—he was always late.*
anxiety, apprehension, disquiet, worry

concern 2

noun someone's duty or responsibility » *The child's health is the parent's concern.*
affair, business, responsibility

concern 3

verb to make someone worried » *It concerns me that Leo doesn't want to talk to the teacher about the problem.*
bother, distress, disturb, trouble, worry, disquiet, perturb

concern 4

verb to affect or involve » *This concerns both of you.*
affect, apply to, be relevant to, involve, bear on, pertain to, touch

concise

adjective using no unnecessary words » *The report was short and concise.*
brief, short, succinct, terse, laconic, pithy
antonym: **long**

conclude 1

verb to decide something » *Dad concluded that I had been right after all.*
decide, deduce, infer, judge, reckon (informal), **suppose, surmise**

conclude 2

verb to finish something » *She concluded the letter by signing her name.*
close, end, finish, round off, wind up
antonym: **begin**

She concluded the letter by signing her name.

conclusion 1

noun a decision made after thinking carefully about something » *I've come to the conclusion that she was lying.*
deduction, inference, judgment, verdict

conclusion 2

noun the finish or ending of something » *A period marks the conclusion of a sentence.*
close, end, ending, finish, termination
antonym: **beginning**

condemn 1

verb to say that something is bad or unacceptable » *The scheme was condemned for being a waste of money.*
blame, censure, criticize, damn, denounce

condemn 2

verb to give a punishment » *The thief was condemned to five years in prison.*
damn, doom, sentence

condition 1

noun the state of something » *The house is in good condition and needs no repairs.*
form, shape, state

condition 2

noun something required for something else to be possible » *Emily was allowed to go to the party on the condition that she first cleaned her room.*
prerequisite, provision, proviso, qualification, requirement, requisite, stipulation, terms

conduct 1

verb to carry out an activity or task » *We conducted an experiment in science class.*
carry out, direct, do, manage, organize, perform, run, execute, implement, orchestrate

conduct 2

noun the way someone behaves » *Mary's conduct was a good example to others.*
attitude, behaviour, manners, ways, comportment, demeanour

conduct yourself

verb to behave in a particular way » *The way you conduct yourself reflects on the school.*
act, behave, acquit yourself

conference

noun a meeting for discussion » *The team held a conference to discuss the new project.*
congress, convention, discussion, forum, meeting, colloquium, convocation, symposium

The team held a conference to discuss the new project.

confess

verb to admit to something » *The boy confessed to eating the entire package of cookies.*
acknowledge, admit, own up
antonym: **deny**

confession

noun the act of confessing » *I have to make a confession—I borrowed your dress without asking first.*
acknowledgement, admission

confidence 1

noun a feeling of trust » *I have complete confidence that you will do well.*
belief, faith, reliance, trust
antonym: **distrust**

confidence 2

noun sureness of yourself » *I've never had much confidence about speaking in class.*
aplomb, assurance, self-assurance, self-possession
antonym: **shyness**

We conducted an experiment in science class.

48

consider »

confident 1
adjective sure about something
» *Angela had worked hard and was confident of success.*
certain, convinced, positive, satisfied, secure, sure
antonym: **uncertain**

confident 2
adjective sure of yourself
» *Hari was a confident actor.*
assured, self-assured, self-possessed
antonym: **shy**

*Hari was a **confident** actor.*

confine 1
verb to limit to something specified » *We confined our discussion to tennis rather than sports in general.*
limit, restrict

confine 2
verb to prevent from leaving
» *His flu confined him to bed for two days.*
hem in, imprison, restrict, shut up, immure, incarcerate, intern

confirm 1
verb to say or show that something is true » *Kate was given a certificate to confirm that she had passed the test.*
bear out, endorse, prove, substantiate, validate, verify, authenticate, corroborate

confirm 2
verb to make something definite » *The date of the election was confirmed.*
fix, settle

*Will resolved the **conflict** between the friends.*

conflict 1
noun disagreement and argument » *Will resolved the conflict between the friends.*
antagonism, disagreement, discord, friction, hostility, opposition, strife

conflict 2
noun a war or battle
» *The man reported on the conflict in the Middle East.*
battle, combat, fighting, strife, war

conflict 3
verb to differ or disagree
» *The team leaders conflicted over who should go first.*
be at variance, be incompatible, clash, differ, disagree

confuse 1
verb to mix two things up
» *It is possible to confuse fact with fiction.*
mistake, mix up, muddle up

confuse 2
verb to puzzle or bewilder
» *The complicated instructions confused me.*
baffle, bewilder, mystify, puzzle, bemuse, faze, nonplus, perplex

confused 1
adjective puzzled or bewildered
» *Hattie was confused—the information didn't make sense.*
baffled, bewildered, muddled, perplexed, puzzled, at a loss, at sea, flummoxed, nonplussed

confused 2
adjective in an untidy mess
» *The papers lay in a confused heap.*
chaotic, disordered, disorganized, untidy
antonym: **tidy**

confusing
adjective bewildering or puzzling » *It was a confusing situation.*
baffling, bewildering, complicated, puzzling

confusion
noun an untidy mess
» *The room was in a state of confusion with furniture all over the place.*
chaos, disarray, disorder, disorganization, mess
antonym: **order**

connect 1
verb to join together
» *The firefighter connected the hose to the tap.*
affix, attach, couple, fasten, join, link
antonym: **separate**

*The firefighter **connected** the hose to the tap.*

connect 2
verb to associate one thing with another » *Laughter is connected to happiness.*
ally, associate, link, relate

connection 1
noun a link or relationship
» *Bridget had connections to a large number of people.*
affiliation, association, bond, correlation, correspondence, link, relation, relationship

*He fixed the loose **connection** in the circuit board.*

connection 2
noun a point where things are joined » *He fixed the loose connection in the circuit board.*
coupling, fastening, junction, link

conscience
noun a sense of right and wrong » *Phil's conscience told him the right thing to do.*
principles, scruples, sense of right and wrong

conservative
adjective unwilling to change
» *People often get more conservative as they grow older.*
conventional, traditional, hidebound, reactionary
antonym: **radical**

consider 1
verb to judge someone or something » *We consider him the perfect candidate.*
believe, judge, rate, regard as, think, deem, hold to be

consider 2
verb to think carefully
» *I will consider your offer.*
contemplate, deliberate, meditate, muse, ponder, reflect, think about, cogitate, mull over, ruminate

consider 3
verb to take into account
» *You should consider Ruth's feelings.*
bear in mind, make allowances for, respect, take into account, think about

consideration

consideration [1]
noun careful thought about something » *Ramon's decision required careful consideration.*
attention, contemplation, deliberation, study, thought

consideration [2]
noun concern for someone » *Please show consideration for others and work quietly.*
concern, kindness, respect, tact

consideration [3]
noun something to be taken into account » *Safety is a major consideration.*
factor, issue, point

consist: consist of
verb to be made up of » *The brain consists of millions of nerve cells.*
be composed of, be made up of, comprise

conspicuous
adjective easy to see or notice » *Sarah wore her bright red coat to be conspicuous.*
apparent, blatant, evident, noticeable, obvious, perceptible, patent, manifest

Sarah wore her bright red coat to be conspicuous.

constant [1]
adjective going on all the time » *There was constant barking from the dog next door.*
continual, continuous, eternal, nonstop, perpetual, relentless, incessant, interminable, sustained, unremitting
antonym: **periodic**

constant [2]
adjective staying the same » *The thermometer showed the temperature was constant.*
even, fixed, regular, stable, steady, uniform, immutable, invariable
antonym: **changeable**

construct
verb to build or make something » *He's constructing a compost bin.*
assemble, build, create, erect, make, put together, put up

He's constructing a compost bin.

consult
verb to go to for advice » *Consult your doctor before training for the race.*
ask for advice, confer with, refer to

contact [1]
noun the state of being in touch with someone » *We must keep in contact.*
communication, in touch

contact [2]
noun someone you know » *He had a contact in the music business.*
acquaintance, connection

contact [3]
verb to get in touch with » *Abbey contacted the company to complain.*
approach, communicate with, get hold of, get in touch with, reach

Abbey contacted the company to complain.

contain [1]
verb to include as a part of » *The glass contains the juice from 10 oranges.*
comprise, include

contain [2]
verb to keep under control » *Hans was finding it difficult to contain his excitement.*
control, curb, repress, restrain, stifle

container
noun something that holds things » *Gail used a plastic container for her food.*
holder, vessel, receptacle, repository

contemplate [1]
verb to think carefully about something » *Maria paused to contemplate her options.*
consider, examine, muse on, ponder, reflect on, think about

contemplate [2]
verb to consider doing something » *He contemplated becoming a vet.*
consider, envisage, plan, think of

contempt
noun complete lack of respect » *Rick's contempt for the club's rules resulted in him being asked to leave.*
derision, disdain, disregard, disrespect, scorn
antonym: **respect**

contest [1]
noun a competition or game » *It was a thrilling contest between two strong teams.*
competition, game, match, tournament

contest [2]
noun a struggle for power » *There was a bitter contest over who should control the nation's future.*
battle, fight, struggle

---

boil **fry** **grill**

cook
verb to prepare food for eating by heating it in some way » *I enjoy cooking for friends.*

bake

50

cool

contest [3]
verb to object formally to a statement or decision » *You have 14 days to contest the plans for the extension.*
challenge, dispute, oppose, question
antonym: accept

continual [1]
adjective happening all the time without stopping » *There was continual rain the afternoon of the fair.*
constant, continuous, endless, eternal, nagging, perpetual, uninterrupted, incessant, interminable, unremitting

continual [2]
adjective happening again and again » *Paolo received continual reminders to renew his club membership.*
frequent, recurrent, regular, repeated
antonym: occasional

continue [1]
verb to keep doing something » *She continued talking even though no one was listening.*
carry on, go on, keep on, persist

She continued talking even though no one was listening.

continue [2]
verb to go on existing » *Their friendship continued even when one of them moved abroad.*
carry on, endure, last, persist, remain, survive

continue [3]
verb to start doing again » *When he returned from vacation, Reg continued to work on his model airplanes.*
carry on, recommence, resume

continuous
adjective going on without stopping » *The continuous building work went on for weeks.*
constant, continued, extended, prolonged, uninterrupted
antonym: periodic

control [1]
noun power over something » *The children learning to ski were under the control of an experienced instructor.*
authority, command, direction, government, management, power, rule, supremacy, jurisdiction, mastery, superintendence

control [2]
verb to be in charge of » *Camilla controlled the rota for cleaning the hamster cage.*
administer, be in charge of, command, direct, govern, have power over, manage, rule

convenient
adjective helpful or easy to use » *Cycling was a convenient way to get around.*
handy, helpful, useful, user-friendly, labour-saving, serviceable
antonym: inconvenient

convention [1]
noun an accepted way of behaving or doing something » *The convention is to shake hands when you strike a deal.*
code, custom, etiquette, practice, tradition, propriety, protocol

The convention is to shake hands when you strike a deal.

convention [2]
noun a large meeting of an organization or group » *The society hosted a convention of children's authors every year.*
assembly, conference, congress, meeting

conventional [1]
adjective relating to what is normally done or believed » *His uniform was conventional school wear.*
conformist, conservative, unadventurous, bourgeois, staid

conventional [2]
adjective familiar, or generally used » *The coach taught us all a conventional tennis serve.*
customary, ordinary, orthodox, regular, standard, traditional

convey
verb to cause information or ideas to be known » *She conveyed her thoughts on global warming to the class.*
communicate, express, get across, impart

convince
verb to persuade that something is true » *I convinced him of my innocence.*
assure, persuade, satisfy

convincing
adjective persuasive » *Jackie had a convincing argument.*
conclusive, effective, persuasive, plausible, powerful, telling, cogent, incontrovertible
antonym: unconvincing

cook
verb to prepare food for eating by heating it in some way
▼ SEE BELOW

cool [1]
adjective having a low temperature » *There was a gust of cool air.*
chilled, chilly, cold, refreshing
antonym: warm

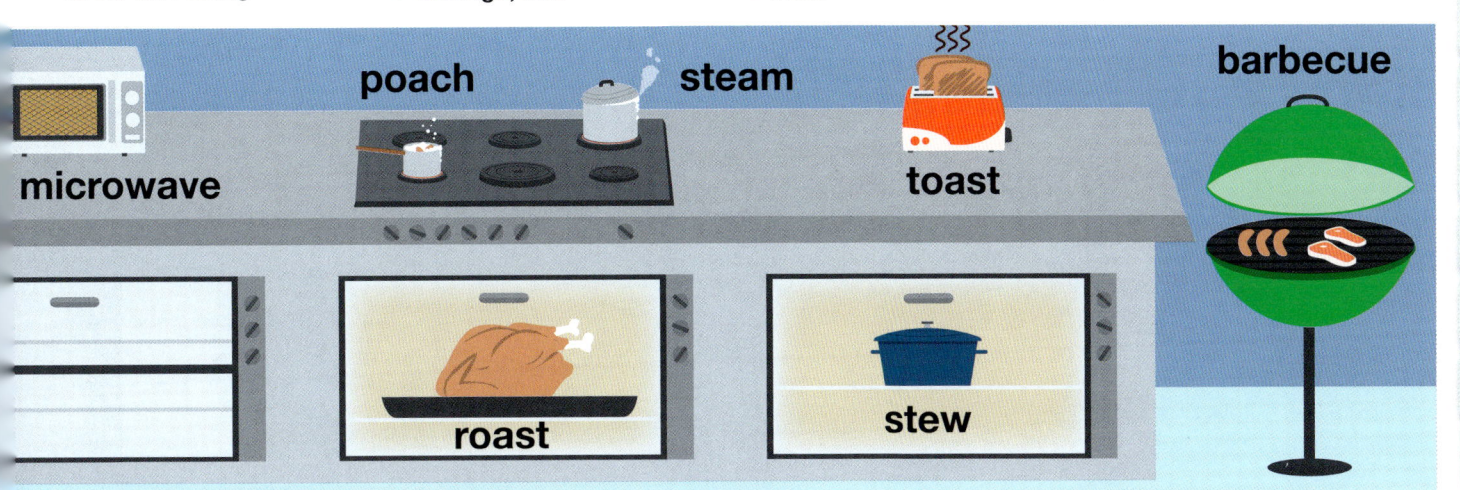

---

microwave · poach · steam · toast · barbecue · roast · stew

cool

cool [2]
adjective staying calm
» José kept cool through the whole incident.
calm, collected, composed, level-headed, relaxed, serene, dispassionate, imperturbable, unemotional, unexcited, unruffled
antonym: **nervous**

cool [3]
verb to make or become cool
» Elsa put the cupcakes on a rack to cool.
chill, cool off, freeze, refrigerate
antonym: **heat**

Elsa put the cupcakes on a rack to cool.

co-operate
verb to work together » Laura co-operated with the rest of the team to finish the task.
collaborate, join forces, pull together, work together

copy [1]
noun something made to look like something else » Tony made a copy of his favourite painting
counterfeit, duplicate, fake, forgery, imitation, replica, reproduction, facsimile, likeness, replication

copy [2]
verb to do the same thing as someone else » My little brother copies everything that I do.
ape, emulate, follow, imitate, mimic, follow suit, parrot, simulate

copy [3]
verb to make a copy of
» The teacher copied the handout and gave a sheet of it to each pupil.
counterfeit, duplicate, reproduce

corny
adjective unoriginal or sentimental » Dad always listens to corny music.
banal, hackneyed, maudlin, sentimental, stale, stereotyped, trite, mawkish, old hat, unoriginal

correct [1]
adjective without mistakes » Jonathan's calculations were correct.
accurate, exact, faultless, flawless, precise, right, true

correct [2]
adjective socially acceptable » Our teacher said the correct way to greet the principal was "Good morning, Mr. Brown".
acceptable, appropriate, fitting, okay or **OK** (informal), **proper, seemly**
antonym: **wrong**

correct [3]
verb to make right » Jimmy corrected the errors in his work.
amend, cure, improve, rectify, reform, remedy, right, emend, redress

correction
noun the act of making something right » We made a correction to our design project.
adjustment, amendment, righting, rectification

We made a correction to our design project.

correspond
verb to be similar or connected to something else » The two maps correspond—they both show the old tower at the top of the hill.
agree, be related, coincide, correlate, fit, match, tally

corrupt [1]
adjective acting dishonestly or illegally » Her scheme was unfair and showed her to be corrupt.
crooked, dishonest, fraudulent, shady (informal), **unscrupulous,** unethical, unprincipled, venal
antonym: **honest**

corrupt [2]
verb to change a computer file by introducing errors » I should make a back-up copy in case the original is corrupted.
alter, contaminate, falsify, manipulate, doctor

corruption
noun dishonest and illegal behaviour » The police arrested him on charges of corruption.
bribery, dishonesty, fraud, extortion, profiteering, venality

cost [1]
noun the amount of money needed » The cost of chocolate has gone up.
charge, expense, outlay, payment, price, rate

cost [2]
noun loss or damage » They extended the house but at the cost of the garden.
detriment, expense, penalty

cost [3]
verb to involve a cost of » The air fares were going to cost a lot of money.
come to, sell at, set someone back (informal)

cosy [1]
adjective warm and comfortable » Guests can relax in the cosy lounge.
comfortable, snug, warm

cosy [2]
adjective pleasant and friendly » She enjoyed a cosy chat with her friends.
friendly, informal, intimate, relaxed

council
noun a governing group of people » The city council had ordered the road closure.
assembly, board, committee, panel, conclave, convocation

count [1]
verb to add up » I counted the money.
add up, calculate, tally, compute, enumerate

I counted the money.

count [2]
verb to be important » Your opinions count.
carry weight, matter, rate, signify, weigh

count [3]
noun a counting or number counted » The count revealed that our group had the most votes.
calculation, reckoning, sum, tally, computation, enumeration

co**ver** »

counteract
verb to reduce the effect of something » *Water the plants to counteract the drying effect of the sun.*
act against, offset, counterbalance, countervail, negate, neutralize

countless
adjective too many to count » *She was the star of countless movies.*
infinite, innumerable, myriad, untold, incalculable, limitless, measureless, multitudinous

country 1
noun a political area » *He drove over the border between the two countries.*
kingdom, land, state

country 2
noun land away from towns and cities » *My friend lives right out in the country.*
boondocks (informal), **bush, countryside, outdoors, the sticks** (slang)
related words:
adjectives **pastoral, rural**

My friend lives right out in the country.

courage
noun lack of fear
▶▶ SEE RIGHT

course 1
noun a policy of action » *Jed took the only course left open to him.*
plan, policy, procedure

She taught a course on algebra.

course 2
noun a series of lessons » *She taught a course on algebra.*
classes, curriculum

course 3
noun a way taken to get somewhere » *The sailor changed the yacht's course to avoid the rocks.*
direction, line, path, route, trajectory, way

court 1
noun a place where legal matters are decided » *He ended up in court for theft.*
bench, law court, tribunal

court 2
verb (old-fashioned) to hope to marry » *Grandpa said he courted grandma for years before she agreed to marry him.*
go steady, woo

courtesy
noun polite and considerate behaviour » *He showed courtesy to other drivers, yielding to them on the busy road.*
civility, courteousness, gallantry, good manners, grace, graciousness, politeness

cover 1
verb to protect or hide » *He covered his face.*
cloak, conceal, cover up, hide, mask, obscure, screen, shade
antonym: **reveal**

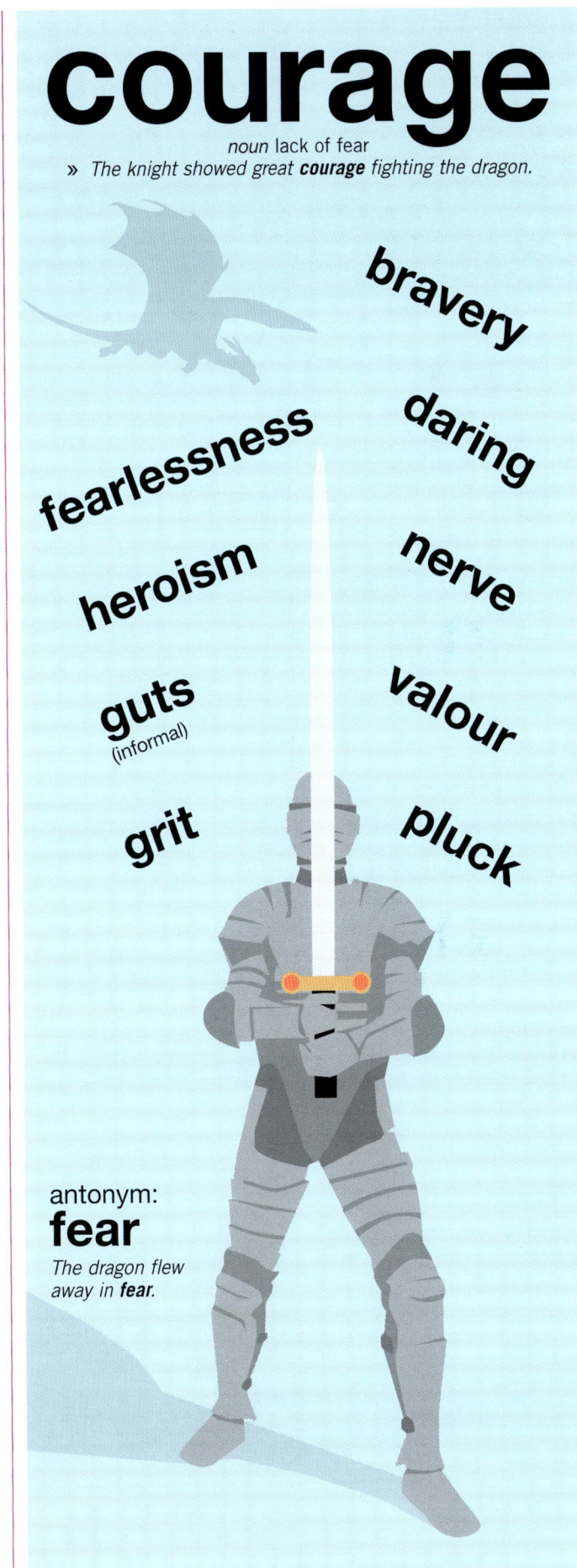

courage
noun lack of fear
» *The knight showed great **courage** fighting the dragon.*

bravery
daring
fearlessness
nerve
heroism
valour
guts (informal)
grit
pluck

antonym:
fear
*The dragon flew away in **fear**.*

cover

cover 2
verb to form a layer over » *The fish was covered with breadcrumbs.*
coat, overlay

cover 3
noun something which protects or hides » *They snuggled down under the covers.*
case, coating, covering, jacket, mask, screen, wrapper

They snuggled down under the covers.

cow
noun a farm animal kept for milk or meat » *A herd of dairy cows stood in the field.*
bovine, cattle

coward
noun someone who is easily scared » *I'm a coward when it comes to the dark so Dad leaves the hall light on.*
chicken (slang), **wimp** (informal)

cowardly
adjective easily scared » *She was too cowardly to get the spider out of the bath.*
chicken (slang), **faint-hearted, gutless** (informal), **craven, lily-livered, pusillanimous, spineless, timorous**
antonym: **brave**

cower
verb to bend down with fear » *The dog cowered before the cat.*
cringe, quail, shrink

crack 1
verb to become damaged, with lines on the surface » *The road surface cracked in the heat.*
break, fracture, snap

crack 2
verb to find the answer to something » *We've managed to crack the problem.*
decipher, solve, work out

crack 3
noun a line or gap caused by damage » *There was a large crack in the wall.*
break, cleft, crevice, fracture, fissure, interstice

crafty
adjective clever and rather dishonest » *The crafty kid managed to get both his parents to give him his allowance money that week.*
artful, cunning, devious, scheming, slippery, sly, wily

cram
verb to stuff something into a container or place » *Minnie crammed chips into her mouth.*
jam, pack, squeeze, stuff

crash 1
noun an accident involving a moving vehicle » *No one was hurt in the car crash.*
accident, bump, collision, pile-up (informal), **smash**

No one was hurt in the car crash.

crash 2
noun a loud noise » *I heard a crash coming from outside.*
bang, clash, din, smash

crash 3
noun the failure of a business » *There was a stock market crash overnight.*
bankruptcy, collapse, depression, failure, ruin

crash 4
verb to have an accident » *His car crashed into the back of a van.*
bump, collide, drive into, have an accident, hurtle into, plow into, wreck

crawl 1
verb to move slowly on hands and knees or near the ground » *The ladybug crawled through the grass.*
creep, drag, edge, inch, slither, on hands and knees

crawl 2
verb to be full of » *The branch was crawling with red ants.*
be alive with, be full of, be overrun (slang), **swarm, teem**

The branch was crawling with red ants.

craze
noun a brief enthusiasm for something » *Yoga is Jasmine's latest fitness craze.*
fad, fashion, trend, vogue

crazy 1
adjective (informal) very strange or foolish » *People thought our plans were crazy.*
foolish, insane, mad, ridiculous, wild, zany
antonym: **sensible**

crazy 2
adjective (informal) very keen on something » *Gavin's crazy about football.*
fanatical, mad, obsessed, passionate, smitten, wild, enamoured, zealous

create 1
verb to make something happen » *The band coming on stage created a buzz of excitement around the room.*
bring about, cause, lead to, occasion

create 2
verb to invent something » *He created a new type of kite.*
coin, compose, devise, formulate, invent, originate

creative
adjective able to invent » *Sheila is so creative—she's writing and illustrating a graphic novel in her spare time.*
fertile, imaginative, inspired, inventive

credit
noun praise for something » *Luca took all the credit for my idea.*
commendation, glory, praise, recognition, thanks, acclaim, Brownie points (informal), **kudos**
antonym: **disgrace**

creepy
adjective (informal) strange and frightening » *The old house is really creepy at night.*
disturbing, eerie, macabre, scary (informal), **sinister, spooky, unnatural**

crime
noun an act that breaks the law » *Shoplifting is a crime.*
misdemeanour, offence, violation, wrong, felony, malfeasance, misdeed, transgression

criminal 1
noun someone who has committed a crime » *The criminal spent 10 years in prison.*
crook (informal), **culprit, delinquent, offender, villain, evildoer, felon, lawbreaker, malefactor**

crumple »

criminal [2]
adjective involving crime
» *Stealing is a criminal offence.*
corrupt, crooked, illegal, illicit, unlawful, culpable, felonious, indictable, iniquitous, nefarious
antonym: **legal**

cripple [1]
verb to injure severely
» *He was crippled for months after the accident.*
disable, lame, maim, paralyze

cripple [2]
verb to prevent from working
» *Snow crippled the bus network and we got the day off.*
bring to a standstill, impair, put out of action

critical [1]
adjective very important
» *It is critical to add the ingredients in the right order.*
crucial, deciding, decisive, momentous, pivotal, vital
antonym: **unimportant**

critical [2]
adjective very serious
» *Her car was in critical need of a new battery.*
grave, precarious, serious

critical [3]
adjective finding fault with something or someone
» *The boy thought his teacher was too critical when she gave his essay a bad mark.*
carping, derogatory, disapproving, disparaging, scathing, captious, censorious, fault-finding
antonym: **complimentary**

criticism
noun expression of disapproval
» *His criticism of the play was harsh.*
censure, disapproval, disparagement, fault-finding, flak (informal)**, panning** (informal), denigration, stricture
antonym: **praise**

criticize
verb to find fault » *The bus driver was criticized for not being on time.*
censure, condemn, find fault with, knock (informal)**, pan** (informal)**, put down,** disparage, excoriate, lambaste
antonym: **praise**

crook
noun (informal) a criminal » *The man is a crook and a liar.*
cheat, rogue, scoundrel (old-fashioned)**, shark, swindler, thief, villain**

crooked [1]
adjective bent or twisted » *The nails were crooked after Dad's attempts to hammer them into the hard wall.*
bent, deformed, distorted, irregular, out of shape, twisted, warped
antonym: **straight**

crooked [2]
adjective dishonest or illegal » *My parents hoped the salesman wasn't crooked.*
corrupt, criminal, dishonest, fraudulent, illegal, shady (informal), dishonourable, nefarious, unprincipled
antonym: **honest**

cross [1]
verb to go across » *The bridge crosses the river.*
ford, go across, span, traverse

The bridge crosses the river.

cross [2]
verb to meet and go across » *The bus stop is near the traffic lights where the roads cross.*
crisscross, intersect

cross [3]
noun a mixture of two things » *The dog was a cross between a collie and a retriever.*
blend, combination, mixture

cross [4]
adjective angry » *I'm very cross with him.*
angry, annoyed, fractious, fretful, grumpy, in a bad mood, irritable, irascible, peevish, testy

crouch
verb to squat down » *We all crouched in the grass.*
bend down, squat

We all crouched in the grass.

crowd [1]
noun a large group of people » *A huge crowd gathered in the square.*
horde, host, mass, mob, multitude, swarm, throng

crowd [2]
verb to gather close together » *Hundreds of fans crowded into the hall.*
congregate, gather, swarm, throng

crowded
adjective full of people » *It was a crowded room.*
congested, full, overflowing, packed

crucial
adjective very important » *He held his nerve at the crucial moment and won the game.*
central, critical, decisive, momentous, pivotal, vital

The monkey used the stone as a crude tool to open the nuts.

crude [1]
adjective rough and simple » *The monkey used the stone as a crude tool to open the nuts.*
primitive, rough, rudimentary, simple

crude [2]
adjective rude and offensive » *He had a crude and embarrassing sense of humour.*
coarse, tasteless, vulgar, boorish, crass
antonym: **refined**

cruel
adjective deliberately causing hurt » *Her words were cruel.*
barbarous, brutal, callous, cold-blooded, heartless, inhumane, sadistic, savage, vicious
antonyms: **compassionate, kind**

cruelty
noun cruel behaviour » *Leaving Maz out of the final match was an act of cruelty.*
barbarity, brutality, callousness, inhumanity, savagery, viciousness
antonyms: **compassion, kindness**

crumple
verb to squash and wrinkle » *She crumpled the paper in her hand.*
crease, crush, screw up, wrinkle

» crush

My little brother loves to crush the garlic.

crush [1]
verb to destroy the shape of by squeezing
» *My little brother loves to crush the garlic.*
crumble, crumple, mash, squash

crush [2]
verb to defeat completely
» *His football team was crushed with a 6–0 defeat.*
overcome, put down, quell, stamp out, vanquish

cry [1]
verb to have tears coming from your eyes » *The movie made her cry.*
bawl, blubber, howl, sob, weep, whimper, wail

cry [2]
verb to call out loudly
» *"See you soon!" they cried.*
call, exclaim, shout, yell

cry [3]
noun a loud or high shout
» *The fans in the stadium gave a cry of disappointment when the player missed the goal.*
call, exclamation, shout, yell

cunning [1]
adjective clever and deceitful
» *The boy had a cunning plan.*
artful, crafty, devious, sly, wily, foxy, Machiavellian
antonym: **open**

cunning [2]
noun cleverness and deceit
» *The goats showed cunning in finding food.*
deviousness, guile

curb [1]
verb to keep something within limits » *Owen must learn to curb his temper.*
check, contain, control, limit, restrain, suppress

curb [2]
noun an attempt to keep something within limits
» *Parents called for stricter curbs on who could be invited to the school party.*
brake, control, limit, limitation, restraint

cure [1]
verb to make well » *The ointment cured the rash.*
heal, remedy

cure [2]
noun something that makes an illness better » *The medicine provided a cure.*
medicine, remedy, treatment

curiosity [1]
noun the desire to know
» *The man showed curiosity in his family tree.*
inquisitiveness, interest

curiosity [2]
noun something unusual
» *The museum was full of relics and curiosities.*
freak, marvel, novelty, oddity, rarity

The museum was full of relics and curiosities.

curious [1]
adjective wanting to know
» *He was curious about the new neighbours.*
inquiring, inquisitive, interested, nosy (informal)
antonym: **incurious**

curious [2]
adjective strange and unusual
» *The store was full of curious trinkets.*
bizarre, extraordinary, odd, peculiar, singular, strange, unusual
antonym: **ordinary**

current [1]
noun a strong continuous movement of water
» *She was almost swept away by the current of water.*
flow, tide, undertow

current [2]
adjective happening, being done, or being used now
» *His current car goes much faster than his last one.*
contemporary, ongoing, present, present-day, today's, up-to-the-minute
antonym: **past**

curve [1]
noun a bending line » *There was a curve in the road.*
arc, bend, trajectory, turn
related word: adjective **sinuous**

curve [2]
verb to move in a curve
» *The road curved sharply to the left.*
arc, arch, bend, swerve

custom [1]
noun a traditional activity
» *The tea-drinking ceremony is an ancient Chinese custom.*
convention, practice, ritual, tradition

custom [2]
noun something a person always does » *It was her custom to get up at 7 o'clock every morning.*
habit, practice, routine, wont

customer
noun someone who buys something » *The store was filled with customers.*
buyer, client, consumer, patron, purchaser, shopper

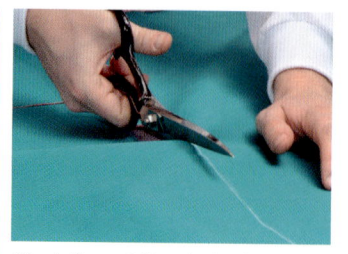

The tailor cut the cloth with a sharp pair of scissors.

cut [1]
verb to mark, injure, or remove part of (something or someone) with something sharp
» *The tailor cut the cloth with a sharp pair of scissors.*
chop, clip, nick, score, slice, slit, trim

cut [2]
verb to reduce something
» *Dad cut the amount of TV we watched.*
cut back, decrease, lower, reduce, slash, abridge, downsize, rationalize
antonym: **increase**

cut [3]
noun a mark or injury made by cutting » *Sofia had a cut on her finger.*
gash, incision, slash, slit

cut [4]
noun a reduction in something
» *There was a cut in the number of books in the library.*
cutback, decrease, lowering, reduction, saving
antonym: **increase**

cute
adjective pretty or attractive
» *You were such a cute baby!*
appealing, attractive, charming, dear, good-looking, gorgeous, pretty
antonym: **ugly**

cynical
adjective always thinking the worst of people
» *Alistair had a cynical attitude that made him seem world-weary.*
distrustful, sceptical

56

Dd

*The ocean can be **dangerous** during a storm.*

dabble
verb to take part in an activity in a casual way
» *She dabbled at playing the piano in her spare time.*
dip into, flirt with, play at, putter, tinker, trifle with

damage [1]
verb to cause harm to something » *Hail damaged the corn crop.*
harm, hurt, injure

*Hail **damaged** the corn crop.*

damage [2]
noun harm that is done to something » *The storm caused damage to the town, flattening several houses.*
harm, injury

damp [1]
adjective slightly wet
» *The towel was damp once he had used it after swimming.*
clammy, dank, humid, moist, sodden, soggy, wet

damp [2]
noun slight wetness
» *The damp all over the walls left a dark stain.*
dampness, humidity, moisture, clamminess, dankness

danger
noun the possibility of harm
» *A stampeding hippo is a great danger in Africa.*
hazard, jeopardy, menace, peril, risk, threat
antonym: **safety**

dangerous
adjective likely to cause harm
» *The ocean can be dangerous during a storm.*
hazardous, perilous, risky, treacherous
antonym: **safe**

dare [1]
verb to challenge someone to do something » *I dare you to jump off the top diving board.*
challenge, defy, throw down the gauntlet

dare [2]
verb to have the courage to do something » *Nobody dared to complain to the angry man.*
risk, venture

daring [1]
adjective willing to take risks
» *They made a daring escape by helicopter.*
adventurous, audacious, bold, brave, fearless, intrepid, valiant
antonym: **cautious**

daring [2]
noun the courage to take risks
» *Ben showed his daring when he spoke in the assembly for five minutes without notes.*
audacity, boldness, bravery, courage, guts (informal)**, nerve** (informal)**, fearlessness, intrepidity, temerity**
antonym: **caution**

dark [1]
adjective lacking light
» *It was too dark to see what was happening.*
black, cloudy, dim, dingy, murky, overcast, shadowy, swarthy
antonym: **light**

dark [2]
noun lack of light
▼ SEE BELOW

dash [1]
verb to rush somewhere
» *Madison dashed towards the finish line.*
bolt, fly, race, run, rush, sprint, tear, make haste, hasten

dash [2]
verb to throw or be thrown violently against something » *The huge waves dashed against the rocks.*
break, crash, hurl, slam, smash

---

dark
[2] noun lack of light » *It is difficult to see where you're going in the dark.*

dimness
*I'm squinting to adjust to the **dimness**.*

darkness
*The room was plunged into **darkness**.*

gloom
*Can you see in the **gloom**?*

dusk
*It's only 6 o'clock. It's **dusk**—it's not pitch dark yet.*

murk
*I can't make much out in this **murk**.*

antonym: **light**
*Let's turn on the **light**.*

dash

dash [3]
verb to ruin or frustrate someone's hopes or ambitions
» *The children's hopes of a picnic were dashed by the rain.*
crush, destroy, disappoint, foil, frustrate, shatter, thwart, confound, quash

dash [4]
noun a sudden movement or rush » *Harper made a dash for the door.*
bolt, race, run, rush, sprint, stampede

dash [5]
noun a small quantity of something » *He added a dash of salt to his meal.*
drop, pinch, splash, sprinkling

daydream [1]
noun a series of pleasant thoughts » *His mind often drifted into a daydream.*
dream, fantasy, pipe dream, reverie

*His mind often drifted into a **daydream**.*

daydream [2]
verb to think about pleasant things » *Noah daydreams of being famous.*
dream, fantasize

dazed
adjective unable to think clearly » *At the end of the interview I felt dazed and exhausted.*
bewildered, confused, dizzy, light-headed, numbed, stunned, disorientated, punch-drunk, stupefied

dead [1]
adjective no longer alive » *He found a dead jellyfish washed up on the beach.*
deceased, departed, extinct, late
antonym: **alive**

dead [2]
adjective no longer functioning » *The radio is dead.*
defunct, not working

deadly
adjective causing death » *The Brazilian wandering spider is the world's most deadly arachnid.*
destructive, fatal, lethal, mortal

deal
verb to cope successfully with something » *Ethan deals with stress by doing yoga.*
attend to, cope with, handle, manage, see to, take care of

dear [1]
noun a person for whom you have affection » *Happy Valentine's Day, dear.*
angel, beloved (old-fashioned)**, darling, love, sweetheart,** treasure (informal)

dear [2]
adjective much loved » *He was a dear friend of mine and I miss him.*
beloved, cherished, darling, esteemed, precious, prized, treasured

*She didn't buy the handbag because it was too **dear**.*

dear [3]
adjective costing a lot » *She didn't buy the handbag because it was too dear.*
costly, expensive, pricey (informal)

deceive
verb to make someone believe something that is untrue » *The ad deceived the public by claiming the product would make them look younger.*
con (informal)**, double-cross, dupe, fool, mislead, take in, trick,** bamboozle, beguile, hoodwink

decent [1]
adjective of an acceptable standard » *The pay was decent although not generous.*
adequate, passable, reasonable, respectable, satisfactory, tolerable

decent [2]
adjective correct and respectable » *She was a decent person who always tried to do the right thing.*
proper, respectable
antonym: **improper**

deceptive
adjective likely to make people believe something untrue » *The deceptive honey badger looks cute, but it can give a painful scratch.*
false, fraudulent, illusory, misleading, unreliable, delusive, specious

*Happy Valentine's Day, **dear**.*

decide
verb to choose to do something » *She decided to sign up for swimming lessons.*
choose, come to a decision, determine (formal)**, elect** (formal)**, make up your mind, reach a decision, resolve** (formal)

decision
noun a judgment about something » *The judges came to a decision about who the winner was.*
conclusion, finding, judgment, resolution, ruling, verdict

declaration
noun a forceful or official announcement » *She made her declaration in public for all to hear.*
affirmation, protestation (formal)**, statement, testimony,** assertion, avowal

*She made her **declaration** in public for all to hear.*

declare
verb to state something forcefully or officially » *Rohan declared that he was going to sail around the world.*
affirm, announce, assert, certify, proclaim, profess (formal)**, pronounce, state,** attest, aver, avow

decline [1]
verb to become smaller or weaker » *The plants in the garden declined during the fall.*
decrease, diminish, drop, fall, go down, plummet, reduce, dwindle, wane
antonym: **increase**

decline [2]
verb to refuse politely to accept or do something » *He declined their invitation as he didn't want to go out.*
abstain, excuse yourself, refuse, turn down
antonym: **accept**

decline [3]
noun a gradual weakening or decrease » *There was a decline in the number of bees visiting the hive this year.*
decrease, downturn, drop, fall, recession, shrinkage, slump
antonym: **increase**

decorate [1]
verb to make more attractive » *She decorated her room with posters and pictures.*
adorn, deck, ornament, beautify, bedeck, embellish, festoon

She decorated her room with posters and pictures.

decorate [2]
verb to put paint or wallpaper on » *They decided to decorate the house and paint her bedroom walls yellow.*
do up (informal), **renovate**

decrease [1]
verb to become or make less » *The dentist said we should decrease the amount of sugar we eat.*
cut down, decline, diminish, drop, dwindle, lessen, lower, reduce, shrink, abate, curtail, subside, wane
antonym: **increase**

The sudden decrease in sales was a shock.

decrease [2]
noun a lessening in the amount of something » *The sudden decrease in sales was a shock.*
decline, drop, lessening, reduction, abatement, curtailment, cutback, diminution
antonym: **increase**

deep [1]
adjective having a long way to the bottom » *The rabbit dug a deep hole.*
bottomless, yawning
antonym: **shallow**

The rabbit dug a deep hole.

deep [2]
adjective great or intense » *Joe had a deep love of sports and played on many teams.*
extreme, grave, great, intense, profound, serious

deep [3]
adjective low in sound » *The man had a deep voice and sang bass in the choir.*
bass, low, resonant, sonorous
antonym: **high**

defeat [1]
verb to win a victory over someone » *I defeated last year's arm-wrestling champion.*
beat, conquer, crush, rout, trounce, vanquish (formal)

defeat [2]
noun a failure to win » *His basketball team suffered a crushing defeat.*
conquest, debacle (formal), **loss, rout, trouncing**
antonym: **victory**

defect
noun a fault or flaw » *A software defect made the phone unusable.*
deficiency, failing, fault, flaw, imperfection, shortcoming, weakness

defence [1]
noun action to protect something » *Many plant-eating dinosaurs had spikes and weapons on their tails as a form of defence.*
cover, protection, resistance, safeguard, security

defence [2]
noun an argument in support of something » *Jason's only defence for taking the chocolate without asking was that he was hungry.*
argument, excuse, explanation, justification, plea

defend [1]
verb to protect from harm » *The cat defended her kittens from the dog next door.*
cover, guard, protect, safeguard, shelter, shield

defend [2]
verb to argue in support of » *I defended his silence, explaining he was shy, not rude.*
endorse, justify, stick up for (informal), **support, uphold**

defender
noun a person who argues in support of something » *The man was a committed defender of human rights.*
advocate, champion, supporter

deficiency
noun a lack of something » *The disease scurvy is caused by a deficiency of vitamin C.*
deficit, deprivation, inadequacy, lack, want (formal)
antonym: **abundance**

deficient
adjective lacking in something » *I watered the lawn to make up for the deficient rainfall.*
inadequate, lacking, poor, short, wanting

definite [1]
adjective unlikely to be changed » *Dad set a definite limit to my vacation money.*
assured, certain, decided, fixed, guaranteed, settled

definite [2]
adjective certainly true » *Hot cocoa was a definite help in getting to sleep.*
clear, positive, black-and-white, clear-cut, cut-and-dried

deformed
adjective abnormally shaped » *The deformed carrot looked as if it had two legs.*
disfigured, distorted

The deformed carrot looked as if it had two legs.

degrade

degrade
verb to humiliate someone
» Ava was sorry that her mean remark had degraded her friend.
demean, humiliate

delay 1
verb to put something off until later » Lunch was delayed by an hour as our guests were late.
defer, postpone, put off, shelve, suspend

delay 2
verb to slow or hinder something » Fallen trees on the road delayed her journey.
hinder, impede, obstruct, set back, hold up, retard

delay 3
noun a time when something is delayed » The fog grounded planes, causing flight delays.
interruption, obstruction, setback

delete
verb to remove something written » She deleted the final paragraph because it repeated an earlier one.
cross out, erase, rub out, edit out, strike out

deliberate 1
adjective done on purpose » When I found the textbook under Doug's desk, I realized it was part of a deliberate attempt to cheat in the exam.
calculated, conscious, intentional, premeditated, studied
antonym: **accidental**

deliberate 2
adjective careful and not hurried » The vet's movements were gentle and deliberate as he felt the cat's leg for bruising.
careful, cautious, measured, methodical
antonym: **casual**

The girl deliberated over what to eat.

deliberate 3
verb to think carefully about a choice
» The girl deliberated over what to eat.
debate, meditate, mull over, ponder, reflect

delicious
adjective tasting very nice
▶▶ SEE RIGHT

delight 1
noun great pleasure or joy » It gives me great delight to welcome you to our new home.
glee, happiness, joy, pleasure, rapture, satisfaction

delight 2
verb to give someone great pleasure » The squeaky toy delighted the baby.
amuse, captivate, charm, enchant, please, thrill

demand
verb to need or require something » Running the obstacle course demanded strength and coordination.
involve, need, require, take, want, call for, entail, necessitate

deny 1
verb to say that something is untrue » He denied he broke the ornament on purpose.
contradict, refute, abjure, disavow, disclaim, gainsay, rebut, repudiate
antonym: **admit**

deny 2
verb to refuse to believe something » She denied the existence of ghosts.
reject, renounce

deny 3
verb to refuse to give something » Pamela's mom denied her any more snacks before dinner.
refuse, withhold

department
noun a section of an organization » The store's sock department was always busier than swimwear in winter.
division, office, section, unit

depend on 1
verb to rely on
» You can depend on me to help you in an emergency.
bank on, count on, rely on, trust

depend on 2
verb to be affected by » The taste depends on the quality of the ingredients.
be determined by, hinge on, be subject to, hang on, rest on

deposit
verb to put down or leave somewhere » She deposited the coin in the piggy bank.
drop, lay, leave, place, put down

She deposited the coin in the piggy bank.

No one knew who owned the derelict building with the broken window.

derelict
adjective abandoned and in poor condition » No one knew who owned the derelict building with the broken window.
abandoned, dilapidated, neglected, ruined

descend
verb to move downwards
» We descended the stairs.
dip, dive, fall, go down, plummet, sink
antonym: **ascend**

describe
verb to give an account of something » The teacher asked Amy to describe what she did in her spare time.
define, depict, portray, characterize, detail

deserve
verb to have a right to something » Mom works hard, so she deserves a rest.
be entitled to, be worthy of, earn, justify, merit, warrant

design 1
verb to make a plan of something » She couldn't wait to design her new bedroom herself.
draft, draw up, plan

design 2
noun a plan or drawing » Brad showed us his design for a vegetable garden.
model, plan, blueprint, schema

design 3
noun the shape or style of something » The design of the clock is unusual.
form, pattern, shape, style

design »

tasty
A cake is a **tasty** after-dinner treat.

luscious
I find lemon-glazed cakes particularly **luscious**.

yummy
(informal)
Marzipan is **yummy**, I prefer it to icing.

delectable
She said that the cupcakes from the local café were **delectable**.

scrumptious
Anything with icing is **scrumptious**!

appetizing
The bakery had an array of **appetizing** cakes.

mouth-watering
The **mouth-watering** smell of cakes baking was so tempting.

delicious
adjective tasting very nice » The cake was **delicious**.

desire

desire [1]
verb to want something
» *We can stay longer at the fair if you desire.*
crave, fancy, long for, want, wish, yearn,
ache for, covet

desire [2]
noun a feeling of wanting something » *I have a strong desire to help people.*
appetite, craving, hankering, longing, wish, yearning, yen (informal)

despair [1]
noun a loss of hope » *Emma felt despair at the thought of yet another long car journey.*
dejection, despondency, gloom, hopelessness

despair [2]
verb to lose hope » *The team despaired of ever winning a game.*
feel dejected, feel despondent, lose heart, lose hope

despite
preposition in spite of
» *He gave a great talk despite his fear of public speaking.*
in spite of, notwithstanding (formal), **regardless of**

destroy
verb to ruin something completely » *The fire destroyed the building.*
annihilate, demolish, devastate, obliterate, raze, ruin, wreck

The fire destroyed the building.

The destruction of the rainforest left many animals homeless.

destruction
noun the act of destroying something » *The destruction of the rainforest left many animals homeless.*
annihilation, demolition, devastation, obliteration

detail
noun an individual feature of something » *We discussed every detail of the play.*
aspect, element, particular, point, respect, fine point, nicety

determination
noun a firm decision to do something » *Adam showed determination in his training for the Olympics.*
perseverance, persistence, resolution, resolve (formal), **tenacity, doggedness, single-mindedness, steadfastness, willpower**

determine [1]
verb to cause or control a situation or result » *The size of the chicken determines the cooking time.*
control, decide, dictate, govern, shape

determine [2]
verb to decide or settle something firmly
» *The date of the match had not yet been determined.*
arrange, choose, decide, fix, resolve, settle

determine [3]
verb to find out the facts about something » *The X-ray will determine if there are any broken bones.*
ascertain (formal), **confirm, discover, establish, find out, verify**

determined
adjective firmly decided » *Mia was determined to finish the race, however long it took her.*
bent on, dogged, intent on, persistent, purposeful, resolute (formal), **single-minded, tenacious,**
steadfast, unflinching, unwavering

develop [1]
verb to grow or become more advanced » *The seedling developed new leaves.*
advance, evolve, grow, mature, progress, result, spring

The seedling developed new leaves.

develop [2]
verb to become affected by an illness or fault » *He developed pneumonia.*
catch, contract (formal), **fall ill, get, go down with, pick up, succumb**

devious
adjective achieving your goal by sly methods » *He got another turn by being devious, claiming he'd missed out last time.*
calculating, scheming, underhand, wily

devoted
adjective very loving and loyal
» *He was a devoted father.*
constant, dedicated, doting, faithful, loving, loyal, true

die [1]
verb to stop living » *The flowers had drooped and died.*
expire (formal), **kick the bucket** (slang), **pass away, pass on, perish** (formal)

die [2]
verb to fade away » *Liam reassured her that the worry she felt would soon die.*
fade away, fade out, peter out

die out
verb to cease to exist
» *Many ancient customs have died out.*
disappear, fade, vanish

difference [1]
noun a lack of similarity between things » *There is a huge difference between the size of a Yorkshire Terrier and a Great Dane.*
contrast, discrepancy, disparity, distinction, divergence, variation
antonym: **similarity**

There is a huge difference between the size of a Yorkshire Terrier and a Great Dane.

difference [2]
noun the amount by which two quantities differ
» *The difference between 17 and 19 is two.*
balance, remainder

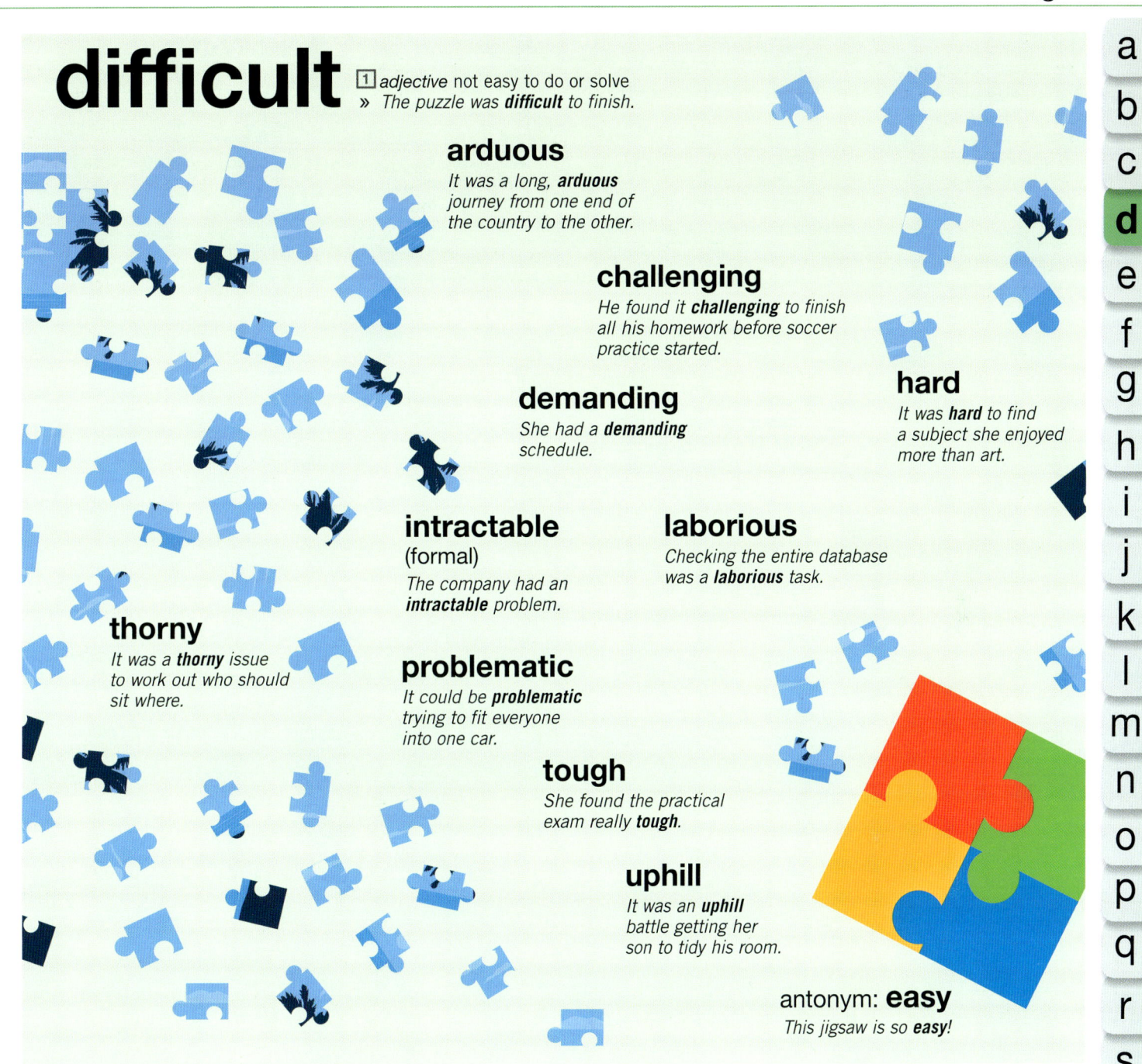

difficult

[1] *adjective* not easy to do or solve
» *The puzzle was **difficult** to finish.*

arduous
*It was a long, **arduous** journey from one end of the country to the other.*

challenging
*He found it **challenging** to finish all his homework before soccer practice started.*

demanding
*She had a **demanding** schedule.*

hard
*It was **hard** to find a subject she enjoyed more than art.*

intractable
(formal)
*The company had an **intractable** problem.*

laborious
*Checking the entire database was a **laborious** task.*

thorny
*It was a **thorny** issue to work out who should sit where.*

problematic
*It could be **problematic** trying to fit everyone into one car.*

tough
*She found the practical exam really **tough**.*

uphill
*It was an **uphill** battle getting her son to tidy his room.*

antonym: **easy**
*This jigsaw is so **easy**!*

---

different [1]
adjective unlike something else » *His shiny green shoes were different to everyone else's.*
contrasting, disparate (formal), **dissimilar, opposed, unlike, at odds, at variance, divergent** (formal)
antonym: **similar**

different [2]
adjective unusual and out of the ordinary » *Jane's hairstyle was different, shaved at the front and long at the back.*
special, unique

different [3]
adjective distinct and separate » *The school supports a different charity every year.*
another, discrete (formal), **distinct, individual, separate**

difficult [1]
adjective not easy to do or solve
▲ SEE ABOVE

difficult [2]
adjective not easy to deal with » *He was difficult to deal with because of his mood swings.*
demanding, troublesome, trying, obstreperous, refractory, unmanageable

difficulty [1]
noun a problem » *The main difficulty was that her car wouldn't start.*
complication, hassle (informal), **hurdle, obstacle, pitfall, problem, snag, trouble, impediment, stumbling block**

difficulty [2]
noun the quality of being difficult » *Getting on and off the bus on crutches was a difficulty she had to overcome.*
hardship, strain, tribulation (formal), **arduousness, laboriousness**

dig [1]
verb to break up soil or sand » *The dog used its front paws to dig a hole in the ground.*
burrow, excavate, gouge, hollow out, quarry, till, tunnel

» dig

dig [2]
verb to push something in » *She could feel the tight bracelet digging into her arm.*
jab, poke, thrust

dig [3]
noun a push or poke » *Daisy silenced Matt with a dig in the arm.*
jab, poke, prod, thrust

*Daisy silenced Matt with a **dig** in the arm.*

dim [1]
adjective not bright or well-lit » *The light from the lamp was dim, and he couldn't see well enough to read his book.*
dark, dull, grey, murky, poorly lit, shadowy

dim [2]
adjective vague or unclear » *She had a dim memory of seeing the girl somewhere before.*
faint, hazy, indistinct, obscure, shadowy, vague, fuzzy, ill-defined, indistinguishable
antonym: **clear**

dim [3]
adjective (informal) slow to understand » *He is rather dim, but don't offend him by saying so!*
dumb (informal), obtuse, slow, stupid, thick (informal)
antonym: **bright**

diminish
verb to reduce or become reduced » *The cookie stash diminished throughout the day.*
contract, decrease, lessen, lower, reduce, shrink, weaken

direct [1]
adjective in a straight line or with nothing in between » *Dad took the most direct route to the airport.*
immediate, straight, uninterrupted
antonym: **indirect**

direct [2]
adjective clear and honest » *He gave a direct answer to her rambling question: "No".*
blunt, candid, forthright, frank, straight, straightforward
antonym: **devious**

direct [3]
verb to control and guide something » *Christopher is captain and directs the team on the field.*
control, guide, lead, manage, oversee, run, supervise

direction [1]
noun the line in which something is moving » *He walked for an hour in the wrong direction.*
course, path, route, way

*He walked for an hour in the wrong **direction**.*

direction [2]
noun control and guidance of something » *He chopped vegetables under the chef's direction.*
charge, command, control, guidance, leadership, management

dirt [1]
noun dust or mud » *The bike was covered in dirt.*
dust, filth, grime, muck, mud

dirt [2]
noun earth or soil » *He drew a circle in the dirt with a stick.*
earth, soil

dirty [1]
adjective marked with dirt
▼ SEE BELOW

dirty [2]
adjective unfair or dishonest » *It was a dirty deal that tricked Joe into doing his brother's chores as well as his own.*
corrupt, crooked
antonym: **honest**

dirty

[1] *adjective* marked with dirt » *He was always getting his clothes dirty.*

filthy
What a **filthy** T-shirt!

grimy
Her boots were **grimy** from the grass and mud.

soiled
Don't put your **soiled** clothes on the carpet.

grubby
The players were told to wash their **grubby** hands before eating.

disable
verb to stop something working » *You need to disable the alarm before you enter.*
deactivate, defuse, immobilize

disadvantage
noun an unfavourable circumstance » *They considered the advantages and disadvantages of moving to a new house.*
drawback, handicap, minus, weakness, downside, hindrance
antonym: **advantage**

disagree 1
verb to have a different opinion » *She disagreed with everything he said.*
differ, dispute, dissent
antonym: **agree**

She disagreed with everything he said.

disagree 2
verb to think that something is wrong » *I disagree with your statement that cats are boring because they sleep all the time.*
object, oppose, take issue with

disagreeable
adjective unpleasant in some way » *The smell of old cabbage was disagreeable.*
horrible, horrid, nasty, objectionable, obnoxious, unfriendly, unpleasant
antonym: **agreeable**

disagreement 1
noun a dispute about something » *My friend and I had a disagreement about which pop group was the best.*
altercation (formal), **argument, difference, dispute, quarrel, squabble, tiff**
antonym: **agreement**

disagreement 2
noun an objection to something » *There was disagreement over the principal insisting we wear our school uniforms on the bus home.*
dissent, objection, opposition

stained
His shorts were stained from the grass.

unclean
The unclean uniform will go straight into the washing machine.

antonym: **clean**
The substitute didn't play and so his uniform remained clean.

disappear 1
verb to go out of sight » *The aircraft disappeared off the radar.*
be lost to view, drop out of sight, fade, recede, vanish
antonym: **appear**

disappear 2
verb to stop existing » *The snow disappeared when the sun came out.*
cease (formal), **die out, go away, melt away, pass, vanish**

disappointed
adjective sad because hopes have not been fulfilled » *I was disappointed that we didn't go swimming.*
dejected, despondent, disenchanted, disillusioned, downcast, saddened, disheartened, let down
antonym: **satisfied**

disappointment 1
noun sadness because hopes have not been fulfilled » *Book early to avoid disappointment.*
dejection, despondency, regret, disenchantment, disillusionment

disappointment 2
noun something that does not meet your expectations » *The movie was a disappointment; it was really boring.*
blow, setback

disapproval
noun the belief that something is wrong » *John's mom expressed disapproval when he wore ripped jeans to school.*
censure, condemnation, criticism
antonym: **approval**

disapprove
verb to think that something is wrong » *Everyone disapproved of the stickers all over Maria's precious violin.*
condemn, deplore (formal), **dislike, find unacceptable, take a dim view of, frown on, take exception to**
antonym: **approve**

disaster
noun a very bad accident » *The flood was a disaster.*
calamity (formal), **catastrophe, misfortune, tragedy**

discard
verb to get rid of something » *She discarded the pieces of paper that held her old notes.*
cast aside, dispose of, dump (informal), **jettison, shed, throw away, throw out**

She discarded the pieces of paper that held her old notes.

discern
verb (formal) to notice or understand something with difficulty » *Abigail discerned someone walking towards her through the mist.*
detect, make out, notice, observe, perceive, see, spot

discharge 1
verb to send something out » *The cleaned water will be discharged into the sea.*
emit, empty, expel, flush, give off, release

discharge 2
verb to allow someone to leave hospital or prison » *He has a broken arm but was discharged from the hospital yesterday.*
free, let go, liberate, release, set free

discharge 3
verb to dismiss someone from a job » *He was discharged for shouting at his boss.*
dismiss, eject, fire (informal), **sack** (informal)

discharge »

65

» **di**scharge

discover

verb to find something or find out about something
» She **discovered** a shell in the rock pool.

come across
The children **came across** the pool when exploring the beach.

unearth
He **unearthed** a shell hidden in the mud.

find
She didn't know what she would **find** in the water.

find out
He wanted to **find out** more about hermit crabs.

learn
He went to the library to **learn** about rock pools.

realize
They **realized** that the tide was coming in.

stumble upon or **stumble across**
Stumbling upon the rock pool was the highlight of their day at the beach.

discharge [4]
noun a sending away from a job or institution
» *A broken leg led to her discharge from the team for the rest of the season.*
dismissal, ejection, expulsion, the sack (informal)

discourage
verb to make someone lose enthusiasm » *Don't let these problems discourage you.*
daunt, deter, dissuade, put off, demoralize, dishearten
antonym: **encourage**

discover
verb to find something or find out about something
◀◀ SEE LEFT

discuss
verb to talk about something » *We discussed what we should do tomorrow.*
debate, exchange views on, go into, talk about

discussion
noun a talk about something » *The teachers sat in another room to have a discussion.*
consultation, conversation, debate, dialogue, discourse, talk

The teachers sat in another room to have a discussion.

disgrace [1]
noun loss of respect because of a dishonourable action
» *By refusing to shake hands after the match, he has brought disgrace upon the whole team.*
scandal, shame, discredit, dishonour
antonym: **credit**

disgrace [2]
verb to bring shame upon » *The dog disgraced itself by ripping the cushions.*
discredit, shame

disgraceful
adjective deserving of shame » *Grace had wasted a disgraceful amount of paper while trying to write the letter.*
scandalous, shameful, shocking, discreditable, dishonourable

disgust [1]
noun a strong feeling of dislike » *Leah felt disgust at the thought of eating a worm.*
nausea, repulsion, revulsion

Leah felt disgust at the thought of eating a worm.

disgust [2]
verb to cause someone to feel disgust » *The foul smell disgusted him.*
repel, revolt, sicken, nauseate, turn your stomach

disgusting
adjective very unpleasant or unacceptable » *That garbage dump is one of the most disgusting things I've ever seen.*
foul, gross, obnoxious, repellent, revolting, sickening, vile, nauseating, repugnant

dishonest
adjective not truthful » *It is dishonest to mislead people.*
corrupt, crooked, deceitful, fraudulent, lying, mendacious, untruthful
antonym: **honest**

dishonesty
noun dishonest behaviour » *Her lies and dishonesty had annoyed people.*
cheating, corruption, deceit, trickery, duplicity, fraudulence, mendacity
antonym: **honesty**

disintegrate
verb to break into many pieces » *The sandcastle disintegrated when the tide came in.*
break up, crumble, fall apart, fall to pieces, fragment

The sandcastle disintegrated when the tide came in.

dislike [1]
verb to consider something unpleasant » *We don't always have liver on the menu because lots of people dislike it.*
abhor (formal)**, be averse to, detest, hate, loathe, not be able to abide, not be able to bear, not be able to stand**
antonym: **like**

dislike [2]
noun a feeling of not liking something » *Mom looked at the weeds in the garden with dislike.*
animosity, antipathy, aversion, distaste, hatred, hostility, loathing
antonym: **liking**

disobey
verb to deliberately refuse to follow instructions » *He was forever disobeying rules.*
break, defy, flout, infringe, violate, contravene (formal)**, transgress**
antonym: **obey**

Her drawer was in disorder, and it was impossible to find an eraser.

disorder [1]
noun a state of untidiness » *Her drawer was in disorder, and it was impossible to find an eraser.*
clutter, disarray, muddle
antonym: **order**

disorder [2]
noun a lack of organization » *The play ended in disorder when they all forgot their lines and stumbled off the stage.*
chaos, confusion, disarray, turmoil

disorder [3]
noun a disease or illness » *It was a rare nerve disorder.*
affliction, complaint, condition, disease, illness

dispose of
verb to get rid of something » *Tie the bag and dispose of it.*
discard, dispense with, dump, get rid of, throw away

disprove
verb to show that something is not true » *The science experiment will either prove or disprove the theory.*
discredit, invalidate, prove false, refute
antonym: **prove**

dispute [1]
noun an argument » *The dispute between them is now settled.*
argument, clash, conflict, disagreement, feud, wrangle

» **di**spute

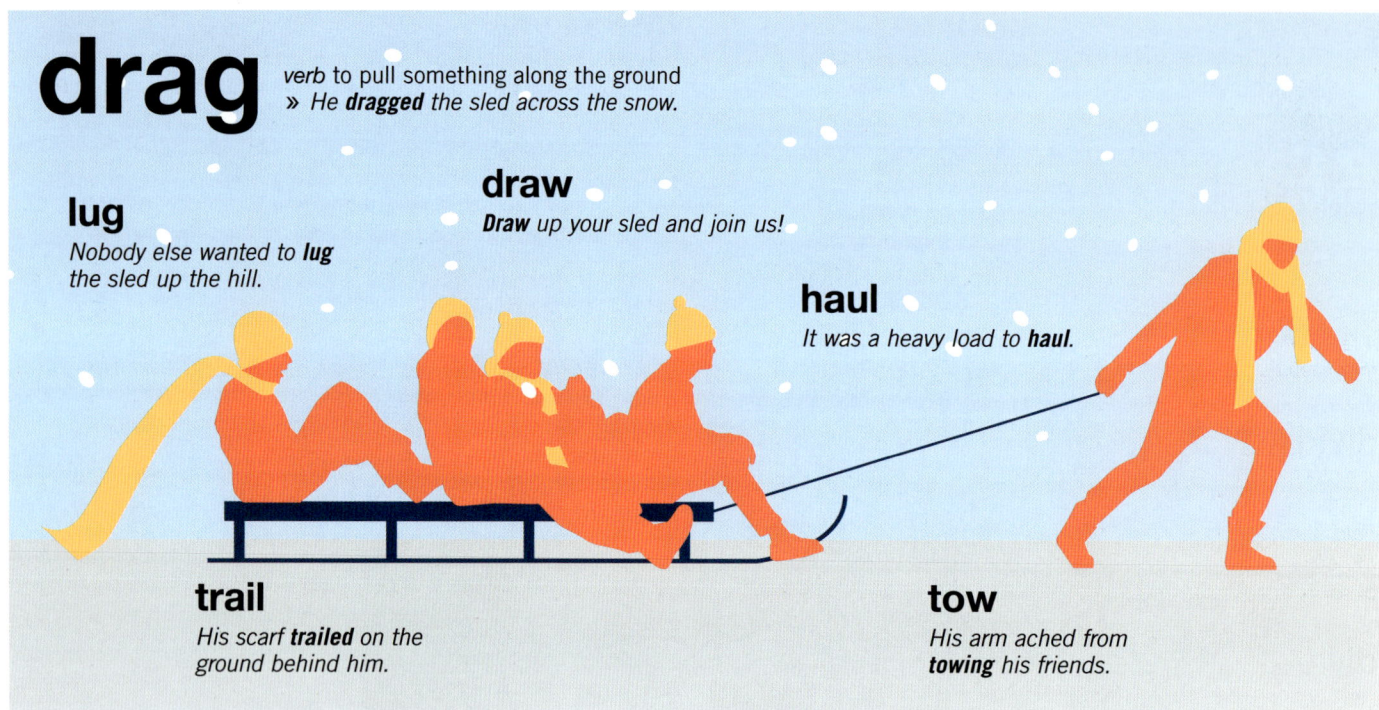

drag
verb to pull something along the ground
» He **dragged** the sled across the snow.

lug
Nobody else wanted to **lug** the sled up the hill.

draw
Draw up your sled and join us!

haul
It was a heavy load to **haul**.

trail
His scarf **trailed** on the ground behind him.

tow
His arm ached from **towing** his friends.

dispute [2]
verb to question something's truth or wisdom
» Tim disputed the claim that he hadn't even tried to win.
challenge, contest, contradict, deny, query, question
antonym: **accept**

distant [1]
adjective far away in space or time » A distant ship appeared on the horizon.
far, outlying, out-of-the-way, remote, faraway, far-flung, far-off
antonym: **close**

A **distant** ship appeared on the horizon.

distant [2]
adjective cold and unfriendly
» He is polite but distant.
aloof, detached, reserved, withdrawn, standoffish, unapproachable
antonym: **friendly**

distinguish [1]
verb to see the difference between things » A pet can't distinguish right from wrong.
differentiate, discriminate, tell, tell apart, tell the difference

distinguish [2]
verb to just recognize something » I heard shouting but was unable to distinguish the words.
discern, make out, pick out, recognize

distract
verb to stop someone from concentrating » Playing computer games distracted John from his homework.
divert, draw away, sidetrack, turn aside

distress [1]
noun great suffering » The pain from her broken arm was causing her distress.
heartache, pain, sorrow, suffering

distress [2]
noun the state of needing help » The ship sent out a signal that it was in distress.
difficulty, need, straits, trouble

distress [3]
verb to cause someone unhappiness » It distressed Mary that her cousins left without saying goodbye.
bother, disturb, grieve, pain, sadden, trouble, upset, worry

distribute [1]
verb to hand something out » The teacher distributed the prizes to the winners.
circulate, hand out, pass around

distribute [2]
verb to spread something through an area » Distribute the sprinkles evenly over the cupcake.
diffuse, disperse, scatter, spread

Distribute the sprinkles evenly over the cupcake.

distribute [3]
verb to divide and share something » Chores were evenly distributed among all family members.
allocate, allot, dispense (formal), **divide, dole out, share, apportion, mete out**

disturb [1]
verb to intrude on someone's peace » She crept past her sleeping father so as not to disturb him.
bother, disrupt, intrude on

disturb [2]
verb to upset or worry someone » The scenes on the news disturbed him.
agitate, distress, shake, trouble, unsettle, upset, worry

dive
verb to go head first into water » Sharon dived into the pool.
jump, leap, submerge

divide [1]
verb to split something up » He divided the can of food between the two cats.
cut up, partition, segregate, separate, split, split up
antonym: **join**

drastic

A fence divides the field between the sheep and the cows.

divide [2]
verb to form a barrier between things » *A fence divides the field between the sheep and the cows.*
bisect, separate

divide [3]
verb to cause people to disagree » *My parents were divided over which colour to paint the walls.*
come between, set against one another, split

division [1]
noun separation into parts » *The city's division into two parts was caused by the railway line that ran through its centre.*
partition, separation

division [2]
noun a disagreement » *There were divisions in the community over where the carnival should be held.*
breach, difference of opinion, rupture, split

division [3]
noun a section of something » *The costume division was in charge of dressing the actors.*
department, section, sector

dizzy
adjective about to lose your balance » *Manuel had a dizzy spell and almost fell over.*
giddy, light-headed

do [1]
verb to carry out a task » *He just didn't want to do any work.*
carry out, execute (formal), **perform, undertake**

do [2]
verb to be sufficient » *It is best to send a birthday card, but an email will do.*
be adequate, be sufficient, suffice (formal)

do [3]
verb to perform at a certain level » *Connie did well at tap.*
fare, get on, manage

dodge [1]
verb to move out of the way » *The player in white dodged the tackle.*
duck, swerve

The player in white dodged the tackle.

dodge [2]
verb to avoid doing something » *He dodged the question by talking about something else.*
avoid, elude, evade, get out of, shirk, sidestep

dog
noun an animal often kept as a pet » *The dog is a loyal pet.*
canine, mongrel, mutt (slang), **pooch** (slang)
related words:
adjective **canine**; female **bitch**; young **pup, puppy**

doomed
adjective certain to fail » *It was a doomed attempt to retrieve the ball—they would never be able to reach it up in the tree.*
condemned, hopeless, ill-fated

double [1]
adjective twice the usual size » *Bad traffic meant it took double the time to get home.*
twice, twofold

double [2]
adjective consisting of two parts » *A double stroller was needed for the twin babies.*
dual, twin, twofold

doubt [1]
noun a feeling of uncertainty » *She had doubts about travelling in snowy weather.*
misgiving, qualm, scepticism, uncertainty
antonym: **certainty**

doubt [2]
verb to feel uncertain about something » *Sam doubted his ability to play a concerto.*
be dubious, be sceptical, query, question
antonym: **believe**

doubtful
adjective unlikely or uncertain » *It's doubtful he'll do another tour as he wants a change.*
debatable, dubious, questionable, uncertain
antonym: **certain**

down [1]
adverb towards the ground, or in a lower place » *He walked down the stairs.*
downwards, downstairs
antonym: **up**

He walked down the stairs.

down [2]
adjective depressed » *He felt down when his team lost.*
dejected, depressed, dispirited, glum, melancholy, miserable, sad, despondent, morose, pessimistic

downfall
noun the failure of a person or thing » *The king's greed had been his downfall.*
collapse, fall, ruin

drab
adjective dull and lacking brightness » *The army truck was painted in drab colours.*
dingy, dismal, dreary, dull, gloomy, grey, sombre, cheerless, lacklustre
antonym: **bright**

The army truck was painted in drab colours.

drag
verb to pull something along the ground
◀◀ SEE LEFT

drain [1]
verb to cause a liquid to flow somewhere » *Kevin pulled out the plug to drain water from the bathtub.*
draw off, pump

drain [2]
verb to flow somewhere » *Some rivers drain into lakes.*
discharge, empty, flow, seep

drain [3]
verb to use something up » *The long day of travelling drained her of energy.*
consume, exhaust, sap, tax, use up

drastic
adjective severe and urgent » *Now is the time for drastic action if we are going to save the day.*
extreme, harsh, radical, severe

draw

draw [1]
verb to make a picture
» Lucas decided to draw the view through the window.
paint, sketch, trace

draw [2]
verb to move somewhere
» The car drew away from the curb.
move, pull

draw [3]
verb to pull something » Max drew his chair nearer to the fire.
drag, haul, pull

drawback
noun a problem that makes something less than perfect
» The only drawback was that the apartment was too small.
difficulty, hitch, problem, snag, trouble

dreadful
adjective extremely bad » She thought the play was dreadful: poor acting and no plot.
appalling, atrocious, awful, frightful, ghastly, horrendous, terrible
antonym: **wonderful**

dream [1]
noun mental pictures while sleeping » Ahmed had a dream that his rabbit could fly.
hallucination, trance, vision, delusion, reverie

dream [2]
noun something that you want very much
» His father's dream was to be promoted in the next year.
ambition, aspiration, daydream, fantasy, Holy Grail, pipe dream

His father's dream was to be promoted in the next year.

dreary
adjective dull and dismal
» It was a dreary, rainy day.
bleak, depressing, drab, dull, gloomy, monotonous
antonym: **cheerful**

dress [1]
noun a piece of clothing
» It was a hot day so she wore a summer dress.
frock, gown, robe

It was a hot day so she wore a summer dress.

dress [2]
noun clothing in general » The invitation said "casual dress."
attire (formal), **clothes, clothing, costume, garb** (formal), apparel, raiment

dress [3]
verb to put on clothes
» The little boy had dressed himself and put his pants on back to front.
attire (formal), **clothe, garb** (formal)
antonym: **undress**

drink
verb to swallow liquid
▶▶ SEE RIGHT

drip [1]
verb to fall in small drops
» Rain dripped from the brim of his cap.
dribble, splash, trickle

drip [2]
noun a small amount of a liquid » There were drips of paint on the carpet when Dad finished painting the wall.
bead, drop, droplet, dribble, globule

drive [1]
verb to operate or power a machine or vehicle » He liked to drive the car on empty roads.
operate, pilot, power, propel, run, steer, work

drive [2]
verb to force someone to do something » Ambition drove Jim to work harder.
compel, force, lead, motivate, prompt, push, spur

drive [3]
verb to force something pointed into a surface » Rick used a sledgehammer to drive the pegs into the ground.
hammer, knock, ram, sink, thrust

Rick used a sledgehammer to drive the pegs into the ground.

drive [4]
noun a journey in a vehicle
» We decided to go for a drive in the car.
excursion, jaunt, journey, ride, run, spin, trip

drive [5]
noun energy and determination
» Justin had the drive to succeed against all odds.
ambition, determination, energy, enterprise, initiative, motivation, vigour

The ball dropped and bounced on the ground.

drop [1]
verb to fall downwards
» The ball dropped and bounced on the ground.
descend, fall, plummet, sink, tumble

drop [2]
verb to become less
» Temperatures can drop to freezing at night.
decline, decrease, fall, plummet, sink, slump, tumble
antonym: **rise**

drop [3]
noun a small amount of a liquid » A drop of ink splashed from the end of the pen.
bead, drip, droplet, dribble, globule

drowsy
adjective tired and sleepy
» It had been an exhausting day and he felt drowsy.
lethargic, sluggish

drug [1]
noun a treatment for disease
» The drug was a type of antibiotic.
medication, medicine

dry [1]
adjective without any liquid
» The path was dry after several days of sunshine.
arid, dried-up, parched
antonym: **wet**

dry [2]
verb to remove liquid from something » You wash the dishes and I'll dry them.
drain, dehumidify, dehydrate, desiccate
antonym: **moisten**

dubious [1]
adjective not entirely honest or reliable » Rachel didn't believe his dubious answer that his bus had broken down.
crooked, dishonest, questionable, suspect, suspicious, unreliable

dubious [2]
adjective doubtful about something » My parents were dubious about the number of friends I'd invited for a sleepover.
doubtful, nervous, sceptical, suspicious, unconvinced, undecided, unsure

dull [1]
adjective not interesting » I found the chess game dull as Millie took so long between moves.
boring, drab, humdrum, monotonous, tedious, uninteresting
antonym: **interesting**

dull [2]
adjective not bright or clear » The weather is always dull and foggy.
cloudy, drab, gloomy, muted, overcast, sombre, subdued
antonym: **bright**

dull [3]
adjective not sharp » I tried to cut the tomato in half, but the knife was dull.
blunt, unsharpened
antonym: **sharp**

dumb [1]
adjective unable to speak » We were all struck dumb with surprise.
mute, silent, speechless

dumb [2]
adjective (informal) slow to understand » She called him dumb for not understanding what the teacher said, and the teacher scolded her for being rude.
dim, obtuse (formal), **stupid, thick** (informal)
antonym: **smart**

They dumped the extra sand back at the quarry.

dump [1]
verb to get rid of something » They dumped the extra sand back at the quarry.
discharge, dispose of, get rid of, jettison, throw away, throw out

dump [2]
verb (informal) to put something down » We dumped our coats and ran off.
deposit, drop

dupe
verb to trick someone » She realized he'd duped her when he pulled a rabbit from her hat.
cheat, con (informal), **deceive, delude, fool, play a trick on, trick**

duty [1]
noun something that you ought to do » We have a duty to look after the environment.
obligation, responsibility

duty [2]
noun a task associated with a job » My main duty as a chauffeur is to drive people from one place to another.
assignment, job, responsibility, role

duty [3]
noun tax paid to the government » There's no duty to pay on perfume at the airport.
excise, levy (formal), **tariff, tax**

dying: be dying for
verb to want something very much » I'm dying for a pizza.
ache for, hunger for, long for, pine for, yearn for

drink
verb to swallow liquid » He **drank** hot chocolate from his favourite mug.

gulp
Gulping the water gave him hiccups.

imbibe
The bride's father **imbibed** rather too much alcohol at the wedding.

quaff
He **quaffed** huge cups of water after the race.

guzzle
Don't **guzzle** all the juice!

sup
She **supped** her soup straight from the mug.

sip
She **sipped** tea from a china cup.

swig (informal)
He **swigged** the lemonade straight from the bottle.

» eager

Ee

eager
adjective wanting very much to do or have something
» Robert was eager to earn some extra money and offered to mow his neighbours' lawns for a fee.
anxious, ardent, avid, enthusiastic, keen, raring to go (informal), **fervent, hungry, zealous**

early [1]
adjective before the arranged or expected time
» Kate was early; none of her friends had arrived yet.
advance, premature, untimely
antonym: **late**

early [2]
adjective near the beginning of a period of time
» Alberta and Saskatchewan joined Confederation in the early 20th century.
primeval, primitive

early [3]
adverb before the arranged or expected time
» We arrived early at the movie theatre to make sure we would get good seats.
ahead of time, beforehand, in advance, in good time, prematurely

earn [1]
verb to get money in return for doing work
» John earns a good wage.
bring in, draw, get, make, obtain, net, procure, reap

earn [2]
verb to receive something that you deserve » Tina earned her scholarship through hard work and determination.
acquire, attain (formal)**, win**

Earth [1]
noun the planet on which we live » Most of the Earth's surface is covered with water.
globe, planet, world
related word:
adjective **terrestrial**

Most of the Earth's surface is covered with water.

Lynn planted the flower and filled the pot with earth.

earth [2]
noun soil from the ground
» Lynn planted the flower and filled the pot with earth.
clay, dirt, ground, soil, loam, topsoil, turf

ease [1]
noun lack of difficulty or worry
» After weeks of practice, Len passed his test with ease.
leisure, relaxation, simplicity

ease [2]
verb to make or become less severe or intense
» The doctor gave him some medicine to ease the pain.
abate, calm, relax, relieve, slacken, allay, alleviate, assuage

eat
[1] *verb* to chew and swallow food
» The dogs **eat** their food with great enthusiasm!

gobble

munch

chew

chomp

snack

guzzle (informal)

ecstasy

ease 3
verb to move slowly or carefully » *He eased open the heavy door and peered outside.*
creep, edge, guide, inch, lower, manoeuvre, squeeze

easy 1
adjective able to be done without difficulty » *This is an easy puzzle with lots of clues.*
light, painless, simple, smooth, straightforward
antonym: **hard**

easy 2
adjective comfortable and without worries » *We had an easy, relaxed day at the beach.*
carefree, comfortable, leisurely, quiet, relaxed

eat 1
verb to chew and swallow food
▼ SEE BELOW

eat 2
verb to have a meal » *We like to eat dinner early.*
breakfast (formal), dine, feed, have a meal, lunch (formal), picnic

The body of the van had been eaten away by rust.

eat away
verb to destroy something slowly » *The body of the van had been eaten away by rust.*
corrode, destroy, dissolve, erode, rot, wear away

eccentric 1
adjective regarded as odd or peculiar » *My friend wears eccentric hats covered with bells.*
bizarre, outlandish, quirky, strange, weird, whimsical

eccentric 2
noun someone who is regarded as odd or peculiar » *Lisa is bit of an eccentric with her strange views on life.*
character, crank

economic 1
adjective concerning the way money is managed » *It is hard to start a business when the economic situation is bad.*
budgetary, commercial, financial, fiscal, monetary

economic 2
adjective making a profit » *Bananas are an economic crop to grow.*
productive, profitable, viable, money-making, profit-making, remunerative

economical 1
adjective cheap to use and saving you money » *Our car may not be fast, but it's very economical to run.*
cheap, cost-effective, economic, inexpensive

economical 2
adjective careful and sensible with money or materials » *It is more economical for us to make hot chocolate at home than to buy it from the café.*
careful, frugal, prudent, thrifty

economy
noun the careful use of things to save money » *Ben always spent too much; he needed to start shopping with economy.*
frugality (formal), prudence, restraint, thrift

ecstasy
noun extreme happiness » *Winning the gold medal was total ecstasy!*
bliss, delight, elation, euphoria, exaltation, joy, rapture

Winning the gold medal was total ecstasy!

---

devour · **swallow** · **feeds (on)** · **scoff** · **nibble** · **wolf down** · **consume**

edge

Don't go near the edge of the cliff!

edge [1]
noun the place where something ends or meets something else » *Don't go near the edge of the cliff!*
border, boundary, brim, fringe, lip, margin, rim, perimeter, periphery
antonym: **centre**

edge [2]
verb to move somewhere slowly » *Finn edged towards the door, ready to make a quick escape.*
creep, inch, sidle

educated
adjective having a high standard of learning » *Our school principal is an educated and wise lady.*
cultivated, cultured, intellectual, learned, erudite, well-educated

education
noun the process of learning or teaching » *A good education is essential for success in life.*
coaching, e-learning, instruction, schooling, training, tutoring

effect
noun a direct result of something » *Regular piano practice had a real effect on my playing.*
consequence, end result, fruit, result, upshot

efficient
adjective able to work well without wasting time or energy » *Kit's an efficient worker who helps us get things done quickly.*
businesslike, competent, economic, effective, organized, productive
antonym: **inefficient**

effort [1]
noun physical or mental energy » *It took a lot of effort to move the heavy box.*
application, energy, exertion, trouble, work

effort [2]
noun an attempt or struggle » *Mom's cake-making efforts are greatly appreciated by her hungry family.*
attempt, bid, stab (informal), **struggle**

elaborate [1]
adjective having many different parts » *She threw an elaborate party with lots of entertainment and music, and huge amounts of food.*
complex, complicated, detailed, intricate, involved
antonym: **simple**

elaborate [2]
adjective highly decorated » *The wooden box had elaborate carvings.*
fancy, fussy, ornate

The wooden box had elaborate carvings.

elaborate [3]
verb to add more information about something » *He promised to elaborate on the plan by giving more details.*
develop, enlarge, expand

eliminate [1]
verb to get rid of someone or something » *My lactose-intolerant friend has to eliminate dairy foods from her diet.*
cut out, do away with, eradicate, get rid of, remove, stamp out

eliminate [2]
verb to beat someone in a competition » *Dan's team was eliminated in the first round.*
knock out, put out

embarrass
verb to make someone feel ashamed or awkward » *My dad likes to embarrass me in front of my friends!*
disconcert, fluster, humiliate, shame, discomfit, faze, mortify

embarrassed
adjective ashamed and awkward » *She was easily embarrassed and turned red when anyone looked at her.*
ashamed, awkward, humiliated, red-faced, self-conscious, sheepish, abashed, bashful, discomfited, mortified

embarrassment
noun shame and awkwardness » *I laughed loudly to cover my embarrassment at falling over.*
awkwardness, bashfulness, humiliation, self-consciousness, shame, chagrin, discomfiture, mortification

emergency
noun an unexpected and difficult situation » *It was an emergency: she was lost and couldn't find her way home.*
crisis, pinch

emit
verb to give out or release something » *The alarm emitted a loud, shrill ring.*
exude, give off, give out, release, send out, utter, produce, radiate, send forth

emphasis
noun special or extra importance » *The book placed more emphasis on the characters than the plot.*
accent, importance, prominence, weight

emphasize
verb to make something seem especially important or obvious » *He emphasized the need for everyone to stay quiet while they visited the reptile house.*
accent, accentuate, highlight, play up, stress, underline, foreground, prioritize, underscore

employ [1]
verb to pay someone to work for you » *The family next door employs me to babysit.*
appoint, commission, engage (formal), **hire, take on**

employ [2]
verb to use something » *When his parents said no, Kieran employed a new strategy to get what he wanted.*
bring to bear, make use of, use, utilize

employee
noun someone who is paid to work for someone else » *Hannah was one of eight employees on the farm.*
hand, worker, workman

employer
noun someone that other people work for » *The new office assistant thanked her employer for giving her the job.*
boss

employment
noun giving someone paid work or having paid work » *Will you stay in school or seek employment?*
engagement, enlistment, hiring, recruitment
▶▶ SEE RIGHT

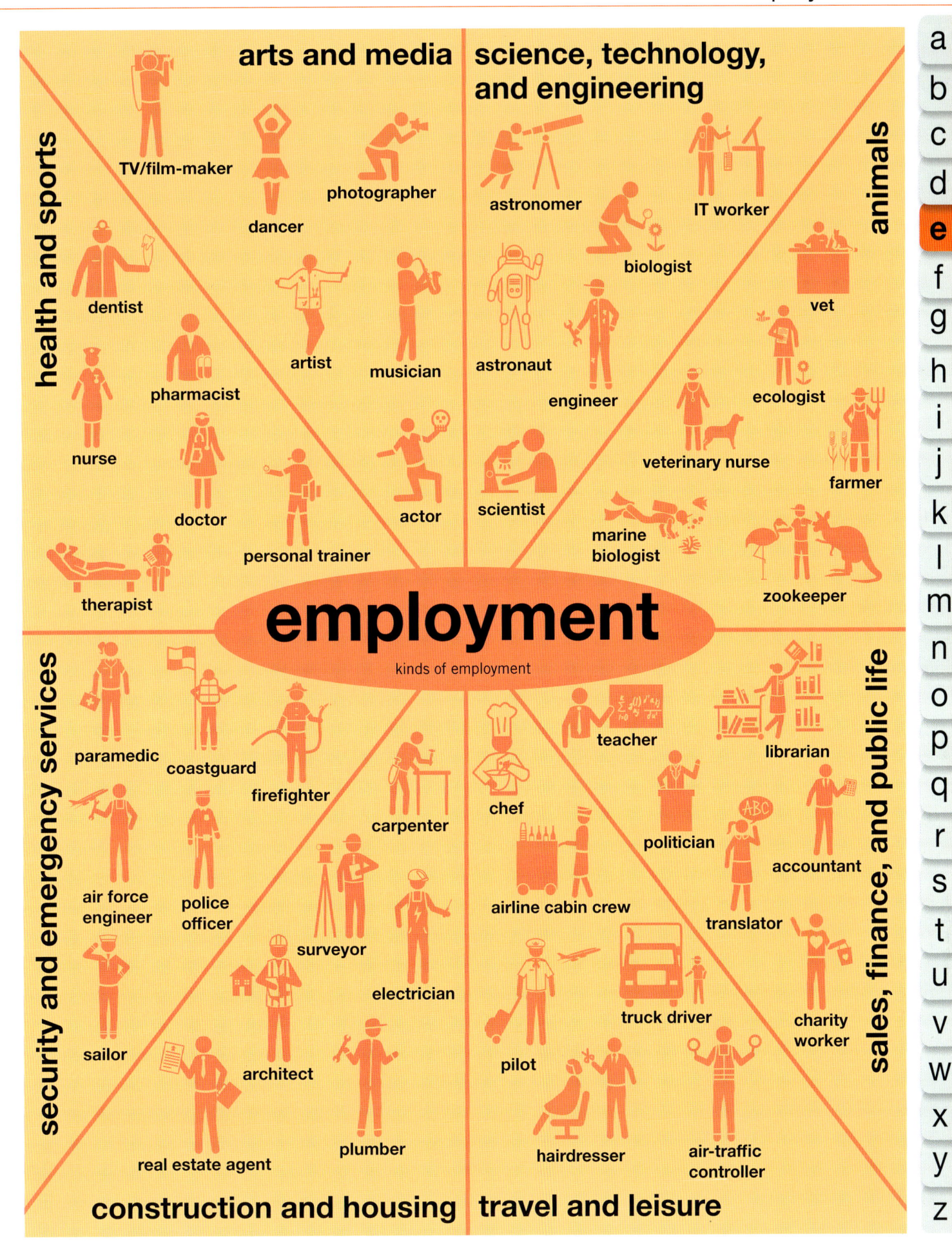

employment

arts and media
- TV/film-maker
- dancer
- photographer
- artist
- musician
- actor
- personal trainer

science, technology, and engineering
- astronomer
- IT worker
- biologist
- astronaut
- engineer
- scientist
- marine biologist

health and sports
- dentist
- pharmacist
- nurse
- doctor
- therapist

animals
- vet
- ecologist
- veterinary nurse
- farmer
- zookeeper

employment
kinds of employment

security and emergency services
- paramedic
- coastguard
- firefighter
- air force engineer
- police officer
- sailor

construction and housing
- carpenter
- surveyor
- electrician
- architect
- real estate agent
- plumber

travel and leisure
- chef
- airline cabin crew
- pilot
- truck driver
- hairdresser
- air-traffic controller

sales, finance, and public life
- teacher
- librarian
- politician
- accountant
- translator
- charity worker

a b c d e f g h i j k l m n o p q r s t u v w x y z

» empty

A B C D **E** F G H I J K L M N O P Q R S T U V W X Y Z

close
climax
ending
finish
conclusion
culmination

end
1 noun the last part of a period or event » The curtains closed at the **end** of the play.

antonym: beginning
The curtains will open at the **beginning** of tomorrow's performance.

empty 1
adjective having no people or things in it » There was no food in the house; the cupboards were empty.
bare, blank, clear, deserted, unfurnished, uninhabited, vacant
antonym: **full**

empty 2
adjective boring or without value or meaning » The offer to go on vacation together was an empty promise.
inane, meaningless, worthless

empty 3
verb to remove people or things » Danny sat down and emptied the water that had got into his boots.
clear, drain, evacuate, unload
antonym: **fill**

*Danny sat down and **emptied** the water that had got into his boots.*

enclose
verb to surround a thing or place completely » The book arrived enclosed in a protective plastic bag.
encircle, fence off, hem in, surround, wrap

encourage 1
verb to give someone confidence » She was encouraged by the teacher's praise for her essay.
cheer, hearten, reassure
antonym: **discourage**

encourage 2
verb to support a person or activity » Her family's cheers encouraged Zoe to run faster.
aid, boost, favour, help, incite, support, foster, further, promote, strengthen

end 1
noun the last part of a period or event
◀◀ SEE LEFT

end 2
noun the furthest point of something » I was staying in a room at the end of the corridor.
boundary, bounds, edge, extremity, limits, margin

end 3
noun the purpose for which something is done » By studying for our exams, we're all working towards the same end, which is to pass!
aim, goal, intention, object, objective, purpose, reason

end 4
verb to come or bring to a finish » Jim waited for the movie to end before going home.
bring to an end, cease, conclude, finish, stop, terminate
antonym: **begin**

endanger
verb to put someone or something in danger » The lack of rain has endangered the plants in my garden.
compromise, jeopardize, put at risk, risk, threaten

endure 1
verb to experience something difficult » The students endured a three-hour exam.
cope with, experience, go through, stand, suffer

endure 2
verb to continue to exist » Phil's jeans endured despite years of wear and tear.
last, live on, remain, survive

76

equal

enemy
noun someone who is against you » *The knight fought a duel against his enemy.*
adversary, antagonist, foe, opponent
antonym: **friend**

energetic
adjective full of energy » *The energetic kitten climbed the curtains.*
animated, dynamic, indefatigable, spirited, tireless, vigorous

energy
noun the ability and strength to do things » *I haven't got the energy to go swimming.*
drive, life, spirit, strength, vigour, vitality, élan, verve, zeal, zest

enjoy
verb to find pleasure in something » *I haven't enjoyed a movie as much as that in ages!*
appreciate, delight in, like, love, relish, revel in, take pleasure from, take pleasure in

enlarge
verb to make something larger » *The team became so successful that they had to enlarge the stadium.*
add to, expand, extend, increase, magnify, augment, broaden, distend, elongate, lengthen, widen

enlarge on
verb to give more information about something » *The teacher told Paul to enlarge on his answers to get more marks in the test.*
develop, elaborate on, expand on

enormous
adjective very large in size or amount » *The enormous monument dominated the skyline.*
colossal, gigantic, huge, immense, massive, tremendous, vast
antonym: **tiny**

ensure
verb to make sure about something » *Fran tried the door again to ensure it was securely locked.*
guarantee, make certain, make sure

enterprise [1]
noun a business or company » *The grocery store was a small family enterprise.*
business, company, concern, establishment, firm, operation

enterprise [2]
noun a project or task » *Lara's latest enterprise was to learn how to drive.*
effort, endeavour, operation, project, undertaking, venture

Lara's latest enterprise was to learn how to drive.

entertain
verb to keep someone amused or interested » *The puppy entertained the whole family.*
amuse, charm, delight, enthral, please

entertainment
noun enjoyable activities » *The television provided the entertainment for the evening.*
amusement, enjoyment, fun, pleasure, recreation

enthusiasm
noun eagerness and enjoyment in something » *Alice showed great enthusiasm for the piano and practised daily.*
eagerness, excitement, interest, keenness, warmth, ardour, fervour, relish, zeal

Some of the volunteers were more enthusiastic than others.

enthusiastic
adjective showing great excitement and eagerness for something » *Some of the volunteers were more enthusiastic than others.*
ardent, avid, devoted, eager, excited, keen, passionate, fervent, wholehearted, zealous
antonym: **apathetic**

entrance [1]
noun the way into a particular place » *I met Barry at the entrance to the station.*
door, doorway, entry, gate, way in

entrance [2]
noun a person's arrival somewhere » *The celebrity made a dramatic entrance.*
appearance, arrival, entry

entrance [3]
noun the right to enter somewhere » *If you buy a special pass, you can gain early entrance to the theme park.*
access, admission, entry

entrance [4]
verb to amaze and delight someone » *The audience was entranced by the singer's voice.*
bewitch, captivate, charm, delight, enthral, fascinate, enchant, enrapture, spellbind

entry [1]
noun a person's arrival somewhere » *The audience fell silent when the hero made his entry onto the stage.*
appearance, arrival, entrance

entry [2]
noun the way into a particular place » *The main entry to the house is around the side.*
door, doorway, entrance, gate, way in

entry [3]
noun something that has been written down » *Writing about the flight home was Liz's final entry in her travel journal.*
item, note, record

envy [1]
noun a feeling of resentment about what someone else has » *He felt envy at the sight of his friend's large garden.*
jealousy, resentment

envy [2]
verb to want something that someone else has » *James envied Peter's new bike.*
be envious, begrudge, be jealous, covet, resent

James envied Peter's new bike.

equal [1]
adjective the same in size, amount, or value » *Everyone at the party had an equal number of jelly beans.*
equivalent, identical, the same

equal [2] : equal to
adjective having the necessary ability for something » *Rhett was equal to the task and could do it with ease.*
capable of, up to

77

equal

equal [3]
verb to be as good as something else » *Mike's swim time equalled his previous best.*
be equal to, match

equip
verb to supply someone with something » *The hikers were equipped with a compass and map.*
arm, endow, fit out, provide, supply

equipment
noun the things you need for a particular job
▶▶ SEE RIGHT

erode
verb to wear something away and destroy it » *The cliffs were being eroded by the constant pounding of the sea.*
corrode, destroy, deteriorate, disintegrate

The cliffs were being eroded by the constant pounding of the sea.

err
verb to make a mistake » *Sophie had erred in her timing and arrived far too late.*
blunder, go wrong, make a mistake, miscalculate

error
noun a mistake » *The error was easy to fix.*
blunder, fault, lapse, mistake, slip

escape [1]
verb to manage to get away » *The dog escaped from the yard.*
break free, break out, get away, make your escape, run away, run off, abscond, bolt

escape [2]
verb to manage to avoid something » *Sid was lucky to escape injury when he fell over.*
avoid, dodge, duck, elude, evade

escape [3]
noun something that distracts you from something unpleasant » *Listening to music provided Kate with an escape from her hard day.*
distraction, diversion, relief

Listening to music provided Kate with an escape from her hard day.

essence [1]
noun the most basic and important part of something » *The essence of the story could be summed up in a few words.*
core, heart, nature, soul, spirit, crux, kernel, substance

essence [2]
noun a concentrated liquid » *Sheryl added a teaspoon of vanilla essence to the chocolate brownies.*
concentrate, extract

essential [1]
adjective extremely important » *A battery is essential for making a phone work.*
crucial, indispensable, vital

essential [2]
adjective basic and important » *Flour is an essential ingredient for any baker.*
basic, cardinal, fundamental, key, main, principal

essentials
plural noun the things that are most important » *We had enough money to buy only the essentials.*
basics, fundamentals, necessities, prerequisites, rudiments

esteem
noun admiration and respect for another person » *Our teacher is popular and held in high esteem by the rest of the staff.*
admiration, estimation, regard, respect, reverence, honour, veneration (formal)

estimate
noun a guess at an amount, quantity, or outcome » *The final fee was five times higher than the original estimate.*
appraisal, assessment, estimation, guess, quote, reckoning, valuation

eternal
adjective lasting forever » *The villain in the movie was seeking the secret to eternal life.*
everlasting, immortal, unchanging

even [1]
adjective flat and level » *Dad used a level to make sure the shelf was even.*
flat, horizontal, level, smooth
antonym: **uneven**

Dad used a level to make sure the shelf was even.

even [2]
adjective without changing or varying » *The dam let through an even flow of water.*
constant, regular, smooth, steady, uniform

even [3]
adjective the same » *At halftime, the scores were even.*
equal, identical, level, neck and neck

event [1]
noun something that happens » *He was still amazed by the events of last week.*
affair, business, circumstance, episode, experience, incident, matter

event [2]
noun a competition » *The next event is the long jump.*
bout, competition, contest

everyday
adjective usual or ordinary » *Getting up early was part of Liam's everyday life.*
common, daily, day-to-day, mundane, ordinary, routine, banal, unexceptional

evident
adjective easily noticed or understood » *Claire's happiness was evident from the smile on her face.*
apparent, clear, noticeable, obvious, palpable, plain, visible, conspicuous, manifest, patent

evil [1]
noun the force that causes bad things to happen » *Many movie plots are based around the conflict between good and evil.*
badness, immorality, sin, vice, wickedness, baseness, depravity, sinfulness
antonym: **good**

evil [2]
noun something unpleasant or harmful » *The dentist lectured the class on the evils of sugary foods.*
affliction, ill, misery, sorrow

examination »

evil [3]
adjective morally wrong or bad » *The evil deeds of the superhero's enemy are too many to count.*
bad, depraved, malevolent, sinful, vile, wicked
antonym: **good**

exact [1]
adjective correct in every detail » *Alf built an exact replica of the first steam engine.*
accurate, authentic, faithful, faultless, precise, true
antonym: **approximate**

exact [2]
verb (formal) to demand and obtain something » *Vicky wanted to exact a positive response from the school for her statement on recycling.*
command, extract, impose, insist on, insist upon, wring

exactly [1]
adverb with complete accuracy and precision » *The train arrived exactly at five o'clock.*
accurately, faithfully, just, on the dot, precisely, quite
antonym: **approximately**

exactly [2]
interjection an expression implying total agreement » *"We'll never know the answer." "Exactly! So let's stop guessing."*
absolutely, indeed, precisely, quite

exaggerate
verb to suggest something is more, better, or worse than it really is » *Lionel exaggerated the size of the wolf he claimed to have seen in his backyard.*
overdo, overestimate, overstate

exam
noun a test to find out how much you know » *The math exam was three hours long.*
examination, oral, test

examination [1]
noun a careful inspection of something » *The divers carried out an examination of the shipwreck to find out where the ship had come from.*
analysis, inspection, study

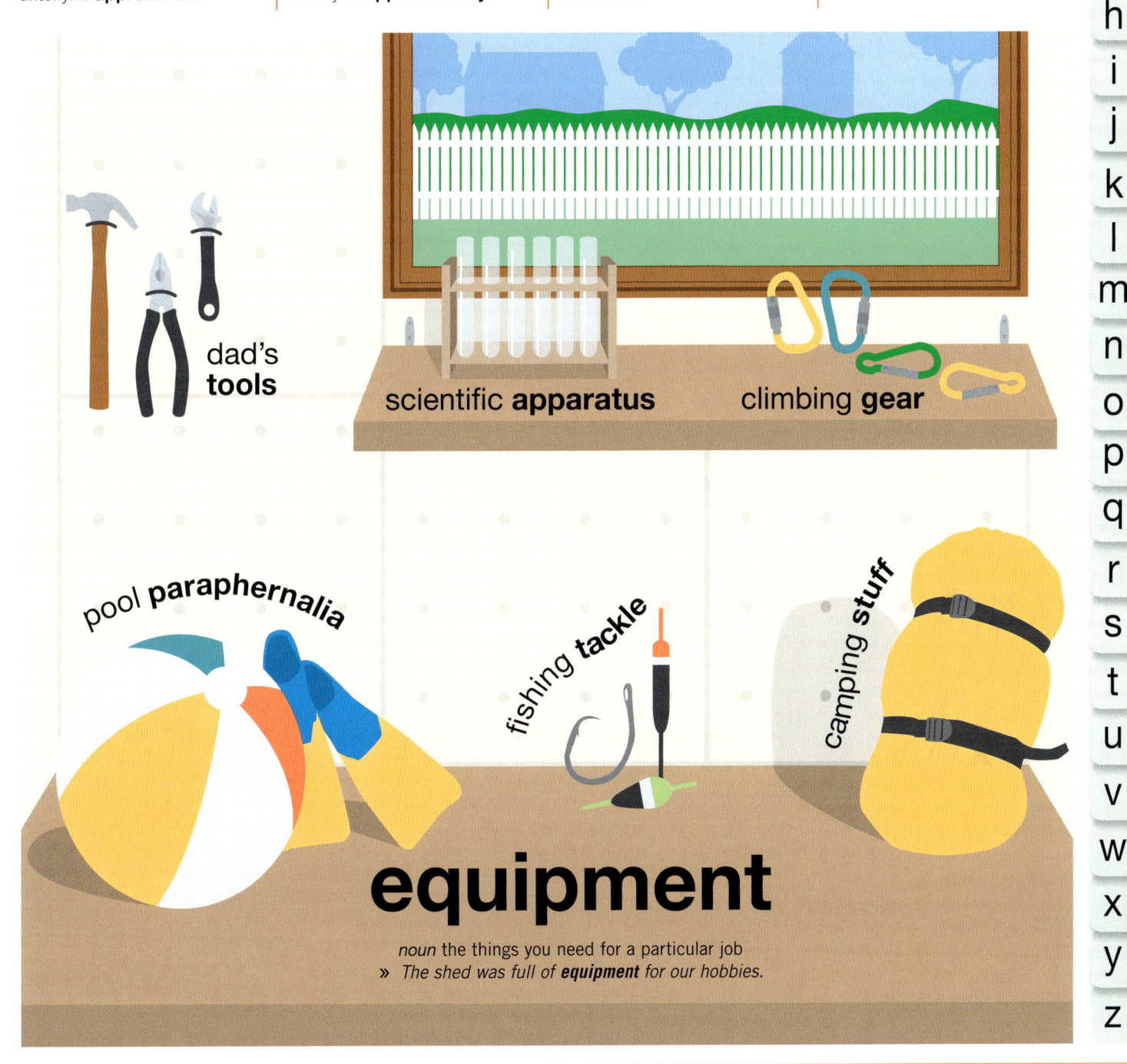

dad's **tools**

scientific **apparatus**

climbing **gear**

pool **paraphernalia**

fishing **tackle**

camping **stuff**

equipment
noun the things you need for a particular job » *The shed was full of **equipment** for our hobbies.*

» examination

The doctor made an examination of the patient's chest.

examination [2]
noun a check carried out on someone by a doctor » *The doctor made an examination of the patient's chest.*
check, checkup, physical

examine [1]
verb to look at something very carefully » *Experts examined the frozen remains of a woolly mammoth.*
analyze, go over, go through, inspect, look over, study, peruse, scrutinize

examine [2]
verb to give someone a medical examination » *The patient was examined by several specialists.*
check, inspect, look at, test

example [1]
noun something that represents a group of things » *The museum held several examples of Roman swords.*
illustration, sample, specimen

example [2]
noun something that people can imitate » *The respect that Grandma showed people is an example to us all.*
ideal, model, paragon, prototype, archetype, exemplar, paradigm

excellent
adjective extremely good » *It's an excellent book—one of my favourites.*
brilliant, extraordinary, fantastic, fine, first-class, great, outstanding, superb
antonym: **terrible**

except
preposition apart from » *Chris always gets the 8:10 train, except when he's running late.*
apart from, but, other than, save (formal), **with the exception of**

exceptional [1]
adjective unusually excellent, talented, or clever » *Lee's piano playing is exceptional; he should be on the stage.*
excellent, extraordinary, outstanding, phenomenal, remarkable, talented
antonym: **mediocre**

exceptional [2]
adjective unusual and likely to happen very rarely » *Having two people win first place was an exceptional event in sports history and had never happened before.*
isolated, out of the ordinary, rare, special, unheard-of, unusual, unprecedented (formal)
antonym: **common**

excess [1]
noun behaviour that goes beyond what is acceptable » *Stacey shopped to excess and regretted her purchases.*
extravagance, indulgence, intemperance, overindulgence

Stacey shopped to excess and regretted her purchases.

excess [2]
noun a larger amount than necessary » *An excess of houseplants made the room look like a jungle.*
glut, overdose, surfeit, surplus, overabundance, plethora, superfluity
antonym: **shortage**

excess [3]
adjective more than is needed » *The airline charged us an additional fee for our excess baggage.*
extra, superfluous, surplus

excessive
adjective too great » *We never travel first class because the cost is excessive.*
enormous, exaggerated, needless, undue, unreasonable, disproportionate, exorbitant, immoderate, inordinate, profligate

exchange [1]
verb to give something in return for something else » *We exchanged phone numbers.*
barter, change, swap, switch, trade

We exchanged phone numbers.

exchange [2]
noun the act of giving something for something else » *There was a useful exchange of ideas in the classroom.*
interchange, swap, switch, trade

excite [1]
verb to make someone feel enthusiastic or nervous » *Zara was extremely excited about her upcoming vacation.*
agitate, animate, thrill, titillate

excite [2]
verb to cause a particular feeling or reaction » *The dull movie failed to excite strong feelings in anyone.*
arouse, elicit, evoke, incite, inspire, provoke, stir up, fire, foment, inflame, kindle, rouse

The children were very excited to get a dog.

excited
adjective happy and enthusiastic » *The children were very excited to get a dog.*
agitated, enthusiastic, feverish, high (informal), **thrilled**
antonym: **bored**

excitement
noun interest and enthusiasm » *The release of his latest song has caused great excitement.*
activity, adventure, agitation, commotion, enthusiasm, thrill, animation, elation, furor, tumult

exciting
adjective making you feel happy and enthusiastic » *It was the most exciting race I've ever seen—no one could predict who would win.*
dramatic, electrifying, exhilarating, rousing, stimulating, thrilling, intoxicating, sensational, stirring
antonym: **boring**

exclude [1]
verb to decide not to include something » *The teacher excluded the easy words from the spelling test.*
eliminate, ignore, leave out, omit, rule out
antonym: **include**

exclude [2]
verb to stop someone going somewhere or doing something » *The cat was excluded from the lounge to stop it scratching the furniture.*
ban, bar, forbid, keep out, blackball, debar

exclusive
adjective available only to a few select people » *The restaurant was so exclusive, you could only get in by invitation.*
chic, elite, posh (informal), **private, restricted, select**

excuse [1]
noun a reason or explanation » *Stop making excuses and get on with your work!*
explanation, justification, pretext, reason

excuse [2]
verb to forgive someone or someone's behaviour » *Please excuse my late arrival.*
forgive, overlook, pardon, turn a blind eye to

exempt
adjective excused from a duty or rule » *Anne was exempt from singing in the choir due to her sore throat.*
excused, immune, not liable

exercise
noun activity that keeps you fit » *Half an hour of exercise is the best way to start the day.*
activity, exertion, training, work, workout

Half an hour of exercise is the best way to start the day.

exhaust [1]
verb to make very tired » *The marathon exhausted her and she felt ready to go to bed.*
drain, fatigue, tire out, wear out

exhaust [2]
verb to use something up completely » *Stuart drank so much tea, he exhausted the supply of tea bags.*
consume, deplete, run through, use up

expand
verb to make or become larger » *The balloon expanded when it was filled with air.*
develop, enlarge, extend, fill out, grow, increase, swell
antonym: **contract**

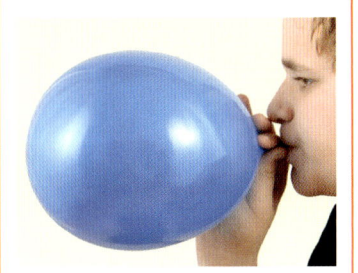

The balloon expanded when it was filled with air.

expand on
verb to give more information about something » *Please expand on your story; I want to hear more details.*
develop, elaborate on, enlarge on

expect [1]
verb to believe that something is going to happen » *The vet expects the baby elephant will be born in the next 12 hours.*
anticipate, assume, believe, imagine, presume, reckon, think, envisage, forecast, foresee, predict

expect [2]
verb to believe that something is your right » *I expect to be given a pay raise.*
demand, rely on, require

expensive
adjective costing a lot of money » *The running shoes were very expensive, and it took Charles a long time to save up for them.*
costly, dear, pricey, exorbitant, overpriced
antonym: **cheap**

We chose the dancers with the most experience to take on the leading roles in the ballet.

experience [1]
noun knowledge or skill in a particular activity » *We chose the dancers with the most experience to take on the leading roles in the ballet.*
expertise, know-how, knowledge, training, understanding

experience [2]
noun something that happens to you » *Mark's round-the-world trip was an experience that he'd never forget.*
adventure, affair, encounter, episode, incident, ordeal

experience [3]
verb to have something happen to you » *We're experiencing a few technical problems.*
encounter, have, meet, undergo

experienced
adjective very skilful as a result of practice » *After 20 dives, Naomi considered herself an experienced diver.*
expert, knowledgeable, practised, seasoned, well-versed
antonym: **inexperienced**

expert [1]
noun a skilled or knowledgeable person » *Nigel is an expert on cheetahs.*
ace (informal), **authority, buff** (informal), **geek, guru, master, professional, specialist, wizard**
antonym: **novice**

expert [2]
adjective skilled and knowledgeable » *Becky's expert performance on the guitar impressed everyone.*
able, adept, experienced, knowledgeable, proficient, skilful, skilled, adroit, dexterous, masterly, practised

explain
verb to make clear by providing extra information » *The teacher explained how the machine worked.*
define, describe, illustrate, elucidate, expound

explanation
noun a helpful or clear description » *The teacher wanted an explanation for why the children were late to class.*
clarification, definition, description, exposition

explode [1]
verb to burst or cause to burst loudly » *The party balloons exploded and made them all jump.*
blow up, burst, detonate, go off, set off

explode [2]
verb to become angry suddenly » *I asked him if he'd move up a seat and he just exploded.*
blow up, go berserk, go mad

explode [3]
verb to increase suddenly and rapidly » *Sales of computer games have exploded in recent years.*
rocket, shoot up, soar

Sales of computer games have exploded in recent years.

explode »

a b c d e f g h i j k l m n o p q r s t u v w x y z

explosion

explosion
noun a violent burst of energy
» *There was an explosion as the fireworks lit up the sky.*
bang, blast

expose 1
verb to make something visible
» *The dog's digging exposed the buried treasure.*
reveal, show, uncover

expose 2
verb to tell the truth about someone or something
» *Joe's real reason for wanting his allowance money early was exposed when he appeared wearing a brand new jacket.*
bring to light, reveal, show up, uncover, unearth

express 1
verb to say what you think
» *Sonia expressed a desire to take part in a foreign language exchange group.*
communicate, phrase, put, put across, utter, voice, articulate, couch, enunciate, verbalize

express 2
adjective very fast
» *The express train was the quickest way to get to the city.*
direct, fast, high-speed, nonstop

The express train was the quickest way to get to the city.

expression 1
noun a look that shows your feelings » *The expression on Dad's face was one of relief when we told him he hadn't missed Mom's birthday.*
countenance, look, aspect, mien

expression 2
noun a word or phrase used to communicate » *Helen hadn't heard that particular expression before, but she understood its meaning.*
idiom, phrase, remark, term

extend 1
verb to have a particular size or position » *The caves extend for miles beneath the hills.*
continue, hang, reach, stretch

extend 2
verb to stick out » *A large rock extended from the cliffs.*
jut out, project, protrude (formal), stick out

A large rock extended from the cliffs.

extend 3
verb to make something larger » *Mom wants to extend the house and build a sunroom.*
add to, develop, enlarge, expand, widen, augment, broaden, supplement

extensive 1
adjective covering a large area » *It took several hours to cross the extensive forest.*
broad, expansive, large, spacious, sweeping, vast, wide

extensive 2
adjective very great in effect » *The flood caused extensive damage across the whole area.*
comprehensive, considerable, far-reaching, great, pervasive, untold, widespread

The giraffe stretched its neck to its full extent to reach the leaves.

extent
noun the length, area, or size of something » *The giraffe stretched its neck to its full extent to reach the leaves.*
degree, level, measure, scale, size, expanse, magnitude

extra 1
adjective more than is usual or expected » *Neha placed an extra blanket on the bed because it was very cold that night.*
added, additional, excess, further, more, new, spare, ancillary, auxiliary, supplementary

extra 2
noun something that is not included with other things » *The parents had to pay extra for private riding lessons.*
addition, bonus

extract 1
verb to take or get something out of somewhere » *Citric acid can be extracted from orange juice.*
draw, mine, obtain, pull out, remove, take out

extract 2
verb to get information from someone » *The police interviewed the suspect in an attempt to extract information from him.*
draw, elicit (formal), get, glean, obtain

extract 3
noun a small section of music or writing » *Joanne read an extract from her story.*
excerpt, passage, reading, section, snatch, snippet

extraordinary
adjective unusual or surprising » *Seeing a shooting star is an extraordinary experience.*
amazing, bizarre, odd, singular, strange, surprising, unusual
antonym: ordinary

extreme 1
adjective very great in degree or intensity » *He felt extreme pain in his knee while jogging.*
acute, deep, dire, great, intense, profound, severe

He felt extreme pain in his knee while jogging.

extreme 2
adjective unusual or unreasonable » *Flora's angry reaction was extreme, and she regretted it once she'd calmed down.*
drastic, exceptional, excessive, extravagant, radical, unreasonable

extreme 3
noun the highest, lowest, or furthest degree or point » *Don was cautious to an extreme—he insisted that everyone wear life jackets in the wading pool.*
boundary, depth, end, height, limit, ultimate, acme, apex, nadir, pinnacle, zenith

Ff

face 1
noun the front part of the head » *A strong wind was blowing in my face, making my eyes water.*
countenance, features, mug (slang), **physiognomy**

face 2
verb to look towards something or someone » *Her room faced onto the street.*
be opposite, look at, overlook

face 3
noun a surface or side of something » *The explorers approached the mountain's summit via its north face.*
aspect, exterior, front, side, surface

The explorers approached the mountain's summit via its north face.

fact
noun a piece of information that is true » *The fact is that only male lions have manes.*
certainty, reality, truth
antonym: **lie**

factor
noun something that helps to cause a result » *A key factor in ice-skating is good balance.*
aspect, cause, consideration, element, influence, part, circumstance, determinant

factory
noun a building where goods are made » *The workers made desks in the furniture factory.*
mill, plant, works

The workers made desks in the furniture factory.

fade
verb to make or become less intense » *The fabric had faded in the bright sunlight.*
die away, dim, discolour, dull, wash out

fail 1
verb to be unsuccessful » *Claire tried to fix her bike but failed, so she had to walk.*
be defeated, be in vain, be unsuccessful, come to grief, fall through, flunk (informal)
antonym: **succeed**

fail 2
verb to omit to do something » *Jamie failed to phone, even though he said he would.*
neglect, omit

fail 3
verb to become less effective » *When Dad's eyesight began to fail, he went for an eye test.*
cease, decline, give out, stop working, crash, sink

failure 1
noun a lack of success » *She tried her best, but it ended in failure.*
breakdown, defeat, downfall, fiasco, miscarriage
antonym: **success**

failure 2
noun an unsuccessful person or thing » *The storm made the barbecue a complete failure.*
disappointment, flop (informal), **loser, incompetent, ne'er-do-well**

failure 3
noun a weakness in something » *A failure in the electrical system stopped the doorbell working.*
deficiency, shortcoming

faint 1
adjective lacking in intensity » *Rick tried to erase the picture, but it left a faint outline behind.*
dim, faded, indistinct, low, muted, vague
antonym: **strong**

Rick tried to erase the picture, but it left a faint outline behind.

faint 2
adjective feeling dizzy and unsteady » *Mira felt a bit faint after rushing around so much.*
dizzy, giddy, light-headed, enervated, vertiginous

faint 3
verb to lose consciousness temporarily » *The soldiers had to stand for hours in the heat, and one fainted.*
black out, collapse, pass out, swoon (literary)

fair 1
adjective reasonable and just » *To keep things fair, they all took turns on the trampoline.*
equal, equitable, impartial, legitimate, proper, upright, disinterested, dispassionate, unbiased
antonym: **unfair**

fair 2
adjective having light-coloured hair or pale skin » *She had long, fair hair.*
blond or **blonde, light**
antonym: **dark**

She had long, fair hair.

fair 3
noun an outdoor entertainment » *Tom had made cupcakes for the school fair.*
bazaar, carnival, exhibition, festival, fête, show

faith 1
noun trust in a thing or a person » *I have faith in you to succeed in whatever you do.*
confidence, trust

faith

faith [2]
noun a person's or community's religion » *Charles followed the Christian faith.*
belief, creed, persuasion, religion

faithful [1]
adjective loyal to someone or something » *The dog was my uncle's faithful companion.*
devoted, loyal, staunch, true, steadfast, unwavering
antonym: **unfaithful**

faithful [2]
adjective accurate and truthful » *The movie was faithful to the novel.*
accurate, exact, strict, true

fake [1]
noun a deceitful imitation of a thing or person » *These paintings are fakes.*
copy, forgery, fraud, imitation, reproduction, sham

fake [2]
adjective imitation and not genuine » *Alice wore a fake moustache as part of her costume.*
artificial, counterfeit, false, imitation, phony (informal)**, assumed**
antonym: **real**
related word: *prefix* **pseudo-**

Alice wore a fake moustache as part of her costume.

fake [3]
verb to pretend to experience something » *She faked a tummy ache so she wouldn't have to eat dinner.*
feign, pretend, simulate

Nicky fell from his bike onto the path.

fall [1]
verb to descend towards the ground » *Nicky fell from his bike onto the path.*
collapse, drop, plunge, topple
antonym: **rise**

fall [2]
verb to become lower or less » *The number of fish in the sea has fallen due to overfishing.*
decline, decrease, diminish, dwindle, plummet, subside, abate, depreciate, ebb
antonym: **increase**

fall [3]
noun a reduction in amount » *There has been a fall in ice-cream sales now that summer is over.*
decline, decrease, drop, reduction, slump
antonym: **rise**

false [1]
adjective not true or correct » *Ellen was accused of spreading false rumours.*
erroneous, fictitious, incorrect, mistaken, untrue
antonym: **true**

false [2]
adjective not genuine but intended to seem so » *The woman was wearing false eyelashes.*
artificial, bogus, fake, forged, simulated, ersatz, spurious
antonym: **genuine**
related word: *prefix* **pseudo-**

false [3]
adjective unfaithful and deceitful » *Ivy was a false friend, betraying Belinda to their teacher.*
deceitful, disloyal, insincere, unfaithful, duplicitous, perfidious

fame
noun the state of being very well-known » *The movie brought him international fame.*
eminence, glory, prominence, renown, reputation

familiar
adjective knowing something well » *Most children are familiar with nursery rhymes.*
acquainted with, aware of, knowledgeable about, versed in
antonym: **unfamiliar**

family [1]
noun a group of relatives » *My family always gets together for dinner.*
descendants, relations, relatives
related word: *adjective* **familial**

My family always gets together for dinner.

family [2]
noun a group of related species » *Tigers are members of the cat family.*
class, classification, kind

famous
adjective very well-known » *The chef's TV show made him famous.*
celebrated, distinguished, illustrious, legendary, noted, renowned, lionized
antonym: **unknown**

fan
noun an enthusiast about something or someone » *George was the band's biggest fan.*
adherent, admirer, devotee, geek (slang)**, lover, supporter, zealot,** aficionado, buff, enthusiast

Domingo and Carla were soccer fanatics and went to every match.

fanatic
noun someone who is extremely enthusiastic about something » *Domingo and Carla were soccer fanatics and went to every match.*
activist, devotee, extremist, militant, zealot

fanatical
adjective showing extreme support for something » *Lisa was fanatical about animal conservation.*
fervent, obsessive, passionate, rabid, wild, immoderate, zealous

fancy [1]
verb to want to have or do something » *Liam fancied a pizza.*
be attracted to, hanker after, have a yen for, would like

fancy [2]
adjective special and elaborate » *She was wearing a fancy hat, full of feathers.*
decorated, elaborate, extravagant, intricate, ornate, baroque, embellished, ornamented
antonym: **plain**

far [1]
adverb at a great distance from something » *The top of the mountain was far above us.*
afar, a great distance, a long way, deep, miles

far [2]
adverb to a great extent or degree » *The computer he bought was far better than the other options.*
considerably, incomparably, much, very much

far 3
adjective very distant
▶▶ SEE RIGHT

fascinate
verb to be of intense interest to someone » *He was fascinated by the fossil collection.*
absorb, bewitch, captivate, enthral, intrigue, beguile, enchant, spellbind, transfix

fashion 1
noun a popular style of dress or behaviour » *Diana dressed according to the latest fashion.*
craze, fad, style, trend, vogue

fashion 2
noun a manner or way of doing something » *Paul thanked my mother for the lift in his usual polite fashion.*
manner, method, mode, way

fashion 3
verb to make and shape something » *The child fashioned a doll from playdough.*
construct, create, make, mould, shape, work

The child fashioned a doll from playdough.

fashionable
adjective very popular » *The fashionable restaurant was a favourite of the rich and famous.*
current, in (informal), **latest, popular, prevailing,** chic, in vogue, trendsetting
antonym: **old-fashioned**

fast 1
adjective moving at great speed » *The fast train sped along the tracks.*
accelerated, hurried, quick, rapid, speedy, swift, fleet, mercurial, winged
antonym: **slow**

fast 2
adverb quickly and without delay » *You'll have to get there fast to make the start of the movie.*
hastily, hurriedly, quickly, rapidly, swiftly
antonym: **slowly**

fast 3
adverb firmly and strongly » *Alex held fast to the swing.*
firmly, securely, tightly

Alex held fast to the swing.

fasten
verb to close or attach something » *Fasten your seat belts.*
attach, fix, join, lock, secure, tie

fat
adjective weighing too much » *The dog had become rather fat in its old age.*
chubby, fleshy, obese, overweight, plump, pudgy (informal), **roly-poly** (informal), **tubby** (informal), **stout**
antonym: **thin**

fatal 1
adjective causing death » *A bite from a funnel web spider can be fatal to humans.*
deadly, incurable, lethal, mortal, terminal

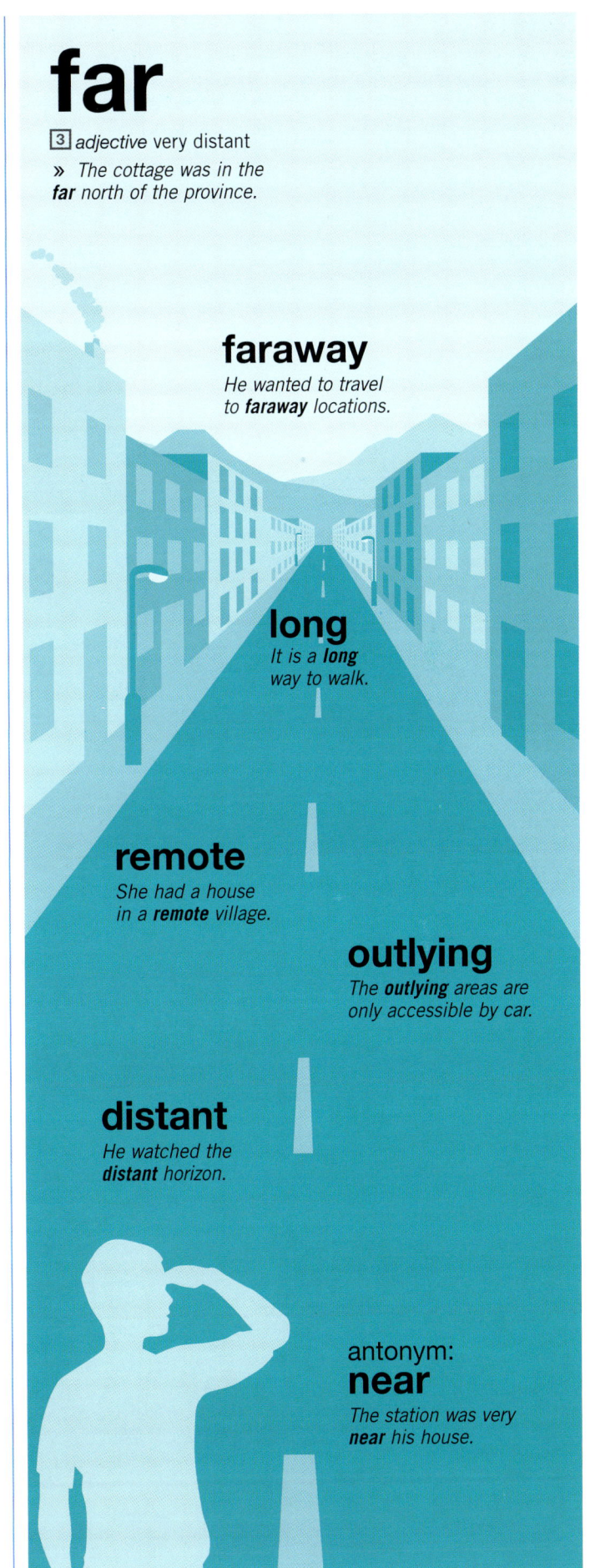

far
3 adjective very distant
» *The cottage was in the far north of the province.*

faraway
He wanted to travel to **faraway** locations.

long
It is a **long** way to walk.

remote
She had a house in a **remote** village.

outlying
The **outlying** areas are only accessible by car.

distant
He watched the **distant** horizon.

antonym:
near
The station was very **near** his house.

»fatal

fatal [2]
adjective having an undesirable effect » *There was a fatal flaw in the plan, and the plot failed.*
calamitous, catastrophic, disastrous, lethal

fate
noun a power believed to control events » *Fate would decide who won the lottery.*
chance, destiny, fortune, providence, kismet, predestination

fault [1]
noun something for which someone is responsible » *It was Eva's fault that the man had fallen over; she'd left her bag in his way.*
blame, liability, responsibility

fault [2]
noun a defective quality in something » *There was a fault with the vending machine and no drinks would come out.*
blemish, defect, deficiency, drawback, failing, flaw, imperfection, weakness
antonym: **strength**

fault [3]
verb to find reasons to be critical of someone » *Lydia's conduct cannot be faulted—she behaves beautifully.*
blame, censure, criticize

faulty
adjective containing flaws or errors » *The sound system was faulty and kept giving out ear-piercing squawks.*
defective, flawed, imperfect, invalid, unsound, fallacious, imprecise, malfunctioning

favour [1]
noun a liking or approval of something » *Everyone was in favour of the new plans; no one argued against them.*
approval, esteem, grace, support
antonym: **disapproval**

favour [2]
noun a kind and helpful action » *Can you do me a favour?*
courtesy, good turn, kindness, service
antonym: **wrong**

favour [3]
verb to prefer something or someone » *James favoured the brown boots over the black.*
prefer, single out

*James **favoured** the brown boots over the black.*

favourable [1]
adjective of advantage to someone » *The wind was favourable for sailing, and we set out on the lake.*
advantageous, beneficial, good, opportune, suitable, auspicious, propitious, timely
antonym: **unfavourable**

favourable [2]
adjective positive and expressing approval » *Jake received a favourable review, which really boosted his confidence.*
affirmative, amicable, approving, friendly, positive, sympathetic, welcoming
antonym: **unfavourable**

favourite [1]
adjective being someone's best-liked person or thing » *Mia's favourite food is toast.*
best-loved, dearest, favoured, preferred

favourite [2]
noun the thing or person someone likes best » *Tracey was the teacher's favourite and was always asked to hand out the books.*
darling, idol, pet, pick

favouritism
noun unfair favour shown to a person or group » *The head boy showed favouritism in picking his friend to help him.*
bias, one-sidedness, nepotism, partiality, partisanship
antonym: **impartiality**

fear [1]
noun an unpleasant feeling of danger » *Julie suffered from a fear of heights.*
alarm, awe, dread, fright, panic, terror, apprehensiveness, cravenness, trepidation

fear [2]
verb to feel frightened of something » *There is no need to fear my dog—she won't bite.*
be afraid, be frightened, be scared, dread, take fright

feature [1]
noun a particular characteristic of something » *The fireplace was an original feature of the old house.*
aspect, attribute, characteristic, mark, property, quality

feature [2]
noun a special article or program » *The magazine included a feature on the season's latest trends.*
article, column, item, piece, report, story

*The magazine included a **feature** on the season's latest trends.*

feature [3]
verb to include and draw attention to something » *The TV program featured an interview with the film's star.*
emphasize, give prominence to, spotlight, star

*Elsa was **feeling** left out.*

feel [1]
verb to experience emotionally » *Elsa was feeling left out.*
experience, suffer, undergo

feel [2]
verb to believe that something is the case » *Grace felt that telling the teacher was the right thing to do.*
believe, consider, deem, judge, think

feel [3]
verb to touch something physically » *Daisy felt the rabbit's soft fur.*
finger, fondle, stroke, touch

feeling [1]
noun the experiencing of an emotion » *Max couldn't hide his feelings of jealousy.*
emotion, fervour, heat, passion, sentiment

feeling [2]
noun a physical sensation » *Zoe had an uneasy feeling, and the hair stood up on the back of her neck.*
sensation, sense

feeling [3]
noun an opinion on something » *Brett had strong feelings about global warming and its effects on the environment.*
inclination, opinion, point of view, view

fellowship [1]
noun a feeling of friendliness within a group » *Lydia felt a sense of fellowship with the new people she'd met on the course.*
brotherhood, camaraderie, companionship

fill

fellowship [2]
noun a group of people with a common interest
» *The fellowship of writers met once a month.*
association, brotherhood, club, league, society

female [1]
noun a person or animal that can have babies » *The baby chimpanzees were cared for by the females in the group.*
girl, lady, woman
antonym: **male**

female [2]
adjective relating to females » *She was the world's fastest female distance runner.*
feminine, girlish, womanly
antonym: **male**

fertile
adjective capable of producing plants or offspring » *The fertile soil produced healthy plants with lots of fruit.*
fruitful, productive, prolific, rich, fecund
antonym: **barren**

fervent
adjective showing sincere and enthusiastic feeling » *Mom is a fervent admirer of this artist and buys his paintings whenever she can.*
ardent, committed, devout, enthusiastic, impassioned, passionate, zealous

festival [1]
noun a time of religious celebration » *Easter, Passover, and Holi are springtime festivals in different religions.*
anniversary, holiday

The music festival was lively.

festival [2]
noun an organized series of events » *The music festival was lively.*
carnival, entertainment, fair, fête, gala

few
adjective small in number » *There were few seats left on the bus, so we had to stand.*
infrequent, meagre, not many, scanty, scarce, sparse
antonym: **many**

fidget
verb to move and change position restlessly » *Stop fidgeting and sit still!*
fiddle (informal), **jiggle, squirm, twitch**

field [1]
noun an area of farmland » *The field was full of sheep.*
green, meadow, pasture

field [2]
noun a particular subject or interest » *The discovery was a breakthrough in the field of physics.*
area, department, domain, province, speciality, territory, discipline, métier

fierce [1]
adjective wild and aggressive » *The fierce lion chased the antelope.*
aggressive, dangerous, ferocious, murderous, barbarous, feral
antonym: **gentle**

fierce [2]
adjective very intense » *There was a fierce contest between the two teams.*
intense, keen, relentless, strong

fight [1]
verb to take part in a battle or contest » *The boxer fought hard to win the final round.*
battle, brawl, grapple, struggle

fight [2]
noun an aggressive struggle » *The kittens would have play fights.*
action, battle, bout, combat, duel, skirmish

The kittens would have play fights.

fight [3]
noun an angry disagreement » *Steve felt bad after his fight with Aaron, so he went back to say sorry.*
argument, dispute, row, squabble

fighter
noun someone who physically fights another person
» *Soldiers are trained fighters.*
soldier, warrior

figure [1]
noun a number, or an amount represented by a number » *Jim was happy with the figure he paid for the new car.*
amount, digit, number, numeral, statistic, total

figure [2]
noun a shape, or the shape of someone's body » *The ballerina has an elegant figure.*
body, build, form, physique, shape, silhouette

The ballerina has an elegant figure.

figure [3]
noun a person » *Terry Fox was an inspirational figure for so many people.*
character, dignitary, person, personality, player

figure [4]
verb (informal) to guess or conclude something » *I figure I'll get it right eventually if I try enough times.*
expect, guess, reckon (informal), **suppose**

fill
verb to make something full
▼ SEE BELOW

---

fill
verb to make something full
» *The hamster filled its cheek pouches with food.*

gorge
He gorges on food until there's no room for any more.

pack
All hamsters pack food into their cheeks.

cram
His cheeks were crammed with sunflower seeds.

stuff
Can he stuff any more in there?

stock
We stock the cupboards with plenty of pet food.

antonym: **empty**
The hamster completely emptied the food bowl.

final

final [1]
adjective being the last one in a series » *It was the final game of the Stanley Cup playoffs.*
closing, concluding, eventual, last, ultimate
antonym: **first**

final [2]
adjective unable to be changed or questioned » *The umpire's decision is final.*
absolute, conclusive, definite, definitive

finally [1]
adverb happening after a long time » *After waiting a week, the package finally arrived.*
at last, at the last moment, eventually, in the end, in the long run

finally [2]
adverb in conclusion of something » *And finally, before I finish, I'd like to talk to you about my favourite book.*
in conclusion, in summary, lastly

finance [1]
verb to provide the money for something » *The school fête raised enough money to finance the new science labs.*
back, fund, pay for, support

finance [2]
noun the managing of money and investments » *Banks play a leading role in the world of finance.*
banking, budgeting, commerce, economics, investment

financial
adjective relating to money » *Simon solved his financial problems by dogsitting to supplement his allowance money.*
economic, fiscal, money, budgetary, monetary, pecuniary

find [1]
verb to discover something » *I can't find my notes.*
come across, discover, locate, track down, turn up, unearth, descry, espy, ferret out
antonym: **lose**

find [2]
verb to realize or learn something » *We found that we got along well.*
become aware, detect, discover, learn, realize

fine [1]
adjective good and admirable » *Loretta wears fine clothes—unlike my shabby outfits.*
admirable, beautiful, excellent, magnificent, outstanding, splendid

fine [2]
adjective small in size or thickness » *A spider's web is made up of fine threads of silk.*
delicate, lightweight, powdery, sheer, small, diaphanous, gauzy, gossamer

A spider's web is made up of fine threads of silk.

fine [3]
adjective subtle and precise » *We had a general plan but needed to sort out the fine details.*
fastidious, keen, precise, refined, sensitive, subtle

finish [1]
verb to complete something » *Tom finished his homework in time to watch TV before bed.*
close, complete, conclude, end, finalize
antonym: **start**

finish [2]
noun the last part of something » *Naomi tried to stay awake to see the movie through to the finish.*
close, completion, conclusion, end, ending, finale, culmination, denouement, termination
antonym: **start**

finish [3]
noun the surface appearance of something » *Would you like a matte or gloss finish on your photos?*
grain, lustre, polish, shine, surface, texture

fire [1]
noun the flames produced when something burns » *A fire flickered in the fireplace.*
blaze, combustion, flames, inferno

A fire flickered in the fireplace.

fire [2]
verb to shoot or detonate something » *Jerry fired the pistol to start the race.*
detonate, explode, launch, set off, shoot

fire [3]
verb (informal) to dismiss someone from a job » *She was fired from her job.*
discharge, dismiss, make redundant, sack (informal)

firm [1]
adjective solid and not soft » *Put the jelly in the fridge until it is completely firm.*
compressed, congealed, hard, rigid, set, solid, stiff
antonym: **soft**

firm [2]
adjective resolute and determined » *The teacher was firm in her decision to keep the class in detention.*
adamant, determined, inflexible, resolute, staunch, unshakable, obdurate, steadfast, unwavering

firm [3]
noun a commercial organization » *We employed a local firm to decorate the house.*
business, company, corporation, enterprise, organization

first [1]
adjective done or in existence before anything else » *Neil Armstrong was the first human to set foot on the Moon.*
earliest, initial, opening, original, primeval
antonym: **last**

first [2]
adverb done or occurring before anything else » *First wash your hands, then you can eat.*
beforehand, earlier, initially, to begin with

first [3]
adjective more important than anything else » *Your safety is our first priority.*
chief, foremost, leading, prime, principal

first-rate
adjective excellent » *Ellis was a first-rate cellist.*
excellent, exceptional, first-class, marvellous, outstanding, splendid, superb, superlative (formal), unparalleled

fissure
noun a deep crack in rock or the ground » *There was a deep fissure in the rock that was too dangerous for the climbers to cross.*
cleft, crack, crevice, fault, rift, split

88

flat

The plug fits the socket exactly.

fit 1
verb to be the right shape or size » *The plug fits the socket exactly.*
belong, correspond, dovetail, go, match

fit 2
verb to place something in position » *Chris fitted the new stereo into the car.*
adapt, arrange, place, position

fit 3
adjective in good physical condition » *The doctor said I was fit and healthy.*
healthy, in good condition, robust, trim, well
antonym: **unfit**

fitting 1
adjective appropriate and suitable for something » *The fireworks were a fitting end to a great day.*
appropriate, correct, proper, right, suitable, apposite, decorous, seemly

fitting 2
noun a part attached to something else » *The bathroom fittings were chrome.*
accessory, attachment, component, part, unit

fix 1
verb to attach or secure something » *Mom fixed the shelves to the wall.*
attach, bind, fasten, secure, stick

fix 2
verb to repair something broken » *Dad fixed the leaky tap.*
correct, mend, patch up, repair

fix 3
noun (informal) a difficult situation » *He was in a fix and wasn't sure what to do.*
difficulty, mess, predicament, quandary

flabby
adjective fat and with loose flesh » *Doing sit-ups can help tone a flabby tummy.*
sagging, slack, flaccid, pendulous
antonym: **taut**

flash 1
noun a sudden short burst of light » *There was a flash of lightning.*
burst, flare, sparkle

flash 2
verb to shine briefly and often repeatedly
▶▶ SEE RIGHT

flashy
adjective showy in a vulgar way » *Ricky wore flashy clothes.*
flamboyant, garish, showy, tacky (informal), **tasteless, ostentatious**
antonym: **modest**

Ricky wore flashy clothes.

flat 1
adjective clearly unmistakeable » *His request was met with a flat refusal.*
absolute, explicit

flash
2 verb to shine briefly and often repeatedly » *The lighthouse's light flashed in the distance.*

twinkle *The stars twinkled in the night sky.*

flare *The beam of light flared.*

glint *Light glinted on the waves.*

glitter *The sea glittered in the moonlight.*

sparkle *The reflected light sparkled like a diamond.*

» flat

*Lisa and Jude upgraded their TV to one with a **flat** screen.*

flat 2
adjective level and smooth » *Lisa and Jude upgraded their TV to one with a flat screen.*
horizontal, level, levelled, smooth, unbroken
antonym: **uneven**

flat 3
adjective without emotion or interest » *The disappointing musical performance left the audience feeling flat.*
boring, dull, insipid, monotonous, weak

flatter 1
verb to praise someone, often insincerely » *Nigel flattered Felix about his violin playing but secretly thought some of the notes were wrong.*
compliment, fawn

flatter 2
verb to make more attractive » *Those clothes really flatter your figure.*
enhance, set off, suit

flattery
noun flattering words and behaviour » *Vicky was suspicious of Dan's flattery—what did he really want?*
adulation, fawning, blandishment, obsequiousness, sycophancy

flaw
noun an imperfection in something » *There was a crucial flaw in their plan.*
blemish, defect, fault, imperfection

flee
verb to run away from something » *The boys fled the park pursued by a dog.*
bolt, escape, fly, leave, run away, take flight

*The boys **fled** the park pursued by a dog.*

*Ben practised yoga and had a **flexible** body.*

flexible 1
adjective able to bend or be bent easily » *Ben practised yoga and had a flexible body.*
elastic, lithe, pliable, supple, ductile, lissom, lissome, pliant

flexible 2
adjective able to adapt or change » *My time is flexible, so let's meet whenever it's best for you.*
adaptable, discretionary, open

flinch
verb to move suddenly with fear or pain » *A sharp pain in her knee made Laura flinch.*
cringe, shrink, start, wince

float 1
verb to be supported by water or air
▼ SEE BELOW

float 2
verb to be carried on the air » *The smell of freshly baked bread floated past my window.*
drift, glide, hang, hover

flood 1
noun a large amount of water coming suddenly » *Many houses and cars were damaged in the flood.*
deluge, downpour, spate, torrent

*Many houses and cars were damaged in the **flood**.*

flood 2
noun a sudden large amount of something » *A flood of people entered the store all at once.*
rush, stream, torrent

float

1 verb to be supported by water or air
» *Many boats were **floating** on the water.*

be on the surface

lie on the surface

drift

stay afloat

bob

90

fold »

flood 3
verb to overflow with water
» *The river flooded its banks.*
deluge, drown, overflow, submerge, swamp

flourish 1
verb to develop or function successfully or healthily
» *The strawberries were flourishing in the garden.*
bloom, boom, do well, prosper, succeed, thrive
antonym: **fail**

flourish 2
verb to wave or display something » *The conductor flourished his baton wildly, lost in the music.*
brandish (literary)**, display, hold aloft, wave**

flourish 3
noun a bold sweeping or waving movement » *Linda gave a flourish as she tried on the coat.*
flick, sweep, wave

Linda gave a flourish as she tried on the coat.

The waterfall flowed down the steep drop.

flow 1
verb to move or happen in a continuous stream
» *The waterfall flowed down the steep drop.*
circulate, glide, roll, run, slide

flow 2
noun a continuous movement of something » *The flow of busy traffic prevented him from crossing the road.*
current, drift, flood, stream, tide

fluent
adjective expressing yourself easily and without hesitation
» *The girl was fluent in three languages.*
articulate, easy, effortless, flowing, ready
antonym: **hesitant**

fly 1
verb to move through the air
» *The child chased the birds, and they flew high out of reach.*
flit, flutter, sail, soar

fly 2
verb to move very quickly
» *Debbie flew down the stairs; she was very late.*
dart, dash, hurry, race, rush, speed, tear

foam 1
verb to swell and form bubbles
» *The soap foamed as I washed my hands.*
bubble, fizz, froth

The soap foamed as I washed my hands.

foam 2
noun a mass of tiny bubbles
» *There was a lot of foam on top of my hot chocolate.*
bubbles, froth, head, lather

focus 1
verb to concentrate your vision on something » *The optician told Ron to focus on the red dot on the screen.*
aim, concentrate, direct, fix

focus 2
noun the centre of attention
» *The celebrity guest was the main focus of the gala dinner.*
centre, focal point, hub, target

foil 1
verb to prevent something from happening » *"Foiled again!" the villain exclaimed as the sheriff arrested him.*
check, counter, defeat, frustrate, thwart,
circumvent, nullify

foil 2
noun a contrast to something
» *Luke is very serious and made the perfect foil for the comedian's jokes.*
antithesis, background, complement, contrast

fold 1
verb to bend something
» *To make an origami boat, fold the paper as shown.*
bend, crease, crumple, tuck, turn under

To make an origami boat, fold the paper as shown.

---

waft

sail

wash

swim

glide

antonym:
sink

91

fold

forest
noun a wooded area of trees and dense vegetation

» Harry spotted a deer in the **forest**.

coppice
The oaks in the **coppice** were cut back to encourage growth.

copse
The **copse** behind the house was too small to shade the garden.

grove
There was no undergrowth in the olive **grove**.

jungle
The **jungle** was dense and swampy.

bush
We headed into the **bush** on a camping trip.

rainforest
The **rainforest** was hot and steamy.

thicket
The **thicket** was thick with brambles.

wood
Tina and Hugo picnicked under a shady tree in the **wood**.

woodland
Tom left the **woodland** and walked across a field.

form »

fold [2]
noun a crease in something » *The fabric of Martha's dress hung in folds.*
bend, crease, pleat, wrinkle

follow [1]
verb to come after someone or something » *Night follows day.*
come after, succeed, supersede
antonym: **precede**

follow [2]
verb to pursue someone » *The goslings followed their mother.*
hound, pursue, stalk, track

The goslings followed their mother.

follow [3]
verb to act in accordance with something » *Follow the instructions carefully.*
comply, conform, obey, observe

follower
noun a supporter of a person or belief » *Steve's blog had thousands of followers.*
believer, disciple, fan, henchman, supporter, adherent, protagonist
antonym: **leader**

fond [1]
adjective feeling affection or liking » *My sister had become very fond of her new hamster.*
adoring, affectionate, devoted, doting, having a liking for, loving

fond [2]
adjective cherished, but unlikely to happen or be fulfilled » *Amy had fond hopes of becoming an actress one day.*
deluded, empty, foolish, naive, unrealistic, vain, delusory, overoptimistic

The refrigerator was full of food for the week ahead.

food
noun things eaten to provide nourishment » *The refrigerator was full of food for the week ahead.*
diet, fare, foodstuffs, nourishment, provisions, refreshment, provender, subsistence, victuals
related word:
noun **gastronomy**

fool [1]
noun an unintelligent person » *Ben is clever, but he likes to play the fool.*
dope (informal), **dunce, idiot, ignoramus**

fool [2]
verb to trick someone » *Don't let Gus fool you with his charm.*
con (informal), **deceive, dupe, mislead, trick, bamboozle, hoodwink**

foolish
adjective silly and unwise » *Emma felt foolish when she wore her shirt inside out.*
inane, nonsensical, senseless, silly, unintelligent, unwise
antonym: **wise**

forbid
verb to order someone not to do something » *Mary was forbidden from watching TV after 9 p.m.*
ban, exclude, outlaw, prohibit, veto
antonym: **allow**

force [1]
verb to compel someone to do something » *The snow forced us to abandon the car and walk.*
compel, drive, make, oblige, pressurize, coerce, impel, obligate

force [2]
noun a pressure to do something » *The rebels took the building by force.*
compulsion, duress, pressure

force [3]
noun the strength of something » *The force of gravity is what causes an apple to fall to the ground.*
impact, might, power, pressure, strength

foreign
adjective relating to other countries » *Jack's passport contained stamps from all the foreign countries he'd visited.*
distant, exotic, overseas

foremost
adjective most important or best » *Nadia is the school's foremost soccer player.*
best, chief, first, greatest, leading, most important, prime, principal, top

Nadia is the school's foremost soccer player.

forest
noun a wooded area of trees and dense vegetation
◀◀ SEE LEFT

forget
verb to fail to remember something » *I forgot my house keys; now I'm locked out.*
fail to remember, omit, overlook
antonym: **remember**

forgive
verb to stop blaming someone for something » *Will you ever forgive me for forgetting your birthday?*
absolve, condone, excuse, pardon
antonym: **blame**

forgiveness
noun the act of forgiving » *I ask for your forgiveness.*
acquittal, mercy, pardon, remission, absolution, exoneration

form [1]
noun a type or kind » *Sam spoke a form of Chinese that Anna couldn't understand.*
class, kind, sort, type, variant, variety

form [2]
noun the shape or pattern of something » *The 3D jigsaw had the form of a globe.*
contours, layout, outline, shape, structure

form [3]
verb to be the elements that something consists of » *Rachel's childhood formed the basis of her novel.*
compose, constitute, make up, serve as

form [4]
verb to organize, create, or come into existence » *Paul formed a bowl from clay.*
assemble, create, develop, draw up, establish, fashion, make

Paul formed a bowl from clay.

93

» formal

friend
noun a person you know and like
» Tim sat with his **friends** most lunchtimes.

companion — Ruby and Lily were constant **companions**.

confidant — Dan is Pete's **confidant**—he tells him everything.

crony — Tony was surrounded by his football **cronies**.

ally — Sam was Ben's **ally** whenever there was an argument.

buddy — Sharon goes out with her **buddies** after school.

soul mate — Jen and Sally are **soul mates** and know what each other is thinking.

sidekick — Ben's **sidekick** feeds him lines so he can tell his jokes.

pal — Sam and Dan are great **pals**.

antonym: **enemy** — I don't have many **enemies**.

formal [1]
adjective in accordance with convention
» We attended a formal dinner at the hotel.
conventional, correct, precise, stiff
antonym: **informal**

formal [2]
adjective official and publicly recognized » No formal announcement has been made.
approved, legal, official, prescribed, regular

former
adjective existing in the past
» The former Olympic champion congratulated this year's winners.
ancient, bygone, old, past

formidable
adjective difficult to overcome
» Climbing the cliff was going to be a formidable challenge.
challenging, daunting, difficult, intimidating, mammoth, onerous

*Climbing the cliff was going to be a **formidable** challenge.*

*The old **fort** was built to defend the harbour from attack.*

fort
noun a building for defence and shelter » The old fort was built to defend the harbour from attack.
castle, citadel, fortification, fortress

fragile
adjective easily broken or damaged » The antique china plate was extremely fragile.
breakable, dainty, delicate, flimsy, frail, frangible, infirm
antonym: **tough**

fragrance
noun a pleasant smell
» The flowers had a sweet fragrance.
aroma, perfume, scent, smell

*The flowers had a sweet **fragrance**.*

frustrate

fragrant
adjective having a pleasant smell » *The lemongrass and ginger made the curry wonderfully fragrant.*
aromatic, perfumed, sweet-smelling

frank
adjective open and straightforward » *Ryan and his mom had a frank discussion about his poor exam results.*
blunt, candid, honest, open, plain, straightforward

fraud 1
noun the act of deceiving someone » *Sid committed fraud by taking on someone else's identity.*
deceit, deception, guile, hoax, trickery, chicanery, duplicity, spuriousness

fraud 2
noun someone or something that deceives you » *Don't believe what that man says—he's a fraud.*
charlatan, cheat, fake, forgery, imposter, quack

free 1
adjective not being held prisoner » *The chicks escaped from their cage and were found running free in the garden.*
at large, at liberty, liberated, loose
antonym: **captive**

The chicks escaped from their cage and were found running free in the garden.

free 2
adjective available without payment » *Tom was giving away free magazines at the local store.*
complimentary, gratis, unpaid, without charge

free 3
verb to release from captivity » *Nathan's friends helped him to free his foot from beneath the rock.*
discharge, liberate, release, set at liberty, set loose, emancipate, unfetter
antonym: **imprison**

freedom 1
noun the ability to choose » *Sara had the freedom to decide for herself what to wear.*
discretion, latitude, leeway, licence, scope

freedom 2
noun the state of being free or being set free » *Lydia felt an amazing sense of freedom now that the holidays were here.*
emancipation, liberty, release, deliverance
antonym: **captivity**

freedom 3: freedom from
noun the absence of something unpleasant » *She enjoyed freedom from pain for the first time that day when she took off her tight shoes.*
exemption, immunity

frenzy
noun wild and uncontrolled behaviour » *The fish darted around in a feeding frenzy.*
agitation, fury, hysteria, madness, rage, delirium, paroxysm

frequent 1
adjective happening often » *Alex walked the dog on a frequent basis.*
common, continual, everyday, habitual, recurrent, repeated
antonym: **rare**

frequent 2
verb to go somewhere often » *When they had nothing else to do, the boys frequented the local park.*
attend, haunt, patronize, visit
antonym: **avoid**

friend
noun a person you know and like
◀◀ SEE LEFT

friendly
adjective kind and pleasant » *Peter had a friendly relationship with his neighbour.*
affectionate, amiable, close, cordial, genial, welcoming, companionable, comradely, convivial
antonym: **unfriendly**

Peter had a friendly relationship with his neighbour.

friendship
noun a state of being friendly with someone » *Their friendship was important to him.*
affection, attachment, closeness, goodwill
antonym: **hostility**

frighten
verb to make someone afraid » *The dog tried to frighten the others away by barking fiercely.*
alarm, intimidate, scare, startle, terrify, terrorize, unnerve

frightened
adjective having feelings of fear about something » *The cat was frightened by the noise of the fireworks.*
afraid, alarmed, petrified, scared, startled, terrified, cowed, panicky, terror-stricken

frightening
adjective causing someone to feel fear » *Thunder and lightning can be quite frightening.*
alarming, hair-raising, intimidating, menacing, terrifying

frivolous
adjective not serious or sensible » *She knew buying another party dress was frivolous.*
flippant, foolish, juvenile, puerile, silly
antonym: **serious**

front 1
noun the part that faces forward » *The front wall of the house was painted blue.*
face, frontage
antonym: **back**

front 2
noun the outward appearance of something » *Despite feeling nervous, Jo put on a brave front.*
appearance, exterior, face, show

front 3: in front
preposition further forward » *The car in front stopped suddenly so Mom slammed on the brakes.*
ahead, before, leading

frown
verb to draw the eyebrows together » *Ann frowned at the naughty child.*
glare, glower, knit your brows, scowl

frozen
adjective extremely cold » *Neil felt frozen, despite his big winter jacket.*
arctic, chilled, frigid, icy, numb

Neil felt frozen, despite his big winter jacket.

frustrate
verb to prevent something from happening » *Jon's efforts to start a fire were frustrated by the rain.*
block, check, foil, thwart, forestall, nullify

fulfill

fulfill
verb to carry out or achieve something » *Sam knew he would fulfill his dream and travel the world one day.*
accomplish, achieve, carry out, perform, realize, satisfy

full [1]
adjective filled with something » *The suitcase was so full of clothes, we couldn't close it.*
filled, loaded, packed, saturated
antonym: **empty**

The suitcase was so full of clothes, we couldn't close it.

full [2]
adjective missing nothing out » *I want to hear the full story of what happened.*
comprehensive, detailed, exhaustive, extensive, maximum, thorough

full [3]
adjective loose-fitting » *Her full skirt was made of a lot of material.*
baggy, loose, voluminous

fun [1]
noun an enjoyable activity
▶▶ SEE RIGHT

fun [2] : make fun of
verb to tease someone » *Don't make fun of him.*
deride, laugh at, mock, ridicule, taunt, lampoon, rib, satirize

function [1]
noun the useful thing that something or someone does » *The function of an oven is to heat food.*
duty, job, purpose, responsibility, role

function [2]
noun a large formal dinner, reception, or party » *Her parents were going to a function in the city.*
dinner, event, gathering, party, reception

function [3]
verb to operate or work » *The heater was not functioning properly—it was stone cold.*
go, operate, perform, run, work

fund [1]
noun an amount of money » *Ali needed to find a way to add to his savings fund.*
capital, foundation, pool, reserve, supply

fund [2]
noun a large amount of something » *She had a fund of knowledge about dinosaurs.*
hoard, mine, reserve, reservoir, store

fund [3]
verb to provide the money for something » *Helen was raising money to fund a local charity.*
finance, pay for, subsidize, support

funny [1]
adjective being strange or odd » *Chris heard a funny noise.*
mysterious, odd, peculiar, puzzling, strange, unusual

funny [2]
adjective causing amusement » *Jessica laughed at her sister's funny story.*
amusing, comic, comical, hilarious, humorous, witty, droll, jocular, risible
antonym: **serious**

Jessica laughed at her sister's funny story.

furious [1]
adjective extremely angry » *The man was furious that my ball had broken his window.*
enraged, fuming, infuriated, livid, mad, raging, frenzied, incensed, tumultuous

furious [2]
adjective involving great energy, effort, or speed » *There was a furious contest between the two racing drivers.*
breakneck, fierce, frantic, frenzied, intense, manic, frenetic

fuss [1]
noun anxious or excited behaviour » *What's all the fuss about?*
agitation, bother, commotion, confusion, stir, to-do, ado, fluster, palaver

fuss [2]
verb to behave in a nervous or restless way » *Waiters fussed around the table.*
bustle, fidget, fret

fussy
adjective difficult to please » *The toddler was a fussy eater and refused to eat pasta.*
choosy (informal), **discriminating, exacting, fastidious, particular,** faddish, finicky, persnickety

futile
adjective having no chance of success » *Kelly made a futile effort to catch the fish, but it slipped through her fingers.*
abortive, forlorn, unsuccessful, useless, vain
antonym: **successful**

future
adjective relating to a time after the present » *Future generations may one day live on the Moon.*
approaching, coming, forthcoming, impending, later, prospective
antonym: **past**

fun

[1] noun an enjoyable activity » *theme park was great fun.*

- amusement
- enjoyment
- entertainment
- pleasure
- recreation

Gg

gadget
noun a small machine or tool » *The kitchen was full of gadgets to make cooking easier.*
appliance, device, machine, tool, implement, instrument, utensil

The kitchen was full of gadgets to make cooking easier.

gain 1
verb to get something gradually » *The motorbike gained speed.*
achieve, acquire, earn, obtain, secure, win, attain, capture, reap

gain 2
verb to obtain an advantage » *I did my training in an office to gain work experience.*
benefit, profit

gain 3
noun an increase or improvement in something » *Jon's financial gains were down to good work and determination.*
advance, growth, improvement, increase, rise

gamble 1
verb to bet money on something » *Louis gambled on the lottery once a year, on his birthday.*
back, bet, wager

gamble 2
verb to take a risk » *He had gambled on it being a sunny day and hadn't brought his umbrella.*
chance, risk, stake, hazard, take a chance, venture

He had gambled on it being a sunny day and hadn't brought his umbrella.

gamble 3
noun a risk that someone takes » *We are taking a gamble on a young player.*
chance, lottery, risk

The atmosphere was great for the first game of the season.

game
noun an occasion on which people compete » *The atmosphere was great for the first game of the season.*
clash, contest, match

gap 1
noun a space or a hole in something
▼ SEE BELOW

gap 2
noun a period of time » *After a two-year gap, the fair came back to town.*
hiatus (formal), **interlude, interval, lull, pause**

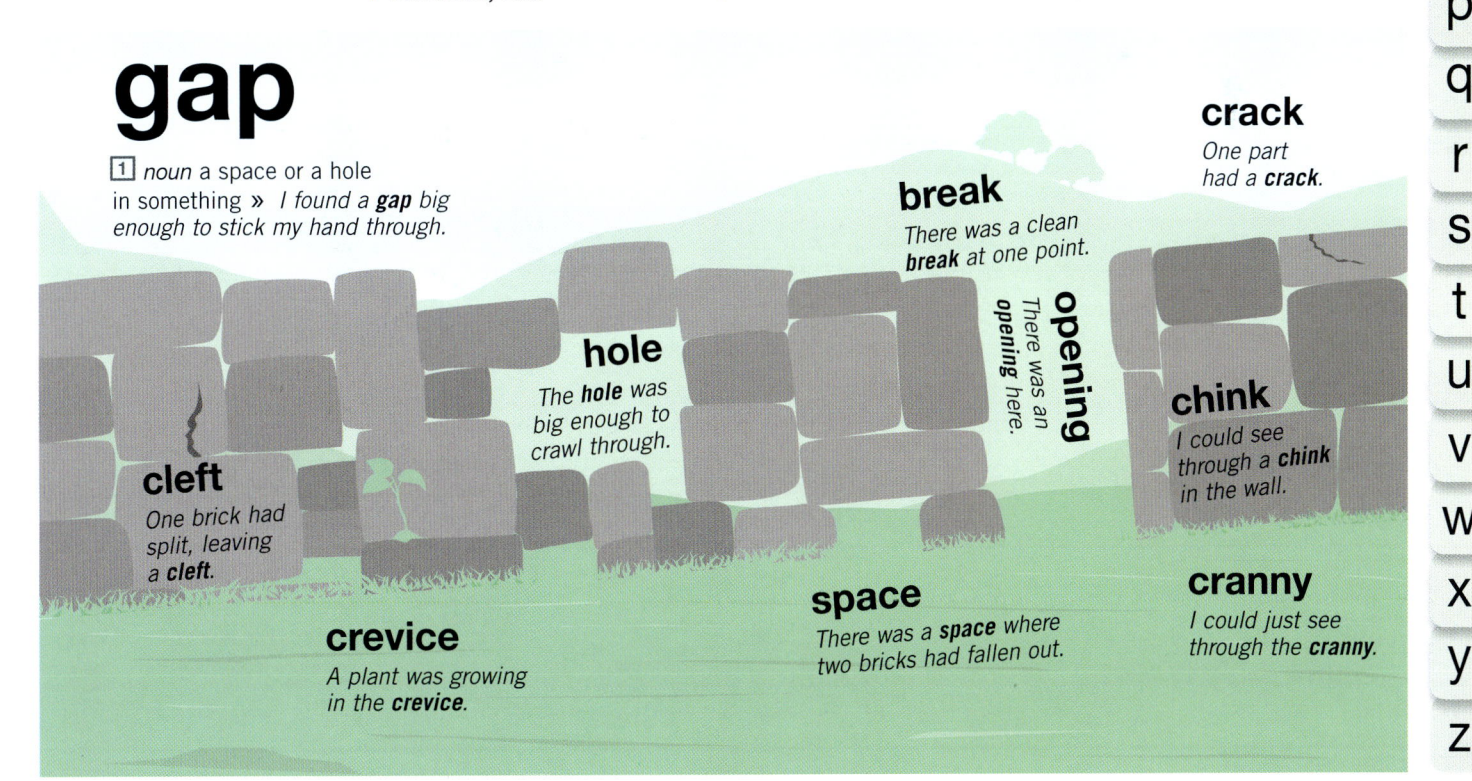

gap

1 noun a space or a hole in something » *I found a gap big enough to stick my hand through.*

cleft — One brick had split, leaving a **cleft**.

crevice — A plant was growing in the **crevice**.

hole — The **hole** was big enough to crawl through.

break — There was a clean **break** at one point.

opening — There was an **opening** here.

space — There was a **space** where two bricks had fallen out.

crack — One part had a **crack**.

chink — I could see through a **chink** in the wall.

cranny — I could just see through the **cranny**.

gap

gap [3]
noun a difference between people or things » There was a gap between what they hoped for, and what they got.
difference, disparity (formal), **inconsistency**

garbage [1]
noun things that people do not want » Garbage was piled on the street, ready to be collected.
debris, junk (informal), **litter, refuse** (formal), **rubbish, trash, waste**

garbage [2]
noun (informal) ideas and opinions that are untrue or unimportant » I personally think that this is garbage.
drivel, gibberish, nonsense, rubbish

garbled
adjective confused or incorrect » Anita couldn't understand the garbled voicemail message.
confused, distorted, incomprehensible, jumbled, unintelligible

gasp [1]
verb to breathe in quickly through your mouth » Beth gasped for air after running so fast.
choke, gulp, pant, puff, catch your breath, fight for breath

Beth gasped for air after running so fast.

gasp [2]
noun a short quick breath of air » The audience gave a gasp as the actor walked on stage.
gulp, pant, puff

gather [1]
verb to come together in a group
>> SEE RIGHT

gather [2]
verb to bring things together » The squirrel gathered the nuts into a pile.
accumulate, amass, collect, hoard, stockpile

The squirrel gathered the nuts into a pile.

gather [3]
verb to learn or believe something » Listening to the headlines, I gathered that the band had broken up over money problems.
assume, conclude, hear, learn, understand

gathering
noun a meeting with a purpose » Luca had been nervous about the hockey team gathering, but it had ended up being fun.
assembly, congregation, get-together (informal), **meeting, rally, conference, congress, convention**

gaudy
adjective colourful in a vulgar way » The fake gems in the jewellery were gaudy.
bright, flashy, garish, loud, showy, tacky (informal), **vulgar, jazzy, ostentatious, tasteless, tawdry**

general [1]
adjective relating to the whole of something » There was a general increase in student numbers across all subjects.
broad, comprehensive, overall, generic, indiscriminate, panoramic, sweeping
antonym: **specific**

general [2]
adjective widely true, suitable, or relevant » The campaign should raise general awareness about bullying.
broad, common, universal, widespread, accepted
antonym: **special**

generosity
noun willingness to give money, time, or help » Elsa is well known for her generosity in sharing her treats.
benevolence, charity, kindness, bounty, liberality, munificence, open-handedness
antonym: **meanness**

generous [1]
adjective very large » Amir donated a generous amount of clothes to charity.
abundant, ample, plentiful
antonym: **meagre**

Amir donated a generous amount of clothes to charity.

generous [2]
adjective willing to give money, time, or help » The offer to make all the invitations was very generous.
charitable, hospitable, kind, lavish, liberal, munificent, open-handed, prodigal, unstinting
antonym: **mean**

genius [1]
noun a very clever or talented person » Lena was a musical genius.
brain, master, mastermind, virtuoso

genius [2]
noun extraordinary ability or talent » Bradley is a mathematician of pure genius.
brains, brilliance, intellect

Bradley is a mathematician of pure genius.

gentle
adjective not violent or rough » The mother reminded her children to be gentle with the toys.
benign, kind, kindly, meek, mild, placid, soft, tender, compassionate, humane, lenient, sweet-tempered
antonym: **cruel**

genuine
adjective not false or pretend » Experts are convinced that the painting is a genuine work by the artist Monet.
authentic, bona fide, honest, real, true
antonym: **fake**

glare

get 1
verb to fetch or receive something » *I'll get us some drinks for the picnic.*
acquire, fetch, obtain, procure (formal)**, receive, secure** (formal)

get 2
verb to change from one state to another » *Once it gets dark, people draw the curtains and put on the lights.*
become, grow, turn

get on
verb to enjoy someone's company » *The two friends always did get on very well.*
be compatible, hit it off (informal)

ghost
noun the spirit of a dead person » *Lots of children dressed up as ghosts on Halloween.*
apparition, phantom, spectre, spirit
related word:
adjective **spectral**

*Ann bought the **gift** for her friend.*

gift 1
noun something you give someone » *Ann bought the gift for her friend.*
bequest (formal)**, contribution, donation, legacy, present**

gift 2
noun a natural skill or ability » *Huan had a gift for music.*
ability, aptitude, flair, talent

give 1
verb to provide someone with something » *I gave her a glass of orange juice.*
award, deliver, donate, grant, hand, present, provide, supply, accord, administer, bestow, confer
antonym: **take**

give 2
verb to collapse or break under pressure » *The bookcase was likely to give if any more books were placed on it.*
buckle, cave in, collapse, give way, yield

give in
verb to admit that you are defeated » *The kids kept whining until their dad gave in and took them to the park.*
capitulate, concede, submit, succumb, surrender, yield

glad
adjective happy about something » *I'm so glad you could make it—I haven't seen you in ages!*
delighted, happy, joyful, overjoyed, pleased
antonym: **sorry**

glance 1
noun a brief look at something » *They exchanged glances when the teacher's back was turned, as they knew they were about to get homework.*
glimpse, look, peek, peep

glance 2
verb to look at something quickly » *Wyatt glanced at his watch.*
glimpse, look, peek, peep, scan

glance 3
verb to hit something quickly and bounce away » *The ball glanced off the goal post.*
bounce, brush, skim, rebound, ricochet

glare 1
verb to look angrily at someone » *Joe glared at his sister.*
frown, glower, scowl

*Joe **glared** at his sister.*

glare 2
noun an angry look » *When the teacher gave them a glare, the class settled down.*
frown, scowl

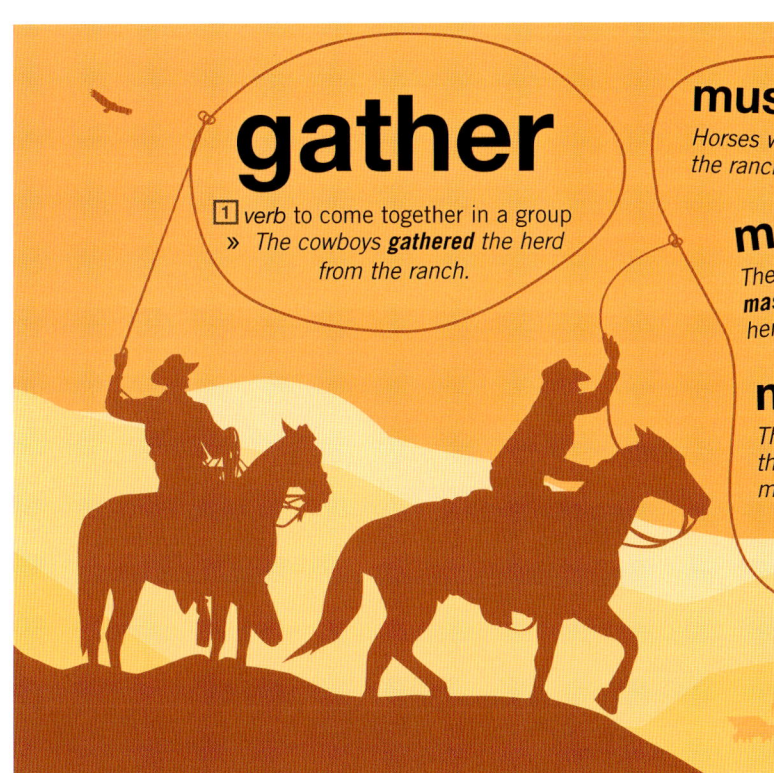

gather

1 verb to come together in a group » *The cowboys gathered the herd from the ranch.*

muster
Horses were mustered at the ranch for inspection.

mass
The cows needed to be massed together before herding back to the ranch.

marshal
The ranch owner marshalled the cowboys for a quick meeting.

congregate
The cows had congregated in the next pasture.

convene
All the cowboys in the area convened for a meal after work.

round up
The aim was to round up all the cattle before midday.

assemble
The cowboys assembled at the ranch before starting work.

antonym:
scatter
There were more cows scattered in distant fields.

99

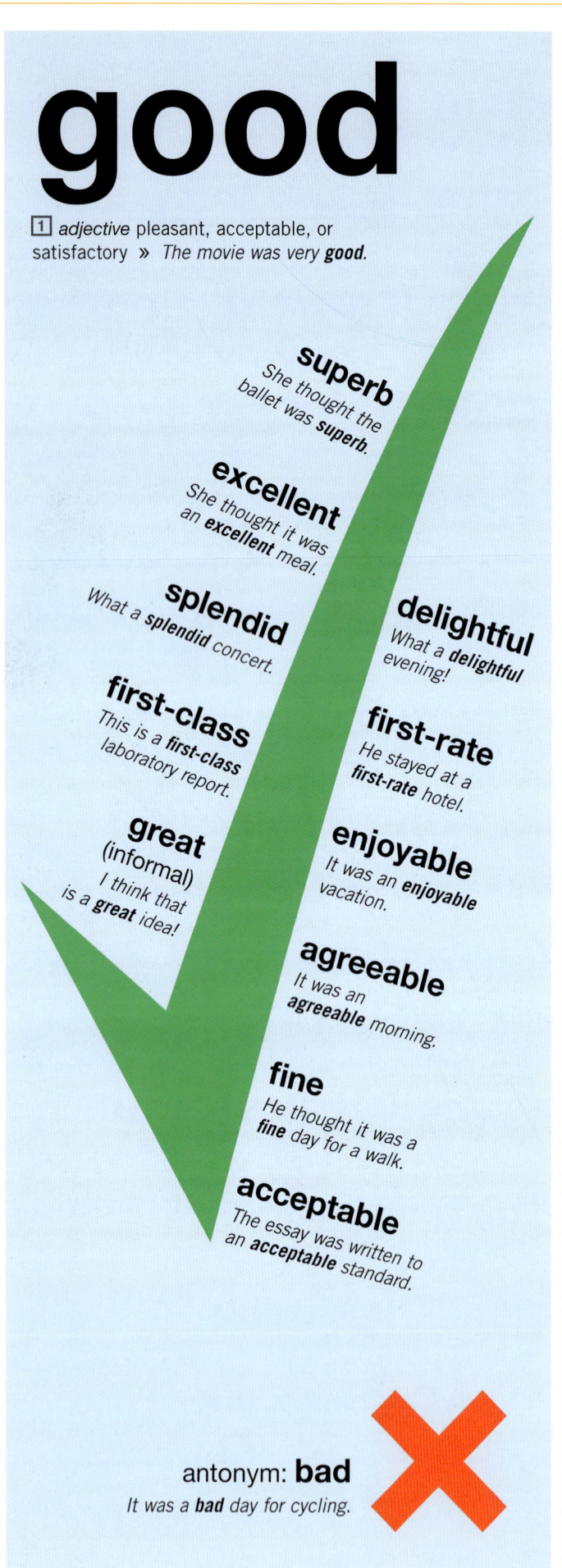

» glare

good

1 *adjective* pleasant, acceptable, or satisfactory » *The movie was very **good**.*

superb
She thought the ballet was **superb**.

excellent
She thought it was an **excellent** meal.

splendid
What a **splendid** concert.

first-class
This is a **first-class** laboratory report.

great (informal)
I think that is a **great** idea!

delightful
What a **delightful** evening!

first-rate
He stayed at a **first-rate** hotel.

enjoyable
It was an **enjoyable** vacation.

agreeable
It was an **agreeable** morning.

fine
He thought it was a **fine** day for a walk.

acceptable
The essay was written to an **acceptable** standard.

antonym: bad
It was a **bad** day for cycling.

glare 3
noun very bright light » *Vicky tilted her rear-view mirror to avoid the glare of the headlights from the car behind.*
blaze, glow

gloomy 1
adjective feeling very sad » *Carla felt gloomy at the prospect of leaving her old house.*
dejected, down, glum, miserable, sad, blue, despondent, downhearted
antonym: **cheerful**

gloomy 2
adjective dark and depressing » *The room was gloomy with all the curtains closed.*
dark, dismal, dreary, dull
antonym: **sunny**

*The room was **gloomy** with all the curtains closed.*

glory 1
noun fame and admiration that someone gets » *Winning the competition was her moment of glory.*
fame, honour, immortality, praise, prestige, acclaim, eminence, renown
antonym: **disgrace**

glory 2
noun something impressive or beautiful » *Spring arrived in all its glory.*
grandeur, magnificence, majesty, splendour

glory 3
verb to enjoy something very much » *The schoolchildren were glorying in the freedom of the holidays.*
gloat, relish, revel

*Use polish to give your shoes a **gloss**.*

gloss
noun a bright shine on a surface » *Use polish to give your shoes a gloss.*
brilliance, gleam, polish, sheen, shine

glossy
adjective smooth and shiny » *The leaves were dark and glossy.*
bright, brilliant, polished, shiny, sleek

glow 1
noun a steady light » *Madison felt soothed by the glow of the fire.*
gleam, glimmer, light

glow 2
verb to shine with a dull steady light » *The sun glowed through the trees.*
gleam, glimmer, shine, smoulder

glue
verb to stick things together » *Glue the two halves together.*
fix, paste, seal, stick

go 1
verb to move or travel somewhere » *I usually go into town on the weekends.*
advance, drive, fly, journey (formal), **leave, proceed** (formal), **set off, travel**

go 2
verb to work properly » *The car won't go.*
function, work

go 3
noun an attempt to do something » *I always wanted to have a go at waterskiing.*
attempt, shot (informal), **stab** (informal), **try**

goal
noun something that a person hopes to achieve » *The goal is to finish the race as fast as you can without dropping the egg from the spoon.*
aim, end, intention, object, objective, purpose, target

gobble
verb to eat food very quickly » *Pete gobbled the pasta as if he hadn't eaten for a week.*
bolt, devour, wolf

Pete gobbled the pasta as if he hadn't eaten for a week.

good 1
adjective pleasant, acceptable, or satisfactory
◀◀ SEE LEFT

good 2
adjective skilful or successful » *Miguel was really good at art.*
accomplished, adept, clever, competent, proficient, skilled, talented
antonym: **incompetent**

good 3
adjective kind, thoughtful, and loving » *You are so good to me, bringing me flowers.*
benevolent, considerate, generous, kind-hearted, obliging, thoughtful

As service was unusually slow, the waiter gave her a free drink as a gesture of goodwill.

goodwill
noun kindness and helpfulness towards other people » *As service was unusually slow, the waiter gave her a free drink as a gesture of goodwill.*
benevolence, favour, friendliness, friendship

gossip
noun informal conversation about other people » *The friends met once a week for coffee and gossip.*
dirt, hearsay, chitchat, gabfest, prattle, scandal

go through
verb to experience an unpleasant event » *I was going through a very difficult time at school.*
endure, experience, undergo

grab
verb to take hold of something roughly » *He grabbed her hand to stop her from falling.*
clutch, grasp, seize, snatch

He grabbed her hand to stop her from falling.

grace
noun an elegant way of moving » *The swans on the river swim with such grace.*
elegance, poise
antonym: **clumsiness**

grade
verb to arrange things according to quality » *Chilies are graded according to how hot they taste.*
class, classify, group, rate, sort, evaluate, sequence

gradual
adjective happening or changing slowly » *There was a gradual introduction of new school rules.*
continuous, progressive, slow, steady
antonym: **sudden**

grand
adjective very impressive in size or appearance » *The grand building in the town centre is the palace.*
imposing, impressive, magnificent, majestic, monumental, splendid, glorious, grandiose, palatial

The grand building in the town centre is the palace.

grandiose
adjective very large in size, effect, or cost » *The governor's grandiose house and party made people wonder about his spending habits.*
massive, overblown, palatial, pompous, regal, royal

grant 1
noun a money award given for a particular purpose » *My application for a music grant has been accepted.*
allocation, allowance, award, handout, subsidy

grant 2
verb to allow someone to have something » *Chloe was granted access to the backstage area.*
allocate, allow, award, give, permit, accord, bestow
antonym: **deny**

Chloe was granted access to the backstage area.

grant 3
verb to admit that something is true » *I grant that the chair was wobbly before you broke it.*
accept, acknowledge, admit, allow, concede
antonym: **deny**

grasp 1
verb to hold something firmly » *Rohan grasped the branch to steady himself.*
clutch, grab, grip, hold, seize, snatch

grasp 2
verb to understand an idea » *She failed to grasp the urgency of the situation.*
absorb, appreciate, assimilate, realize, take in, understand

grasp 3
noun a firm hold » *Logan loosened his grasp on the camera.*
clasp, embrace, grip, hold

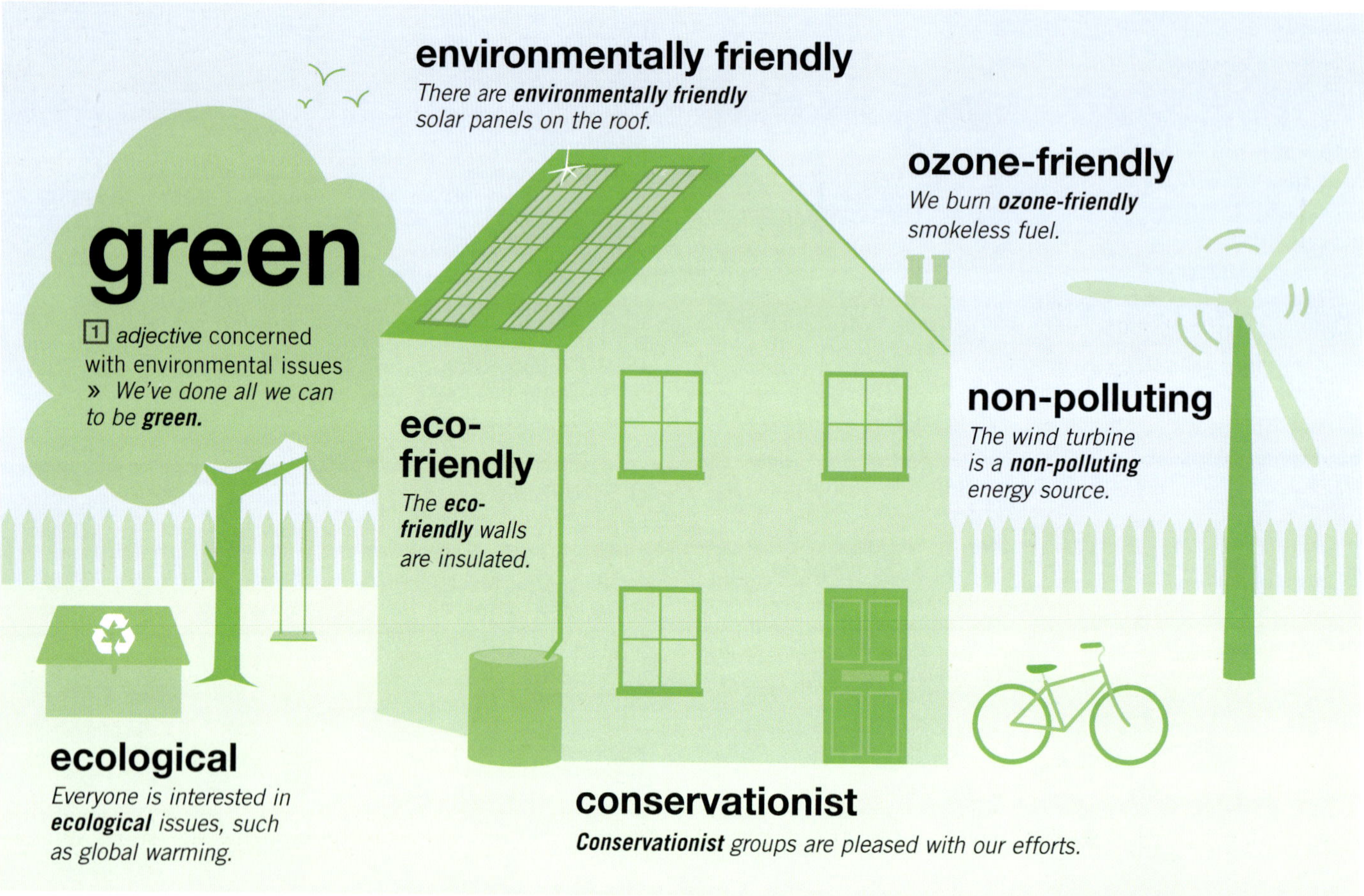

grasp

green
[1] adjective concerned with environmental issues
» We've done all we can to be **green**.

environmentally friendly
There are **environmentally friendly** solar panels on the roof.

ozone-friendly
We burn **ozone-friendly** smokeless fuel.

eco-friendly
The **eco-friendly** walls are insulated.

non-polluting
The wind turbine is a **non-polluting** energy source.

ecological
Everyone is interested in **ecological** issues, such as global warming.

conservationist
Conservationist groups are pleased with our efforts.

grasp [4]
noun a person's understanding of something » My brother has a good grasp of foreign languages.
awareness, comprehension (formal), **grip, knowledge, understanding**

grateful
adjective pleased and wanting to thank someone » Grace was grateful for the wonderful birthday party.
appreciative, indebted, thankful
antonym: **ungrateful**

Grace was grateful for the wonderful birthday party.

gratitude
noun the feeling of being grateful » After the walk, the dog wagged its tail in gratitude.
appreciation, recognition, thanks
antonym: **ingratitude**

grave [1]
noun a place where someone is buried when they die » They visited her grave twice a year.
mausoleum, pit, sepulchre, tomb, burial chamber, catacomb

grave [2]
adjective (formal) very serious » The students looked grave as they filed into the hall for the assembly.
acute, critical, heavy (informal), **serious, sober, solemn, sombre**

graze [1]
verb to slightly injure your skin » Anton fell over and grazed his left arm.
scrape, scratch, skin

graze [2]
noun a slight injury to your skin » Oskar just has a graze, not a major cut.
abrasion (formal), **scrape, scratch**

great [1]
adjective very large in size » There are great glaciers in the Arctic Ocean.
big, colossal, huge, large, enormous, extensive, gigantic, immense, stupendous, tremendous, vast
antonym: **small**

*There are **great** glaciers in the Arctic Ocean.*

great [2]
adjective important or famous » They erected a statue to honour the great leader.
celebrated, chief, distinguished, eminent, famed, famous, illustrious, important, main, major, momentous, notable, principal, prominent, renowned, serious, significant

*They erected a statue to honour the **great** leader.*

grow

great [3]
adjective (informal) very good » *Fran thought the surprise birthday party was a great idea and joined in with the planning.*
excellent, fantastic (informal), **fine, first-rate, marvellous** (informal), **outstanding, superb, terrific** (informal), **tremendous** (informal), **wonderful**
antonym: **terrible**

greedy
adjective wanting more than you need » *The greedy cat ate more than it needed.*
materialistic, acquisitive, avaricious, grasping, ravenous, voracious

The greedy cat ate more than it needed.

green [1]
adjective concerned with environmental issues
◀◀ SEE LEFT

green [2]
noun or adjective
Shades of green:
apple green, avocado, bottle green, chartreuse, emerald, grass green, jade, khaki, lime, Lincoln green, olive, pea green, pistachio, sage, sea green, turquoise
related word:
adjective **verdant**

The Prime Minister was greeted by local political leaders.

greet
verb to say hello to someone when they arrive » *The Prime Minister was greeted by local political leaders.*
meet, receive (formal), **welcome, hail, salute**

grey [1]
adjective being dull and dismal » *The rush hour crowds looked fed-up and grey.*
colourless, dull, nondescript, unremarkable

grey [2]
noun or adjective
Shades of grey:
ash, charcoal, gunmetal, hoary, leaden, pewter, platinum, silver, silvery, slate, steel grey, stone, taupe, whitish

grief
noun a feeling of extreme sadness » *She felt a sense of grief when her best friend moved abroad.*
distress, heartache, misery, sadness, sorrow, unhappiness, anguish, dejection, heartbreak, woe
antonym: **happiness**

grieve [1]
verb to feel extremely sad » *The nation grieved for the loss of their much-loved president at the state funeral.*
lament, mourn

grieve [2]
verb to make someone feel extremely sad » *It grieved Elaine to be away from her pets when she was on vacation.*
distress, pain, sadden, upset
antonym: **cheer**

grim
adjective looking very serious » *Her face was grim upon hearing the bad news.*
grave, severe, solemn, stern

grip [1]
noun a firm hold on something » *Aiden's grip on the bag was strong and fast.*
clasp, grasp, hold

grip [2]
noun someone's control over something » *The principal kept a tight grip on the school budget.*
clutches, control, influence, power

grip [3]
verb to hold something firmly » *The girl gripped the rope and began to climb.*
clutch, grasp, hold

The girl gripped the rope and began to climb.

ground
noun the surface of the Earth » *We sat on the ground and had a picnic.*
dirt, earth, land, soil, terrain

The school's grounds were used for sporting activities.

grounds [1]
plural noun the land surrounding a building » *The school's grounds were used for sporting activities.*
estate, gardens, land

grounds [2]
plural noun the reason for doing or thinking something » *Owen was against buying a new car on the grounds of expense.*
basis, cause, excuse, justification, reason, foundation, pretext, rationale

group [1]
noun a number of people or things » *The group of soccer fans cheered on their team.*
band, bunch, collection, crowd, gang, pack, party, set, aggregation, assemblage, coterie

group [2]
verb to link people or things together » *The pupils were grouped into four teams.*
arrange, class, classify, organize, sort, assort, marshal

grow [1]
verb to increase in size or amount » *The girl's hair grew very long.*
develop, expand, increase, multiply
antonym: **shrink**

grow [2]
verb to pass gradually into a particular state » *I grew more tired as the day went on.*
become, get, turn

103

» grow

A B C D E F G H I J K L M N O P Q R S T U V W X Y Z

grow [3]
verb to be alive or exist
▼ SEE BELOW

growth
noun the act of getting bigger
» *The doctor measured the child's growth.*
development, enlargement, expansion, increase

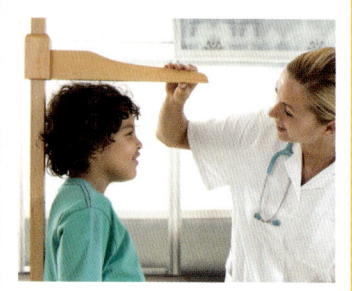

The doctor measured the child's growth.

grumble [1]
verb to complain in a bad-tempered way » *"This is very inconvenient," he grumbled.*
carp, complain, groan, moan, mutter, whine

grumble [2]
noun a bad-tempered complaint » *I didn't hear any grumbles when we were first planning what food should be served at the party.*
complaint, moan, murmur, objection, protest

grumpy
adjective bad-tempered and annoyed » *Alex was grumpy because he had forgotten his homework.*
irritable, sulky, sullen, surly, bad-tempered, cantankerous, ill-tempered

guarantee [1]
noun something that makes another thing certain » *The digital radio came with a guarantee that it would be replaced or fixed if anything was wrong with it.*
assurance, pledge, promise, undertaking, word

guarantee [2]
verb to make it certain that something will happen » *The free cupcakes were guaranteed to attract customers to the stall.*
ensure, pledge, promise

guard [1]
verb to protect someone or something » *The dog guarded the house, barking at any intruders.*
defend, protect, safeguard, shelter, shield, watch over

guard [2]
verb to stop someone making trouble or escaping » *Police guarded the angry crowds as they marched through the town.*
patrol, police, supervise

The security guard kept watch on the store's parking lot.

guard [3]
noun someone who guards people or places » *The security guard kept watch on the store's parking lot.*
sentry, warden, sentinel, warder, watchman

guess [1]
verb to form an idea or opinion about something » *I guess I'll have the cake for dessert.*
estimate, imagine, reckon, speculate, suppose, suspect, think, conjecture, hazard, surmise

guess [2]
noun an attempt to give the right answer » *Stefan made a guess that the time was three o'clock.*
feeling, reckoning, speculation, conjecture, hypothesis

guide [1]
verb to lead someone somewhere » *Ella took Elliott by the arm and guided him out.*
accompany, direct, escort, lead, conduct, convoy, shepherd, usher

guide [2]
verb to influence someone » *Guided by her father's advice, Priya bought the red bicycle.*
counsel (formal)**, govern, influence**

guilty [1]
adjective having done something wrong » *The dog was guilty of eating all the biscuits.*
convicted, criminal, blameworthy, culpable, felonious
antonym: **innocent**

guilty [2]
adjective unhappy because you have done something bad » *Sadie felt guilty for spilling tea on the carpet.*
ashamed, regretful, remorseful (formal)**, sorry, conscience-stricken, contrite, shamefaced**

gullible
adjective easily tricked » *Ivan was very gullible and believed everything the other boy said.*
naive, trusting, credulous, unsuspecting
antonym: **suspicious**

gush
verb to flow in large quantities » *Water gushed from the tap.*
flow, pour, spurt, stream, cascade, issue, jet

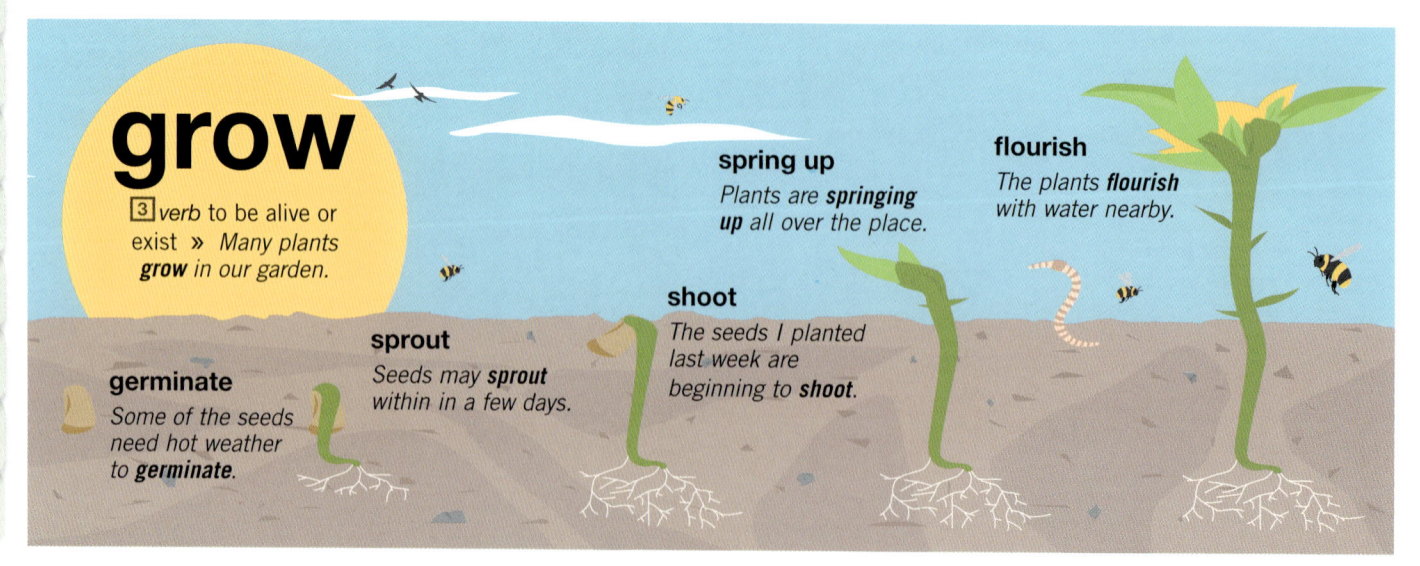

grow

[3] verb to be alive or exist » *Many plants grow in our garden.*

germinate
Some of the seeds need hot weather to **germinate**.

sprout
Seeds may **sprout** within in a few days.

shoot
The seeds I planted last week are beginning to **shoot**.

spring up
Plants are **springing up** all over the place.

flourish
The plants **flourish** with water nearby.

Hh

habit [1]
noun something that is done regularly » *Jonathan has an annoying habit of leaving the top off the toothpaste.*
convention, custom, practice, routine, tradition

habit [2]
noun an addiction to something » *Jess has a bad chocolate habit—she eats one chocolate bar every day.*
addiction, dependence

habitat
noun the natural home of a plant or animal » *Crocodiles live in tropical habitats.*
environment, territory
▼ SEE BELOW

hackneyed
adjective used too often to be meaningful » *Diego could only find hackneyed postcards of Mounties and the Parliament Buildings when he went to Ottawa.*
banal, clichéd, stale, tired, trite, run-of-the-mill, threadbare, timeworn
antonym: **original**

hail
verb to attract someone's attention » *Hannah hailed me from across the street.*
call, signal to, wave down

halt [1]
verb to bring something to an end » *The barbecue was finally halted by a rainstorm.*
cease, check, curb, cut short, end, terminate
antonym: **begin**

halt [2]
verb to come or bring to a stop » *She held her hand out and halted the cars.*
draw up, pull up, stop

She held her hand out and halted the cars.

halt [3]
noun an interruption or end to something » *When the bell rang for lunch, she brought the class to a halt.*
close, end, pause, standstill, stop, stoppage, impasse, termination

hamper
verb to make movement or progress difficult for someone » *I was hampered by a lack of information.*
frustrate, hinder, impede, obstruct, restrict, encumber, fetter

hand down
verb to pass from one generation to another » *Recipes are handed down from parents to their children.*
bequeath, give, pass down, pass on, bestow, will

---

habitat
types of habitat

forest
Forests are found in cooler, wetter areas where there is enough rain for trees to grow.

desert
With little annual rainfall, **deserts** are the driest places on Earth.

polar regions
The icy Arctic and Antarctic are **polar regions**.

Mediterranean
The **Mediterranean** can be very hot and humid.

grasslands
Grasslands are usually very dry and home to many grazing animals.

rainforest
More species of wildlife are found in **rainforests**, or jungles, than anywhere else in the world.

» **ha**ndicap

happy
[1] *adjective* feeling or causing joy
» *The children were so **happy** when dessert arrived.*

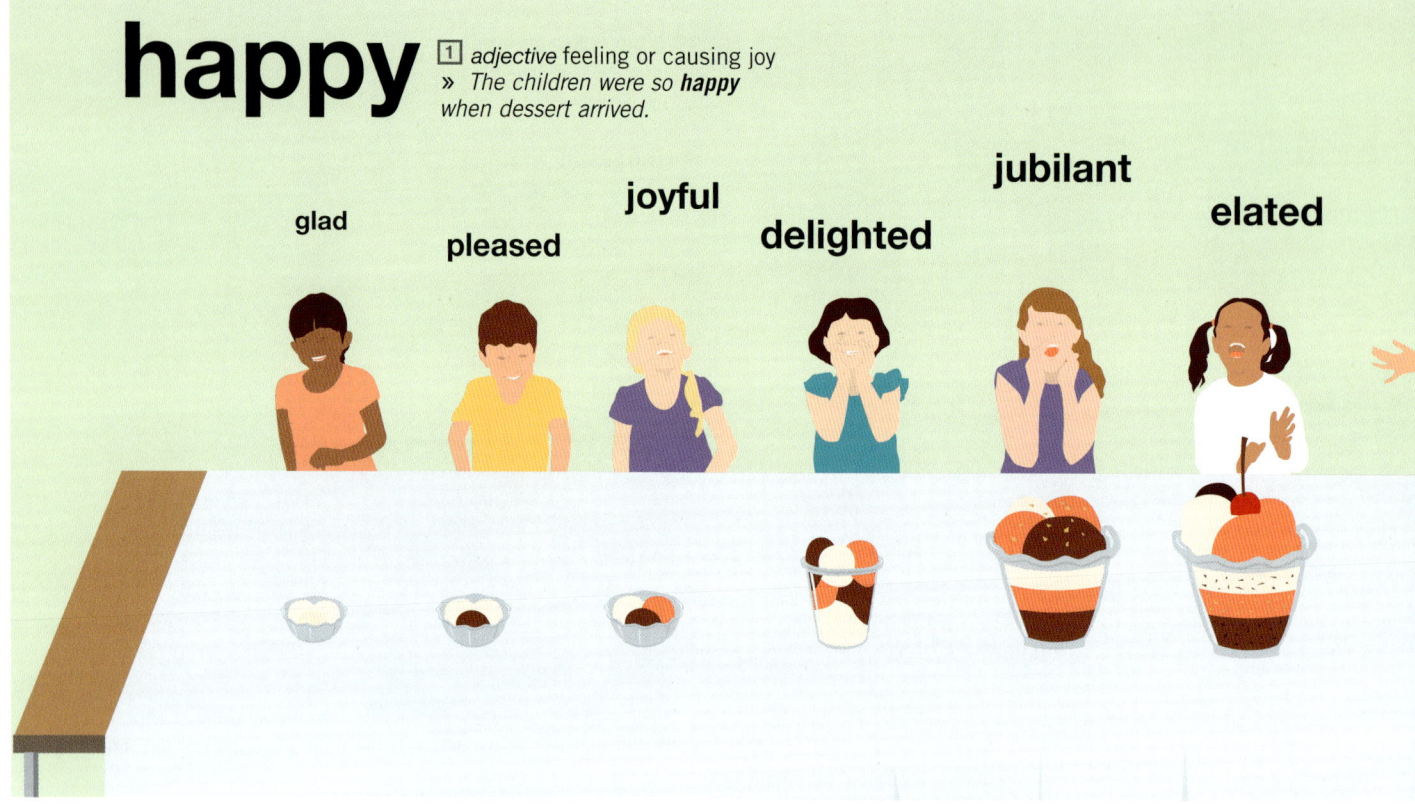

glad • pleased • joyful • delighted • jubilant • elated

handicap [1]
noun something that makes progress difficult » *Not speaking the same language was a real handicap.*
barrier, disadvantage, drawback, hindrance, impediment, obstacle

handicap [2]
verb to make something difficult for someone » *Lack of proper tools handicapped my father's attempt to build a wardrobe.*
burden, hamper, hinder, impede, restrict

handle [1]
noun the part of an object by which it is held » *The broom handle suddenly broke.*
grip, hilt

*The broom **handle** suddenly broke.*

handle [2]
verb to hold or move with the hands » *Please remember to wear gloves when handling cleaning products.*
feel, finger, grasp, hold, touch

handle [3]
verb to deal with or control something » *Thalia handled the travel arrangements.*
administer, conduct, deal with, manage, supervise, take care of

handsome [1]
adjective very attractive in appearance » *The main actor was talented and very handsome.*
attractive, good-looking
antonym: **ugly**

handsome [2]
adjective large and generous » *They made a handsome profit from the bake sale.*
ample, considerable, generous, liberal, plentiful, sizable
antonym: **small**

*Keep a pencil and paper **handy** so you can take notes during the telephone call.*

handy [1]
adjective conveniently near » *Keep a pencil and paper handy so you can take notes during the telephone call.*
at hand, at your fingertips, close, convenient, nearby, on hand

handy [2]
adjective easy to handle or use » *Paul gave me some handy hints on how to look after indoor plants.*
convenient, easy to use, helpful, neat, practical, useful, user-friendly

hang [1]
verb to be attached at the top with the lower part free » *Miguel's jacket hung from a hook behind the door.*
dangle, droop

hang [2]
verb to fasten something to another thing at the top » *Sara hung clothes on the line.*
attach, drape, fasten, fix, suspend

*Sara **hung** clothes on the line.*

happen
verb to take place » *Claire's surprise party happened on the weekend after her birthday.*
follow, go down (slang), **occur, result, take place, ensue, materialize**

106

harmful »

thrilled   overjoyed   over the moon (informal)   ecstatic   euphoric

happiness
noun a feeling of great pleasure » *Shreya was overwhelmed with happiness.*
delight, ecstasy, elation, joy, pleasure, satisfaction, exuberance, felicity, merriment
antonym: **sadness**

happy 1
adjective feeling or causing joy
▲ SEE ABOVE

happy 2
adjective fortunate or lucky » *By happy coincidence, Joe bumped into an old friend on the train.*
auspicious, convenient, favourable, fortunate, lucky, opportune, timely
antonym: **unlucky**

hard 1
adjective firm, solid, or rigid » *The cheese was so hard he struggled to cut it.*
firm, rigid, solid, stiff, strong, tough
antonym: **soft**

hard 2
adjective requiring a lot of effort » *Clearing out the garage was hard work, so he always put it at the bottom of his to-do list.*
arduous, exhausting, laborious, rigorous, strenuous, tough
antonym: **easy**

hard 3
adjective difficult to understand » *Ava found her algebra homework very hard.*
baffling, complex, complicated, difficult, puzzling
antonym: **simple**

Ava found her algebra homework very hard.

harden
verb to make or become stiff or firm » *The cement finally hardened so we could walk on it.*
freeze, set, solidify, stiffen
antonym: **soften**

hardly
adverb almost not or not quite » *There is hardly any water left in the bottle.*
barely, just, only just, scarcely

There is hardly any water left in the bottle.

hardship
noun difficult circumstances » *There are many countries suffering financial hardship.*
adversity, destitution, difficulty, misfortune, want, oppression, privation, tribulation

harm 1
verb to injure someone or damage something » *The bear ate our supplies, but didn't harm anyone.*
abuse, damage, hurt, ill-treat, ruin, wound

harm 2
noun injury or damage » *She accidentally stepped on his toe but didn't mean to cause him harm.*
abuse, damage, hurt, injury

harmful
adjective having a bad effect on something » *Eating chocolate is harmful to dogs.*
damaging, destructive, detrimental, hurtful, pernicious, baleful, baneful, deleterious, injurious
antonym: **harmless**

» **ha**rmless

catch He **caught** a snatch of conversation from people in the carriage.

overhear He couldn't avoid **overhearing** someone else's music.

heed He **heeded** the warning to stay off of the train tracks.

listen in He **listened in** on the businessman's phone call.

eavesdrop He **eavesdropped** on two teenagers gossiping.

listen to He tried to **listen to** the announcements.

hear

1 *verb* to listen to something
» *He could **hear** so many noises in the train.*

hear

harmless
adjective safe to use or be near » *This experiment is harmless to plants.*
innocuous, nontoxic, not dangerous, safe
antonym: **harmful**

harsh
adjective severe, difficult, and unpleasant » *The weather conditions were harsh in the mountains.*
austere, cruel, hard, ruthless, severe, stern, draconian, spartan
antonym: **mild**

The weather conditions were harsh in the mountains.

hassle 1
noun (informal) something that is difficult or causes trouble » *I wouldn't bring in the heavy history textbook—it's not worth the hassle.*
bother, effort, inconvenience, trouble, upheaval

hassle 2
verb (informal) to annoy someone by nagging or making demands » *My sister started hassling me to go to the movies with her.*
badger, bother, go on at, harass, nag, pester

hasty
adjective done or happening suddenly and quickly » *Saul made a hasty exit just before the train door closed.*
brisk, hurried, prompt, rapid, swift

hate 1
verb to have a strong dislike for something or someone » *I really hate mustard.*
abhor, be sick of, despise, detest, dislike, loathe
antonym: **love**

hate 2
noun a strong dislike » *Bullies are people who are full of hate.*
animosity, aversion, dislike, hatred, hostility, loathing, animus, detestation, enmity, odium
antonym: **love**

hateful
adjective extremely unpleasant » *It was a hateful thing to say.*
abhorrent, despicable, horrible, loathsome, obnoxious, offensive

hatred
noun an extremely strong feeling of dislike » *The bully made her feel full of hatred.*
animosity, antipathy, aversion, dislike, hate, revulsion
antonym: **love**

haughty
adjective showing excessive pride » *Ben was self-important and spoke to them in a haughty tone.*
arrogant, conceited, disdainful, proud, snobbish, stuck-up (informal)
antonym: **humble**

have 1
verb to own something » *Riley has two tickets for the concert.*
hold, keep, own, possess

Riley has two tickets for the concert.

have 2
verb to experience something » *Alex had a marvellous time.*
endure, enjoy, experience, feel, sustain, undergo

head 1
noun a person's mind and mental abilities » *I don't have a head for languages.*
aptitude, brain, common sense, intelligence, mind, wits, intellect, rationality

head 2
noun the top, front, or start of something » *We finally reached the head of the line.*
beginning, front, source, start, top
antonym: **tail**

head 3
noun the person in charge of something » *Our school hired a new head of the music program.*
boss, chief, director, leader, manager, president, principal

head 4
verb to be in charge of something » *Our teacher heads the department.*
be in charge of, control, direct, lead, manage, run

health 1
noun the condition of your body » *Exercise is good for your health.*
condition, constitution, shape

health 2
noun a state in which a person is feeling well » *In the hospital, they nursed me back to health.*
fitness, good condition, wellbeing
antonym: **illness**

healthy 1
adjective having good health » *Zoe was a very healthy child.*
active, fit, in good shape (informal), robust, strong, well
antonym: **ill**

I always eat a healthy breakfast.

healthy 2
adjective producing good health » *I always eat a healthy breakfast.*
beneficial, bracing, good for you, nourishing, nutritious, wholesome, invigorating, salubrious, salutary
antonym: **unhealthy**

heap 1
noun a pile of things » *As the bulldozers worked, the heap of rubble grew.*
hoard, mass, mound, pile, stack

heap 2
verb to pile things up » *Cora heaped potatoes onto Tom's plate.*
pile, stack

heaps
plural noun (informal) plenty of something » *Ivan always seems to have heaps of cash.*
loads (informal), lots (informal), plenty, stacks, tons (informal)

hear 1
verb to listen to something
◀◀ SEE LEFT

hear 2
verb to learn about something » *I heard that they didn't enjoy their holiday, which is a shame.*
ascertain, discover, find out, gather, learn, understand

heat

heat [1]
noun the quality of being warm or hot » *The heat of the midday sun was intense.*
high temperature, warmth
antonym: **cold**
related word: *adjective* **thermal**

heat [2]
noun a state of strong emotion » *In the heat of the argument, he said things he didn't mean.*
excitement, fervour, intensity, passion, vehemence

heat [3]
verb to raise the temperature of something » *Heat the oil in a frying pan.*
reheat, warm up
antonym: **cool**

Heat the oil in a frying pan.

heaven [1]
noun the place where good people are believed to go when they die » *She told them that he was now in heaven.*
next world, paradise, Elysium (Greek), **happy hunting ground** (Native American legend), **nirvana** (Buddhism and Hinduism), **Valhalla** (Norse)
antonym: **hell**

heaven [2]
noun a place or situation liked very much » *Martin was in musical heaven as he listened to the orchestra.*
bliss, ecstasy, paradise, rapture

The strawberry birthday cake was heavenly.

heavenly
adjective delightful or blissful » *The strawberry birthday cake was heavenly.*
blissful, delightful, excellent, glorious, superb

heavy [1]
adjective great in weight or force » *The bag was so heavy, I had to carry it using both hands.*
bulky, massive
antonym: **light**

heavy [2]
adjective serious or important » *The mood was heavy following the sad news.*
deep, grave, profound, serious, solemn, weighty
antonym: **trivial**

heed [1]
verb to pay attention to someone's advice » *No one heeded my warning about the spicy food.*
follow, listen to, pay attention to, take notice of

heed [2]
noun careful attention » *He pays too much heed to her.*
attention, notice

hell [1]
noun the place where souls of evil people are believed to go after death » *Some people believe that hell is where the devil lives.*
abyss, inferno, fire and brimstone, Hades (Greek), **hellfire, underworld**
antonym: **heaven**

hell [2]
noun (informal) an unpleasant situation or place » *Cancelled trains can make your journey hell.*
agony, anguish, misery, nightmare, ordeal

hello
interjection a greeting » *I stopped by to say hello.*
good afternoon (formal), **good evening** (formal), **good morning** (formal), **hey** (informal), **hi** (informal), **how do you do?** (formal), **how's it going?** (informal)
antonym: **goodbye**

help [1]
verb to make something easier or better for someone » *Dan began to help with the chores.*
aid, assist, lend a hand, support

Dan began to help with the chores.

help [2]
noun assistance or support » *The textbooks gave her the help she needed to study for her exams.*
advice, aid, assistance, guidance, helping hand, support

helper
noun a person who gives assistance » *There is an adult helper for every two children on the school trip.*
aide, assistant, deputy, right-hand man, supporter, henchman

helpful [1]
adjective giving assistance or advice » *The staff in the office are very helpful.*
accommodating, cooperative, kind, supportive
antonym: **unhelpful**

helpful [2]
adjective making a situation better » *Having the right equipment is always helpful.*
advantageous, beneficial, constructive, profitable, useful

helpless
adjective weak or unable to cope » *The newborn kittens were helpless.*
defenceless, powerless, unprotected, vulnerable, weak

hesitant
adjective uncertain about something » *At first Isaac was hesitant to accept the role.*
diffident, doubtful, reluctant, unsure, wavering, irresolute, vacillating

hesitate
verb to pause or show uncertainty » *Sue hesitated before replying to the question.*
dither, pause, waver

hide [1]
verb to put something where it cannot be seen » *The kitten hid under the basket.*
cache, conceal, secrete, stash (informal)

The kitten hid under the basket.

hide ②
noun the skin of a large animal » *They wrapped themselves in animal hides to keep warm.*
pelt, skin

high ①
adjective tall or a long way above the ground » *The Burj Khalifa is so high it towers over neighbouring buildings.*
elevated, lofty, soaring, steep, tall, towering
antonym: **low**

*The Burj Khalifa is so **high** it towers over neighbouring buildings.*

high ②
adjective great in degree, quantity, or intensity » *There is a high risk of sunstroke on beach vacations.*
acute, excessive, extraordinary, extreme, great, severe
antonym: **low**

hill
noun an area of high ground » *There is a large hill behind our house.*
down, dune, elevation, fell, foothill, height, hillock, hump, knoll, mound, prominence, rise, tor

hinder
verb to get in the way of someone or something » *A thigh injury hindered her ability to run.*
block, check, delay, frustrate, hamper, impede, encumber, stymie

hint ①
noun an indirect suggestion » *Victor gave a strong hint that we might go out to eat later.*
clue, indication, intimation, suggestion

hint ②
noun a helpful piece of advice » *I hope my cousin will give me some fashion hints.*
advice, pointer, suggestion, tip

hint ③
verb to suggest something indirectly » *My mother hinted at her disapproval of the TV program.*
imply, indicate, insinuate, intimate, suggest

hire ①
verb to employ the services of someone » *They are hiring staff to work in the store on Saturdays.*
appoint, commission, employ, engage, sign up

hire ②
verb to pay money to use something » *She hired the witch costume for the party.*
charter, lease, rent

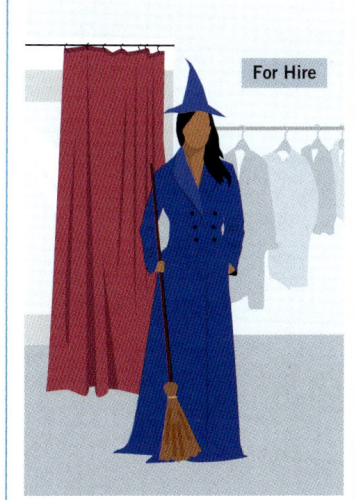

*She **hired** the witch costume for the party.*

hit ①
verb to strike someone or something forcefully
▶▶ SEE RIGHT

hit
① *verb* to strike someone or something forcefully » *He **hit** the machine with a big mallet.*

- hammer
- batter
- pound
- wallop
- belt
- beat
- strike
- whack
- bash
- punch
- thump
- smack
- slap
- bang
- knock
- swat
- rap
- tap
- pat

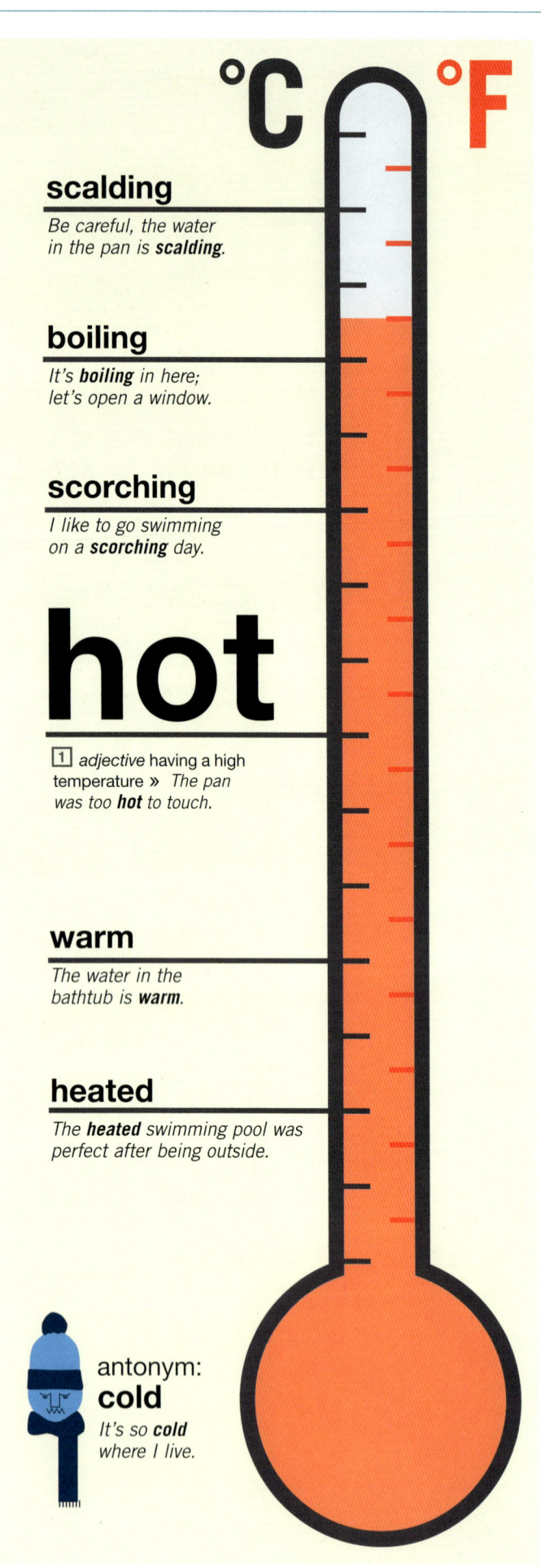

hit

scalding
Be careful, the water in the pan is **scalding**.

boiling
It's **boiling** in here; let's open a window.

scorching
I like to go swimming on a **scorching** day.

hot

[1] *adjective* having a high temperature » The pan was too **hot** to touch.

warm
The water in the bathtub is **warm**.

heated
The **heated** swimming pool was perfect after being outside.

antonym: **cold**
It's so **cold** where I live.

hit [2]
verb to collide with something » The car hit a traffic sign.
bang into, bump, collide with, meet head-on, run into, smash into

hit [3]
noun the action of hitting something » Give it a good hard hit with a hammer.
blow, knock, rap, slap, smack, stroke

hoard [1]
verb to store for future use » People began to hoard cans of food after the flood warning.
save, stockpile, store

People began to **hoard** cans of food after the flood warning.

hoard [2]
noun a store of things » Mia found a hoard of Roman silver buried in the field.
cache, fund, reserve, stockpile, store, supply

hoarse
adjective rough and unclear » Nick's voice was hoarse with screaming.
croaky, gruff, husky, rasping
antonym: **clear**

hobby
noun an enjoyable activity pursued in your spare time » My hobbies are music and photography.
diversion, leisure activity, leisure pursuit, pastime

Ellie **held** her bag up so her friend could see what she had bought.

hold [1]
verb to carry or support something » Ellie held her bag up so her friend could see what she had bought.
carry, clasp, clutch, embrace, grasp, grip

hold [2]
noun power or control over someone or something » The teacher has a considerable hold over her pupils.
control, dominance, sway

hold [3]
noun the act or a way of holding something » Ethan tightened his hold on the rope so he didn't fall.
grasp, grip

hole [1]
noun an opening or hollow in something » The builders cut holes into the stone.
gap, hollow, opening, pit, split, tear

hole [2]
noun a weakness in a idea or argument » There are some holes in that idea.
defect, error, fault, flaw, loophole

hole [3]
noun (informal) a difficult situation » Due to the crisis, he admitted the government was in a hole.
fix (informal), **hot water** (informal), **mess, predicament, tight spot**

holiday
noun time spent away from school, work, or home for rest or enjoyment » *Roshni couldn't wait to go on holiday.*
break, leave, recess, time off, vacation

holy 1
adjective relating to God or a particular religion » *The Bible is a holy book for Christians.*
blessed, consecrated, hallowed, sacred, sacrosanct, venerated

holy 2
adjective religious and leading a good life » *Monks are holy men.*
devout, pious, religious, saintly, virtuous, god-fearing, godly
antonym: **wicked**

home 1
noun the building in which someone lives » *Her parents stayed at home to watch a movie.*
abode, dwelling, house, residence

home 2
adjective involving your own home or region » *The home team won the match easily.*
domestic, internal, local, national, native
antonym: **foreign**

homely
adjective simple, ordinary, and comfortable » *The room was small and homely.*
comfortable, cosy, modest, simple, welcoming
antonym: **grand**

honest
adjective truthful and trustworthy » *He is a very honest, decent man.*
law-abiding, reputable, trustworthy, truthful, virtuous
antonym: **dishonest**

honour 1
noun personal integrity » *It was an honour to be part of a team that worked so hard.*
decency, goodness, honesty, integrity
antonym: **dishonour**

honour 2
noun an award or mark of respect » *The star was showered with honours, including the top trophy.*
accolade, commendation, homage, praise, recognition, tribute, acclaim, kudos

*The star was showered with **honours**, including the top trophy.*

honour 3
verb to give someone special praise » *The soloist was honoured by the conductor.*
commemorate, commend, decorate, glorify, praise

hooligan
noun a destructive and violent young person » *The hooligans damaged two buses.*
delinquent, ganster, goon, lout, punk, thug, tough, troublemaker, vandal

hope
noun a wish or feeling of desire and expectation » *Sam had high hopes that the weather would improve before his camping trip.*
ambition, dream, expectation

hopeless 1
adjective certain to fail or be unsuccessful » *Marooned on the desert island, our situation seemed hopeless.*
forlorn, futile, impossible, pointless, useless, vain

hopeless 2
adjective bad or inadequate » *The buses in the morning are hopeless, so it is difficult to get to school on time.*
inadequate, pathetic, poor, useless (informal)

horrible 1
adjective disagreeable or unpleasant » *The burger from the mall's food court was horrible.*
awful, disagreeable, horrid, mean, nasty, unpleasant

horrible 2
adjective causing shock, fear, or disgust » *A horrible crime was committed last night.*
appalling, dreadful, grim, gruesome, terrifying

horrify
verb to cause to feel horror or shock » *This latest robbery will horrify homeowners.*
appal, disgust, dismay, outrage, shock, sicken

horror 1
noun a strong feeling of alarm or disgust » *Mila gazed in horror at the mess the dog had made in the kitchen.*
alarm, dread, fear, fright, panic, terror

horror 2
noun a strong fear of something » *Felix had a horror of deep water and avoided it whenever he could.*
abhorrence, aversion, disgust, hatred, loathing, revulsion, abomination, odium, repugnance

horse
noun an animal domesticated for riding » *Maria rode her horse daily so that she was ready for the competition.*
bronco, equine, nag (informal), **pony, mount, steed**
related words:
adjectives **equestrian, equine, horsey;** noun **equitation;** male **stallion;** female **mare;** young **colt, filly, foal**

hostile
adjective unfriendly, aggressive, and unpleasant » *His suggestion received a hostile response.*
antagonistic, belligerent, malevolent, unkind
antonym: **friendly**

*His suggestion received a **hostile** response.*

hostility
noun aggressive or unfriendly behaviour towards someone or something » *The fans showed hostility to the opposing team.*
animosity, antagonism, hatred, ill will, malice, resentment, animus, detestation, enmity
antonym: **friendship**

hot 1
adjective having a high temperature
◂◂ SEE LEFT

» hot

hot [2]
adjective very spicy
» *The curry was so hot, it stung his mouth.*
peppery, spicy
antonym: **bland**

house
noun a building in which people live » *They live in a large house with eight rooms.*
abode, building, dwelling, home, residence

hug [1]
verb to hold someone close to you » *Lynn and I hugged each other.*
clasp, cuddle, embrace, squeeze

Lynn and I hugged each other.

hug [2]
noun the act of holding someone close to you » *Deeksha gave him a hug.*
clinch (slang), **embrace**

huge
adjective extremely large in amount, size, or degree » *A huge crowd gathered to watch the match.*
colossal, enormous, giant, immense, massive, vast, gargantuan, prodigious
antonym: **tiny**

humane
adjective showing kindness and sympathy towards others » *They hoped to create a fairer, more humane society.*
benevolent, caring, charitable, compassionate, kind, merciful, thoughtful, altruistic, humanitarian

humble [1]
adjective not vain or boastful » *The musician gave a great performance, but he was humble and wouldn't accept the praise.*
meek, modest, unassuming
antonym: **haughty**

humble [2]
adjective ordinary or unimportant » *A few herbs will transform a humble stew into a dish fit for a king.*
lowly, modest, ordinary, simple

humble [3]
verb to make someone feel humiliated » *The young chess player humbled his experienced opponent.*
chasten, deflate, disgrace, humiliate

humid
adjective damp and hot » *It was hot and humid in the jungle, making the journey hard.*
clammy, muggy, steamy, sticky

It was hot and humid in the jungle, making the journey hard.

humiliate
verb to hurt someone's pride » *I was upset that he humiliated me in front of all my friends.*
disgrace, embarrass, humble, put down, shame

humour [1]
noun something that is thought to be funny » *The movie's humour contains a serious message.*
comedy, wit, drollery, jocularity

John agreed to wear the blue shirt, but with bad humour.

humour [2]
noun the mood someone is in » *John agreed to wear the blue shirt, but with bad humour.*
frame of mind, mood, spirits, temper

humour [3]
verb to please someone so that they will not become upset » *As he ranted, she nodded, partly to humour him.*
flatter, indulge, mollify, pander to

hungry
adjective wanting to eat » *I didn't have any lunch, so I'm really hungry.*
famished, ravenous, starving

hurry [1]
verb to move or do something as quickly as possible » *Emma hurried through the train station to get to her platform on time.*
dash, fly, get a move on (informal), **rush, scurry**

hurry [2]
verb to make something happen more quickly » *Nina tried to hurry Gemma, so they wouldn't miss the bus.*
accelerate, hasten, quicken, speed up
antonym: **slow down**

hurt [1]
verb to cause someone to feel pain » *I didn't mean to hurt her, but she fell over when I gave her a playful push.*
harm, injure, wound

hurt [2]
verb to upset someone or something » *That lie you told really hurt me.*
distress, sadden, upset, wound

hurt [3]
adjective upset or offended » *He felt hurt by all the lies.*
aggrieved, offended, upset, wounded, piqued, rueful

hygiene
noun the principles and practice of health and cleanliness » *Kristina cared about her personal hygiene and showered every day.*
cleanliness, sanitation

hypnotize
verb to put someone into a state in which they seem to be asleep but can respond to suggestions » *He will hypnotize you and stop you from biting your nails.*
put in a trance, put to sleep, entrance, mesmerize

hysterical [1]
adjective in a state of uncontrolled excitement or panic » *Calm down—don't get hysterical.*
frantic, frenzied, overwrought, raving

hysterical [2]
adjective (informal) extremely funny » *We loved listening to his stand-up routine; it was always hysterical.*
comical, hilarious

We loved listening to his stand-up routine; it was always hysterical.

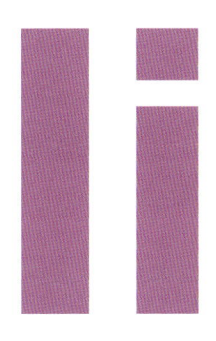

Ii

icon
noun a picture that represents a person or thing » *The tablet screen is full of app icons.*
avatar, representation, thumbnail

The tablet screen is full of app icons.

idea 1
noun what you know about something » *I think we're lost—I have no idea where we are.*
clue, guess, hint, inkling, notion, suspicion

idea 2
noun an opinion or belief about something » *My grandmother has old-fashioned ideas about clothes and refuses to leave the house without her hat.*
belief, conviction, impression, notion, opinion, view

idea 3
noun a plan or suggestion for something
▼ SEE BELOW

ideal 1
noun a principle or idea you try to achieve » *My father has high ideals and always tries to live up to them.*
principle, standard, value

ideal 2
noun the best example of something » *She's my ideal of what a best friend should be.*
epitome, example, model, paragon, prototype, standard, archetype, criterion, paradigm

ideal 3
adjective being the best example of something » *He was the ideal person for the Saturday job as he already had lots of experience.*
classic, complete, consummate, model, perfect, supreme

identify 1
verb to recognize or name someone or something » *Joe tried to identify the handwriting on the letter, as the sender hadn't signed their name.*
diagnose, label, name, pinpoint, place, recognize

identify 2 : identify with
verb to understand someone's feelings » *I can't identify with the book's main character.*
associate with, empathize with, feel for, relate to, respond to

idiot
noun a stupid person » *You're an idiot for carrying too much at once!*
fool, imbecile, nitwit, oaf, twit (informal)

idiotic
adjective extremely foolish or silly » *Sending the letter to the wrong person was an idiotic thing to do.*
daft (informal), **dumb** (informal), **foolish, senseless, silly, stupid,** foolhardy, insane

idle
adjective doing nothing » *I was idle that vacation, and simply read books and relaxed.*
jobless, unemployed, unproductive, inactive, stationary
antonym: **busy**

I was idle that vacation, and simply read books and relaxed.

---

idea 3 noun a plan or suggestion for something » *He had a great idea for a new game.*

plan — *He had a cunning plan to take over the market.*

recommendation — *The producer gave recommendations for improvements.*

scheme — *She asked if he had a scheme for the game.*

solution — *He came up with a solution to the problem.*

suggestion — *People had lots of suggestions for what to call the game.*

theory — *He had a theory that there was a gap in the market for the new game.*

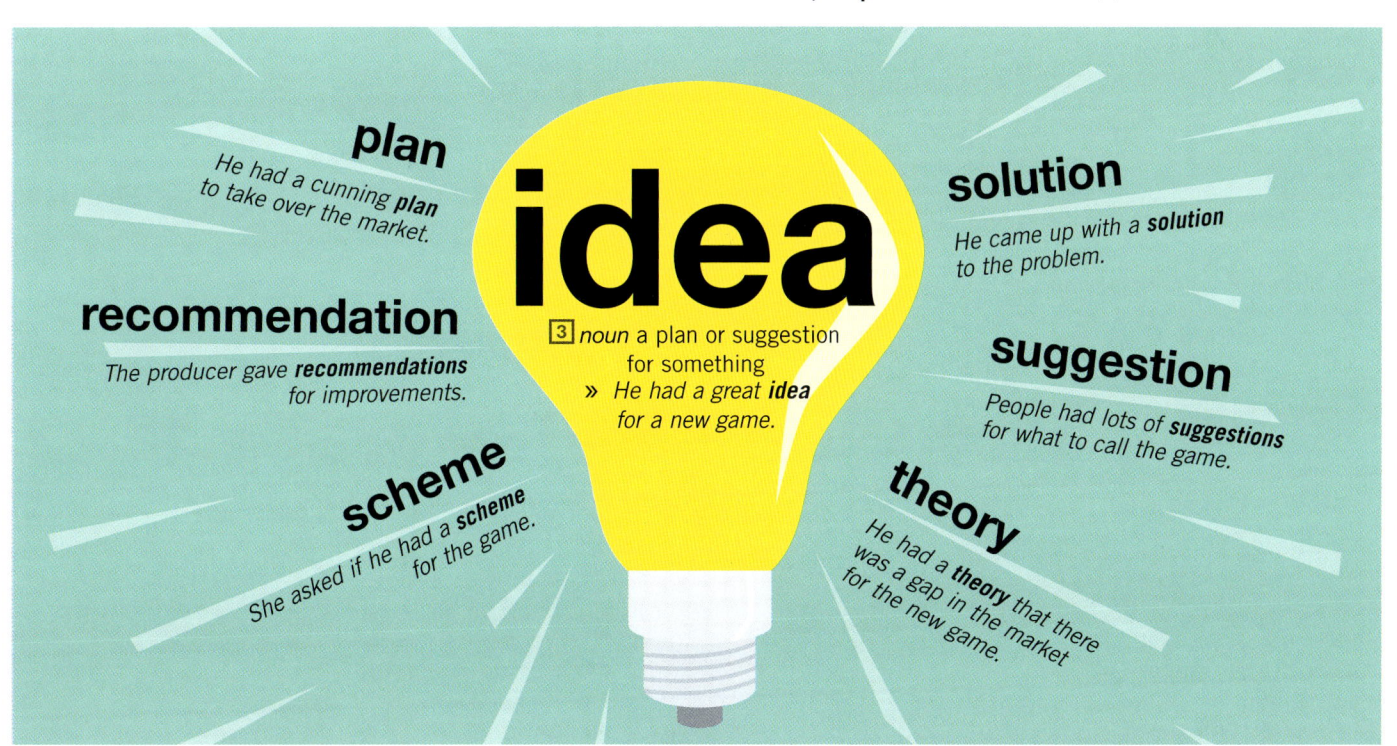

»**ig**norant

imaginary

adjective existing in your mind but not in real life
» *Kevin's little sister, Karina, had an **imaginary** friend.*

Kevin's little sister, Karina, had an **imaginary** friend, who lived in a **fictional** place called Wonderland and had the **fictitious** name of Elsanna. They rode on **mythical** unicorns and acted out all sorts of **hypothetical** scenarios. In an **ideal** world, they would be best friends forever. Karina knew her friend was **illusory**, but still liked to play her **invented** games.

fictional
fictitious
mythical
hypothetical
illusory
ideal
invented

antonym: **real**
*In the **real** world, Karina's brother could be grumpy.*

impede »

ignorant [1]
adjective not knowing about something » *He was ignorant of the rules and didn't wear a tie on the first day of school.*
inexperienced, innocent, oblivious, unaware, unconscious

ignorant [2]
adjective not knowledgeable about things » *Elijah was determined not to be ignorant, so he read the news every day.*
green, naive, unaware, uneducated, unlearned, untutored

ignore
verb to take no notice of someone or something » *Julia ignored Huan when he came into the room.*
discount, disregard, neglect, overlook, reject

ill
adjective unhealthy or sick » *Patricia was ill with the flu.*
ailing, poorly (informal)**, queasy, sick, unhealthy, unwell, indisposed, infirm, under the weather**
antonym: **healthy**

*Patricia was **ill** with the flu.*

illegal
adjective forbidden by the law » *Shoplifting is an illegal activity.*
banned, criminal, illicit, outlawed, prohibited, unlawful, proscribed, unauthorized, wrongful
antonym: **legal**

illness
noun a particular disease » *His illness was a mystery—no one knew what was wrong.*
affliction, ailment, bug (informal)**, complaint, disease, disorder, infirmity, malady, sickness**

illusion [1]
noun a false belief » *Pedro is under the illusion that he is very important.*
delusion, fallacy, fancy, misconception

illusion [2]
noun a thing that you think you can see » *Seeing its reflection gave the fox the illusion of another fox.*
hallucination, mirage, semblance, chimera, phantasm

*Seeing its reflection gave the fox the **illusion** of another fox.*

imaginary
adjective existing in your mind but not in real life
◀◀ SEE LEFT

imagination
noun the ability to form new ideas » *Harry is clever, but lacks imagination—he just copied the project.*
creativity, ingenuity, inventiveness, originality, vision

imagine [1]
verb to have an idea of something » *Clara could not imagine a more peaceful scene.*
conceive, envisage, fantasize, picture, visualize

imagine [2]
verb to believe that something is the case » *I imagine you're talking about my brother.*
assume, believe, gather, guess (informal)**, suppose, suspect, fancy, surmise**

imitate
verb to copy someone or something » *My son imitates everything I do.*
ape, copy, emulate, impersonate, mimic, simulate, mirror, mock, parody

*My son **imitates** everything I do.*

immediate [1]
adjective happening or done without delay » *Mia's immediate reaction was to laugh.*
instant, instantaneous

immediate [2]
adjective most closely connected to you » *I live with my immediate family.*
close, direct, near

immediately [1]
adverb right away » *Logan replied to my message immediately.*
at once, directly, instantly, now, promptly, right away, right now, straight away, forthwith, posthaste

immediately [2]
adverb very near in time or position » *The playing field was immediately behind the school.*
closely, directly, right

*An **immense** cloud turned the sky black.*

immense
adjective very large or huge » *An immense cloud turned the sky black.*
colossal, enormous, giant, gigantic, huge, massive, vast
antonym: **tiny**

imminent
adjective going to happen very soon » *I was excited about my sister's imminent arrival.*
close, coming, forthcoming, impending, looming, near

immune
adjective not subject to or affected by something » *He seems immune to the cold.*
exempt, free, protected, resistant, safe, unaffected, insusceptible, invulnerable

impatient [1]
adjective easily annoyed » *You are too impatient with others.*
brusque, curt, irritable, intolerant, snappy
antonym: **patient**

impatient [2]
adjective eager to do something » *Maya was impatient to leave.*
eager, restless

impede
verb to make someone's or something's progress difficult » *Fallen trees impeded our walk to school this morning.*
block, delay, disrupt, get in the way, hamper, hinder, obstruct

imperfect

imperfect
adjective having faults or problems » *We live in an imperfect world.*
broken, damaged, defective, faulty, flawed, deficient, impaired, rudimentary
antonym: **perfect**

impersonal
adjective not concerned with people and their feelings » *She found him strangely distant and impersonal.*
aloof, cold, detached, formal, neutral, remote, bureaucratic, businesslike, dispassionate

implore
verb to beg someone to do something » *"Tell me what to do!" Stefan implored Sara.*
beg, beseech (literary), **plead with**

important 1
adjective necessary or significant » *Her friends are the most important people in her life.*
momentous, serious, significant, weighty, salient, seminal
antonym: **unimportant**

important 2
adjective having great influence or power » *The principal is the most important person in the school.*
eminent, foremost, influential, leading, notable, powerful, pre-eminent, prominent

impose 1
verb to force something on someone » *Fines were imposed on the culprits.*
dictate, enforce, inflict, levy, ordain

impose 2 : **impose on**
verb to take advantage of someone » *I should stop imposing on your hospitality.*
abuse, take advantage of, use

impossible
adjective unable to happen or be believed » *Finishing the race seemed impossible.*
absurd, hopeless, inconceivable, ludicrous, out of the question, unthinkable, outrageous, unattainable, unworkable
antonym: **possible**

impression 1
noun the way someone or something seems to you » *Conor's first impressions of the hotel were good.*
feeling, hunch, idea, notion, sense

impression 2 : **make an impression**
verb to have a strong effect on people » *He certainly made a good impression on his teachers when he turned in his homework early.*
cause a stir, influence, make an impact

impressionable
adjective easy to influence » *Parents were worried about the effect the movie might have on impressionable teenagers.*
gullible, open, receptive, sensitive, susceptible, vulnerable, ingenuous, suggestible

impressive
adjective tending to impress » *Winning so many medals was an impressive achievement.*
awesome, exciting, great, powerful, stirring, striking, dramatic, moving

*Winning so many medals was an **impressive** achievement.*

*He was **imprisoned** for theft.*

imprison
verb to lock someone up » *He was imprisoned for theft.*
confine, detain, incarcerate, jail, lock-up (informal), **send to prison,** constrain, immure, intern
antonym: **free**

improbable
adjective unlikely or unbelievable » *Helen told an improbable story about the dog eating her homework.*
doubtful, dubious, far-fetched, implausible, unbelievable, unlikely
antonym: **probable**

improve
verb to get or make better » *My grades have definitely improved over the school year.*
advance, better, enhance, look up (informal), **progress, upgrade,** ameliorate, develop, reform, revise
antonym: **worsen**

improvement
noun the fact or process of getting better » *There was a dramatic improvement in the food since he'd taken the cooking class.*
advance, development, enhancement, progress, upturn

impudence
noun disrespectful talk or behaviour towards someone » *Have you ever heard such impudence?*
audacity, boldness, cheek (informal), **chutzpah** (informal), **gall, impertinence, insolence, nerve, sass**

inability
noun a lack of ability to do something » *Ava's inability to run was due to her injured left knee.*
impotence, inadequacy, incompetence, ineptitude
antonym: **ability**

inadequate 1
adjective not enough in quantity » *Our supplies of popcorn were inadequate for the long movie.*
insufficient, lacking, poor, scarce, short
antonym: **adequate**

inadequate 2
adjective not good enough » *He had no idea what he was supposed to be doing and felt inadequate to the task.*
deficient, incapable, incompetent, inept, pathetic, useless

*He had no idea what he was supposed to be doing and felt **inadequate** to the task.*

inappropriate
adjective not suitable for a purpose or occasion » *Running around is inappropriate behaviour for the classroom.*
improper, unfit, unseemly, unsuitable, untimely, wrong, incongruous
antonym: **appropriate**

incentive
noun something that encourages you to do something » *Luca had an incentive to study now that he'd booked his vacation.*
bait, encouragement, inducement, motivation, stimulus, lure, motive, spur

incident
noun an event » *This morning's incident of calling the teacher "Dad" was rather embarrassing.*
circumstance, episode, event, happening, occasion, occurrence

incite
verb to excite someone into doing something » *The campaigners incited a protest.*
agitate for, goad, instigate, provoke, whip up

include
verb to have as a part » *A cake recipe usually includes eggs, flour, and sugar.*
contain, cover, embrace, encompass, incorporate, involve
antonym: **exclude**

income
noun the money someone or something earns » *Jake was thrilled—he had an income at last.*
earnings, pay, profits, salary, takings, wages, proceeds, receipts, revenue

Jake was thrilled—he had an income at last.

incomparable
adjective too good to be compared with anything else » *The view from the peak was one of incomparable beauty.*
inimitable, peerless (literary), superlative, supreme, unparalleled, unrivalled, matchless, unequalled

John was an incompetent carpenter.

incompetent
adjective lacking the ability to do something properly » *John was an incompetent carpenter.*
bungling, incapable, inept, unable, unfit, useless, ineffectual, inexpert, unskilful
antonym: **competent**

incomplete
adjective not finished or whole » *An incomplete letter lay on the desk.*
deficient, insufficient, partial, sketchy, imperfect, undeveloped, unfinished
antonym: **complete**

increase 1
verb to make or become larger in amount » *The population continues to increase.*
enlarge, expand, extend, grow, multiply, swell, augment, escalate
antonym: **decrease**

increase 2
noun a rise in the amount of something » *Valeria asked for a pay increase.*
gain, growth, increment, rise, upsurge
antonym: **decrease**

incredible 1
adjective totally amazing
▶▶ SEE RIGHT

incredible
1 adjective totally amazing
» *The juggler at the circus had **incredible** skill.*

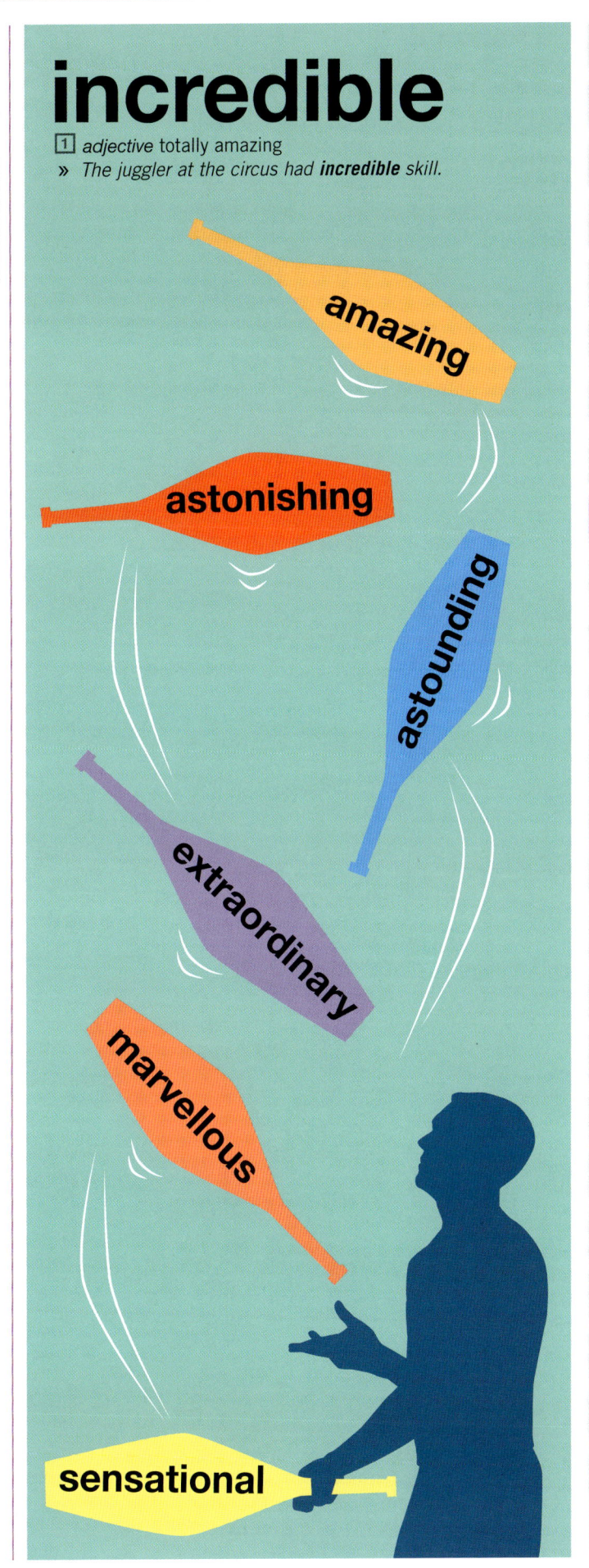

- amazing
- astonishing
- astounding
- extraordinary
- marvellous
- sensational

incredible

incredible [2]
adjective impossible to believe » Sofia told an incredible story about a dragon trapped in a mountain cave.
absurd, far-fetched, improbable, unbelievable, unimaginable, unthinkable, implausible, inconceivable, preposterous

indecent
adjective shocking or rude » Carter refused to play the song because its lyrics were indecent.
crude, improper, rude, vulgar

independent [1]
adjective separate from other people or things » Each hiker had their independent tent in the clearing.
autonomous, free, separate, unrelated

Each hiker had their independent tent in the clearing.

independent [2]
adjective not needing other people's help » Zoe is a fiercely independent child.
individualistic, liberated, self-sufficient, unaided

indicate
verb to show something » He smiled to indicate his relief.
denote, reveal, show, signal, signify, imply, manifest, point to

indication
noun a sign of something » Ahmed gave no indication that he had heard me.
clue, hint, sign, signal, suggestion, warning, intimation

indirect
adjective not done or going directly but by another way » We took an indirect route to avoid the traffic jam.
meandering, oblique, rambling, roundabout, tortuous, wandering
antonym: **direct**

individual [1]
adjective relating to separate people or things » Maria made individual chocolate cakes for the twins' birthday celebration.
discrete (formal), **independent, separate, single**

individual [2]
adjective different and unusual » I have developed my own individual writing style.
characteristic, distinctive, idiosyncratic, original, personal, special, unique

individual [3]
noun a person, different from any other person » Tim took part in the competition as an individual.
character, party, person, soul, personage

industrious
adjective tending to work hard » The industrious bees were making honey in their hive.
busy, conscientious, diligent, hard-working, tireless
antonym: **lazy**

The industrious bees were making honey in their hive.

inefficient
adjective badly organized and slow » We live in the countryside and have an inefficient bus service.
disorganized, incapable, incompetent, inept, sloppy, ineffectual, inexpert, slipshod
antonym: **efficient**

inexperienced
adjective lacking experience of a situation or activity » Inexperienced drivers should avoid roads in big cities.
green (informal), **naive, new, raw, unaccustomed**
antonym: **experienced**

infect
verb to cause disease in something » One mosquito can infect many people.
affect, blight, contaminate, taint

infectious
adjective spreading from one person to another » My cold was infectious—my whole family caught it.
catching, contagious, spreading, communicable, virulent

My cold was infectious—my whole family caught it.

inferior [1]
adjective having a lower position than something or someone else » The status of a prince is inferior to that of a king.
lesser, lower, minor, secondary, second-class, subordinate
antonym: **superior**

inferior [2]
adjective of low quality » Ruben gave an inferior performance because he was feeling unwell.
mediocre, poor, second-class, second-rate, shoddy
antonym: **superior**

inferior [3]
noun a person in a lower position than another » You must be polite to your inferiors.
junior, menial, subordinate, underling
antonym: **superior**

infinite
adjective without any limit or end » The start of the school holidays presented an infinite number of possibilities.
boundless, eternal, everlasting, inexhaustible, perpetual, untold, bottomless, interminable, limitless

influence [1]
noun power over other people » Ethan has quite a lot of influence over his classmates.
authority, control, importance, power, sway, ascendancy, domination

influence [2]
noun an effect that someone or something has » Lily stayed up late, under the influence of her friend.
effect, hold, magnetism, spell, weight

influence [3]
verb to have an effect on someone or something » Older siblings can influence their younger siblings.
affect, control, direct, guide, manipulate, sway

inform
verb to tell someone about something » Please inform me of any delays.
advise (formal), **brief, enlighten, notify, tell,** apprise, communicate

inspect »

*The party was **informal** so they wore shorts.*

informal
adjective relaxed and casual » *The party was informal so they wore shorts.*
casual, colloquial, easy, familiar, natural, relaxed
antonym: **formal**

information
noun the details you know about something » *Our teacher would not give us any information about the exam questions.*
data, facts, info (slang)**, knowledge, material, news, notice, report, word**

inform on
verb to tell the police about someone who has committed a crime » *Somebody must have informed on the vandals.*
betray, denounce, snitch (slang)**, tattle, tell on** (informal)

ingredient
noun a thing that something is made from » *Lisa bought the necessary ingredients to bake a cake.*
component, constituent, element

*Lisa bought the necessary **ingredients** to bake a cake.*

inhabit
verb to live in a place » *The people who inhabit these islands are used to the cold.*
dwell, live, lodge, occupy, populate, reside (formal)

inhabitant
noun someone who lives in a place » *I am an inhabitant of British Columbia.*
citizen, inmate, native, occupant, resident

inheritance
noun something that is passed on » *The house will be his son's inheritance.*
bequest, heritage, legacy

injure
verb to damage part of someone's body » *The dog had injured its leg.*
harm, hurt, maim, wound

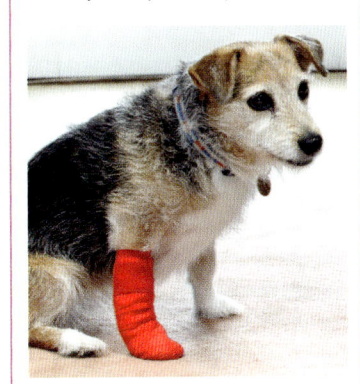

*The dog had **injured** its leg.*

injury
noun damage to part of the body » *Although the cat fell from quite high up, it had suffered no injuries.*
damage, harm, wound

injustice
noun unfairness and lack of justice » *The players complained about the injustice of the referee.*
bias, discrimination, inequality, prejudice, unfairness, wrong
antonym: **justice**

innocence
noun inexperience of evil or unpleasant things » *The baby's face was a picture of innocence.*
gullibility, inexperience, naïveté, purity, simplicity, artlessness, ingenuousness, unworldliness

innocent 1
adjective not guilty of a crime » *The man had an alibi and was clearly innocent.*
blameless, clear, not guilty
antonym: **guilty**

innocent 2
adjective without experience of evil or unpleasant things » *They were so young and innocent.*
childlike, guileless, naive, pure, spotless, artless, ingenuous, unworldly

insane
adjective crazy » *I would go insane if I stayed indoors every day.*
crazy, deranged, mad, mentally ill, nuts (informal)**, out of your mind, unhinged**

insert
verb to put something into something else » *Emil inserted the key into the lock.*
enter, implant, introduce, place, put, set

*Emil **inserted** the key into the lock.*

inside
adjective surrounded by the main part and often hidden » *On the ship we had an inside cabin with no window.*
inner, innermost, interior, internal
antonym: **outside**

insides
plural noun (informal) the parts inside your body » *My insides ached from eating too much.*
entrails, guts, innards, internal organs, viscera, vitals

*My **insides** ached from eating too much.*

insignificant
adjective small and unimportant » *The flaw was so insignificant you could barely see it.*
irrelevant, little, minor, petty, trifling, trivial, unimportant, inconsequential
antonym: **significant**

insincere
adjective saying things you do not mean » *Eric told Ida what she wanted to hear, but his words were insincere.*
deceitful, dishonest, false, two-faced
antonym: **sincere**

insist
verb to demand something forcefully » *My mother always insists that I eat everything on my plate.*
demand, press, urge

inspect
verb to examine something carefully » *Alice inspected her salad for caterpillars.*
check, examine, eye, investigate, scan, survey, audit, scrutinize, vet

instant

instant [1]
noun a short period of time
» *The rain stopped in an instant.*
flash, minute, moment, second, split second, trice

instant [2]
adjective immediate and without delay » *He took an instant liking to her.*
immediate, instantaneous, prompt

instinct
noun a natural tendency to do something » *My dog has a strong instinct to chase rabbits.*
feeling, impulse, intuition, sixth sense, urge

instruct [1]
verb to tell someone to do something » *The teacher instructed the class to be quiet.*
command, direct, order, tell
antonym: **forbid**

instruct [2]
verb to teach someone about a subject or skill » *Liam instructs budding sailors on how to raise the sail.*
coach, educate, school, teach, train, tutor

Liam instructs budding sailors on how to raise the sail.

insufficient
adjective not enough for a particular purpose » *There were insufficient refreshments for the hungry players.*
deficient, inadequate, lacking, scant, short
antonym: **sufficient**

insult [1]
verb to offend someone by being rude to them » *I did not mean to insult you.*
abuse, affront, offend, put down, ridicule, slander, slight, snub
antonym: **compliment**

insult [2]
noun a rude remark that offends someone » *The two men exchanged insults.*
abuse, affront, offence, put-down, slight, snub
antonym: **compliment**

The two men exchanged insults.

intelligence
noun the ability to understand and learn things » *The tricky quiz really tested the teams' intelligence.*
cleverness, comprehension, intellect, perception, sense, understanding, wit, acumen, capacity

intelligent
adjective able to understand and learn things » *Dolphins are an intelligent species.*
acute, brainy (informal)**, bright, clever, quick, sharp, smart**
antonym: **stupid**

intend [1]
verb to decide or plan to do something » *Harper intended to stay for lunch.*
aim, be determined, mean, plan, propose, resolve

intend [2]
verb to mean for a certain use » *This book is intended for younger children.*
aim, design, earmark, mean

Michaela watched the screen with intense concentration.

intense [1]
adjective very great in strength or amount » *Michaela watched the screen with intense concentration.*
acute, deep, extreme, fierce, great, powerful, profound, severe

intense [2]
adjective tending to have strong feelings » *The actor's intense performance was gripping.*
ardent, earnest, fervent, fierce, impassioned, passionate, vehement

intention
noun a plan to do something » *Layla announced her intention of going to the party.*
aim, goal, idea, object, objective, purpose

interest [1]
noun a feeling of wanting to know about something » *I have a great interest in that period of history.*
attention, concern, curiosity, fascination

interest [2]
noun a hobby » *Of her many interests, Nora enjoyed knitting the most.*
activity, hobby, pastime, pursuit

Of her many interests, Nora enjoyed knitting the most.

interest [3]
verb to attract someone's attention and curiosity » *This picture interests me most—I love the colours.*
appeal, captivate, fascinate, intrigue, stimulate
antonym: **bore**

interesting
adjective making you want to know, learn, or hear more » *In the car this morning, we had an interesting conversation about bats.*
absorbing, compelling, entertaining, gripping, intriguing, stimulating
antonym: **boring**

interfere [1]
verb to try to influence a situation » *Stop interfering and leave her alone.*
butt in, intervene, intrude, meddle, tamper

interfere [2]
verb to have a damaging effect on a situation » *The loud music interfered with her sleep.*
conflict, disrupt

internet
noun a worldwide network of computers » *Hazel used the internet to book her vacation.*
blogosphere, cloud, cyberspace, net, web, world wide web

Hazel used the internet to book her vacation.

interrogate
verb to question someone thoroughly » *I interrogated everyone involved.*
examine, grill (informal)**, question, quiz,** cross-examine, cross-question

interrupt [1]
verb to start talking when someone else is talking » *He tried to speak, but she interrupted him.*
butt in, heckle, talk over

interrupt [2]
verb to stop a process or activity for a time » *The match was interrupted by rain.*
break, discontinue, suspend

interval
noun a period of time between two moments or dates » *Maria ate an ice cream in the interval between the first and second acts of the play.*
break, gap, hiatus, interlude, intermission, pause, period

Piper had agreed to intervene when things got heated.

intervene
verb to step in to prevent conflict » *Piper had agreed to intervene when things got heated.*
arbitrate, mediate

introduction [1]
noun the act of presenting someone or something new » *The introduction of a new uniform was discussed.*
establishment, inauguration, initiation, institution, launch

introduction [2]
noun a piece of writing at the beginning of a book » *The book contains a new introduction by the author.*
foreword, preface, prologue

intrude
verb to disturb someone or something » *I don't want to intrude on your privacy.*
butt in, encroach, infringe, interrupt, trespass, violate

invade
verb to enter a country by force » *The Vikings invaded much of Europe.*
attack, enter, occupy, violate

invent [1]
verb to be the first person to think of a device or idea
▼ SEE BELOW

invent [2]
verb to make up a story or excuse » *I tried to invent a plausible excuse for why I was late.*
concoct, fabricate, make up, manufacture

investigate
verb to find out all the facts about something » *Police are still investigating the incident.*
examine, explore, probe, research, sift, study

---

invent

[1] verb to be the first person to think of a device or idea » *The busy professor invented a Walkomatic robot to walk his dog for him.*

conceive
The professor conceived the idea when his dog whined for a walk.

coin
He coined the name "Walkomatic."

come up with (informal)
He was the first person to come up with the idea of a dog-walking robot.

design
The professor designed several models.

formulate
He formulated plans to make the robot move.

improvise
He improvised by using empty cans to make the robot's body.

originate
I want to be as famous as the professor who originated the Walkomatic.

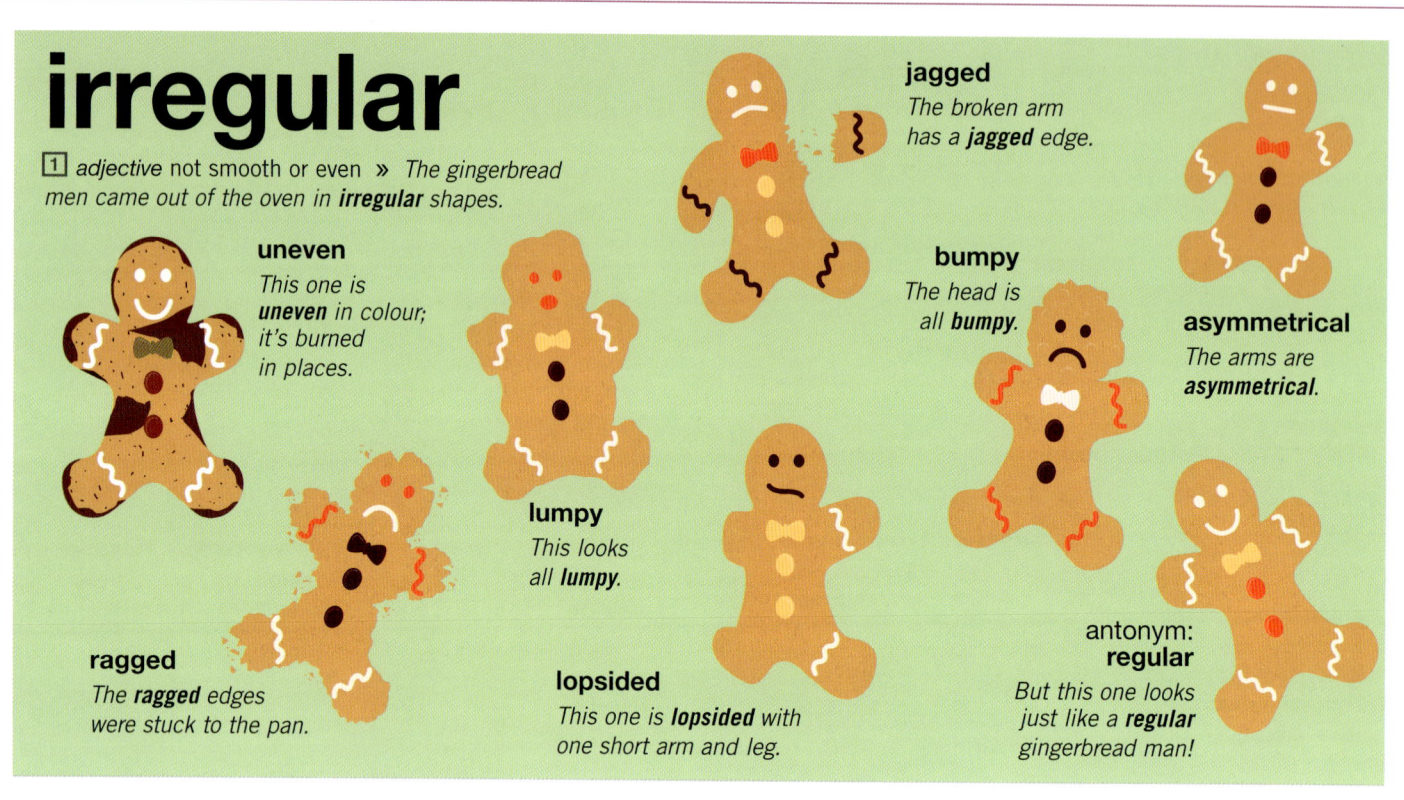

irregular

1 *adjective* not smooth or even » The gingerbread men came out of the oven in **irregular** shapes.

uneven
This one is **uneven** in colour; it's burned in places.

ragged
The **ragged** edges were stuck to the pan.

lumpy
This looks all **lumpy**.

lopsided
This one is **lopsided** with one short arm and leg.

jagged
The broken arm has a **jagged** edge.

bumpy
The head is all **bumpy**.

asymmetrical
The arms are **asymmetrical**.

antonym: **regular**
But this one looks just like a **regular** gingerbread man!

invincible
adjective unable to be defeated » When the defending champion is playing well, he is invincible.
impregnable, indomitable, unbeatable, indestructible, insurmountable, unassailable

invisible
adjective unable to be seen » Hugo's face was invisible beneath his hat.
concealed, disguised, hidden, inconspicuous, unseen, imperceptible, indiscernible
antonym: **visible**

involve
verb to have as a necessary part » Preparing for an exam involves a great deal of discipline.
incorporate, require, take or **take in, entail, necessitate**

irrational
adjective not based on logical reasons » Her fear of ghosts is irrational—they don't exist.
absurd, crazy, illogical, nonsensical, unsound, silly, unreasonable

irregular 1
adjective not smooth or even
▲ SEE ABOVE

irregular 2
adjective not forming a regular pattern » Stephen worked irregular hours.
erratic, haphazard, occasional, patchy, random, variable, fitful, sporadic
antonym: **regular**

irresponsible
adjective not concerned with the consequences of your actions » His irresponsible attitude often got him into trouble with his parents.
careless, reckless, thoughtless, wild
antonym: **responsible**

irritable
adjective easily annoyed » My mother had slept badly and was tense and irritable.
bad-tempered, cantankerous, cranky, petulant, surly, testy, touchy, irascible, tetchy

irritate
verb to annoy someone » Nathan's tuneless whistling always irritates me.
anger, annoy, bother, exasperate, irk, needle (informal), **ruffle, wind up** (informal), **gall, provoke**

issue 1
noun a subject that people are talking about » There were several issues to be discussed at the teacher-parent meeting.
concern, matter, problem, question, subject, topic

issue 2
noun a particular edition of a newspaper or magazine » Jade bought the latest issue of her favourite magazine.
copy, edition, instalment

Jade bought the latest issue of her favourite magazine.

issue 3
verb to make a formal statement » They have issued a statement explaining what really happened.
deliver, give, make, pronounce, read out, release
antonym: **withdraw**

issue 4
verb to give something officially » Staff will be issued passes to get into the building.
equip, furnish (formal), **give out, provide, supply**

item 1
noun one of a collection or list of things » When Chloe opened her suitcase, several items were missing.
article, matter, point, thing

item 2
noun a newspaper or magazine article » There was an item in the paper about his daring rescue of the cat.
article, feature, notice, piece, report

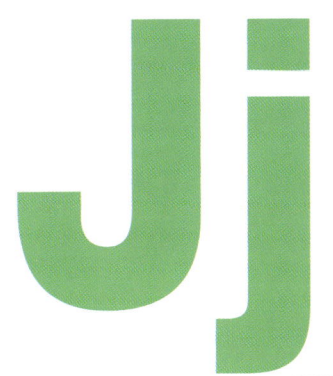

Jj

jagged
adjective sharp and spiky » *The waves broke against the jagged rocks.*
barbed, craggy, rough, serrated, sharp
antonym: **smooth**

jail 1
noun a place where prisoners are held » *Chris was sentenced to 18 months in jail.*
clink (slang), **prison, slammer** (informal), **lock-up** (informal), **penal institution, penitentiary**

jail 2
verb to put in prison » *He was jailed for 20 years.*
detain, imprison, incarcerate

jam 1
noun a crowded mass of people or things » *Nora was late because she was stuck in a traffic jam.*
crowd, crush, mass, mob, multitude, throng

Nora was late because she was stuck in a traffic jam.

jam 2
noun a difficult situation » *We're in a real jam now.*
bind, dilemma, fix (informal), **hole** (slang), **hot water** (informal), **pickle** (informal), **plight, predicament, quandary, trouble**

jam 3
verb to push something somewhere roughly » *Martin jammed his hat on to his head.*
cram, force, ram, stuff

jam 4
verb to become stuck » *She tried to leave the room, but the door jammed.*
stall, stick

jealous
adjective wanting to have something that someone else has » *I was jealous of my friend's new shoes.*
envious, resentful, covetous

job 1
noun the work someone does to earn money » *I'm looking for a job on a farm.*
employment, occupation, position, post, profession, trade

job 2
noun a duty or responsibility » *It's your job to wash the dishes.*
concern, duty, function, responsibility, role, task

join 1
verb to become a member of something » *Adam joined a band as the lead singer.*
enlist, enrol, sign up
antonym: **resign**

join 2
verb to fasten two things together
▶▶ SEE RIGHT

join

2 verb to fasten two things together » *The paper dolls were joined at their hands and feet.*

attach
She attached a strap to her bag.

connect
The two rooms were connected by a passage.

couple
An engine is coupled to a gearbox.

fasten
The bench was fastened to the floor.

link
He linked a clip to the chain.

splice
The ropes were spliced together.

tie
He tied the dog to the post with its leash.

antonym: **separate**
Grace separated a doll from the chain to give to her friend.

joke

That joke was so funny.

joke [1]
noun something that makes people laugh » *That joke was so funny.*
gag (informal), **jest, lark, prank, quip, wisecrack** (informal), **witticism,** jape

joke [2]
verb to say something funny » *Alex was always joking about her appearance.*
banter, chaff, jest, kid (informal), **quip, tease**

journey [1]
noun the act of travelling from one place to another » *We took a train journey through the mountains.*
excursion, expedition, passage, tour, trek, trip, voyage

We took a train journey through the mountains.

journey [2]
verb to travel from one place to another » *We journeyed through France to reach Spain.*
go, proceed, tour, travel, trek, voyage

joy
noun great happiness » *Her face shone with joy.*
bliss, delight, ecstasy, elation, rapture, exaltation, exultation, felicity
antonym: **misery**

joyful
adjective extremely happy » *My father gave a joyful smile when he saw me.*
delighted, elated, jubilant, over the moon (informal), **enraptured**

judge [1]
noun the person in charge of a law court » *The judge called for order in court.*
adjudicator, justice, magistrate
related word: adjective **judicial**

The judge called for order in court.

judge [2]
noun someone who picks the winner or keeps control of a competition » *The judges inspected each dog carefully before selecting the finalists.*
adjudicator, referee, umpire

judge [3]
verb to form an opinion about someone or something » *Don't judge me for having another slice of cake.*
appraise, assess, consider, estimate, evaluate, rate

judge [4]
verb to pick the winner or keep control in a competition » *Entrants will be judged in two age categories.*
referee, umpire, adjudge, adjudicate

judgment
noun an opinion or decision based on evidence » *It's hard to form a judgment without all the facts.*
appraisal, assessment, conclusion, opinion, ruling, verdict, view

jump [1]
verb to leap up or over something » *I jumped over the fence.*
bound, clear, hurdle, leap, spring, vault

I jumped over the fence.

jump [2]
verb to increase suddenly » *Sales of coats jumped when the temperature dropped below zero.*
escalate, increase, rise, surge

jump [3]
noun a leap into the air » *Ryan misjudged his jump and landed in the stream.*
bound, leap, vault

junior
adjective having a relatively low position compared to others » *I started as a junior waitress, but now I run the restaurant.*
inferior, lesser, lower, subordinate
antonym: **senior**

What are you going to do with all that junk?

junk
noun old articles that people usually throw away » *What are you going to do with all that junk?*
clutter, odds and ends, refuse, rubbish, scrap, trash

justice [1]
noun fairness in the way that people are treated » *He had been treated unfairly and wanted justice.*
equity, fairness, impartiality
antonym: **injustice**

justice [2]
noun the person in charge of a law court » *They were married by the Justice of the Peace.*
judge, magistrate

justify
verb to show that something is reasonable or necessary » *Tina justified eating a large lunch by going for a long walk afterwards.*
defend, excuse, explain, vindicate, warrant

Kk

*Hugo was a **keen** amateur wildlife photographer.*

keen [1]
adjective showing eagerness and enthusiasm for something » *Hugo was a keen amateur wildlife photographer.*
ardent, avid, eager, enthusiastic, fond of, into (informal)

keen [2]
adjective quick to notice or understand things » *She has a keen eye for a bargain.*
astute, brilliant, clever, perceptive, quick, shrewd

keep [1]
verb to have and look after something » *His father keeps sheep and pigs.*
care for, maintain, preserve

keep [2]
verb to store something » *Zoe kept her toys in a box.*
deposit, hold, store

keep [3]
verb to do what you said you would do » *I always keep my promises.*
carry out, fulfill, honour

kidnap
verb to take someone away by force » *Lisa's brother kidnapped her teddy bear.*
abduct, capture, seize

kill
verb to make someone or something die » *The terrier killed a rat.*
assassinate, destroy, execute, exterminate, massacre, murder, slaughter, slay, annihilate, dispatch

kin
plural noun the people who are related to you » *She has gone to live with her husband's kin.*
family, kindred, people, relations, relatives

kind [1]
noun a particular type of person or thing » *That's my favourite kind of cheese.*
brand, breed, category, class, classification, genre, grade, sort, species, type, variety

kind [2]
adjective considerate towards other people » *Thank you for being so kind to me.*
benevolent, benign, charitable, compassionate, considerate, good, humane, kind-hearted, kindly, thoughtful, unselfish, lenient, philanthropic
antonym: **cruel**

*Thank you for being so **kind** to me.*

kindness
noun the quality of being considerate towards other people » *Everyone has treated me with great kindness.*
benevolence, charity, compassion, gentleness, humanity, kindliness, magnanimity, philanthropy, tenderness
antonym: **cruelty**

*He wore a crown and robe to play the **king** in the school show.*

king
noun a man who is the head of a royal family » *He wore a crown and robe to play the king in the school show.*
monarch, sovereign
related words: *adjectives* **royal, regal, monarchical**

know [1]
verb to understand or be aware of something » *I don't know anything about cars.*
apprehend, be aware of, comprehend, perceive, see, understand

know [2]
verb to be familiar with a person or thing » *I believe you two already know each other.*
be acquainted with, be familiar with, recognize

knowledge
noun all you know about something
▼ SEE BELOW

knowledge
noun all you know about something » *She had no **knowledge** of French.*

command
comprehension
education
grasp
learning
scholarship
understanding
wisdom

Ll

label 1
noun a piece of paper or plastic attached to something for information » *The label said the shirt was made of cotton.*
sticker, tag, ticket

The label said the shirt was made of cotton.

label 2
verb to put a label on something » *The toy was labelled "Made in China."*
flag, sticker, tag

labour 1
noun very hard work » *Fred soon discovered that weeding and digging the garden was hard labour.*
effort, exertion, industry, toil, work

labour 2
noun the workforce of a country or industry » *Some businesses take on extra labour to help at busy times.*
employees, workers, workforce

labour 3
verb to work very hard » *The farm workers laboured all night to finish the harvest.*
slave, toil, work
antonym: **relax**

She couldn't buy new clothes due to a lack of money.

lack 1
noun the shortage or absence of something that is needed » *She couldn't buy new clothes due to a lack of money.*
absence, deficiency, scarcity, shortage, want, dearth, insufficiency
antonym: **abundance**

lack 2
verb to be without something that is needed » *Katie was a good baker, but didn't enter any competitions because she lacked confidence.*
be deficient in, be short of, miss

lag
verb to make slower progress than other people or things » *The runner-up is lagging 10 points behind the champion.*
fall behind, trail

lake
noun a large area of water surrounded by land » *Jay went for a swim in the lake.*
lagoon, mere, pond, reservoir, tarn

lame 1
adjective unable to walk properly because of an injured leg » *The old soldier was lame in one leg.*
crippled, hobbling, limping

lame 2
adjective weak or unconvincing » *No one believed Sam's lame excuse for arriving late.*
feeble, flimsy, pathetic, poor, unconvincing, weak

lament 1
verb to express sorrow or regret over something » *Freya lamented the loss of her favourite sweater.*
grieve, mourn, wail, weep, bemoan, bewail, whine

lament 2
noun something you say to express sorrow or regret » *The old man sang a lament for his lost youth.*
moan, wail, gripe, lamentation, plaint

laugh
1 verb to make a noise that shows you are amused or happy » *The comedian told such a funny joke that we all laughed.*

chuckle   chortle   titter   giggle   snigger

lawyer

land 1
noun an area of ground that someone owns » *My parents keep horses on their land.*
estate, grounds, property

land 2
noun a region or country » *Nunavut is an Inuktitut word meaning "our land."*
country, nation, province, region, territory

land 3
verb to arrive on the ground after flying or sailing » *The plane landed in Toronto at noon.*
alight, dock, touch down

The plane landed in Toronto at noon.

language 1
noun the system of words people use to communicate » *She speaks four languages.*
dialect, idiom, jargon, lingo (informal), **tongue, vernacular, vocabulary,** argot, cant, lingua franca, patois

language 2
noun the style in which you speak or write » *The poem was written in flowery language.*
phrasing, style, wording, phraseology, terminology

large
adjective of a greater size or amount than usual » *We have a large kitchen with lots of cupboards.*
big, colossal, enormous, giant, gigantic, great, huge, immense, massive, vast, gargantuan, sizable
antonym: **small**

last 1
adjective the most recent » *Our last vacation was a year ago.*
latest, most recent, preceding, previous
antonym: **first**

last 2
adjective happening or remaining after all the others of its kind » *She read the last page and closed the book.*
closing, concluding, final, ultimate
antonym: **first**

last 3
verb to continue to exist or happen » *The movie lasted for two and a half hours.*
carry on, continue, endure, persist, remain, survive

late 1
adjective after the expected time » *The train was nearly an hour late.*
behind, behind time, belated, delayed, last-minute, overdue, tardy, unpunctual
antonym: **early**

late 2
adjective dead, especially recently » *My late husband would have loved this place.*
dead, deceased, departed, defunct, perished

laugh 1
verb to make a noise that shows you are amused or happy
▼ SEE BELOW

laugh 2
noun the noise you make when amused or happy » *He let out a loud laugh at the joke.*
chortle, chuckle, giggle, guffaw, snigger, titter

law 1
noun a country's system of rules » *Vandalism is against the law.*
charter, code, constitution
related words: *adjectives* **legal, judicial**

law 2
noun one of the rules of a country » *The government introduced a new law to help reduce crime rates.*
act, code, decree, regulation, rule, statute, edict, ordinance

lawyer
noun someone who advises people about the law » *The lawyer spoke in court.*
advocate, attorney, barrister, counsel, solicitor

The lawyer spoke in court.

cackle   guffaw   howl   roar

129

lay

lay [1]
verb to put something somewhere » *Lay a sheet of newspaper on the floor.*
place, put, set, set down, settle, spread

lay [2]
verb to arrange or set something out » *A man came to lay the carpet.*
arrange, set out

layer
noun something that covers a surface or comes between two other things » *A fresh layer of snow covered the street.*
blanket, coat, coating, covering, film, sheet, stratum

layout
noun the way in which something is arranged » *The hotel layout was so confusing, it was hard to find our rooms.*
arrangement, design, format, plan

laze
verb to relax and do no work » *Tanya spent a few days lazing on the beach.*
idle, loaf, lounge
antonym: **work**

Tanya spent a few days lazing on the beach.

lazy
adjective not willing to work or move » *Our lazy dog refused to come out for a walk.*
idle, slack, good-for-nothing, indolent, shiftless, slothful, torpid
antonym: **industrious**

lead [1]
verb to guide or take someone somewhere » *She led him towards the door.*
conduct, escort, guide, steer, usher

lead [2]
verb to be in charge of » *The captain led his team to a convincing victory.*
command, direct, govern, head, manage, supervise

The captain led his team to a convincing victory.

lead [3]
noun a clue that may help solve a crime » *The police are following up several leads.*
clue, indication, trace

leader
noun the person in charge of something » *Sophie was the expedition leader.*
boss (informal)**, captain, chief, commander, director, head, principal, ringleader**
antonym: **follower**

leading
adjective particularly important, respected, or advanced » *He was a leading authority on modern art.*
chief, eminent, key, main, major, principal, prominent, top, foremost, pre-eminent

lead to
verb to cause something to happen » *Regular exercise leads to a healthier life.*
cause, contribute to, produce, bring on, conducive to, result in

The hotel lobby had leaflets of nearby tourist attractions.

leaflet
noun a piece of paper with information about a subject » *The hotel lobby had leaflets of nearby tourist attractions.*
booklet, brochure, circular, flyer, pamphlet, handbill

leak [1]
verb to escape from a container or other object » *The bottle of lemonade had leaked all over the sandwiches.*
escape, ooze, seep, spill

leak [2]
noun a hole that lets gas or liquid escape » *The plumber plugged the leaks in the pipe.*
chink, crack, fissure, hole, puncture

leap [1]
verb to jump a great distance or height » *The deer leapt into the air.*
bounce, bound, jump, spring, vault

leap [2]
noun a jump of great distance or height » *He made a huge leap right over the creek.*
bound, jump, spring

learn [1]
verb to gain knowledge by studying or training » *I am trying to learn French.*
grasp, master, pick up

learn [2]
verb to find out about something » *On learning who she was, I asked to meet her.*
ascertain, determine, discover, find out, gather, hear, understand

learned
adjective having gained a lot of knowledge by studying » *My father is a very learned man in the field of history.*
academic, erudite, intellectual, literate, scholarly, lettered, well-read

least
adjective as small or few as possible » *Which cheese contains the least fat?*
fewest, lowest, minimum, slightest, smallest
antonym: **most**

leave [1]
verb to go away from a person or place
▶▶ SEE RIGHT

leave [2]
noun a period of time off work » *Why don't you take a few days' leave?*
holiday, time off, vacation, furlough, sabbatical

lecture [1]
noun a formal talk about a particular subject » *The professor gave a lecture on the basics of chemistry.*
address, discourse, presentation, sermon, speech, talk, exposition, oration

The professor gave a lecture on the basics of chemistry.

length »

leave

abandon
The late passenger **abandoned** his coffee to rush for the train.

abscond
One sneaky passenger **absconded** when the guard came through to check the tickets.

decamp
A person **decamped** quickly after realizing they were on the wrong train!

depart
The crowd cheered as the train **departed**.

leave
1 *verb* to go away from a person or place » *The train **left** the platform on time.*

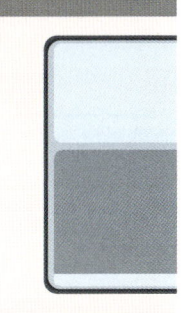

desert
The crowd **deserted** the platform after the train had gone.

forsake
He decided to **forsake** his window seat for a trip to the dining car.

go
There was an announcement that the train was about to **go**.

quit
Tom decided to **quit** his job as a train guard.

withdraw
The crowd **withdrew** from the platform edge as the train moved away.

---

lecture 2
noun a talk intended to tell someone off » *The police gave us a stern lecture on personal safety.*
bawling out (informal), **reprimand, scolding, warning**

lecture 3
verb to teach by giving formal talks to audiences » *The eminent scientist lectures all over the world.*
give a talk, speak, talk, teach

left-wing
adjective believing in reforming, socialist policies » *People said Mary had left-wing views.*
leftist, liberal, radical, socialist

legacy
noun objects or money someone leaves you when he or she dies » *Lord Brown left his sons a generous legacy.*
bequest, estate, heirloom, inheritance

legal 1
adjective relating to the law » *Each country has its own legal system.*
forensic, judicial, judiciary

legal 2
adjective allowed by the law » *My parents are the legal owners of our house.*
authorized, lawful, legitimate, permissible, rightful, valid, constitutional, sanctioned
antonym: **illegal**

leisure
noun time when you can relax » *A long holiday meant plenty of time for leisure.*
free time, recreation, relaxation, time off
antonym: **work**

A long holiday meant plenty of time for leisure.

leisurely
adjective unhurried or calm » *We enjoyed a leisurely walk along the beach.*
comfortable, easy, gentle, relaxed, unhurried
antonym: **hasty**

length 1
noun the distance from one end of something to the other » *The fish was about a metre in length.*
distance, extent, span

length 2
noun the amount of time something lasts for » *The movie is two hours in length.*
duration, period, space, span, term

a b c d e f g h i j k l m n o p q r s t u v w x y z

» lengthen

like

2 *verb* to find someone or something pleasant » *I really **like** this music.*

adore
*She **adored** her pug.*

appreciate
*I **appreciate** good food.*

be fond of
*I **am fond of** him.*

be keen on
*He **was** really **keen on** the band's latest song.*

be partial to
*She **is partial to** action movies.*

enjoy
*He **enjoyed** swimming in the lake.*

go for (informal)
*What kind of music do you **go for**?*

have a soft spot for (informal)
*I **have a soft spot for** people with red hair.*

have a weakness for
*He **had a weakness for** chocolate.*

love
*She **loved** getting presents.*

relish
*He **relished** the idea of celebrating his birthday.*

antonym: **dislike**
*I **dislike** playing hockey.*

lengthen
verb to make something longer » *My pants had to be lengthened because I'd grown.*
extend, make longer, prolong, stretch, elongate, protract
antonym: **shorten**

lessen
verb to decrease in size or amount » *Andy put on an extra sweater to lessen the risk of getting cold.*
abate, decrease, diminish, dwindle, lower, minimize, reduce, shrink, de-escalate, downsize
antonym: **increase**

lesson
noun a period of time for being taught » *Johanna took piano lessons once a week.*
class, coaching, lecture, period, tutoring

let
verb to allow someone to do something » *Leah's parents wouldn't let her go to the party.*
allow, give permission, permit, sanction
antonym: **forbid**

level 1
adjective completely flat » *An ice rink should have a perfectly level surface.*
flat, horizontal
antonym: **uneven**

level 2
verb to make something flat » *We levelled the ground.*
flatten, plane, smooth

level 3
noun a point on a scale that measures something » *Crime levels have started to decline.*
grade, rank, stage, standard, status

lie 1
verb to rest somewhere horizontally » *He was lying on his back, reading a book.*
loll, lounge, recline, sprawl, be prostrate, be recumbent, be supine, repose

lie 2
verb to say something that is not true » *The actor lied about his age and told the reporter he was much younger.*
be dishonest, fib, perjure yourself, tell a lie, prevaricate

lie 3
noun something you say that is not true » *His whole story was a lie—none of it was true.*
deceit, fabrication, falsehood, fib, fiction

life
noun the time during which you are alive » *My grandmother has had a long and active life.*
existence, life span, lifetime, time
related words:
adjectives **animate, vital**

lift 1
verb to move something to a higher position » *Ria strained to lift the heavy pile of books.*
elevate, hoist, pick up, raise
antonym: **lower**

lift 2
verb to remove something such as a ban or law » *They wore earrings to school when the ban on jewellery was lifted.*
cancel, end, relax, remove, rescind, revoke

light 1
noun brightness that enables you to see things » *The Sun's light filtered through the shutters.*
brightness, brilliance, glare, glow, illumination, radiance, incandescence, luminescence, luminosity, phosphorescence
antonym: **dark**
related word: *prefix* **photo-**

132

light 2
adjective pale in colour » *Steve wore a light blue shirt.*
bleached, fair, pale, pastel, blonde or **blond**
antonym: **dark**

light 3
adjective not weighing much » *Now it was empty, the cardboard box was light.*
flimsy, lightweight, portable, slight
antonym: **heavy**

light 4
verb to make a place bright » *The dining room was lit by a single candle.*
brighten, illuminate, light up
antonym: **darken**

light 5
verb to make a fire start burning » *It's time to light the barbecue.*
ignite, kindle
antonym: **extinguish**

like 1
preposition similar to » *He looks just like his father.*
akin, analogous, parallel, similar
antonym: **unlike**

like 2
verb to find someone or something pleasant
◀◀ SEE LEFT

likely
adjective having a good chance of happening » *It's likely my brother will have a mushroom pizza as usual.*
anticipated, expected, liable, possible, probable
antonym: **unlikely**

limit 1
noun a point beyond which something cannot go » *My father never drives above the speed limit.*
bounds, deadline, maximum, ultimate, utmost

limit 2
verb to prevent something from going any further » *Don't limit yourself to one activity.*
confine, curb, fix, ration, restrict, circumscribe, delimit, demarcate

limp
adjective not stiff or firm » *The week-old lettuce had limp leaves.*
drooping, flabby, floppy, slack, soft, flaccid, pliable
antonym: **stiff**

line 1
noun a long thin mark on something » *Use a ruler to draw a line down the centre of the page.*
rule, score, streak, stripe

line 2
noun a row of people or things » *A long line of fans waited to get a glimpse of the singer.*
column, file, queue, rank, row

line 3
noun the route along which something moves » *The golfer studied the ball's line of flight.*
course, path, route, track, trajectory

The golfer studied the ball's line of flight.

link 1
noun a connection between two things » *The wedding guest had links to both the bride's and groom's families.*
affiliation, association, attachment, bond, connection, relationship, tie, affinity, liaison

The friends linked hands as they ran across the field.

link 2
verb to connect two things » *The friends linked hands as they ran across the field.*
attach, connect, couple, fasten, join, tie
antonym: **separate**

liquid 1
noun a substance that is not solid and can be poured » *Make sure you drink enough liquids, particularly water.*
fluid, liquor, solution
antonym: **solid**

liquid 2
adjective in the form of a liquid » *Liquid detergent comes in a bottle, not a box.*
fluid, molten, runny
antonym: **solid**

list 1
noun a set of things written down one below the other » *There were six names on the list.*
catalogue, directory, index, inventory, listing, record, register

list 2
verb to set things down in a list » *The cookies' ingredients are listed on the package.*
catalogue, index, record, register, enumerate, itemize, tabulate

listen
verb to hear and pay attention to something » *I'll repeat that for those of you who weren't listening.*
attend, hark, hear, pay attention

little 1
adjective small in size or amount » *The girl was too little to ride on the rollercoaster.*
dainty, dwarf, mini, miniature, minute, pygmy, small, tiny, wee
antonym: **large**

little 2
noun a small amount or degree » *We offered her plenty to eat but she would only take a little.*
hardly any, meagre, measly, not much, paltry, scant

live 1
verb to have your home somewhere » *Carrie has lived in Montreal for 20 years.*
dwell, inhabit, reside, stay

live 2
verb to be alive » *The tortoise has lived for over 100 years.*
be alive, exist

live 3
adjective not dead or artificial » *I was horrified to find a live mouse sitting in my shoe.*
alive, animate, living

lively
adjective full of life and enthusiasm » *My sister has a lively personality.*
active, animated, energetic, perky, sparkling, sprightly, vivacious
antonym: **dull**

load 1
noun something being carried » *The crane can lift huge, heavy loads.*
cargo, consignment, freight, shipment

The crane can lift huge, heavy loads.

load »

load

load [2]
verb to put a lot of things on or into » *We loaded the car with supplies for the camping trip.*
fill, pack, pile, stack

loan [1]
noun a sum of money that you borrow » *He asked his father for a loan so he could buy a new bicycle.*
advance, credit, mortgage

loan [2]
verb to lend something to someone » *She loaned me her best coat to wear to the party.*
advance, lend

local [1]
adjective belonging to the area where you live » *The local store is on the corner of the next road.*
community, district, neighbourhood, regional

local [2]
noun a person who lives in a particular area » *Every week, the locals met at the café at the end of the street.*
inhabitant, native, resident

locate
verb to find out where someone or something is » *We located our missing friend in the café.*
find, pinpoint, track down

We located our missing friend in the café.

locate: be located
verb being in a particular place » *The restaurant is located near the theatre.*
be placed, be sited, be situated

The castle has a beautiful hilltop location.

location
noun a place or position » *The castle has a beautiful hilltop location.*
place, point, position, site, situation, spot, whereabouts, locale, locus

lock [1]
verb to close and fasten something with a key » *Lock the door when you leave the house.*
latch, padlock
antonym: **unlock**

lock [2]
noun a device used to fasten something » *No one could open the door because the lock was stiff.*
latch, padlock

logical [1]
adjective using logic to work something out » *His argument was logical and made sense.*
consistent, rational, reasoned, sound, valid, cogent, coherent
antonym: **illogical**

logical [2]
adjective sensible in the circumstances » *There has to be a logical explanation for the mysterious noise we heard.*
judicious, obvious, plausible, reasonable, sensible, wise
antonym: **illogical**

lonely [1]
adjective unhappy because of being alone » *The old lady was lonely and wished for visitors.*
alone, forlorn, forsaken, lonesome

lonely [2]
adjective isolated and not visited by many people » *A lonely tree blew in the wind on the bleak hillside.*
deserted, desolate, isolated, remote, secluded, uninhabited, godforsaken, out-of-the-way, unfrequented

long [1]
adjective continuing for a great amount of time » *A long and awkward silence followed her shocking announcement.*
extended, interminable, lengthy, lingering, long-drawn-out, prolonged, protracted, slow, sustained
antonym: **short**

long [2]
adjective great in length or distance » *There was a long line to enter the building.*
elongated, extensive, lengthy
antonym: **short**

There was a long line to enter the building.

long [3]
verb to want something very much » *He longed for a relaxing holiday.*
ache, covet, crave, hunger, lust, pine, yearn

longing
noun a strong wish for something » *She had a real longing for a hot drink.*
craving, desire, hankering, hunger, thirst, yearning

look [1]
verb to turn your eyes towards something and see it
▶▶ SEE RIGHT

look [2]
verb to appear or seem to be » *He looked younger than his age.*
appear, look like, seem, seem to be

look [3]
noun the action of turning your eyes towards something » *Lucy took a look at her reflection in the mirror.*
gaze, glance, glimpse, peek

look [4]
noun the way someone or something appears » *He had the look of a happy man.*
air, appearance, bearing, expression, face, semblance

look after
verb to take care of someone or something » *Will you look after my cats next week?*
care for, mind, nurse, take care of, tend, watch

lookalike
noun a person who looks like someone else » *He makes a living as an Elvis lookalike.*
dead ringer (informal), **double, spitting image** (informal)

look for
verb to try to find a person or thing » *I'm looking for my bag—have you seen it?*
forage, hunt, search, seek

loose [1]
adjective not firmly held or fixed » *The little girl had a loose tooth.*
free, unsecured, wobbly
antonym: **secure**

The little girl had a loose tooth.

134

*Chris wore his shirt **loose** to cool off.*

loose [2]
adjective not fitting closely » *Chris wore his shirt loose to cool off.*
baggy, slack, sloppy
antonym: **tight**

loosen
verb to make something looser » *Harry loosened the knot in his tie.*
slacken, undo, untie
antonym: **tighten**

loot [1]
verb to steal from a place during a riot or battle » *Gangs began breaking windows and looting stores.*
pillage, plunder, raid, ransack

loot [2]
noun stolen or illegal money or goods » *Sadly, the loot was never recovered.*
booty, haul, plunder, spoils, swag (slang)

lose [1]
verb to be unable to find » *I've lost my keys.*
drop, mislay, misplace
antonym: **find**

lose [2]
verb to be beaten » *We lost the match.*
be beaten, be defeated
antonym: **win**

lost [1]
adjective not knowing where you are » *I think we're lost.*
adrift, astray, off-course

lost [2]
adjective unable to be found » *She missed her lost toy.*
mislaid, misplaced, missing, vanished

lot [1] : a lot or lots
noun a large amount of something » *Remember to drink lots of water.*
abundance, a great deal, masses (informal), **piles** (informal), **plenty, quantities, scores**

lot [2]
noun an amount or number » *My mom said my friends were a noisy lot.*
batch, bunch (informal), **crowd, group, quantity, set**

loud [1]
adjective having a high level of sound » *We heard a loud bang from downstairs.*
blaring, deafening, noisy, resounding, strident, thunderous, clamorous, sonorous, stentorian
antonym: **quiet**

loud [2]
adjective too brightly coloured » *He wore a loud tie to the costume party.*
flamboyant, flashy, garish, gaudy, lurid
antonym: **dull**

lovable
adjective easy to love » *I find puppies cute and lovable, but my friend doesn't like them nipping at her ankles.*
adorable, charming, enchanting, endearing, sweet, captivating, engaging, winsome
antonym: **hateful**

love [1]
verb to feel strong affection for someone » *I love my family so much.*
adore, cherish, worship, be in love with, dote on, hold dear, idolize
antonym: **hate**

look
[1] *verb* to turn your eyes towards something and see it » *She **looked** out of the window.*

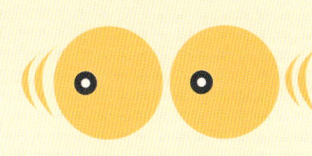

peek
She **peeked** at him through the curtains.

scan
He **scanned** the article in the newspaper.

regard
He **regarded** me curiously.

stare
She **stared** towards the horizon.

observe
He **observed** the scene before him.

survey
He stood up and **surveyed** the crowd.

scrutinize
She **scrutinized** the essay.

glare
He **glared** at her for eating the last slice.

squint
She **squinted** at the writing on the blackboard.

gape
She **gaped** at the price of the dress.

love

love [2]
verb to like something very much » *We both love fishing and go every weekend.*
appreciate, enjoy, like, relish, delight in, have a weakness for, take pleasure in
antonym: **hate**

love [3]
noun a strong feeling of affection » *There is nothing like a mother's love for her children.*
adoration, affection, ardour, devotion, infatuation, passion
antonym: **hatred**

There is nothing like a mother's love for her children.

love [4]
noun a strong liking for something » *Her love of animals has inspired her to become a vet.*
devotion, fondness, liking, weakness, partiality, penchant
antonym: **hatred**

lovely
adjective very attractive and pleasant » *You look lovely in that outfit.*
attractive, beautiful, delightful, enjoyable, pleasant, pretty
antonym: **horrible**

loving
adjective feeling or showing love » *He is a loving husband and father.*
affectionate, devoted, doting, fond, tender, warm, demonstrative, solicitous, warm-hearted
antonym: **cold**

low [1]
adjective short or not far above the ground » *The Sun was low in the sky.*
little, short, small, squat, stunted, sunken
antonym: **high**

low [2]
adjective small in degree or quantity » *The prices were low so we bought more clothes.*
minimal, modest, poor, reduced, scant, small
antonym: **high**

lower [1]
verb to move something downwards » *Sara lowered herself into the bathtub.*
drop, let down, take down
antonym: **raise**

lower [2]
verb to make something less in amount » *The government promised to lower taxes.*
cut, decrease, diminish, lessen, minimize, reduce, slash
antonym: **increase**

loyal
adjective firm in your friendship or support » *Kim was a loyal friend, visiting Ted every day while he was unwell.*
constant, dependable, faithful, staunch, true, trusty, steadfast, true-hearted, unswerving, unwavering
antonym: **treacherous**

Kim was a loyal friend, visiting Ted every day while he was unwell.

luck
noun something that happens by chance » *It was just luck that we happened to meet.*
accident, chance, destiny, fate, fortune, fortuity, predestination

lucky [1]
adjective having a lot of good luck » *Colin has always been lucky at games, winning every time.*
blessed, charmed, fortunate
antonym: **unlucky**

lucky [2]
adjective happening by chance with good consequences » *Suhel was lucky to be dealt such a good hand of cards that he easily won the game.*
fortuitous, fortunate, opportune, timely, adventitious, propitious, providential
antonym: **unlucky**

lump [1]
noun a solid piece of something » *Jane kneaded the big lump of dough.*
ball, cake, chunk, hunk, piece, wedge

Jane kneaded the big lump of dough.

lump [2]
noun a bump on the surface of something » *I've got a big lump on my head from when I walked into the shelf.*
bulge, bump, hump, swelling, protrusion, protuberance

lure [1]
verb to attract someone somewhere or into doing something » *We lured the ducks out of the water with breadcrumbs.*
attract, beckon, draw, entice, tempt

lure [2]
noun something that you find very attractive » *It was a hot day, and the lure of the swimming pool was strong.*
attraction, bait, magnet, pull, temptation

lurk
verb to wait hidden for someone or something » *He thought he saw someone lurking in the doorway.*
lie in wait, loiter, skulk

luxurious
adjective expensive and full of luxury » *We stayed in a luxurious hotel; it had the biggest pool I've ever seen.*
deluxe, lavish, opulent, plush (informal), **posh** (informal), **sumptuous, upscale** (informal)
antonym: **plain**

luxury [1]
noun comfort in expensive surroundings » *We led a life of luxury while on vacation and didn't care how much it cost.*
affluence, opulence, sumptuousness

luxury [2]
noun something enjoyable that you do not have often » *Hiring a sports car was a real luxury for my dad.*
extra, extravagance, indulgence, treat

lying [1]
noun the action of telling lies » *I've had enough of his lying; why can't he just tell the truth for once?*
deceit, dishonesty, fabrication, fibbing, perjury, dissimulation, duplicity, mendacity

lying [2]
adjective telling lies » *Don't trust him— he is a lying cheat.*
deceitful, dishonest, false, untruthful, dissembling, mendacious
antonym: **honest**

Mm

machine
noun a piece of equipment » *The sailors used a machine to pump the water out of the bottom of the ship.*
apparatus, appliance, contraption, device, instrument, mechanism

mad [1]
adjective very foolish or insane » *Craig would be mad to refuse such a generous offer.*
batty (slang), **crazy** (informal), **deranged, foolhardy, foolish, insane, loony** (slang), **stupid**
antonym: **sane**

mad [2]
adjective (informal) angry about something » *My friends got mad at me for interfering.*
angry, enraged, fuming, furious, incensed, infuriated, irate, livid (informal)

magic
noun a special power » *Do you believe in magic?*
sorcery, witchcraft, necromancy, occultism

magical
adjective wonderful and exciting » *I've heard that Paris is a magical city.*
bewitching, enchanting, entrancing, spellbinding

main
adjective most important » *Our main reason for going to Paris is to see the Eiffel Tower.*
cardinal, chief, foremost, leading, major, predominant, primary, prime, principal

mainly
adverb true in most cases » *The kittens were mainly tabbies.*
chiefly, generally, largely, mostly, predominantly, primarily, principally, for the most part, in general, on the whole

The kittens were mainly tabbies.

major
adjective very important or serious » *There's a major problem with your car's engine—it won't start.*
critical, crucial, leading, outstanding, significant
antonym: **minor**

majority
noun more than half » *The majority of our basketball team are girls.*
best part, better part, bulk, mass, most, lion's share, preponderance

The majority of our basketball team are girls.

make [1]
verb to construct something
▼ SEE BELOW

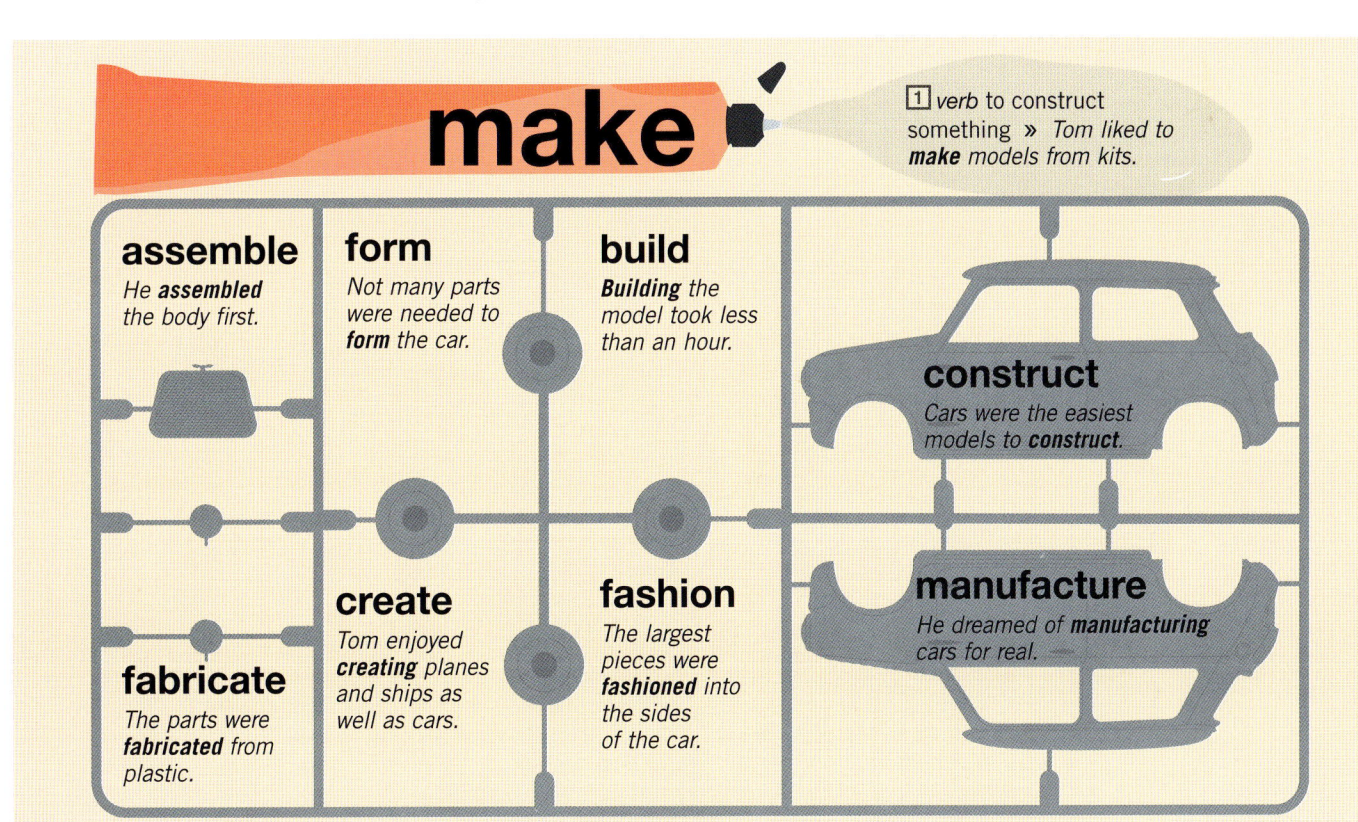

---

make

[1] verb to construct something » *Tom liked to make models from kits.*

assemble
He **assembled** the body first.

form
Not many parts were needed to **form** the car.

build
Building the model took less than an hour.

construct
Cars were the easiest models to **construct**.

fabricate
The parts were **fabricated** from plastic.

create
Tom enjoyed **creating** planes and ships as well as cars.

fashion
The largest pieces were **fashioned** into the sides of the car.

manufacture
He dreamed of **manufacturing** cars for real.

make

Her mother made her clean up the mess.

make [2]
verb to force someone to do something » *Her mother made her clean up the mess.*
compel, drive, force, oblige, coerce, impel

make [3]
noun a particular type » *My uncle always wears a certain make of wristwatch.*
brand, model

make up [1]
verb to form the parts of something » *Boys make up more than half of our history class.*
compose, comprise, constitute, form

make up [2]
verb to invent a story » *Tessa made up a story about why she was late—she didn't admit she'd just overslept.*
concoct, fabricate, invent, formulate, manufacture

making [1]
noun the act of creating something » *More than 100 people were involved in the making of this movie.*
assembly, building, construction, creation, fabrication, manufacture, production

making [2]: in the making
adjective about to become something » *The new recruit was a soldier in the making.*
budding, emergent, potential, up-and-coming

male
adjective relating to men » *I knew my father was at the door as soon as I heard the deep male voice.*
manly, masculine
antonym: **female**

malicious
adjective having the intention of hurting someone » *Pete was accused of spreading malicious rumours about Rita.*
cruel, malevolent (formal), **mean, spiteful, vicious,** malignant, rancorous (formal)

man [1]
noun an adult male human being » *James is a charming young man.*
dude (informal), **fellow, gentleman, guy** (informal), **male**
antonym: **woman**

man [2]
noun people in general » *All men are equal.*
humanity, human race, mankind, Homo sapiens, humankind

manage [1]
verb to succeed in doing something » *The crew managed to stop the fire from spreading any further.*
cope with, succeed in

The crew managed to stop the fire from spreading any further.

manage [2]
verb to be in charge of something » *Within two years Joe was managing the store.*
be in charge of, command, control, direct, run

management [1]
noun the act of running an organization » *The zoo needed better management to reduce the entrance lineups.*
control, direction, running

management [2]
noun the people who run an organization » *The management is investing more in research.*
administration, board, bosses (informal), **directors, employers**

manager
noun a person in charge of running an organization » *We welcomed our new manager in the morning meeting.*
boss (informal), **director, executive**

We welcomed our new manager in the morning meeting.

manifest
adjective (formal) obvious or easily seen » *His manifest failure to notice the puddle resulted in Len getting wet feet.*
blatant, clear, conspicuous, glaring, obvious, patent, plain

manner [1]
noun the way that you do something » *She smiled again in a friendly manner.*
fashion, mode, style, way

manner [2]
noun the way someone behaves » *Kim's kind manner made her feel at ease.*
bearing, behaviour, conduct, demeanour, comportment, deportment

manoeuvre [1]
verb to move something skilfully » *It took expertise to manoeuvre the boat so close to the shore.*
guide, navigate, negotiate, steer

manoeuvre [2]
noun a clever action » *With a series of cunning manoeuvres, Sam won the game of chess.*
dodge, ploy, ruse, tactic, machination, stratagem, subterfuge

manufacture [1]
verb to make goods in a factory » *Several models of car are manufactured at the factory.*
assemble, fabricate, make, mass-produce, process, produce

manufacture [2]
noun the making of goods in a factory » *His job is to supervise the manufacture of cars.*
assembly, fabrication, making, mass production, production

His job is to supervise the manufacture of cars.

many [1]
adjective a large number » *Sue has many friends.*
countless, innumerable, myriad, numerous, umpteen (informal), multifarious, multitudinous
antonym: **few**

138

maybe

many 2: many of
pronoun a large number of people or things » *I'd read many of my books already, so I went to the library to take out more.*
a lot, a mass, a multitude, large numbers, lots (informal), **plenty, scores**
antonym: **few**

mark 1
noun a small stain » *I can't get this mark off the curtain, and it's spoiling the pattern.*
blot, line, smudge, spot, stain, streak

mark 2
verb to stain something » *The pen in Marianna's pocket leaked and marked her trousers.*
smudge, stain, streak

market
noun a place to buy or sell things » *We bought fresh fish at the market today.*
bazaar, fair

marriage 1
noun the formal union of two people who live together » *We have a happy marriage—we've been together for 20 years.*
matrimony (formal), **wedlock** (formal)
related words:
adjectives **conjugal, connubial, marital, nuptial**

marriage 2
noun a union » *The dessert was a perfect marriage of chocolate and whipped cream.*
alliance, association, coupling, link, match, merger, union

*Tall grasses grew in the **marsh**.*

marsh
noun an area of low-lying, poorly drained land that is sometimes flooded » *Tall grasses grew in the marsh.*
bog, fen, mire, morass, mudflats, quagmire, quicksands, saltmarsh, slough, swamp, wetland

marvellous
adjective wonderful or excellent » *The class had a marvellous time at the zoo.*
brilliant, excellent, first-rate, magnificent, remarkable, splendid, superb, wonderful
antonym: **terrible**

mass 1
noun a large number or amount » *Fleur had masses of homework to get through.*
crowd, heap, load, lump, mob, pile, throng

mass 2
adjective involving a large number of people » *There were mass protests about the school holidays being reduced.*
general, popular, universal, widespread

mass 3
verb to gather together in a large group » *The children massed to watch the relay race.*
assemble, congregate, gather, group

master
verb to learn how to do something » *Eloise found it easy to master the recorder.*
become proficient in, get the hang of (informal), **grasp, learn**

match 1
noun an organized game » *Ken was looking forward to the soccer match.*
competition, contest, game

match 2
verb to be similar to » *The shoes matched her dress.*
agree, correspond, fit, go with, suit,
accord, harmonize

material 1
noun any type of cloth » *Sara's skirt was made of thick material.*
cloth, fabric

material 2
noun a solid substance » *He gathered the materials needed for repairing the wall.*
matter, stuff, substance

*He gathered the **materials** needed for repairing the wall.*

matter 1
noun something that you have to deal with » *Rachel found business matters rather dull.*
affair, business, issue, question, situation, subject

matter 2
noun any substance » *The atom is the smallest divisible particle of matter.*
material, stuff, substance

matter 3
verb to be important » *It does not matter what you wear for the party.*
be of consequence, count, make a difference

mature 1
verb to become fully developed » *Children seem to mature earlier these days.*
come of age, grow up, reach adulthood

mature 2
adjective fully developed » *He's very mature for his age.*
adult, full-grown, fully fledged, grown, grown-up

maximum 1
adjective being the most that is possible » *The maximum number of books that will fit on a shelf is 20.*
top, utmost
antonym: **minimum**

maximum 2
noun the most that is possible » *Matt turned the volume of the radio up to the maximum.*
ceiling, height, most, upper limit, utmost
antonym: **minimum**

*Matt turned the volume of the radio up to the **maximum**.*

maybe
adverb it is possible that » *Maybe it would have been quicker to take the bus.*
conceivably, it could be, perhaps, possibly, perchance

139

meagre

*The restaurant served **meagre** portions, and we went home hungry.*

meagre
adjective very small and inadequate » *The restaurant served meagre portions, and we went home hungry.*
inadequate, measly (informal), **paltry, scant, sparse,** exiguous, **insubstantial, scanty, skimpy**

meal
noun an occasion when people eat » *My mother cooked a special meal for my birthday.*
banquet, dinner, feast, repast, spread

mean 1
verb to convey a message » *A red traffic light means that you have to stop.*
denote, indicate, signify

mean 2
verb to intend to do something » *I meant to phone you, but didn't have time.*
aim, intend, plan

meaning
noun the idea expressed by something » *Tom had to look up the meaning of the word in the dictionary.*
drift, gist, message, significance, connotation, import

measure 1
verb to check the size of something » *We measured how tall our little brother was.*
gauge, survey, calibrate, quantify

measure 2
noun an amount of something » *There was a measure of silence after the actor's shocking announcement.*
amount, degree, portion, proportion

measure 3
noun an action to achieve something » *Tough measures are needed to maintain order.*
act, action, deed, expedient, manoeuvre, means, procedure, step

medicine
noun something you take to make you better » *The doctor prescribed some medicine for my sore throat.*
cure, drug, medication, pill, tablet, remedy

medium 1
adjective average in size » *Ella was of medium height.*
average, medium-sized, middling

*Ella was of **medium** height.*

medium 2
noun a means of communication » *The government released the news through the medium of TV.*
channel, vehicle, agency, instrument

meek
adjective quiet and timid » *Janet was a meek girl, always agreeing with whatever her friends said.*
deferential, docile, mild, submissive, timid, unassuming, acquiescent, compliant, mild-mannered
antonym: **bold**

meet 1
verb to be in the same place as someone » *I met my cousin quite by chance.*
bump into (informal), **come across, come upon, encounter, run across, run into**

meet 2
verb to gather in a group » *We meet for lunch at a café once a week.*
assemble, congregate, convene, gather, get together

*We **meet** for lunch at a café once a week.*

meet 3
verb to fulfill a need » *Meals must meet the needs of growing children.*
answer, fulfill, satisfy

meeting 1
noun an event at which people come together for a purpose » *All the parents went to a meeting about the new playground.*
audience, conference, congress, convention, gathering, get-together (informal), **reunion,** conclave, convocation

meeting 2
noun an occasion when you meet someone » *I had a chance meeting with an old friend while I was shopping.*
assignation (literary), **encounter, rendezvous, tryst**

melodramatic
adjective behaving in an exaggerated way » *Elodie was so melodramatic, flouncing out of the café because she didn't like the table they gave her.*
histrionic, sensational, theatrical

melt 1
verb to become liquid » *The ice cream started melting into a puddle.*
dissolve, thaw, liquefy

*The ice cream started **melting** into a puddle.*

melt 2
verb to disappear » *Isabella's anger melted when she saw what Leo had brought her.*
disappear, disperse, dissolve, evaporate, vanish

memorable
adjective likely to be remembered » *The cup final was a memorable victory over the league champions.*
catchy, historic, notable, striking, unforgettable

memory
noun the ability to remember » *I have an excellent memory for phone numbers.*
recall, remembrance (formal), **recollection, retention**

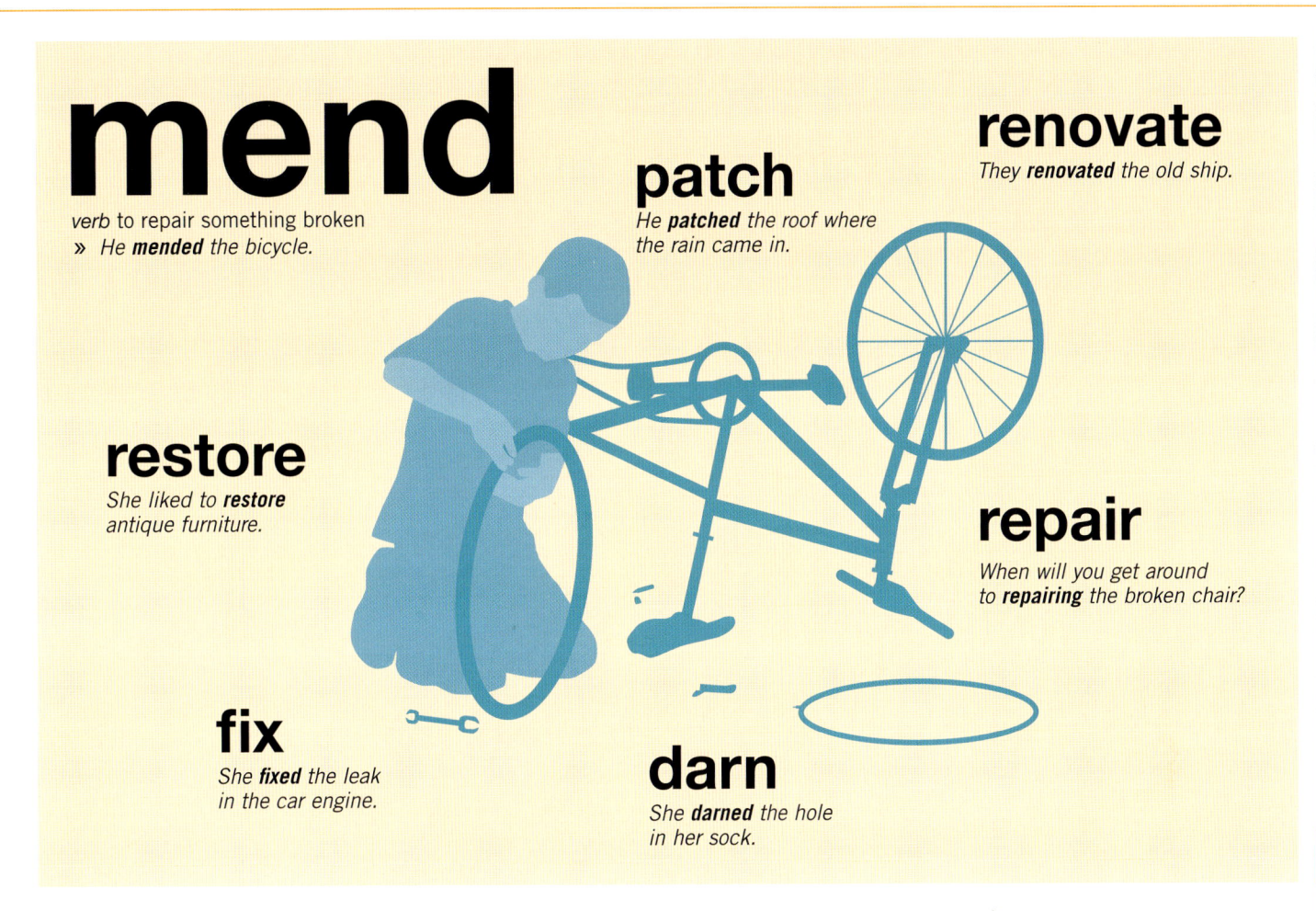

mend
verb to repair something broken
» He **mended** the bicycle.

patch
He **patched** the roof where the rain came in.

renovate
They **renovated** the old ship.

restore
She liked to **restore** antique furniture.

repair
When will you get around to **repairing** the broken chair?

fix
She **fixed** the leak in the car engine.

darn
She **darned** the hole in her sock.

---

mend
verb to repair something broken
▲ SEE ABOVE

mention 1
verb to talk about something briefly » *I mentioned the party to Lisa, but I don't know if she'll come.*
allude to, bring up, broach, hint, intimate, refer to, touch on, touch upon

mention 2
noun a brief comment about something » *There was no mention in the program of my role in the show.*
allusion, reference

merciful 1
adjective showing kindness » *The merciful king treated his subjects with kindness.*
compassionate, humane, kind
antonym: **merciless**

merciful 2
adjective showing forgiveness » *The teacher was merciful and didn't give us a detention for being late.*
forgiving, lenient
antonym: **merciless**

merciless
adjective showing no kindness or forgiveness » *The airport staff were merciless when I forgot my passport and wouldn't let me on the plane.*
callous, cruel, heartless, implacable, ruthless, hard-hearted, pitiless, unforgiving
antonym: **merciful**

mercy 1
noun the quality of kindness » *The wrestler showed no mercy to his opponent.*
compassion, kindness, pity, benevolence, charity

mercy 2
noun the quality of forgiveness » *The criminal threw himself upon the mercy of the court.*
forgiveness, leniency, clemency, forbearance

merit 1
noun worth or value » *The film's producer argued that profits mattered more than artistic merit.*
excellence, value, virtue, worth

merit 2
noun a good quality that something has » *They discussed the merits of the different cakes on offer.*
advantage, asset, strength, strong point, virtue

merit 3
verb to deserve something » *Buying a new camera merits careful consideration.*
be entitled to, be worthy of, deserve, earn, warrant

mess 1
noun a state of untidiness » *The room was in a mess after the party.*
chaos, disarray, disorder

*The room was in a **mess** after the party.*

mess 2
noun a situation that is full of problems » *How are we going to get out of this mess?*
fix (informal), jam (informal), muddle, turmoil

mess 3: mess up
verb to spoil something » *He messed up his career.*
botch, bungle, foul up (informal), ruin, screw up (slang), spoil

message

message [1]
noun a piece of information for someone
▼ SEE BELOW

message [2]
verb to send information to » *Fred messaged his friends to tell them about the match.*
email or **e-mail, IM, instant message, text**

messenger
noun someone who carries a message » *We will send a messenger to the airport to collect the photographs.*
courier, envoy, runner, emissary, go-between, herald

method
noun a way of doing something » *Emily used a traditional method to make jam.*
approach, mode, procedure, technique, way

middle [1]
noun the part furthest from the edges » *There was a large table in the middle of the room.*
centre, halfway point, midst, midpoint, midsection

middle [2]
adjective furthest from the edges » *Carl sat down on the middle seat, between his parents.*
central, halfway

mild [1]
adjective not strong or powerful » *Flo used a mild shampoo to wash her hair.*
insipid, weak
antonym: **strong**

mild [2]
adjective gentle and good-tempered » *My uncle is a mild man who is very good with animals.*
affable, gentle, meek, placid, easy-going, equable, pacific, peaceable

mild [3]
adjective warmer than usual » *The area is famous for its mild winter climate.*
balmy, temperate

mind [1]
noun your ability to think » *Our teacher is really clever and has a sharp mind.*
brain, head, imagination, intellect, psyche
related word: adjective **mental**

mind [2]
verb to be annoyed by something » *I don't mind what you get me for my birthday.*
be bothered, care, object

mind [3]
verb to look after something » *I'm minding my younger brother while my mother is out.*
keep an eye on, look after, take care of, watch

minimum
adjective being the least possible » *My little sister was just tall enough to be the minimum height for the fairground ride.*
least possible, minimal
antonym: **maximum**

minor
adjective less important » *Henry fell off his bike but sustained only minor injuries.*
lesser, petty, secondary, slight, trifling, trivial
antonym: **major**

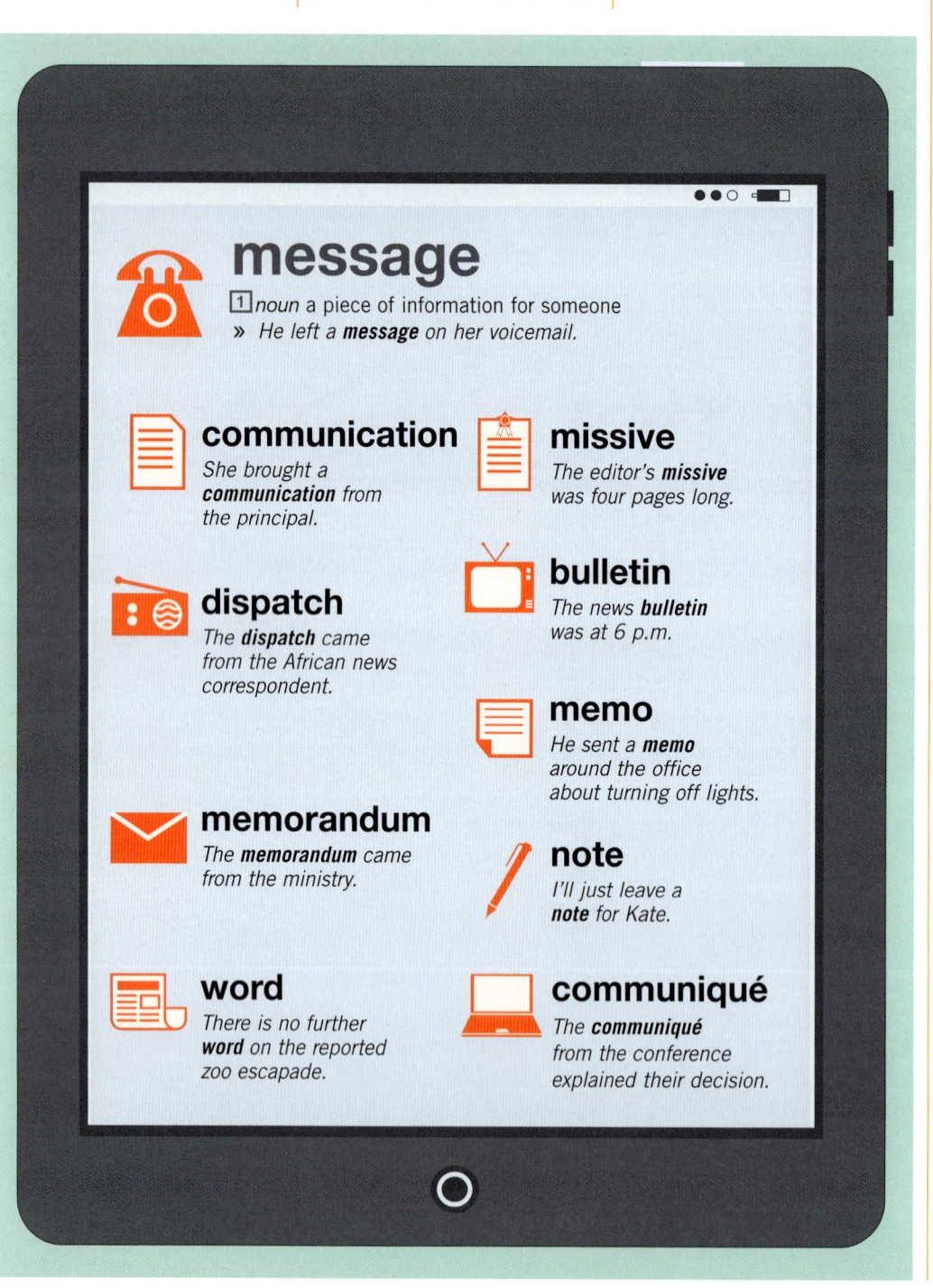

message
[1] noun a piece of information for someone
» *He left a message on her voicemail.*

communication
She brought a **communication** from the principal.

dispatch
The **dispatch** came from the African news correspondent.

memorandum
The **memorandum** came from the ministry.

word
There is no further **word** on the reported zoo escapade.

missive
The editor's **missive** was four pages long.

bulletin
The news **bulletin** was at 6 p.m.

memo
He sent a **memo** around the office about turning off lights.

note
I'll just leave a **note** for Kate.

communiqué
The **communiqué** from the conference explained their decision.

model »

minute [1]
noun a short period of time » *I'll be with you in a minute.*
flash, instant, moment, second, trice

minute [2]
adjective extremely small » *The insect was so minute that Kayla needed a magnifying glass to see it clearly.*
microscopic, negligible, slender, small, tiny, diminutive, minuscule
antonym: **vast**

*The insect was so **minute** that Kayla needed a magnifying glass to see it clearly.*

miracle
noun a surprising and fortunate event » *It was a miracle that everyone escaped unharmed.*
marvel, wonder

miserable [1]
adjective very unhappy » *All this rain makes me miserable.*
dejected, depressed, down, downcast, low, melancholy, mournful, sad, unhappy, wretched, disconsolate, sorrowful
antonym: **cheerful**

miserable [2]
adjective causing unhappiness » *Damp, dark, and tiny—it was a miserable apartment.*
gloomy, pathetic, sorry, wretched

misery
noun unhappiness » *He felt such misery when his pet died.*
depression, despair, grief, melancholy, sadness, sorrow, unhappiness, woe
antonym: **joy**

misfortune
noun an unfortunate event » *I had the misfortune to fall off my bike.*
adversity, bad luck

misrepresent
verb to give a false account of something » *My brother deliberately misrepresented what happened when we argued earlier.*
distort, falsify, twist

miss [1]
verb to fail to notice » *Go to the first floor. You can't miss it.*
fail to notice, mistake, overlook

miss [2]
verb to feel the loss of » *I miss my family when I'm away.*
long for, pine for, yearn for

mistake [1]
noun something that is wrong » *There were a lot of spelling mistakes in his work.*
blunder, error, gaffe, oversight, slip, inaccuracy, miscalculation

*There were a lot of spelling **mistakes** in his work.*

mistake [2]
verb to think one thing is another thing » *I mistook him for the owner of the house.*
confuse with, misinterpret as, mix up with, take for

mistreat
verb to treat someone badly » *The dog had been mistreated, so we gave it a new home.*
abuse, ill-treat

mix
verb to combine things » *Mix the ingredients together slowly.*
amalgamate, blend, combine, merge, mingle, intermingle, interweave

mixture
noun a combination of things » *We used a mixture of flour and water to make dough.*
alloy, amalgamation, blend, combination, compound, fusion, medley, amalgam, composite, conglomeration, mix

*We used a **mixture** of flour and water to make dough.*

mix up
verb to confuse two things » *People often mix us up because we both wear glasses.*
confuse, muddle

mix-up
noun a mistake in something planned » *There has been a mix-up with the bookings.*
mistake, misunderstanding, muddle

moan [1]
verb to make a low sound » *Laura moaned in her sleep.*
groan, grunt

moan [2]
verb to complain about something » *Carol is always moaning about her husband.*
complain, groan, grumble, whine, bleat, carp

moan [3]
noun a low sound » *She let out a faint moan.*
groan, grunt

mock [1]
verb to make fun of someone » *My sister mocked my haircut.*
deride (formal)**, laugh at, make fun of, poke fun at, ridicule, scoff at**

mock [2]
adjective not genuine » *The adults displayed mock surprise when the children performed the same old magic tricks.*
artificial, bogus, counterfeit, dummy, fake, false, feigned, imitation, phony (informal)**, pretended, sham,** ersatz, pseudo

mockery
noun the act of mocking someone » *Was there a glint of mockery in his eyes when he said he liked her new shoes?*
derision, jeering, ridicule

model [1]
noun a copy of something » *We saw a model of what this building used to look like.*
dummy, replica, representation, facsimile, mock-up

model [2]
noun a perfect example of something » *My obedient dog is a model of good behaviour.*
epitome, example, ideal, paragon, archetype, exemplar

model [3]
verb to make something into a shape » *Jo modelled the clay into an animal.*
carve, fashion, form, mould, sculpt, shape

*Jo **modelled** the clay into an animal.*

143

moderate

moderate [1]
adjective neither too much nor too little » *Moderate exercise is good for the health.*
average, fair, medium, middling, reasonable

moderate [2]
verb to become or make less extreme » *The children persuaded their father to moderate his views on pets in bedrooms.*
abate, curb, ease, relax, soften, temper, tone down

modern [1]
adjective relating to the present time » *The modern world increasingly relies on the internet.*
contemporary, current, present, present-day, recent

modern [2]
adjective new and involving the latest ideas » *The house was full of modern technology.*
latest, new, up-to-date, up-to-the-minute
antonym: **old-fashioned**

modest [1]
adjective small in size or amount » *Olivia made a modest donation to charity each month.*
limited, middling, moderate, small

modest [2]
adjective not boastful » *The famous athlete was modest about his achievements.*
humble, unassuming, self-effacing, unpretentious
antonym: **conceited**

moment [1]
noun a short period of time » *Ted paused for a moment to get his breath back.*
instant, minute, second, split second, flash, trice

moment [2]
noun a point in time » *The phone rang at the exact moment I stepped into the bathtub.*
instant, point, time

*Sue enjoyed counting the **money** she had earned.*

money
noun coins or banknotes » *Sue enjoyed counting the money she had earned.*
bread (slang), **bucks** (slang), **capital, cash, dough** (informal), **funds**

mood
noun a state of mind » *Liz has been in a really cheerful mood since getting a kitten.*
frame of mind, humour, spirits, state of mind, temper

moody [1]
adjective depressed or unhappy » *Tony was moody because his father had woken him up.*
irritable, morose, sulky, sullen, huffy, ill-tempered, testy, touchy

moody [2]
adjective liable to change your mood » *We were nervous of visiting the moody old man.*
temperamental, volatile, capricious, mercurial

more
adjective greater than something else » *Belle has more books than Peter.*
added, additional, extra, further
antonym: **less**

*Belle has **more** books than Peter.*

move
[1] *verb* to change position » *The race started and the competitors began to move.*

1 wriggle creep scurry inch
slither crawl scuttle scamper edge

2 run bolt stampede fly shoot dash
jog hasten gallop dart sprint rush

144

motivate
verb to cause a particular behaviour » *The teacher used a sticker chart to motivate the children to work hard.*
drive, inspire, lead, move, prompt, provoke

mountain
noun an area of high ground that is higher and steeper than a hill » *After hours of climbing, we finally reached the top of the mountain.*
alp, elevation, height, mount, peak, precipice, range, ridge

*After hours of climbing, we finally reached the top of the **mountain**.*

move 1
verb to change position
▼ SEE BELOW

move 2
verb to change residence » *Lori moved from Guelph to London.*
migrate, move house, relocate

move 3
verb to cause a deep emotion » *We were moved to tears.*
affect, touch

movement 1
noun a change of position » *The cameras monitor the movement of fish in the river.*
flow, motion

movement 2
noun a group of people with similar aims » *Vicky joined the peace movement.*
campaign, faction, group, organization

moving
adjective causing deep emotion » *The father of the bride gave a moving speech.*
affecting, emotional, poignant, stirring, touching

muddle 1
noun a state of disorder » *The drawer is in a muddle; I can't find what I want.*
chaos, confusion, disarray, disorder, disorganization, jumble, mess, tangle

muddle 2
verb to mix things up » *Gran muddles my sister and me.*
confuse, jumble, mix up

multiply
verb to increase in number » *The number of children in the park multiplied in summer.*
increase, proliferate, spread

mumble
verb to speak quietly » *Speak up—don't mumble!*
murmur, mutter

mysterious 1
adjective strange and not well understood » *My favourite socks went missing under mysterious circumstances.*
arcane (formal)**, baffling, cryptic, enigmatic, mystifying, abstruse, obscure, recondite**

mysterious 2
adjective secretive about something » *Stop being so mysterious and tell me where you've hidden the keys.*
furtive, secretive

mystery
noun something that is not understood » *There is a mystery surrounding our tortoise's disappearance.*
conundrum, enigma, puzzle, riddle

---

tear

hurry   race

» nag

Nn

nag
verb to keep complaining about something to someone » *My dad nagged me to keep the bathroom clean.*
badger, bother, go on at, pester

naked [1]
adjective not wearing any clothes » *Anna's most famous painting was of a naked woman.*
bare, nude, stark-naked, unclothed, undressed
antonym: **clothed**

naked [2]
adjective openly displayed or shown » *His naked ambition was evident in his hard work.*
blatant, evident, manifest, open, unmistakable, overt, **patent, stark**
antonym: **secret**

name [1]
noun a word that identifies a person or thing » *My name is Joe.*
designation, epithet, nickname, term, title, appellation, denomination, sobriquet
related word:
adjective **nominal**

name [2]
noun the opinion people have about someone » *He lied to protect Janet's good name.*
character, reputation

name [3]
verb to give a name to someone » *She named her daughter Kit, after her grandmother.*
baptize, call, christen, dub, style, term

We crossed a narrow stream.

narrow
adjective having a small distance from side to side » *We crossed a narrow stream.*
fine, slender, slim, thin
antonym: **wide**

narrow-minded
adjective unwilling to consider new ideas or other people's opinions » *My friend is rather narrow-minded and doesn't like exploring new ideas.*
biased, bigoted, insular, opinionated, prejudiced, parochial, reactionary
antonym: **tolerant**

nasty
adjective very unpleasant » *The rotten apple left a nasty taste in my mouth.*
disagreeable, disgusting, foul, horrible, repellent, unpleasant, vile
antonym: **pleasant**

natural [1]
adjective normal and to be expected » *Her natural reaction was to laugh at jokes.*
common, everyday, normal, ordinary, typical, usual
antonym: **unnatural**

natural [2]
adjective not trying to pretend » *The new babysitter was so natural with the children.*
candid, frank, genuine, real, unaffected, artless, ingenuous
antonym: **false**

natural [3]
adjective existing from birth and not learned » *I'm a terrible dancer—I have no natural rhythm.*
inborn, inherent, innate, instinctive, intuitive, native, immanent, indigenous

nature
noun someone's character » *It's not in my nature to sit still for long.*
character, makeup, personality

naughty
adjective tending to behave badly » *The teacher told Tony off for being naughty.*
bad, disobedient, impish, mischievous, wayward
antonym: **well-behaved**

navigate
verb to work out the direction in which a ship, plane, or car should go » *Sam navigated the plane through the fog.*
guide, pilot, steer

near [1]
preposition not far from » *The cat curled up near the fire.*
adjacent to, alongside, close to, next to, not far from

The cat curled up near the fire.

near [2]
adjective not far away in distance » *The restaurant we're going to is very near.*
adjacent, adjoining, close, nearby
antonym: **far**

near [3]
adjective not far away in time » *Our final exams are near.*
approaching, forthcoming, imminent, looming, near at hand, nigh, upcoming

nearly
adverb not completely but almost » *The beach was nearly empty after the storm.*
almost, as good as, just about, practically, virtually

neat
adjective having everything arranged in a tidy way » *Anna liked to keep her desk neat.*
orderly, smart, spruce, tidy, trim
antonym: **untidy**

Anna liked to keep her desk neat.

necessary [1]
adjective needed so that something can happen » *Juan made the necessary arrangements for his vacation.*
essential, imperative, indispensable, required, vital, de rigueur, requisite
antonym: **unnecessary**

necessary [2]
adjective (formal) certain to happen or exist » *Wrinkles are a necessary result of getting old.*
certain, inevitable, inexorable, unavoidable

need
verb to require something or be required to do something » *You need a ticket to enter.*
demand, require, want

146

news »

neglect [1]
verb to fail to look after someone or something
» *My toast burned because I had neglected it.*
ignore, overlook, turn your back on

neglect [2]
verb (formal) to fail to do something » *Alex neglected to give me his address, so I don't know where to send the card.*
fail, forget, omit

neglect [3]
noun lack of care » *Most of her plants died from neglect.*
disregard, indifference, unconcern

nervous
adjective worried about something
▶▶ SEE RIGHT

neutral
adjective not supporting either side » *I stayed neutral during my friends' argument.*
disinterested, dispassionate, impartial, nonaligned, nonpartisan, unbiased, unprejudiced
antonym: **biased**

never
adverb at no time at all
» *I never said I was leaving.*
at no time, not ever

new
adjective recently created or discovered » *A new hotel has opened in our town.*
advanced, current, fresh, ground-breaking, latest, modern, recent, ultra-modern, up-to-date, up-to-the-minute
antonym: **old**

news
noun information about things that have happened » *Jackie waited for news of his arrival.*
bulletin, disclosure, dispatch, information, intelligence, latest (informal), **tidings** (formal), **word**

antonym: **calm**
*The coach was **calm** and helped them to relax.*

He was **anxious** to play well.

He felt **apprehensive** until he started to play.

Nerves made his performance **edgy.**

He was still feeling **jittery** when he scored a basket.

The new player was obviously **jumpy.**

He was too **tense** to throw the ball correctly.

He felt **uptight** and uneasy.

He had me **worried** for a moment.

nervous
adjective worried about something
» *He was always **nervous** before a game.*

nice
[1] *adjective* attractive or enjoyable

*Did you have a **nice** time at the wedding?*

*Yes, it was really **good**, and the party afterwards was **enjoyable** too. A **delightful** day in which a **pleasurable** time was had by all.*

*I heard they got married at a **beautiful** old church in a **lovely** little village.*

*The bride looked so **pretty** and her husband so **handsome**. They make a **gorgeous** couple.*

*Her parents are **pleasant** people too—they're such an **agreeable** family.*

*And the food they provided was **delicious**, with a **mouthwatering** dessert.*

next [1]
adjective coming immediately after something else » *Their next child was a girl.*
ensuing, following, subsequent, succeeding

next [2]
adverb coming immediately after something else » *After Sue and Dan, Steve arrived next at the party.*
afterwards, subsequently

next [3]
adjective in a position nearest to something » *I shut the dog in the next room.*
adjacent, adjoining, closest, nearest, neighbouring

nice [1]
adjective attractive or enjoyable
◀◀ SEE LEFT

nice [2]
adjective kind or friendly » *Sending flowers was a nice gesture.*
amiable, charming, considerate, engaging, friendly, good-natured, kind, kindly, likeable, thoughtful

nice [3]
adjective good or satisfactory » *The builder made a nice job of the new garden wall.*
fine, neat, tidy, trim

no
interjection not at all » *"Any problems?" "No, everything is fine, thanks."*
absolutely not, certainly not, definitely not, nope (informal), **not at all, of course not**
antonym: **yes**

noble [1]
adjective deserving admiration because of honesty, bravery, and unselfishness » *Giving his prize money away was noble.*
generous, honourable, magnanimous, upright, virtuous, worthy
antonym: **ignoble**

noble [2]
noun someone from the highest social rank » *The old castle belonged to a family of nobles.*
aristocrat, lord, nobleman, peer
antonym: **peasant**

noise
noun a loud or unpleasant sound » *Bill wore earmuffs while using the jackhammer to muffle the noise.*
commotion, din, hubbub, pandemonium, racket, row, uproar, clamour, rumpus, tumult
antonym: **silence**

*Bill wore earmuffs while using the jackhammer to muffle the **noise**.*

noisy
adjective making a lot of noise » *The bus was full of noisy schoolchildren shrieking with excitement.*
deafening, loud, piercing, strident, tumultuous, vociferous, clamorous, riotous, uproarious
antonym: **quiet**

nominate
verb to suggest someone for a position or role » *My teacher nominated me for the award.*
name, propose, recommend, select, submit, suggest

nonsense
noun foolish words or behaviour » *Stop talking such nonsense!*
drivel, garbage (informal), **inanity, rubbish**

148

normal
adjective usual and ordinary » *A normal journey to school takes 20 minutes.*
average, conventional, habitual, ordinary, regular, routine, standard, typical, usual
antonym: **unusual**

nosy
adjective trying to find out about other people's business » *Our nosy neighbour is always watching us through the curtains.*
curious, eavesdropping, inquisitive, prying

note 1
noun a short letter » *I wrote a note asking him to come by.*
communication (formal), **letter, memo, memorandum, message, reminder,** epistle, missive (old-fashioned)

note 2
noun a written record that helps you remember something » *The secretary made a note of the rescheduled meeting.*
account, jotting, record, register

The secretary made a note of the rescheduled meeting.

note 3
noun an atmosphere, feeling, or quality » *I detected a note of envy in Reg's voice when he talked about his cousin's designer shoes.*
hint, tone, touch, trace

note 4
verb to become aware of or mention a fact » *Paul noted that the rain had stopped and went outside.*
mention, notice, observe (formal)**, perceive, register, remark, see**

notice 1
verb to become aware of something » *I noticed that Billy was the only person who wasn't laughing.*
detect, discern, note, observe, perceive, see, spot

notice 2
noun a written announcement » *The students looked at the notice on the board.*
advertisement, bill, poster, sign

The students looked at the notice on the board.

notice 3
noun warning that something is going to happen » *She was transferred to another group without notice.*
advance warning, intimation, notification, warning

noticeable
adjective obvious and easy to see » *There has been a noticeable improvement in Sam's piano playing since he started practising.*
conspicuous, evident, obvious, perceptible, unmistakable, manifest, **salient**

The airport display board notified the passengers of the delay.

notify
verb to inform someone officially of something » *The airport display board notified the passengers of the delay.*
advise (formal)**, inform, tell, warn**

notorious
adjective well-known for something bad » *The district was notorious for crime.*
disreputable, infamous, scandalous

now
adverb at the present time or moment » *I need to see Gary now, before he leaves.*
at once, currently, immediately, nowadays, right now, straight away, without delay

nuisance
noun someone or something that is annoying » *Dom was a nuisance, always teasing her.*
annoyance, bother, hassle (informal)**, inconvenience, irritation, pain** (informal)**, pest,** plague, **vexation**

Dom was a nuisance, always teasing her.

numb 1
adjective unable to feel anything » *My leg went numb after I sat on it too long.*
dead, frozen, insensitive, paralyzed, benumbed, **insensible**

numb 2
verb to make you unable to feel anything » *The cold numbed my fingers, and I wished I was wearing gloves.*
dull, freeze, paralyze, stun, benumb, deaden, **immobilize**

number 1
noun a word or symbol used for counting » *Pick a number between one and ten.*
digit, figure, numeral, character, integer

number 2
noun a quantity of things or people » *A large number of people attended the carnival.*
collection, crowd, horde, multitude

A large number of people attended the carnival.

numerous
adjective existing or happening in large numbers » *We've met before on numerous occasions.*
lots of, many, several

Oo

oaf
noun a clumsy or aggressive person » *My brother can be such an oaf, always knocking things over.*
brute, lout

oath
noun a formal promise » *When you join the Scouts, you take an oath.*
pledge, promise, vow

obedient
adjective tending to do what you are told » *The horse was calm and obedient—perfect for young riders.*
law-abiding, submissive, subservient, biddable, compliant
antonym: **disobedient**

obey
verb to do what you are told » *Everyone should obey the law.*
abide by, adhere to, comply with, follow, observe
antonym: **disobey**

object [1]
noun anything solid and non-living » *My dog likes to chew on all sorts of objects.*
article, thing

My dog likes to chew on all sorts of objects.

object [2]
noun an aim or purpose » *The object of the exercise is to raise money for the charity.*
aim, goal, idea, intention, objective, purpose

object [3]
verb to express disapproval » *Al objected to seeing the movie because it was too long.*
oppose, protest, demur, expostulate
antonym: **approve**

objection
noun disapproval of something » *Despite objections from her father, Jacqui wore shorts and running shoes.*
opposition, protest
antonym: **support**

obligatory
adjective required by a rule or law » *He said that attendance was obligatory; no one was allowed to miss the class.*
compulsory, forced, mandatory, required, requisite

obscure [1]
verb to make something difficult to see
▶▶ SEE RIGHT

obscure [2]
adjective known by only a few people » *We went to an obscure restaurant on a side street, away from the crowds.*
little-known, unknown
antonym: **famous**

obscure [3]
adjective difficult to understand » *The author used such obscure language in his book, Ciara needed to look up some of the words in a dictionary to understand them.*
arcane, cryptic, opaque, abstruse, esoteric
antonym: **simple**

observant
adjective good at noticing things » *The artist was very observant and captured every detail of the flowers in his painting.*
attentive, perceptive, vigilant, watchful, eagle-eyed, sharp-eyed

The artist was very observant and captured every detail of the flowers in his painting.

observe [1]
verb to watch something carefully » *The zoologists spent years observing the behaviour of chimpanzees.*
monitor, scrutinize, study, survey, view, watch

observe [2]
verb to notice something » *The teacher took the class for a walk in the woods and asked them to write down what wildlife they observed.*
discover, note, notice, see, spot, witness

observe [3]
verb to make a comment about something » *"You've had your hair cut," Dad observed.*
comment, mention, remark, say, state

obsession
noun a compulsion to think about something » *Wayne had always had an obsession with trains.*
complex, fixation, mania, preoccupation, thing (informal)

obstacle
noun something that makes it difficult to go forward » *The main obstacle to cleaning my bedroom is the broken vacuum cleaner.*
barrier, difficulty, hindrance, hurdle, impediment, obstruction, bar, stumbling block

obstinate
adjective unwilling to change your mind » *He is obstinate and will not give up.*
dogged, headstrong, inflexible, intractable, stubborn, wilful, intransigent, recalcitrant
antonym: **flexible**

obstruct
verb to block a road or path » *The fallen tree obstructed the road.*
bar, block, choke, clog

The fallen tree obstructed the road.

*My elder sister **obtained** highest honours in her ballet exam.*

obtain
verb to get something
» My elder sister obtained highest honours in her ballet exam.
acquire, get, get hold of, get your hands on (informal), **procure** (formal), **secure** (formal)

obvious
adjective easy to see or understand » It was obvious that Jessica was trying to impress the teacher as she was always the first to put up her hand to volunteer.
apparent, blatant, clear, evident, overt, palpable, plain, self-evident, conspicuous, manifest, patent

occasion 1
noun an important event
» The launch of a ship is a grand occasion.
affair, event

occasion 2
noun an opportunity to do something
» The family meal was the perfect occasion for telling everyone about his travel plans.
chance, opportunity, time

occasional
adjective happening sometimes » We look forward to our occasional trips to the beach; they are always a lot of fun!
intermittent, odd, periodic, sporadic
antonym: **frequent**

occur 1
verb to happen or exist
» Thunderstorms often occur in late summer.
appear, arise, be present, exist, happen, take place

occur 2
verb to come into your mind
» It didn't occur to me to check the calendar, and I turned up on the wrong day.
cross your mind, dawn on, strike

odd
adjective strange or unusual
» He looked odd, wearing sunglasses at night.
bizarre, curious, funny, peculiar, queer (old-fashioned), **singular** (formal), **strange, weird**
antonym: **ordinary**

offend
verb to upset or embarrass someone » I didn't mean to offend you when I commented on your hat.
affront, insult, outrage
antonym: **please**

offensive
adjective rude and upsetting
» Some people found the words of the song offensive.
abusive, insulting, objectionable

*Catherine **offered** us one of the cakes she'd baked.*

offer 1
verb to make something available for someone to take
» Catherine offered us one of the cakes she'd baked.
give, make available, propose, put forward, suggest, tender, extend, proffer, submit

offer 2
noun something that someone offers you » Sue had refused several job offers because they were too far away.
proposition, tender

---

cloud
The Sun was **clouded** with fog.

conceal
They heard birds **concealed** in the trees.

cloak
The lake was **cloaked** in mist.

shroud
The boat was **shrouded** by the haze.

hide
The lake was partly **hidden** by trees.

mask
There were many leaves **masking** the view of the Sun.

screen
The trees **screened** the lake.

obscure
1 verb to make something difficult to see
» The trees **obscured** their view of the lake.

»official

old

2 *adjective* something in the past » In the **old** days, knights went into battle to defend their king.

ancient
In **ancient** times, the Romans conquered much of Europe.

bygone
Archaeology can tell us about **bygone** eras.

earlier
The painter's **earlier** work is more colourful.

early
In the **early** days of television, programs were in black and white.

ex
He felt awkward seeing his **ex**-wife.

former
She always greeted her **former** teacher with a hug.

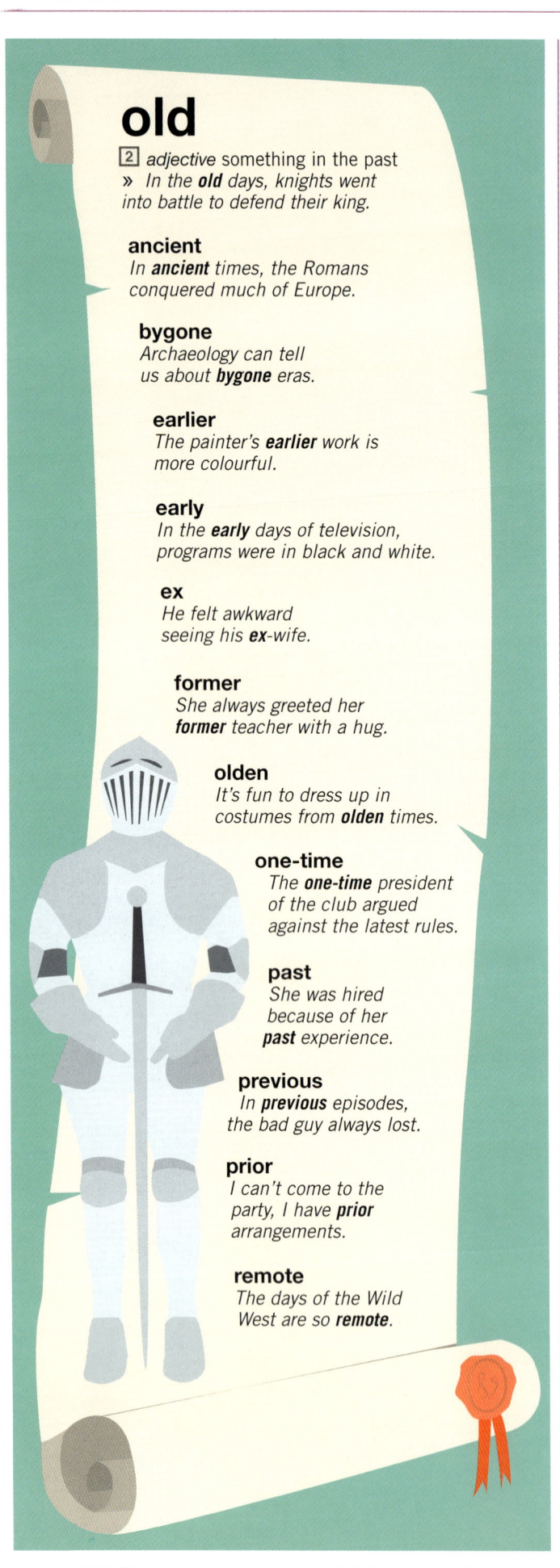

olden
It's fun to dress up in costumes from **olden** times.

one-time
The **one-time** president of the club argued against the latest rules.

past
She was hired because of her **past** experience.

previous
In **previous** episodes, the bad guy always lost.

prior
I can't come to the party, I have **prior** arrangements.

remote
The days of the Wild West are so **remote**.

official 1
adjective approved by someone in authority » *Official figures show that more people use the pool in summer than winter.*
authorized, certified, formal, licensed
antonym: **unofficial**

official 2
noun someone in authority » *We asked an official for directions to our seats.*
executive, officer, representative, bureaucrat, functionary

often
adverb happening many times » *My parents often go to Italy on vacation.*
frequently, repeatedly

okay or OK
adjective (informal) acceptable or satisfactory » *Is it okay if I bring a friend to your party?*
acceptable, all right

old 1
adjective having lived for a long time » *Gareth helped the old lady with her shopping.*
aged, ancient, elderly, venerable
antonym: **young**

old 2
adjective something in the past
◀◀ SEE LEFT

old-fashioned
adjective no longer fashionable » *Granny has an old-fashioned record player.*
antiquated, archaic, dated, obsolete, outdated, outmoded, out of date, passé, behind the times, obsolescent, old-time
antonym: **fashionable**

*Granny has an **old-fashioned** record player.*

omen
noun a sign of what will happen » *There is a proverb that says a black cat crossing your path is an omen of disaster.*
sign, warning, augury, portent

ominous
adjective suggesting that something bad will happen » *There was an ominous silence in the store after Tom broke the expensive vase.*
sinister, threatening, inauspicious, portentous, unpropitious

omit
verb to not include something » *Omit the ham to make the pie suitable for vegetarians.*
exclude, leave out, miss out, skip

only 1
adverb involving one person or thing » *Only Keith knows whether or not he'll be well enough to play.*
just, merely, purely, simply, solely

only 2
adjective having no other examples » *The only tree in the field is an oak.*
one, sole

*The **only** tree in the field is an oak.*

open 1
verb to cause something not to be closed » *Mom opened the door to let us in.*
uncover, undo, unlock, unfasten, unseal
antonym: **shut**

orderly »

*I left an **open** box of chocolates on the table, and my sister ate them.*

open [2]
adjective not closed » *I left an open box of chocolates on the table, and my sister ate them.*
ajar, uncovered, undone, unlocked, unfastened, unsealed
antonym: **shut**

open [3]
adjective not trying to deceive someone » *Ashwin had always been open with his mother and had no secrets from her.*
candid, frank, honest

opening [1]
adjective coming first » *We've got tickets for the opening game of the season.*
first, inaugural, initial, introductory

opening [2]
noun the first part of something » *Lots of people went to the opening of the store.*
beginning, commencement (formal), start
antonym: **conclusion**

*Lots of people went to the **opening** of the store.*

opening [3]
noun a hole or gap » *A fox came into our garden through a narrow opening in the fence.*
chink, cleft, crack, gap, hole, slot, space, vent, aperture, fissure, orifice

opinion
noun a belief or view » *Please tell me what you think about my book—I value your opinion.*
assessment, belief, estimation, judgment, point of view, view, viewpoint

oppose
verb to disagree with something » *The workers opposed the proposed pay cut.*
fight against, resist, speak out against, take a stand against, take issue with
antonym: **support**

*The workers **opposed** the proposed pay cut.*

opposite [1]
adjective completely different from something » *We had opposite views: she wanted to go out and I wanted to stay home.*
conflicting, contrary, contrasting, opposed, reverse, antithetical, diametrically opposed

*Hot is the **opposite** of cold.*

opposite [2]
noun a completely different person or thing » *Hot is the opposite of cold.*
antithesis (formal), contrary, converse, reverse, inverse, obverse

opposition
noun disagreement about something » *Much of the opposition to the school's plan for a new cafeteria came from the pupils.*
disapproval, hostility, resistance
antonym: **support**

oppressed
adjective treated cruelly or unfairly » *The oppressed villagers led a revolt against the king.*
abused, downtrodden, enslaved, tyrannized

oppression
noun cruel or unfair treatment » *The townspeople's fight against oppression became a famous story of bravery.*
persecution, tyranny, subjection, subjugation

optimistic
adjective hopeful about the future » *David woke in an optimistic mood: it was going to be a good day.*
buoyant, confident, hopeful, positive, sanguine
antonym: **pessimistic**

oral
adjective spoken rather than written » *Marie did well in her French oral test.*
spoken, verbal

orange
noun or adjective
Shades of orange:
amber, apricot, carrot, ochre, peach, tangerine

ordeal
noun a difficult and unpleasant experience » *Putting up the tent in the rain was an ordeal.*
hardship, nightmare, torture, trial, tribulation (formal)

order [1]
noun a command by someone in authority » *The crew must follow the orders of the captain.*
command, decree, dictate, directive, instruction

order [2]
noun a well-organized situation » *The kitchen was a mess—it took hours to restore order.*
harmony, regularity, symmetry
antonym: **disorder**

order [3]
verb to tell someone to do something » *The policeman ordered the driver to stop.*
command, decree, direct, instruct, ordain
antonym: **forbid**

orderly
adjective well-organized or well-arranged » *The vehicles were parked in orderly rows.*
neat, regular, tidy
antonym: **disorderly**

*The vehicles were parked in **orderly** rows.*

153

ordinary

ordinary
adjective not special or different » *Fred lived in an ordinary house in the suburbs.*
conventional, normal, regular, routine, standard, usual, run-of-the-mill, unexceptional, unremarkable
antonym: **special**

organization [1]
noun a group or business » *My mother volunteers at many charitable organizations, and is well known in the community.*
association, body, company, confederation, group, institution, outfit (informal)

organization [2]
noun the planning and arranging of something » *Emma was involved in the organization of the party.*
organizing, planning, structuring

organize
verb to plan and arrange something » *Organizing a concert takes a lot of time and effort.*
arrange, establish, plan, set up

origin [1]
noun the beginning or cause of something » *The origins of television date back to the 1920s.*
derivation, root, source, genesis, provenance

origin [2]
noun someone's family background » *Elsa was of Swedish origin.*
ancestry, descent, extraction, lineage, stock

original [1]
adjective being the first example of something » *The original owner of our house lived in it all his life.*
first, initial

original [2]
adjective imaginative and clever » *Adam had a stunningly original idea for the school play—no one had ever seen anything like it before.*
fresh, new, novel, innovative, innovatory
antonym: **unoriginal**

ornament
noun an object that you display » *The shelves were crammed with ornaments.*
adornment, bauble, decoration, knick-knack, trinket

ostentatious
adjective intended to impress people with appearances » *You couldn't miss his ostentatious car—it's large and shiny gold!*
extravagant, flamboyant, flashy, grandiose, pretentious, showy

*You couldn't miss his **ostentatious** car—it's large and shiny gold!*

OUTSTANDING

[1] *adjective* extremely good » *Natalie is an **outstanding** tennis player.*

- brilliant
- superb
- excellent
- great
- exceptional
- first-rate
- first-class

outbreak
noun a sudden occurrence of something » *An outbreak of influenza led to the school being closed for a few days.*
eruption, explosion

outdo
verb to do something better than another person » *She was very competitive and always tried to outdo her sister.*
go one better than, outshine, surpass, top, best, eclipse

outline 1
verb to describe something in a general way » *The mayor outlined his plans to clean up the town.*
sketch, summarize, delineate

outline 2
noun a general description of something » *Peter gave an outline of his presentation to the teacher for review.*
rundown (informal)**, summary, synopsis,** résumé, thumbnail sketch

outline 3
noun the shape of something » *Helena traced around the outline of the rabbit.*
contours, figure, form, shape, silhouette

Helena traced around the outline of the rabbit.

outlook 1
noun your general attitude towards life » *I adopted a positive outlook on life.*
attitude, perspective, view

outlook 2
noun the future prospects of something » *The weather outlook for our vacation next week looks promising.*
future, prospects

out of date
adjective no longer useful » *The information on last week's chart is out of date.*
antiquated, archaic, obsolete, old-fashioned, outdated, outmoded
antonym: **modern**

outside 1
noun the outer part of something » *She stuck leaves on the outside of the glass to decorate it.*
exterior, facade, face, surface
antonym: **inside**

She stuck leaves on the outside of the glass to decorate it.

outside 2
adjective not inside » *We had to use outside showers at the campsite.*
exterior, external, outdoor, outer, outward, surface
antonym: **inside**

outskirts
plural noun the edges of an area » *We live in the outskirts of the city, far from the centre.*
edge, perimeter, periphery, environs

outstanding 1
adjective extremely good
◀◀ SEE LEFT

outstanding 2
adjective still owed » *I have an outstanding debt to my mom, but I'm paying it off slowly.*
due, overdue, owing, payable, unpaid

over
adjective completely finished » *I am glad my exams are finally over.*
at an end, complete, done, finished, gone, past, up

overcome
verb to manage to deal with something » *Molly had overcome her fear of flying and happily boarded the plane.*
conquer, get the better of, master, surmount, triumph over, vanquish (literary)

overlook
verb to ignore or fail to notice something » *Mom overlooked the road sign and missed the turning.*
disregard, forget, ignore, miss, neglect, turn a blind eye to

overrule
verb to reject a decision officially » *The referee's decision was overruled.*
overturn, reverse, countermand, override

oversee
verb to make sure a job is done properly » *The teacher oversaw the pupils' experiment.*
be in charge of, coordinate, direct, manage, preside, supervise

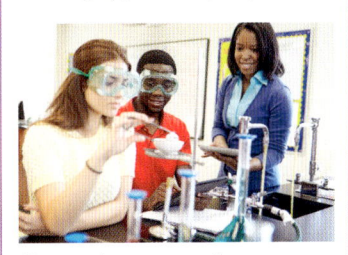

The teacher oversaw the pupils' experiment.

overthrow
verb to remove someone from power by force » *The government was overthrown in a military coup.*
bring down, depose, oust, topple

owner

Fred's fast ball easily overturned the bowling pins.

overturn 1
verb to knock something over » *Fred's fast ball easily overturned the bowling pins.*
capsize, knock down, knock over, tip over, topple, upset, upend, upturn

overturn 2
verb to reject a decision officially » *The school board overturned the principal's decision.*
overrule, reverse, countermand, override

overweight
adjective too fat, and therefore unhealthy » *Being overweight increases your risk of health problems.*
fat, hefty, obese, stout, corpulent, rotund

own 1
adjective belonging to a particular person or thing » *Use your own pencils and stop taking mine!*
personal, private

own 2
verb to have something that belongs to you » *My aunt owns the local corner store.*
have, keep, possess

own 3 : on your own
adverb without other people » *I work best on my own with no one to disturb me.*
alone, by yourself, independently, unaided

owner
noun the person to whom something belongs » *I tried to find the owner of the lost dog.*
possessor, proprietor

155

» **pa**cify

Pp

pacify
verb to calm down someone who is angry » *She shrieked again, refusing to be pacified.*
appease, calm, mollify, placate, soothe, assuage, propitiate

pain 1
noun an unpleasant feeling of physical hurt » *I felt a sharp pain in my neck.*
ache, discomfort, irritation, soreness, trouble, twinge

I felt a sharp pain in my neck.

pain 2
noun a feeling of deep unhappiness » *He felt the pain of rejection when he wasn't picked for the team.*
agony, anguish, distress, grief, misery

painful 1
adjective causing emotional pain » *Driving past our old home brings back painful memories.*
distressing, grievous, saddening, unpleasant

painful 2
adjective causing physical pain » *She fell off her bike, taking a painful knock to the knee.*
aching, excruciating, sore, tender

pale
adjective rather white or without much colour » *Migrating birds filled the pale, misty sky.*
ashen, colourless, faded, sallow, wan, white

panic 1
noun a very strong feeling of fear or anxiety
» *The power outage caused panic among shoppers, who were plunged into darkness.*
alarm, dismay, fear, fright, hysteria, terror

panic 2
verb to become afraid or anxious » *The hikers panicked when the cows began to charge.*
become hysterical, go to pieces, lose it (informal)

The hikers panicked when the cows began to charge.

parade
noun a line of people moving as a display » *A military parade marched through the streets.*
cavalcade, march, pageant, procession, tattoo

paralyze
verb to make someone lose feeling and movement » *She was paralyzed with fear at the sight of the spider.*
cripple, disable

parent
noun your father or your mother
» *I told my parents that I was going out.*
father, folks, mother

parody
noun an amusing imitation of someone else's style
» *Our new play is a parody of a well-known movie.*
imitation, satire, spoof (informal), **takeoff** (informal), lampoon, skit

part 1 : **take part in**
verb to do something with other people » *Thousands took part in this year's marathon.*
be instrumental in, be involved in, have a hand in, join in, participate in, play a part in

Thousands took part in this year's marathon.

part 2
noun a person's involvement in something
» *He tried to conceal his part in the accident.*
capacity, duty, function, involvement, role

pass

1 verb to exceed or go past something

» *Brandon gave a triumphant wave as he passed the finish line.*

go beyond
Wright's speed that day went beyond any of his past records.

outdo
Erikson outdid Wright.

156

passage

part 3
noun a piece or section of something » *I like that part of town.*
bit, fraction, fragment, piece, portion, section

participate
verb to take part in an activity » *Everyone participates in the school quiz.*
be involved in, engage in, enter into, join in, take part

particular 1
adjective relating to only one thing or person » *That particular place is dangerous.*
distinct, exact, express, peculiar, precise, specific

particular 2
adjective especially great or intense » *He took particular care to wash the back of his neck, which was very dirty.*
exceptional, marked, notable, singular, special, uncommon, especial, noteworthy

particular 3
adjective not easily satisfied » *Ted was particular about the colours he used when decorating the room.*
choosy (informal)**, exacting, fastidious, fussy, meticulous**

partly
adverb to some extent but not completely » *This is partly my fault.*
in part (formal)**, in some measure** (formal)**, partially, to some degree, to some extent**

partner 1
noun either member of a couple in a relationship » *My uncle is very happy with his new partner.*
husband, mate, spouse, wife

partner 2
noun the person someone is doing something with » *I have a new tennis partner.*
companion, teammate

party 1
noun an enjoyable social event » *I like to have a party for my birthday every year.*
affair, bash (informal)**, celebration, function, gathering, get-together** (informal)**, reception, shindig** (informal)

I like to have a party for my birthday every year.

party 2
noun an organization for people with the same political beliefs » *Ray joined the party in order to meet like-minded people.*
alliance, clique, coalition, faction, grouping

party 3
noun a group who are doing something together » *The landing party crossed the water to the research station.*
band, crew, gang, squad, team, unit

The landing party crossed the water to the research station.

pass 1
verb to exceed or go past something
▼ SEE BELOW

pass 2
verb to be successful in a test » *Wendy has just passed her cycling proficiency test.*
get through, graduate, qualify, succeed
antonym: **fail**

pass 3
noun a document that allows you to go somewhere » *You'll need your pass to get into the building.*
identification, passport, ticket

passage 1
noun a narrow, empty space that connects places » *He cleared a passage for himself through the crammed streets.*
channel, course, path, road, route, way

passage 2
noun a narrow, built space that connects one place with another » *The passage leads to the courtyard of the old building.*
aisle, corridor, hall, lobby

The passage leads to the courtyard of the old building.

passage 3
noun a section of a book or piece of music » *My flute teacher makes this difficult passage look easy.*
excerpt, extract, quotation, section

---

exceed
Blake **exceeded** his past performance by coming in seventh.

overtake
Khan **overtook** Blake at the last moment.

surpass
Booth **surpassed** his personal best.

outstrip
Abraham tried hard to **outstrip** Booth.

157

passing

passing
adjective lasting only for a short time » *She hoped her son's pink hair was a passing phase.*
fleeting, momentary, short-lived, transitory

passion
noun any strong emotion » *His voice trembled with passion as he spoke of her.*
emotion, excitement, fire, intensity, warmth, zeal

passionate
adjective expressing very strong feelings about something » *I'm passionate about art—I see every exhibition that's on.*
ardent, emotional, heartfelt, impassioned, intense, strong

passive
adjective submissive or not playing an active part » *His passive attitude made it easier for me to take charge.*
docile, receptive, resigned, submissive, acquiescent, compliant, inactive, quiescent

past 1 : the past
noun the period of time before the present » *We would like to put the past behind us.*
antiquity, days gone by, former times, long ago

past 2
adjective happening or existing before the present » *We have wonderful pictures of past generations of our family.*
ancient, bygone, former, olden, previous, erstwhile, quondam
antonym: **future**

*We have wonderful pictures of **past** generations of our family.*

past 3
preposition situated on the other side of somewhere » *My house is just past the shop on the right.*
beyond, by, over

pastime
noun a hobby or something done for pleasure » *My favourite pastime is reading.*
activity, diversion, hobby, recreation

*My favourite **pastime** is reading.*

path 1
noun a strip of ground for people to walk on » *We followed the path along the clifftops.*
footpath, pathway, towpath, track, trail, way

path 2
noun the space ahead of someone as they move along » *A group of reporters stood in the actor's path.*
course, direction, passage, route, way

pathetic 1
adjective causing someone to feel pity » *The shivering dog looked rather pathetic.*
heartbreaking, sad, pitiable, plaintive

pathetic 2
adjective very poor or unsuccessful » *She gave me a pathetic excuse—homework—for not coming to the party.*
feeble, lamentable, pitiful, poor, sorry

patience
noun the ability to stay calm in a difficult situation » *Dealing with four tired, hungry children required all his patience.*
calmness, composure, cool (slang), restraint, tolerance, equanimity, forbearance, imperturbability

patient 1
adjective staying calm in a difficult situation » *Please be patient—we are very busy today.*
calm, composed, long-suffering, philosophical, serene
antonym: **impatient**

patient 2
noun a person receiving medical treatment » *She enjoyed the company of other patients during her stay in the hospital.*
case, invalid, sick person, sufferer

pattern 1
noun a decorative design of repeated shapes » *The cushions have a pattern of colourful stripes.*
design, motif

*The cushions have a **pattern** of colourful stripes.*

pattern 2
noun a diagram or shape used as a guide for making something » *I can knit, but only if I follow a pattern.*
design, diagram, plan, stencil, template

pause 1
verb to stop doing something for a short time » *On leaving, Mel paused at the door to say goodbye again.*
break, delay, halt, rest, take a break, wait

pause 2
noun a short period when activity stops » *There was a pause in conversation while the waiter set down two plates.*
break, gap, halt, interruption, interval, rest, stoppage, hiatus

pay 1
verb to give money to someone to settle a debt » *You can pay with cash or a card.*
compensate, honour, settle, recompense, reimburse, remunerate

*You can **pay** with cash or a card.*

pay 2
verb to give someone a benefit » *It pays to be honest.*
be advantageous, be worthwhile

pay 3
noun money paid to someone for work done » *The factory workers went on strike over pay and conditions.*
earnings, fee, income, payment, salary, wages, emolument, recompense, reimbursement, remuneration, stipend

payment
noun an amount of money that is paid to someone » *Mom made the initial payment for my new computer over the telephone.*
advance, deposit, instalment, premium, remittance

permission »

peace [1]
noun a state of undisturbed calm and quiet » *Hanna left me in peace to finish my book.*
calm, quiet, silence, stillness, tranquillity, quietude, repose

peace [2]
noun freedom from war » *The government is trying to establish peace in the region.*
armistice, cessation of hostilities, truce
antonym: **war**

peaceful
adjective quiet and calm » *The house was peaceful once the children had left for school.*
calm, placid, quiet, serene, still, tranquil

peak [1]
noun the point at which something is at its greatest or best » *Madison was at the peak of her career as a golfer when she won the gold medal.*
climax, culmination, height, high point, zenith, acme, apogee,

peak [2]
noun the pointed top of a mountain » *We flew over snow-covered peaks.*
brow, crest, pinnacle, summit, top, apex

We flew over snow-covered peaks.

peak [3]
verb to reach the highest point or greatest level » *The band's fame peaked some years ago.*
be at its height, climax, come to a head, culminate, reach its highest point

peculiar [1]
adjective strange and perhaps unpleasant » *Lee has a peculiar sense of humour.*
bizarre, curious, funny, odd, queer, strange, weird

peculiar [2]
adjective associated with one particular person or thing » *My uncle has his own peculiar way of doing things.*
distinctive, distinguishing, individual, personal, special, unique, idiosyncratic

peek [1]
verb to have a quick look at something » *The squirrel peeked at me through a hole in the tree trunk.*
glance, peep, snatch a glimpse, sneak a look

The squirrel peeked at me through a hole in the tree trunk.

peek [2]
noun a quick look at something » *Jon took a peek at the presents hidden in the drawer.*
glance, glimpse, look, peep

pent-up
adjective held back for a long time without release » *She had a lot of pent-up anger, which suddenly erupted.*
inhibited, repressed, suppressed

people [1]
plural noun men, women, and children » *Hundreds of people visit the palace every day.*
folk, human beings, humanity, humans, mankind

people [2]
plural noun all the men, women, and children of a particular place » *It's a triumph for the Canadian people.*
citizens, inhabitants, population, public

perceptive
adjective good at noticing or realizing things » *I was impressed by her perceptive account of the poet's life.*
acute, astute, aware, penetrating, sharp, insightful, percipient, perspicacious

perfect [1]
adjective of the highest standard and without fault » *Paolo's English was perfect.*
expert, faultless, flawless, masterly, polished, skilled
antonym: **imperfect**

perfect [2]
adjective complete or absolute » *You have a perfect right to say so, even though I disagree.*
absolute, complete, consummate, sheer, unmitigated, utter

perfect [3]
verb to make something as good as it can be » *She perfected her back flip before the competition.*
hone, improve, polish, refine

She perfected her back flip before the competition.

perform [1]
verb to carry out a task or action » *The people who had performed acts of bravery were awarded medals.*
carry out, complete, do, execute, fulfill

perform [2]
verb to act, dance, or play music in public » *This year, our students are performing a musical.*
act, do, play, present, put on, stage

This year, our students are performing a musical.

perhaps
adverb maybe » *Perhaps you're right.*
conceivably, it could be, maybe, possibly

period
noun a particular length of time » *Imogen will be away for a period of a few months, so she has a lot to organize.*
interval, spell, stretch, term, time, while

permanent
adjective lasting for ever or present all the time » *The farmer built a permanent fence to stop the sheep escaping.*
abiding, constant, enduring, eternal, lasting, perpetual, immutable, imperishable, steadfast
antonym: **temporary**

permission
noun authorization to do something » *I asked permission to leave the table.*
approval, assent, authorization, consent, go-ahead, licence
antonym: **ban**

159

» permit

permit 1
verb to allow something or make it possible » *The guards permitted me to take photographs in the museum when I explained they were for a school project.*
allow, authorize, enable, give the green light to, grant, sanction
antonym: **ban**

permit 2
noun an official document allowing someone to do something » *Mom needed a parking permit to use that parking lot.*
authorization, licence, pass, passport, permission, warrant

persecute
verb to treat someone with continual cruelty and unfairness » *As we trudged through the swamp, we were persecuted by mosquitoes.*
hound, ill-treat, oppress, pick on, torment, torture

person
noun a man, woman, or child » *The amount of sleep we need varies from person to person.*
human, human being, individual, living soul, soul

personal
adjective belonging to a particular person or thing » *Jake put his personal belongings into a locker for safekeeping.*
individual, own, particular, peculiar, private, special

personality 1
noun a person's character and nature » *Shreya has such a kind, friendly personality.*
character, identity, individuality, makeup, nature, psyche

personality 2
noun a famous person in entertainment or sport » *A well-known television personality came to open our new sports centre.*
big name, celebrity, famous name, household name, star

persuade
verb to make someone do something by reason or charm » *Cy persuaded his mother to let him stay up late.*
bring around (informal), **coax, entice, induce, sway, talk into, win over,** impel, inveigle

persuasive
adjective convincing » *Leah gave a persuasive argument against playing computer games.*
compelling, conclusive, effective, plausible, powerful, winning, cogent, incontrovertible
antonym: **unconvincing**

pessimistic
adjective believing that bad things will happen » *He has a pessimistic view of life.*
despondent, gloomy, glum, hopeless, negative
antonym: **optimistic**

pest 1
noun an insect or animal that damages crops or livestock » *The farmer was dismayed to see that half of the crop had been lost to pests.*
blight, scourge

picture

drawing — I used pencils to make a **drawing** of my cat.

photograph — I took a **photograph** of the boat.

portrait — Wilf's **portrait** really looks like him.

1 *noun* a drawing, painting, or photograph » *What a lovely picture of our house!*

illustration — I think the **illustrations** in that book bring the story to life.

selfie (informal) — My friend makes silly expressions when she takes **selfies**.

sketch — I made a series of **sketches** of the dog playing with the ball.

painting — We went to the art gallery to look at the **painting** by Emily Carr.

pink »

My friend's little brother is a pest.

pest [2]
noun an annoying person » *My friend's little brother is a pest.*
bane, bore, nuisance, pain (informal), **pain in the neck** (informal)

pester
verb to bother someone continually » *Our father gets annoyed when we pester him for candy.*
annoy, badger, bother, bug (informal), **drive someone up the wall** (slang), **get on someone's nerves** (informal), bedevil, chivvy

petty [1]
adjective small and unimportant » *The competition organizers have to abide by endless rules and petty regulations.*
insignificant, measly (informal), **trifling, trivial, unimportant**

petty [2]
adjective selfish and small-minded » *I think that attitude is a bit petty.*
cheap, mean, small-minded

phone [1]
noun a device that allows you to speak to someone in another place » *Will you please answer the phone?*
cell, cellphone, horn (slang), **mobile, mobile phone, smartphone, telephone**

phone [2]
verb to contact a person by phone » *Phone me when you get home.*
call, contact, ring, telephone

phony
adjective (informal) false and intended to deceive » *We found out later that his account of events was phony.*
bogus, counterfeit, fake, false, forged, sham, feigned, spurious
antonym: **genuine**

pick [1]
verb to choose something » *Mom picked the biggest, juiciest oranges that she could find.*
choose, decide upon, handpick, opt for, select, settle on

Mom picked the biggest, juiciest oranges that she could find.

pick [2]
verb to remove a flower or fruit with your fingers » *Gareth helps his mother pick apples.*
gather, harvest, pluck

pick [3]
noun the best » *Only the pick of the school's athletes are chosen to go to the national championships.*
best, elite, flower, pride

pick on
verb to criticize someone unfairly or treat them unkindly » *The teacher always picks on me to answer the question.*
bait, tease, torment

picture [1]
noun a drawing, painting, or photograph
◀◀ SEE LEFT

picture [2]
verb to imagine something clearly » *Sam pictured her with long black hair.*
conceive of, imagine, see, visualize, envision, see in the mind's eye

piece [1]
noun a portion or part of something » *He helped himself to the biggest piece of cake.*
bit, chunk, fragment, part, portion, slice

He helped himself to the biggest piece of cake.

piece [2]
noun something that has been written, created, or composed » *Our music teacher composed this piece for the school choir.*
article, composition, creation, study, work

piece together
verb to assemble things or parts to make something complete » *Archaeologists painstakingly pieced together the fragments of bone.*
assemble, join, mend, patch together, repair, restore

pierce
verb to make a hole in something with a sharp instrument » *She pierced the potatoes with a fork so they wouldn't explode in the oven.*
bore, drill, lance, penetrate, puncture

pig
noun a farm animal kept for meat » *The pigs wallowed gleefully in the thick mud.*
hog, piggy (informal), **porker, swine**
related words:
adjective **porcine**; male **boar**; female **sow**; young **piglet**; collective noun **litter**; habitation **sty**

pile [1]
noun a quantity of things lying one on top of another » *Piles of books covered the floor.*
heap, hoard, mound, mountain, stack

pile [2]
noun the raised fibres of a soft surface » *My feet sank into the carpet's luxurious pile.*
down, fur, nap

pile [3]
verb to put things one on top of another » *He piled his plate with sandwiches.*
heap, hoard, stack

He piled his plate with sandwiches.

pink
noun or adjective » *Shades of pink:*
coral, fuchsia, oyster pink, rose, salmon, shell pink, shocking pink

» **pit**

*Tim carefully crawled away from the edge of the **pit**.*

pit
noun a large hole in something » *Tim carefully crawled away from the edge of the pit.*
chasm, hole, pothole

pity 1
verb to feel sorry for someone » *I pitied Austin for not being allowed out to the fair.*
feel for, feel sorry for, sympathize with

pity 2
noun sympathy for other people's suffering » *She saw no pity in their stony faces.*
charity, compassion, kindness, mercy, sympathy, understanding, clemency, forbearance

pity 3
noun a regrettable fact » *It's a pity we can't all have the same opportunities.*
crying shame, shame

place 1
noun any point or area » *We meet in the same place every week.*
area, location, point, position, site, spot

place 2 : take place
verb to happen » *The meeting took place on Thursday.*
go on, happen, occur, transpire

place 3
verb to put something somewhere » *Chairs were placed in rows for the parents.*
deposit, locate, plant, position, put, situate

plain 1
adjective very simple in style with no decoration » *It was a plain, grey stone house.*
austere, bare, spartan, stark
antonym: **fancy**

plain 2
adjective obvious and easy to recognize or understand » *It was plain to me that we were lost.*
clear, comprehensible, distinct, evident, obvious, unmistakable

plain 3
noun a level, often treeless, extent of land » *The plain stretched as far as the horizon.*
flat, flatland, grassland, lowland, mesa, plateau, prairie, savannah, steppe, tableland

*The **plain** stretched as far as the horizon.*

plan 1
noun a way thought out to do something » *We made a plan of what to do during the holiday.*
method, proposal, scheme, strategy, system

plan 2
noun a detailed diagram of something » *The receptionist gave us a plan of the hotel.*
blueprint, diagram, layout, scale drawing

plan 3
verb to decide in detail what is to be done » *I always plan my birthday party months in advance.*
arrange, design, devise, draft, formulate

play 1
verb to take part in games or use toys » *Polly was playing with her teddy bear.*
amuse yourself, entertain yourself, frolic, have fun

play 2
verb to take part in a sport or game » *Alan was playing cards with his friends.*
compete, participate, take on, take part, vie with

play 3
noun a piece of drama performed on stage, radio, or television » *The school took us to see a play by Shakespeare.*
comedy, drama, pantomime, show, tragedy

plead
verb to beg someone for something » *She pleaded with her mother to let her go on the ride.*
appeal, ask, beg, beseech (literary), **implore**

pleasant 1
adjective enjoyable or attractive » *We have a pleasant garden full of flowers.*
agreeable, delightful, enjoyable, lovely, nice, pleasurable
antonym: **unpleasant**

*We have a **pleasant** garden full of flowers.*

pleasant 2
adjective friendly or charming » *The hotel staff were pleasant and helpful.*
affable, amiable, charming, friendly, likeable, nice
antonym: **unpleasant**

please
verb to give pleasure to » *I tidied my bedroom to please my mother.*
amuse, charm, delight, entertain

pleased
adjective happy or satisfied » *I'm pleased my best friend is coming on vacation with us.*
contented, delighted, glad, happy, satisfied

pleasure
noun a feeling of happiness and satisfaction » *The dog takes pleasure in having its chest scratched.*
amusement, enjoyment, happiness, joy, satisfaction

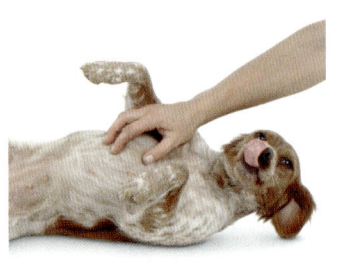

*The dog takes **pleasure** in having its chest scratched.*

plentiful
adjective existing in large amounts » *We have a plentiful supply of food for our expedition.*
abundant, ample, bountiful, copious, infinite, lavish, profuse
antonym: **scarce**

plenty
noun a lot of something » *Our pet hamster has plenty of energy and loves to run in its wheel.*
enough, a great deal, heaps (informal), lots (informal), **plethora**

plot 1
noun a secret plan made by a group of people » *The boys made a plot to ambush their little sister.*
conspiracy, intrigue, plan, scheme, cabal, machination, stratagem

162

polite

1 *adjective* having good manners
» He is **polite** and always remembers to say thank you.

civil
He is **civil** to his parents except when he's tired and hungry.

courteous
He is **courteous** and gives up his seat on the bus.

respectful
He is **respectful** of his grandparents' views.

well behaved
He is **well behaved** in front of the teachers.

well mannered
He is **well mannered** and thinks of other people.

antonym:
rude
She is **rude** and always interrupts.

---

plot 2
noun the story of a novel or play » The movie has a ludicrously complicated plot.
narrative, scenario, story, story line

plot 3
verb to plan something secretly with others » The students plotted to leave school early so they didn't have to play soccer in the rain.
conspire, hatch, plan, scheme, cabal, collude, machinate

plug 1
noun a small, round object for blocking a hole » She pulled the plug out and the water flowed away.
bung, cork, stopper

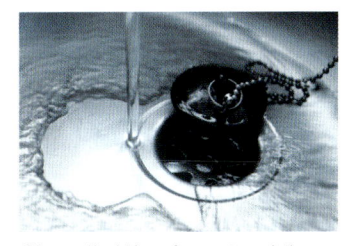

She pulled the plug out and the water flowed away.

plug 2
verb to block a hole with something » The plumber worked all night to plug the leak.
block, fill, seal

plump
adjective rather fat » That cat is starting to look plump.
beefy (informal)**, burly, chubby, fat, stout, tubby**

point 1
noun the purpose or meaning something has » The point of wearing a coat is to be warm.
aim, goal, intention, object, purpose

point 2
noun a quality or feature » Tact was never her strong point.
attribute, characteristic, feature, quality, side, trait

point 3
noun the thin sharp end of something » He pricked his finger on the point of a needle.
nib, prong, tip

poison
noun a substance that can harm or kill people or animals » Mercury is a known poison.
toxin, venom
related word: *adjective* **toxic**

poisonous
adjective containing something that causes death or illness » A few plants are poisonous.
noxious, toxic, venomous

poke 1
verb to jab or prod someone or something » She poked a knife into the cake to see if it was cooked.
dig, elbow, jab, nudge, prod, stab

poke 2
noun a jab or prod » She gave Richard a playful poke.
dig, jab, nudge, prod

polish 1
verb to improve a skill or technique » I need to polish my writing skills.
brush up, improve, perfect, refine

Every morning, he polished his shoes until they shone.

polish 2
verb to make smooth and shiny by rubbing » Every morning, he polished his shoes until they shone.
buff, shine, wax

polish 3
noun elegance or refinement » The lyrics lack the polish of his later songs.
class (informal)**, elegance, finesse, grace, refinement, style,** politesse, suavity, urbanity

polite 1
adjective having good manners
▲ SEE ABOVE

ponder

verb to think about something deeply
» He **pondered** which course of action to take.

contemplate
He sat and **contemplated** his plans.

consider
He **considered** what was the right thing to do.

think
He **thought** about what to do next.

mull over
He **mulled over** what options to choose.

brood
He **brooded** over the meaning of life.

reflect
He **reflected** on the dream he'd had last night.

possession »

polite [2]
adjective cultivated or refined » *Certain words are not acceptable in polite society.*
cultured, genteel, refined, sophisticated, urbane

politeness
noun the quality of being civil to someone » *She listened to him, but only out of politeness.*
civility, courtesy, decency, etiquette

pollute
verb to contaminate with something harmful » *Heavy industry pollutes our rivers with nasty chemicals.*
contaminate, infect, poison, taint, adulterate, befoul, smirch

Heavy industry pollutes our rivers with nasty chemicals.

pompous
adjective behaving in a way that is too serious and self-important » *Cecil is a pompous man with a high opinion of himself.*
arrogant, grandiose, presumptuous, pretentious, puffed up, pontifical, portentous, vainglorious

ponder
verb to think about something deeply
◀◀ SEE LEFT

poor [1]
adjective having little money » *He was poor until he took a well-paid job.*
broke (informal)**, destitute, hard up** (informal)**, impoverished, penniless, poverty-stricken**
antonym: **rich**

poor [2]
adjective of a low quality or standard » *The lead character was a poor actor.*
feeble, inferior, mediocre, second-rate, shoddy, unsatisfactory

popular [1]
adjective liked or approved of by a lot of people » *These delicious pastries are popular.*
fashionable, favourite, in demand, in favour, sought-after, well-liked
antonym: **unpopular**

popular [2]
adjective involving or intended for ordinary people » *The down-to-earth politician was hoping to win the popular vote.*
common, conventional, general, universal

portion
noun a part or amount of something » *I have spent a large portion of my life here.*
bit, chunk, helping, part, piece, segment, serving

pose [1]
verb to ask a question » *When I finally posed the question "Why?" she merely shrugged.*
ask, put, submit, posit

When I finally posed the question "Why?" she merely shrugged.

pose [2]
verb to pretend to be someone else » *Gadi posed as a singer to gain backstage access.*
impersonate, masquerade as, pass yourself off as, pretend to be

posh [1]
adjective (informal) smart, fashionable, and expensive » *We stayed in a posh hotel.*
classy (informal)**, elegant, exclusive, fashionable, smart, stylish, up-market**

posh [2]
adjective upper-class » *He sounded very posh on the phone.*
aristocratic, genteel, upper-class, patrician (formal)
antonym: **common**

position [1]
verb to put something somewhere » *Plants were positioned on either side of our front door.*
arrange, lay out, locate, place, put

Plants were positioned on either side of our front door.

position [2]
noun the place where someone or something is » *The ship's name and position were reported to the coastguard.*
location, place, point, whereabouts

positive [1]
adjective completely sure about something » *I was positive I'd been there before.*
certain, confident, convinced, sure

positive [2]
adjective providing definite proof of the truth or identity of something » *We found positive evidence that the cupboard raider was a mouse.*
clear, clear-cut, conclusive, concrete, firm, incontrovertible, indisputable, unequivocal

positive [3]
adjective tending to emphasize what is good » *I'm hoping for a positive response.*
constructive, helpful
antonym: **negative**

possess [1]
verb to have something as a quality » *The athlete possesses both stamina and great technique.*
be blessed with, be born with, enjoy, have

possess [2]
verb to own something » *He was said to possess a huge fortune.*
control, hold, occupy, own

possession
noun ownership of something » *Carl had possession of the ball.*
control, custody, ownership, tenure

Carl had possession of the ball.

a b c d e f g h i j k l m n o **p** q r s t u v w x y z

» possessions

*We packed up our **possessions**, ready for moving house.*

possessions
plural noun the things owned by someone » *We packed up our possessions, ready for moving house.*
assets, belongings, effects, estate, property, things

possibility
noun something that might be true or might happen » *Daisy cheered up at the possibility of an ice cream.*
chance, hope, likelihood, odds, prospect, risk

possible 1
adjective likely to happen or able to be done » *She was grateful to her music teacher for making the concert possible.*
attainable, feasible, practicable, viable, workable
antonym: **impossible**

possible 2
adjective likely or capable of being true or correct » *It's possible there's an explanation for the delay.*
conceivable, imaginable, likely, potential

postpone
verb to put off to a later time » *The visit has been postponed until tomorrow.*
adjourn, defer, delay, put back, put off, shelve

potential 1
adjective possible but not yet actual » *Suhel was looking for potential sponsors for his marathon attempt.*
likely, possible, probable

potential 2
noun ability to achieve future success » *The tennis coach recognized the potential of the young player.*
ability, aptitude, capability, capacity, power, wherewithal

pour
verb to flow quickly and in large quantities » *She put her umbrella up as it was pouring with rain.*
course, flow, gush, run, spout, stream

*She put her umbrella up as it was **pouring** with rain.*

poverty
noun the state of being very poor » *I'm raising money for a charity that aims to tackle poverty in developing countries.*
destitution, hardship, insolvency, want, beggary, indigence, penury, privation

power 1
noun control over people and activities » *A Prime Minister has great power and influence.*
ascendancy, control, dominion, sovereignty, supremacy

power 2
noun authority to do something » *The police have the power of arrest.*
authority, authorization, licence, privilege, right

power 3
noun physical strength » *Power and bulk are vital to success in football.*
brawn, might, strength, vigour

powerful 1
adjective able to control people and events » *The USA is one of the world's most powerful countries.*
commanding, dominant, influential

powerful 2
adjective physically strong
▶▶ SEE RIGHT

powerful 3
adjective having a strong effect » *It was a powerful argument, but I remained unconvinced.*
compelling, convincing, effective, forceful, persuasive, telling

powerless
adjective unable to control or influence events » *I was powerless to stop her.*
helpless, impotent, incapable

practical 1
adjective involving experience rather than theory » *The book is full of practical suggestions for healthy eating.*
applied, pragmatic, sensible

practical 2
adjective likely to be effective » *The clothes are lightweight and practical for hot weather.*
functional, sensible
antonym: **impractical**

practical 3
adjective able to deal effectively with problems » *She has the practical common sense essential in a team leader.*
accomplished, experienced, proficient, seasoned, skilled, veteran

practice 1
noun something that people do regularly » *We've been getting to know the local practices since moving to the village.*
custom, habit, method, routine, way

practice 2
noun regular training or exercise » *I need more practice to improve my skills.*
drill, exercise, preparation, rehearsal, training

practise 1
verb to do something repeatedly so as to gain skill » *Louis practises cycling for half an hour every day.*
polish, rehearse, train

*Louis **practises** cycling for half an hour every day.*

practise 2
verb to take part in the activities of a religion, craft, or custom » *Acupuncture has been practised in China for thousands of years.*
do, follow, observe

praise 1
verb to express strong approval of someone » *The teacher praised Rob for his test results.*
admire, applaud, approve, congratulate, pay tribute to, acclaim, eulogize, extol, laud
antonym: **criticize**

praise 2
noun something said or written to show approval » *She is full of praise for her students.*
accolade, approval, commendation, congratulation, tribute, eulogy, panegyric
antonym: **criticism**

precaution
noun an action intended to prevent something from happening » *When on a boat, wearing a life jacket is an essential precaution.*
insurance, preventative measure, protection, provision, safeguard

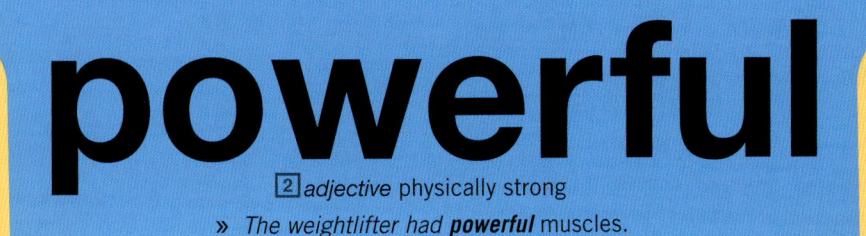

precaution »

powerful

[2] *adjective* physically strong
» The weightlifter had **powerful** muscles.

mighty
He was as **mighty** as a giant.

strapping
He was a **strapping** lad.

strong
He was as **strong** as an ox.

sturdy
He had a **sturdy** build.

vigorous
He was young and **vigorous**.

antonym: **weak**
After his illness, he was too **weak** to lift anything.

precious

*My mother keeps her **precious** ring in a small case.*

precious
adjective of great value and importance » *My mother keeps her precious ring in a small case.*
expensive, invaluable, priceless, prized, valuable
antonym: **worthless**

precise
adjective exact and accurate » *Millie gave such precise answers that she got full marks.*
accurate, actual, correct, exact, particular, specific
antonym: **vague**

predicament
noun a difficult situation » *The decision to go will leave my aunt in a predicament.*
fix (informal), **hot water** (informal), **jam** (informal), **scrape** (informal), **tight spot**

predict
verb to say that something will happen in the future » *The judges are predicting a close contest.*
forecast, foresee, foretell, prophesy, forebode, portend, presage, soothsay

prediction
noun something that is forecast in advance » *His prediction that it would rain turned out to be true.*
forecast, prophecy

prefer
verb to like one thing more than another thing » *Does he prefer a particular sort of music?*
be partial to, favour, go for, incline towards, like better

prejudice 1
noun an unreasonable or unfair dislike or preference » *Edie complained that the company had shown prejudice against her because of her age.*
bias, partiality, preconception

prejudice 2
noun intolerance towards certain people or groups » *As outsiders, we experienced some prejudice when we first moved to the area, but that has gone now people know us.*
bigotry, chauvinism, discrimination, racism, sexism

premonition
noun a feeling that something unpleasant is going to happen » *He had a premonition that there would be an earthquake.*
foreboding, funny feeling (informal), **omen, sign,** portent, presage, presentiment

preoccupied
adjective totally involved with something or deep in thought » *I am preoccupied with the book I'm writing.*
absorbed, engrossed, immersed, oblivious, wrapped up

present 1
adjective being at a place or event » *Dad was present when Simon received his prize.*
at hand, here, in attendance, there
antonym: **absent**

present 2
noun something given to someone » *Vicky gave me a birthday present.*
donation, gift, offering

present 3
verb to give something to someone » *The Mayor presented the prizes.*
award, bestow, donate, give, grant, hand out

press 1
verb to apply force or weight to something » *Press the blue button.*
compress, crush, mash, push, squeeze

press 2
verb to try hard to persuade someone to do something » *My parents are pressing me to invite more people to my birthday party.*
beg, implore, petition, plead, pressurize, urge, entreat, exhort, importune

pretend
verb to claim or give the appearance of something untrue » *Vince pretended to be asleep, but I knew better.*
counterfeit, fake, falsify, feign, pass yourself off as

pretentious
adjective making unjustified claims to importance » *Many critics thought her work and ideas pretentious and empty.*
affected, conceited, ostentatious, pompous, snobbish, bombastic, vainglorious

pretty 1
adjective attractive in a delicate way » *The bouquet of colourful flowers looked pretty.*
attractive, beautiful, cute, lovely

*The bouquet of colourful flowers looked **pretty**.*

pretty 2
adverb (informal) quite or rather » *He spoke English pretty well.*
fairly, kind of (informal), **quite, rather**

prevent
verb to stop something from happening » *Loella was prevented from going on the fairground ride because she wasn't tall enough.*
avert, foil, hinder, impede, stop, thwart

*Loella was **prevented** from going on the fairground ride because she wasn't tall enough.*

previous
adjective happening or existing before something else » *Zac had won the competition the previous year.*
earlier, former, one-time, past, preceding, prior

price 1
noun the amount of money paid for something » *The price of milk has gone up recently.*
amount, charge, cost, fee, figure, value

price 2
verb to fix the price or value of something » *I don't know why it has been priced so high.*
cost, estimate, put a price on, value

pride 1
noun satisfaction about your achievements » *The chef took pride in the meal he'd made.*
delight, pleasure, satisfaction

pride 2
noun an excessively high opinion of yourself » *His pride made him unpopular.*
arrogance, conceit, egotism, smugness, snobbery, vanity, haughtiness, hauteur, hubris, superciliousness
antonym: **humility**

prim
adjective behaving very correctly and easily shocked by anything rude » *My great grandmother's generation were all rather prim and proper.*
proper, prudish, puritanical, straitlaced, uptight (informal)

prime 1
adjective main or most important » *Our prime reason for wanting to visit Italy is to eat a lot of pasta.*
chief, leading, main, principal

prime 2
adjective of the best quality » *He bought a prime cut of meat for the barbecue.*
best, choice, first-rate, select, superior

primitive
adjective very simple or basic » *She made a primitive shelter in the garden.*
crude, rough, rude, rudimentary, simple

*She made a **primitive** shelter in the garden.*

principal
adjective main or most important » *Jay's principal concern is winning the race.*
chief, first, foremost, main, major, primary, prime

principle 1
noun a set of moral rules guiding personal conduct » *She resigned from her job out of principle.*
conscience, integrity, morals, scruples, sense of duty

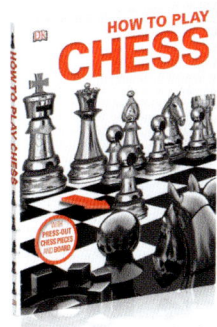

*The book explains the **principles** of chess.*

principle 2
noun a general rule or scientific law » *The book explains the principles of chess.*
axiom, canon, doctrine, fundamental, law, dictum, precept, verity

prison
noun a building where criminals are kept in captivity » *The prison had high fences and security cameras everywhere.*
dungeon, jail, joint (slang), **slammer** (slang), **lock-up** (informal), **penal institution, penitentiary**

prisoner
noun someone kept in prison or captivity » *Prisoners are allowed out for an hour's exercise each day.*
captive, convict, hostage

private 1
adjective for few people rather than people in general » *We hired a private room for the party.*
exclusive, individual, personal, special

private 2
adjective taking place among a small number of people » *They were married in a private ceremony.*
clandestine, confidential, secret
antonym: **public**

prize 1
noun a reward given to the winner of something
▶▶ SEE RIGHT

prize

1 *noun* a reward given to the winner of something » *He won first prize in the piano competition.*

accolade
*She received the ultimate **accolade** of a scholarship.*

*He won the **award** for creative writing.*

*She was showered with **honours**, among them the swimming trophy.*

award

honour

*The cup was a **reward** for winning the school quiz.*

*She won the **trophy** for athletics.*

reward

trophy

» **pr**ize

promise

[1] *verb* to say that you will definitely do or not do something
» *I **promise** I'll come back.*

give your word
I give my word I'll be here.

pledge
I pledge to return.

assure
I assure you I'll return.

vow
I vow that I will be back.

guarantee
I guarantee you'll see me soon.

prize [2]
adjective of the highest quality or standard » *The farmer led his **prize** bull into the ring.*
award-winning, first-rate, outstanding, top

*The farmer led his **prize** bull into the ring.*

prize [3]
verb to value highly » *These vases are **prized** by collectors.*
cherish, esteem, treasure, value

probability
noun the likelihood of something happening » *There's a **probability** that we'll miss the train.*
chances, likelihood, odds, prospect

probable
adjective likely to be true or to happen » *The **probable** cost of our vacation to the Bahamas will be high.*
apparent, feasible, likely, on the cards, plausible, credible, ostensible
antonym: **improbable**

probably
adverb in all likelihood » *The party is **probably** going to be in late August.*
doubtless, in all probability, likely, presumably

problem [1]
noun an unsatisfactory situation causing difficulties » *The teacher asked the unruly student what the **problem** was.*
difficulty, predicament, quandary, trouble

*Flora worked out the math **problem** on the board.*

problem [2]
noun a puzzle that needs to be solved » *Flora worked out the math **problem** on the board.*
conundrum, puzzle, riddle

procedure
noun the correct or usual way of doing something » *He did not follow the correct **procedure** in booking his ticket.*
method, policy, practice, process, strategy, system

proceed [1]
verb to start doing or continue to do something » *I had no idea how to **proceed**.*
begin, carry on, continue, get underway, go on, start

proceed [2]
verb (formal) to move in a particular direction » *She **proceeded** along the hallway.*
advance, continue, go on, make your way, progress, travel

process [1]
noun a method of doing or producing something » *The building **process** would take three years.*
course of action, means, method, procedure, system

process [2]
verb to deal with or treat something » *Your application is being **processed**.*
deal with, dispose of, handle, take care of

produce [1]
verb to make something » *Chocolate is **produced** from cocoa beans.*
construct, create, invent, make, manufacture

produce 2
verb to bring out something so it can be seen or discussed » *To rent a car, you must produce a driver's licence.*
advance, bring forward, bring to light, put forward

product
noun something that is made to be sold » *All of our products are made with natural ingredients.*
commodity, goods, merchandise, produce

productive 1
adjective producing a large number of things » *Our apple trees are very productive this year.*
fertile, fruitful, prolific, fecund, generative
antonym: **unproductive**

Our apple trees are very productive this year.

productive 2
adjective bringing favourable results » *I hope that all this extra work will be productive.*
constructive, useful, valuable, worthwhile
antonym: **unproductive**

profession
noun a job that requires advanced education or training » *Harper was a doctor by profession.*
business, career, occupation

proficient
adjective able to do something well » *Erin is proficient in several languages.*
able, accomplished, adept, capable, competent, efficient, skilful, skilled
antonym: **incompetent**

profit 1
noun money gained in business or trade » *The new business made a huge profit in its first year.*
earnings, proceeds, revenue, surplus, takings
antonym: **loss**

profit 2
verb to gain or benefit from something » *We profited from the low turnout—there was a lot of leftover food.*
capitalize on, exploit, make the most of, take advantage of

program 1
noun a set of instructions that a computer follows to perform a task » *The architect used a computer program to draw up his plans for the house.*
app, application, software

The architect used a computer program to draw up his plans for the house.

program 2
verb to make a plan or plot out instructions » *Diana programmed the TV to record the Saturday show.*
compile, formulate, lineup, list, map out, set up

program 3
noun a planned series of events » *The orchestra has a program of 12 concerts over the next few months.*
agenda, schedule, timetable

program 4
noun a broadcast on radio or television » *He enjoys watching programs about space travel.*
broadcast, show

He enjoys watching programs about space travel.

progress 1
noun improvement or development » *Lou is making progress in writing her novel.*
advance, breakthrough, headway, improvement

progress 2
verb to become more advanced or skilful » *My litttle brother is progressing—he can count to 10 now and he knows colours.*
advance, blossom, develop, improve

prohibit
verb to forbid something or make it illegal » *Littering is prohibited in all provincial parks.*
ban, forbid, outlaw, prevent
antonym: **allow**

prominent 1
adjective important » *A prominent scientist gave us an inspiring lecture.*
eminent, famous, important, notable, noted, renowned, well-known

The castle stood in a prominent position at the top of a steep hill.

prominent 2
adjective very noticeable, or sticking out a long way » *The castle stood in a prominent position at the top of a steep hill.*
conspicuous, eye-catching, jutting, noticeable, obvious, pronounced, striking, blatant, salient

promise 1
verb to say that you will definitely do or not do something
◀◀ **SEE LEFT**

promise 2
verb to show signs of » *This promises to be a great book.*
hint at, indicate, show signs of, augur, bespeak, betoken

promise 3
noun an undertaking to do or not do something » *If you make a promise, you should keep it.*
assurance, guarantee, pledge, undertaking, vow

promising
adjective seeming likely to be good or successful » *He was a promising young athlete.*
gifted, rising, talented, up-and-coming

promote 1
verb to encourage the progress or success of something » *My parents have always promoted healthy eating.*
back, support

promote »

promote

promote [2]
verb to encourage the sale of a product by advertising » *She's in Europe promoting her new movie.*
advertise, plug (informal), **publicize**

promote [3]
verb to raise someone to a higher rank or position » *Mom has been promoted twice in two years.*
elevate, upgrade

prompt [1]
verb to make someone decide to do something » *Rising bus fares have prompted people to walk more.*
cause, induce, inspire, motivate, spur

prompt [2]
verb to encourage someone to say something » *"What was that you were saying about a guided tour?" he prompted her.*
coax, remind

prompt [3]
adjective done without any delay » *The road needs prompt repairs following the storm.*
immediate, instant, instantaneous, quick, rapid, swift

promptly
adverb exactly at the time mentioned » *He arrived promptly at 8 p.m. for the party.*
exactly, on the dot, precisely, promptly, sharp

He arrived promptly at 8 p.m. for the party.

prone [1]
adjective having a tendency to be affected by or to do something » *Lucy is prone to forgetfulness.*
disposed, given, inclined, liable, susceptible

prone [2]
adjective lying flat and face downwards » *She lay prone on the grass.*
face down, prostrate

She lay prone on the grass.

proof
noun evidence that confirms that something is true or exists » *At last, we had proof that rabbits were eating our lettuce.*
confirmation, evidence, testimony, verification, authentication, certification, corroboration, substantiation

proper [1]
adjective correct or most suitable » *Mick decided that the proper course of action would be to say nothing.*
appropriate, apt, correct, fitting, right, suitable
antonym: **improper**

proper [2]
adjective accepted or conventional » *Jess wanted a proper, white wedding.*
accepted, conventional, orthodox

property [1]
noun the things that belong to someone » *Mark was protective of his personal property, and rarely let anyone borrow anything.*
assets, belongings, effects, estate, possessions

property [2]
noun a characteristic or quality » *Peppermint leaves have powerful healing properties when drunk as an infusion or eaten as a herb.*
attribute, characteristic, feature, hallmark, quality, trait

proportion
noun part of an amount or group » *A small proportion of the class chose to study a second language.*
percentage, quota, segment, share

prospect
noun expectation or something anticipated » *Mia was excited by the prospect of arriving back home as she had been away for a long time.*
expectation, hope, outlook, promise

protect
verb to prevent someone or something from being harmed » *The traffic cones protected the man while he was mending the road.*
defend, guard, safeguard, shelter, shield

The traffic cones protected the man while he was mending the road.

He wears plenty of layers for protection against the cold.

protection
noun something that protects » *He wears plenty of layers for protection against the cold.*
barrier, buffer, cover, safeguard, shelter

protest [1]
verb to disagree with someone or object to something » *Bethany protested that she was innocent.*
complain, disagree, disapprove, object, oppose, demur, expostulate, remonstrate

protest [2]
noun a strong objection » *The teacher ignored their protests and sent them out for a run in the rain.*
complaint, objection, outcry

proud
adjective feeling pleasure or satisfaction » *I was proud of our players today.*
gratified by, honoured, pleased

prove
verb to provide evidence that something is definitely true » *This proves that you were right all along.*
ascertain, confirm, demonstrate, establish, verify, authenticate, corroborate, evince, substantiate
antonym: **disprove**

provide
verb to make something available to someone » *We'll provide refreshments after the game.*
contribute, equip, furnish, outfit, supply

provoke 1
verb to try to make someone angry » *I didn't want to do anything to provoke the bulldog.*
anger, annoy, enrage, goad, insult, irritate, tease

provoke 2
verb to cause an unpleasant reaction » *His sister's teasing finally provoked the little boy to hit her.*
cause, evoke, produce, prompt, rouse, set off, spark off

pry
verb to try to find out about someone else's private business » *Our neighbour is always prying into our business.*
interfere, intrude, poke your nose in (informal), **poke your nose into** (informal), **snoop** (informal)

*Our neighbour is always **prying** into our business.*

public 1
noun people in general » *Members of the public were picked at random to appear on the TV show.*
masses, nation, people, populace, society

public 2
adjective relating to people in general » *There was a lot of public support for the new sports centre.*
civic, general, popular, universal

public 3
adjective provided for everyone to use or open to anyone » *Public swimming pools can be very busy.*
communal, community, open to the public, universal
antonym: **private**

***Public** swimming pools can be very busy.*

publicity
noun information or advertisements about an item or event » *The actor gave several interviews as part of the publicity campaign for his new movie.*
advertising, plug (informal), **promotion**

publicize
verb to advertise something or make it widely known » *The author appeared on TV to publicize her book.*
advertise, plug (informal), **promote**

publish
verb to make a piece of writing available for reading » *We publish a range of titles.*
print, put out

*He had been running so hard that he was **puffing**.*

puff
verb to breathe loudly and quickly with your mouth open » *He had been running so hard that he was puffing.*
breathe heavily, gasp, pant, wheeze

pull 1
verb to draw an object towards you » *We saw the sights of the city from an open carriage pulled by two white horses.*
drag, draw, haul, tow, tug, yank
antonym: **push**

pull 2
noun the attraction or influence of something » *The pull of the bakery was too strong, and she went in and bought fresh bread.*
attraction, lure, magnetism

punctual
adjective arriving or leaving at the correct time » *Our first flight was punctual, so we easily caught our connection.*
in good time, on time, prompt

punish
verb to make someone suffer a penalty for some misbehaviour » *I was punished for insolence, though I didn't mean to sound rude.*
discipline, penalize, rap knuckles, sentence, throw the book at

punishment
noun a penalty for a crime or offence » *The punishment must always fit the crime.*
penalty, retribution, chastening, chastisement, just deserts

puny
adjective very small and weak » *The newborn kittens were puny and helpless.*
feeble, frail, sickly, skinny, weak

pupil
noun a student taught at a school » *Our school has 500 pupils.*
scholar, schoolboy, schoolchild, schoolgirl, student, undergrad

pure 1
adjective clean and free from harmful substances » *The water from the spring is pure enough to drink.*
clean, germ-free, pasteurized, spotless, sterilized, unadulterated, unblemished, uncontaminated, unpolluted, untainted
antonym: **impure**

*The water from the spring is **pure** enough to drink.*

pure 2
adjective complete and total » *Anita won the prize through pure luck.*
absolute, complete, outright, sheer, unmitigated, utter

» purple

push

1 *verb* to apply force to something in order to move it » He **pushed** his friend on the swing.

press

He **pressed** his hands against his friend's back to help her swing.

ram

He **rammed** his shoulder against the playground gate to open it.

shove

He **shoved** the merry-go-round to make it spin.

thrust

She was **thrust** forward on the swing.

antonym: **pull**
She **pulled** her legs back to swing higher.

purple
noun or *adjective*
Shades of purple:
amethyst, aubergine, gentian, heather, heliotrope, indigo, lavender, lilac, magenta, mauve, mulberry, plum, puce, royal purple, violet

purpose **1**
noun the reason for something » The purpose of Fleur's shopping trip was to buy a new winter coat.
aim, function, intention, object, point, reason

purpose **2** :
on purpose
adverb deliberately » Did you do that on purpose?
by design, deliberately, intentionally, knowingly, purposely

push **1**
verb to apply force to something in order to move it
◀◀ SEE LEFT

push **2**
verb to persuade someone into doing something » His mother pushed him into auditioning for a part in the play.
encourage, persuade, press, urge

pushy
adjective (informal) unpleasantly forceful and determined » Our new swimming coach can be rather pushy.
aggressive, ambitious, assertive, bossy, forceful, obtrusive

put **1**
verb to place something somewhere » Angela put the photograph on her desk.
deposit, lay, place, position, rest

put **2**
verb to express something » I think you put that very well.
phrase, word

put down **1**
verb to criticize someone and make them appear foolish » My big sister is always putting me down.
belittle, criticize, find fault with, humiliate

put down **2**
verb to kill an animal that is ill or dangerous » The dog was so ill that it had to be put down.
destroy, euthanize, kill, put out of its misery, put to sleep

put off
verb to delay something » We have put off making a decision about where to go until next week.
defer, delay, postpone, put back, put on ice, reschedule

put up with
verb to tolerate something disagreeable » He put up with his daughter's loud music for an hour before asking her to turn it down.
abide, bear, stand, stand for, stomach, tolerate, brook, countenance

puzzle **1**
verb to perplex and confuse » There was something about Renata that puzzled me.
baffle, bewilder, confuse, mystify, stump, confound, flummox, nonplus, perplex

puzzle **2**
noun a game or question that requires a lot of thought to solve » I enjoy doing crossword puzzles.
brain-teaser (informal)**, poser, problem, riddle**

*I enjoy doing crossword **puzzles**.*

Qq

qualification [1]
noun a skill or achievement » *Sam's qualifications mean he can fly an airplane.*
ability, accomplishment, achievement, capability, quality, skill, attribute

qualification [2]
noun something added to modify, limit, or restrict » *The board accepted the principal's changes to the school with a couple of qualifications.*
condition, exception, modification, reservation

qualify
verb to pass the tests necessary for an activity » *My mom qualified as a doctor 30 years ago.*
become licensed, gain qualifications, get certified, graduate

quality [1]
noun the measure of how good something is » *The head chef always makes sure that the food is of the highest quality.*
calibre, distinction, grade, merit, value, worth

*The head chef always makes sure that the food is of the highest **quality**.*

quality [2]
noun a characteristic of something » *His best quality is his kindness.*
aspect, characteristic, feature, mark, property, trait, attribute, peculiarity

quantity [1]
noun an amount you can measure or count » *Petra made a large quantity of cupcakes for the hockey club.*
amount, number, part, sum, portion, quota

quantity [2]
noun the amount of something that there is » *Our teacher likes to emphasize the importance of quality over quantity when it comes to creative writing.*
extent, measure, size, volume, bulk, expanse, magnitude

quarrel [1]
noun an angry argument » *I had a terrible quarrel with my brother.*
argument, disagreement, dispute, feud, fight, row, squabble, altercation, fracas, fray

quarrel [2]
verb to have an angry argument
▼ SEE BELOW

queasy
adjective feeling slightly sick » *Freya felt queasy so her mom comforted her.*
ill, nauseous, sick, unwell

*Freya felt **queasy** so her mom comforted her.*

query [1]
noun a question » *If you have any queries, please contact us.*
inquiry, question
antonym: response

query »

---

quarrel

[2] verb to have an angry argument
» *My sister **quarrelled** with my brother.*

!@?#%   %&?£!

argue
She **argued** with her mother about bedtime.

fall out
She **fell out** with her best friend.

bicker
They **bickered** endlessly over whose turn it was to let the dog out.

fight
They often **fought** about who was right.

clash
They **clashed** over what colour to paint the bedroom.

squabble
They **squabbled** over the remote control.

query

query [2]
verb to question something because it seems wrong » *Gary queried the referee's decision to disallow the goal.*
challenge, dispute, object to, question

question [1]
noun a problem that needs to be discussed » *Can we get back to the question of who's organizing the party?*
issue, motion, point, subject, topic

question [2]
verb to ask someone questions » *A man is being questioned by the police.*
examine, interrogate, probe, quiz, cross-examine, interview, investigate
antonym: **answer**

question [3]
verb to express doubts about something » *I'm fed up with my parents always questioning my decisions.*
challenge, dispute, distrust, doubt, query, suspect

quick [1]
adjective moving with great speed » *The students made a quick exit from the classroom when the bell rang.*
brisk, express, fast, hasty, hurtle, rapid, speedy, swift
antonym: **slow**

quick [2]
adjective lasting only a short time » *We only had time for a quick chat.*
brief, cursory, hasty, hurried, perfunctory
antonym: **long**

quick [3]
adjective happening without any delay » *I received a quick response to my email.*
hasty, prompt, sudden

quickly
adverb with great speed
▶▶ SEE RIGHT

quiet [1]
adjective making very little noise » *The radio was so quiet, we couldn't hear it.*
hushed, inaudible, low, silent, soft, noiseless, soundless
antonym: **noisy**

quiet [2]
adjective peaceful and calm » *We had a quiet day at home.*
calm, mild, peaceful, restful, serene, tranquil, motionless, placid, untroubled

quiet [3]
noun silence or lack of noise » *The teacher called for quiet.*
calmness, peace, serenity, silence, stillness, tranquillity
antonym: **noise**

*The teacher called for **quiet**.*

quit
verb to leave a place or stop doing something » *Keira quit her job and went travelling.*
discontinue, give up, leave, resign, retire, stop, abandon, cease

quite [1]
adverb fairly but not very » *My uncle is quite old.*
fairly, moderately, rather, reasonably, somewhat

quite [2]
adverb completely and totally » *The doctor asked John to lie quite still during the x-ray.*
absolutely, completely, entirely, fully, perfectly, totally, precisely, wholly

quote
verb to repeat the exact words someone has said » *Naz always quotes from TV shows.*
cite, extract, recite, repeat

fast
hastily
hurriedly
rapidly
speedily
swiftly

quickly

adverb with great speed
» *The rocket took off and **quickly** gained height.*

antonym: **slowly**
*The tortoise moves **slowly**.*

Rr

race 1
noun a group of human beings with shared physical or genetic characteristics » *People of different races live side by side in this city.*
ethnic group, nation, people

race 2
verb to move very quickly » *Dan raced to catch the bus, but he was too late.*
dash, fly, hurry, run, speed, tear

Dan raced to catch the bus, but he was too late.

racket
noun a lot of noise » *The builders' drills made such a racket.*
clamour, commotion, din, hubbub, noise, rumpus, cacophony, tumult

rage 1
noun a feeling of extremely strong anger » *She was trembling with rage.*
anger, frenzy, fury, wrath

Mariana was raging at the fact that she'd been on hold for 20 minutes.

rage 2
verb to be angry or speak angrily » *Mariana was raging at the fact that she'd been on hold for 20 minutes.*
be furious, fume, lose your temper, rave, storm

rage 3
verb to continue with great force » *The storm raged all night.*
be at its height, rampage, storm, surge

raid 1
verb to attack suddenly » *Oliver came home hungry and raided the fridge.*
assault, attack, break into, invade, plunder, pillage, rifle, sack

raid 2
noun an attack on something » *The street was closed following the bank raid.*
attack, break-in, foray, incursion, sortie

rain 1
noun water falling from the clouds » *The rain came as a relief after the drought.*
deluge, downpour, drizzle, rainfall, showers

It rained as Caroline was on her way to meet a friend.

rain 2
verb to fall from the sky in drops » *It rained as Caroline was on her way to meet a friend.*
drizzle, pour, teem

raise 1
verb to make something higher » *Flags were raised to signal the start of the national holiday.*
elevate, heave, hoist, lift
antonym: **lower**

raise 2
verb to look after children until they are grown up » *Natasha was raised in a large house in the country.*
bring up, nurture, rear

raise 3
verb to mention or suggest something » *He had raised no objections at the time.*
advance, bring up, broach, introduce, suggest

ramble 1
verb to wander without a specific direction » *We rambled across the fields, taking care to avoid any puddles.*
amble, stray, stroll, walk, wander, perambulate, rove

ramble 2
verb to talk in a confused way » *Garth started rambling and repeating himself.*
babble, chatter

rampage 1
verb to rush about wildly or out of control » *The children rampaged around the yard dressed as cowboys.*
go berserk, rage, run amok, run riot

rampage 2 : on the rampage
adjective rushing about in a wild and uncontrolled way » *The bull escaped from the field and went on the rampage through the village.*
amok, berserk, wild

random 1
adjective not based on a definite plan » *Melissa came to the sleepover in a random selection of clothes—a coat, skirt, and pyjamas!*
aimless, arbitrary, haphazard, indiscriminate, desultory, fortuitous, unpremeditated

Melissa came to the sleepover in a random selection of clothes—a coat, skirt, and pyjamas!

random 2 : at random
adverb without any definite plan » *Children will be chosen at random to represent the school in the parade.*
aimlessly, arbitrarily, haphazardly, indiscriminately, randomly, unsystematically, willy-nilly

range 1
noun the maximum limits of something » *I tried to phone but was not in range of a signal.*
bounds, extent, field, limits, province, scope

range

range
2 noun a number of different things of the same kind
» The sunglasses are available in a **range** of colours.

assortment There is an **assortment** of shapes.

class The designer **class** is more expensive.

gamut Stock covers the whole **gamut** of shapes and sizes.

selection There is a wide **selection**.

series This style comes in a **series** of sizes.

variety There is a **variety** of styles.

range 2
noun a number of different things of the same kind
◀◀ SEE LEFT

range 3
verb to vary between two extremes » *The shelves were filled with goods ranging from the everyday to the exotic.*
extend, go, run, stretch, vary

rank 1
noun someone's level in a group » *Franklin rose to the rank of captain.*
class, echelon, grade, level, position, standing, station, status

rank 2
noun a row of people or things » *Ranks of Mounted Police participated in the parade.*
column, file, line, row

Ranks of Mounted Police participated in the parade.

rank 3
adjective complete and absolute » *Going hiking without a map and compass is rank stupidity.*
absolute, complete, downright, sheer, unmitigated, utter, arrant, egregious

rare
adjective not common or frequent » *We saw a rare species of bird that hardly ever appears in the city.*
exceptional, few, scarce, sparse, sporadic, uncommon, unusual
antonym: **common**

rash 1
adjective acting in a hasty and foolish way » *Sven made a rash decision to go swimming in the freezing lake.*
foolhardy, hasty, impetuous, impulsive, reckless, heedless, injudicious, unthinking

rash 2
noun an irritated area on your skin » *The rash on my leg is really itchy.*
eruption, outbreak

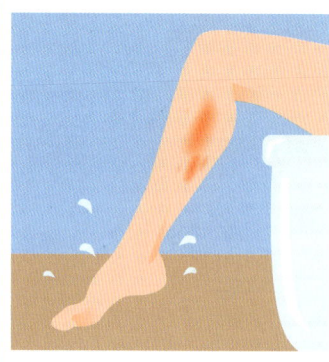

The rash on my leg is really itchy.

rash 3
noun a large number of events happening together » *A rash of bookings followed the television program about the resort.*
epidemic, flood, plague, spate, wave

rate 1
noun the speed or frequency of something » *Our hen lays eggs at the rate of one a day.*
frequency, pace, speed, tempo, velocity

rate 2
noun the cost or charge for something » *We were offered phone calls at cheap rates as part of the package.*
charge, cost, fee, price, tariff

rate 3
verb to give an opinion of someone's or something's qualities » *The app was rated very highly by its users.*
appraise, class, consider, count, rank, regard, adjudge, esteem, evaluate

realize »

rather
adverb to a certain extent » *We got along rather well.*
fairly, pretty (informal), **quite, relatively, slightly, somewhat**

rational
adjective using reason rather than emotion » *There must be a rational explanation for the lights going out.*
enlightened, logical, reasonable, sensible

rave 1
verb to talk in an uncontrolled way » *Ed started raving about being treated badly.*
babble, rage, rant

rave 2
verb (informal) to be enthusiastic about something » *She raved about how good the facilities were at the hotel.*
be wild about (informal), **enthuse, gush**

reach 1
verb to arrive somewhere » *Len did not stop until he reached the end of the trail.*
arrive at, attain, get as far as, get to, make

reach 2
verb to extend as far as something » *Annabel used a ladder to reach the book she wanted.*
extend to, go as far as, touch

Annabel used a ladder to reach the book she wanted.

reach 3
verb to arrive at a certain stage or level » *Exam results have reached record highs.*
arrive at, attain, climb to, fall to, rise to

reaction 1
noun a person's response to something » *When she spotted the spider, Louise's reaction was one of horror.*
acknowledgement, answer, feedback, response

When she spotted the spider, Louise's reaction was one of horror.

reaction 2
noun a response to something unpopular » *There has been a fierce reaction to the suggestion that the school day be made longer.*
backlash, counterbalance

read 1
verb to look at and absorb something written » *Nancy read the article with interest.*
glance at, look at, pore over, scan, study

Nancy read the article with interest.

read 2
verb to understand the true nature or mood » *Rob wished he could read her thoughts.*
comprehend, decipher, interpret

We were packed and ready to go on our trip.

ready 1
adjective prepared for action or use » *We were packed and ready to go on our trip.*
organized, prepared, primed, ripe, set

ready 2
adjective willing to do something » *Kyle was always ready to help with the dishes.*
agreeable, eager, happy, keen, willing, minded, predisposed

ready 3
adjective easily produced or obtained » *There was a ready supply of wood for the campfire.*
accessible, available, convenient, handy

real 1
adjective genuine and not imitation » *The jeweller inspected the gem to see if it was real or a fake.*
authentic, bona fide, genuine, honest, legitimate, rightful, sincere, true, unaffected
antonym: **fake**

The jeweller inspected the gem to see if it was real or a fake.

real 2
adjective actually existing and not imagined » *The movie is based on the real story of a famous scientist.*
actual, authentic, concrete, factual, genuine, legitimate, tangible, true
antonym: **imaginary**

realistic 1
adjective accepting the true situation » *She was realistic that her chances of winning the lottery were virtually nil.*
down-to-earth, level-headed, matter-of-fact, practical, sensible, sober

realistic 2
adjective true to real life » *My sister's paintings are very realistic.*
authentic, faithful, lifelike, true, naturalistic, representational

My sister's paintings are very realistic.

reality
noun something that is true and not imagined » *The reality of the situation is that we are lost.*
authenticity, fact, realism, truth

realize
verb to become aware of something » *Nicole hadn't realized how difficult the recipe was.*
appreciate, comprehend, grasp, recognize, understand

really

1 adverb very or certainly
» The friends had a **really** good time at the party.

I'm **absolutely** delighted to see everyone.

I'm **certainly** enjoying myself.

The food is **extremely** tasty.

You must be **incredibly** tired after all that dancing.

They organized it in a **remarkably** short time.

I'm having a **truly** wonderful time.

I'm **very** glad I came.

really 1
adverb very or certainly
◀◀ SEE LEFT

really 2
adverb in fact
» *Simon really is asleep; he's not pretending.*
actually, in fact, in reality, truly

reason 1
noun the cause of something that happens » *I had no reason to go out, so I stayed at home.*
cause, grounds, incentive, motive, purpose

reason 2
noun the ability to think » *Ivy desperately wanted the bag, but reason told her not to buy it because it was too small.*
intellect, judgment, rationality, reasoning, sense

reason 3
verb to try to persuade someone of something » *I tried to reason with my mother, but she wouldn't listen.*
bring around (informal), **persuade, win over**

I tried to reason with my mother, but she wouldn't listen.

reasonable 1
adjective fair and sensible » *It was only reasonable to share the chores between us.*
fair, moderate, rational, sane, sensible, sober, steady, wise, judicious, plausible

reasonable 2
adjective based on good reasoning » *Ali had a reasonable argument based on the facts.*
justifiable, legitimate, logical, sensible, sound, understandable

reasonable 3
adjective not too expensive » *The cost of my haircut was reasonable; I'd go there again.*
cheap, competitive, fair, inexpensive, low, modest

reassure
verb to put someone's mind at ease » *Sonia reassured me that everything was fine.*
bolster, cheer up, comfort, encourage, buoy up, hearten, inspirit

rebel
verb to fight against authority and accepted values » *Amy rebelled against school policy and dyed her hair pink.*
defy, mutiny, resist, revolt

Amy rebelled against school policy and dyed her hair pink.

rebellion
noun an organized opposition to authority » *Fed up with extra work every night, the students staged a rebellion.*
insurrection, mutiny, revolt, revolution, uprising

receive 1
verb to accept something from someone » *Did you receive my letter?*
accept, be given, get, pick up, take

receive 2
verb to experience something » *We received a very warm welcome.*
encounter, suffer, sustain, undergo

receive 3
verb to welcome visitors » *Jim and Marie were there to receive the guests when they arrived for the party.*
entertain, greet, meet, take in, welcome

Jim and Marie were there to receive the guests when they arrived for the party.

recent
adjective happening a short time ago » *Our most recent vacation was to Chile.*
current, fresh, new, present-day, up-to-date, contemporary, latter-day

reckon 1
verb (informal) to think or believe something is the case » *I reckon they'll be here soon; I told them to come at 3 p.m.*
assume, believe (formal), **consider, judge, suppose, think,** deem (formal), hold to be, surmise (formal)

reckon 2
verb to calculate an amount » *The figure is now reckoned to be 15 percent.*
calculate, count, estimate, figure out, work out

recognize 1
verb to know who or what someone or something is » *I recognized Darren by his red hair.*
identify, know, place, spot

recognize 2
verb to accept or acknowledge something » *William was recognized as an outstanding pilot by the academy.*
acknowledge, appreciate, honour, salute

reconstruct 1
verb to rebuild something that has been damaged » *The old city centre was falling down and has been reconstructed.*
rebuild, recreate, regenerate, renovate, restore, reassemble, remodel

reconstruct 2
verb to build up from small details » *Archaeologists reconstruct the past from the evidence they find.*
build up, deduce, piece together

record 1
noun a stored account of something » *The shelves were bulging with medical records.*
account, archives, file, journal, minute, register

record 2
noun what someone has done in the past » *The interviewer asked for a record of my previous work experience.*
background, career, curriculum vitae, track record (informal)

record 3
verb to note and store information » *Julia records her daily life in her diary.*
blog, document, enter, log, note, register, write down

Julia records her daily life in her diary.

record »

181

recover

recover 1
verb to get better again
» *Pete has still not fully recovered from a nasty cold.*
convalesce, get better, get well, improve, recuperate, revive

recover 2
verb to get something back again » *Lynn's father managed to recover the lost book from behind the shelves.*
get back, recapture, recoup, regain, retrieve

recovery 1
noun the act of getting better again » *He made a remarkable recovery after his operation.*
healing, improvement, recuperation, revival, convalescence, rally

recovery 2
noun the act of getting something back » *The art gallery offered a reward for the recovery of the stolen painting.*
recapture, reclamation, restoration, retrieval

recruit 1
verb to persuade people to join a group » *Ali helped to recruit volunteers for picking up litter.*
draft, enlist, enrol, muster

recruit 2
noun someone who has recently joined a group » *The army recruits were given their new uniforms.*
beginner, convert, novice, trainee, neophyte

The army recruits were given their new uniforms.

I gave my daughter a red apple.

red
noun or adjective
Shades of red:
burgundy, cardinal, carmine, cherry, claret, coral, crimson, flame, maroon, poppy, rose, ruby, scarlet, vermilion, wine
related words:
adjective **rubicund, ruddy**

reduce 1
verb to make something smaller in size or amount » *Mom reduced her hours at work so she could spend more time at home.*
curtail, cut, cut down, decrease, diminish, lessen, lower, shorten
antonym: **increase**

reduce 2
verb to bring to a weaker or inferior state » *The village was reduced to rubble in the earthquake.*
degrade, demote, downgrade, drive, force

refer 1
verb to mention something » *In his speech, Len referred to a recent trip to Vancouver.*
allude, bring up, cite, mention

refer 2
verb to look at something to find something out » *We had to refer to the recipe to make the sauce.*
confer, consult, look up

We had to refer to the recipe to make the sauce.

regular

1 adjective even or equally spaced » *A clock pendulum has regular movement.*

consistent

constant

even

periodic

rhythmic

uniform

antonym: **irregular**

182

relax

*He was a **refined** gentleman with impeccable manners.*

refined [1]
adjective well-mannered and polite » *He was a refined gentleman with impeccable manners.*
civilized, genteel, gentlemanly, ladylike, polite
antonym: **common**

refined [2]
adjective processed to remove impurities » *White sugar is refined from raw sugar cane.*
distilled, filtered, processed, pure, purified

reform [1]
noun a major change or improvement » *The new principal is planning a reform of the school timetable.*
amendment, correction, improvement, rehabilitation, amelioration, **betterment,** rectification

reform [2]
verb to make major changes or improvements to something » *He reformed the athletics team to improve results.*
amend, better, correct, rectify, rehabilitate, ameliorate, emend, revolutionize

refresh
verb to make you feel more energetic » *A glass of fruit juice will refresh you.*
brace, enliven, rejuvenate, revive, stimulate, freshen, invigorate, revitalize, revivify

refuge
noun a place where you go for safety » *We hid from the storm in a tiny mountain refuge.*
asylum, harbour, haven, sanctuary, shelter

refuse [1]
verb to say you will not do something » *He refused to talk about the contents of the letter.*
abstain, decline, withhold

refuse [2]
verb to say you will not allow or accept something » *I politely refused the offer of a drink as I wasn't thirsty.*
decline, reject, spurn, turn down
antonym: **accept**

refuse [3]
noun garbage or waste » *Our household refuse is collected weekly.*
garbage, junk (informal), **litter, rubbish, trash, waste**

regard [1]
verb to think of someone or something in a particular way » *I regard Isabella as my best friend.*
consider, judge, look on, see, think of, view

regard [2]
verb (literary) to look at someone in a particular way » *Janine regarded the magician's trick with interest.*
contemplate, eye, gaze, look, scrutinize, watch

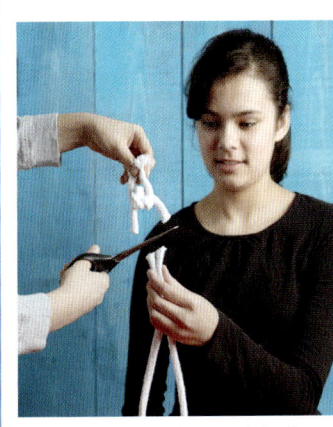

*Janine **regarded** the magician's trick with interest.*

region
noun a large area of land » *We live in a mountainous region.*
area, district, land, locality, quarter, sector, territory, tract, zone

regret [1]
verb to be sorry something has happened » *Michael regretted forgetting his girlfriend's birthday again.*
be sorry, grieve, lament, mourn, repent, bemoan, bewail, rue

*Michael **regretted** forgetting his girlfriend's birthday again.*

regret [2]
noun the feeling of being sorry about something » *He expressed regret that he had caused offence.*
grief, pang of conscience, penitence, remorse, repentance, sorrow, compunction, contrition, ruefulness, self-reproach

regular [1]
adjective even or equally spaced
◀◀ SEE LEFT

regular [2]
adjective usual or normal » *Tom was filling in for the regular store assistant.*
customary, everyday, habitual, normal, ordinary, routine, typical, usual

reject
verb to refuse to accept or agree to something » *Dad rejected the job offer because the office was too far away.*
decline, deny, rebuff, refuse, renounce, say no to, spurn, turn down, disallow, repudiate
antonym: **accept**

rejoice
verb to be very happy about something » *Today we can rejoice in our success.*
be overjoyed, celebrate, delight, glory, exult, revel

relation [1]
noun a connection between two things » *The movie bears no relation whatsoever to the book.*
bearing, bond, connection, correlation, link, relationship

relation [2]
noun a member of your family » *I stayed with my relations while I was in Germany.*
kin, kinsman, kinswoman, relative

relationship [1]
noun the way people act towards each other » *Valerie has a friendly relationship with her customers.*
affinity, association, bond, connection, rapport

*Valerie has a friendly **relationship** with her customers.*

relationship [2]
noun the connection between two things » *There is a clear relationship between happiness and good health.*
connection, correlation, link, parallel

relax
verb to be calm and become less worried » *You can relax during the holidays after working hard all semester.*
laze, rest, take it easy, unwind

relaxed

*I spent a **relaxed** evening listening to music.*

relaxed [1]
adjective calm and peaceful » *I spent a relaxed evening listening to music.*
calm, casual, comfortable, informal, peaceful
antonym: **tense**

relaxed [2]
adjective calm and not worried or tense » *My parents have a relaxed attitude and often let my friends stay over.*
at ease, calm, comfortable, cool, easy, serene, unflustered
antonym: **tense**

relay
verb to give information to someone else » *Ariana relayed your message to me.*
communicate, convey, impart

release [1]
verb to set someone or something free » *Our teacher finally released us from the lesson.*
deliver, discharge, extricate, free, let go, liberate, set free, emancipate, unfetter

release [2]
verb to make something available » *The new album will be released next week.*
issue, launch, publish, put out

release [3]
noun the setting free of someone or something » *The charity's aim was the release of animals in captivity back into the wild.*
discharge, emancipation, freedom, liberation, liberty, deliverance, manumission

relentless
adjective never stopping or becoming less intense » *The rain was relentless and did not let up the whole week.*
incessant, nonstop, persistent, sustained, unrelenting, unremitting

relevant
adjective connected with what is being discussed » *Please stick to the point and just talk about what's relevant.*
applicable, apposite, appropriate, apt, pertinent, germane, material
antonym: **irrelevant**

reliable
adjective able to be trusted » *Mike was reliable and turned up on time every day.*
dependable, faithful, safe, sound, staunch, sure, true, trustworthy
antonym: **unreliable**

religious [1]
adjective connected with religion » *We joined in the religious worship.*
devotional, divine, doctrinal, holy, sacred, scriptural, spiritual, theological

religious [2]
adjective having a strong belief in a god or gods » *Paul is very religious and goes to church every week.*
devout, God-fearing, godly, pious, righteous

reluctant
adjective unwilling to do something » *Dad was reluctant to ask for help.*
averse, disinclined, hesitant, loath, slow, unwilling
antonym: **eager**

remain [1]
verb to stay somewhere » *My friends went out while I remained at home.*
be left, linger, stay behind, wait

*My friends went out while I **remained** at home.*

remain [2]
verb to stay the same » *No matter how much she tried to curl her hair, it remained straight.*
continue, endure, go on, last, stay, survive

remember
verb to bring to mind something from the past
» ***Remember** to feed the cat.*

retain
*I must **retain** all those geography facts.*

recall
*Try to **recall** the words of that poem.*

recognize
*Do you **recognize** this name?*

184

renovate »

remainder
noun the part that is left
» After six weeks of French, we studied Spanish for the remainder of the term.
balance, last, others, remains, remnants, rest

remains
plural noun the parts left over
» We put the remains of lunch in the fridge.
debris, dregs, leftovers, relics, remnants, residue, scraps, vestiges, detritus, leavings

remark 1
verb to mention or comment on something » She remarked that my hair was looking nice.
comment, mention, observe, say, state

remark 2
noun something you say » Trudy's remark about my new coat pleased me.
comment, observation, statement, utterance, word

remember
verb to bring to mind something from the past
▼ SEE BELOW

remind
verb to make someone remember something
» Please remind me to water the plants before we go out.
bring back to, jog someone's memory, make someone remember, put in mind, refresh someone's memory

remote 1
adjective far off in distance » We stayed for a week on a remote farm in the hills.
distant, far-off, inaccessible, isolated, lonely, outlying

We stayed for a week on a **remote** farm in the hills.

remote 2
adjective far away in time » The days of knights in armour riding into battle are from the remote past.
distant, far-off

remote 3
adjective not wanting to be friendly » I tried to talk to her, but she was very remote.
aloof, cold, detached, distant, reserved, withdrawn

remote 4
adjective not very great » The chances of us winning the lottery are pretty remote.
poor, slender, slight, slim, small

remove
verb to take something off or away » Sue had already bought milk, so she removed it from the shopping list.
delete, detach, eject, eliminate, erase, extract, get rid of, take away, take off, take out, withdraw, efface, excise, expunge

Sue had already bought milk, so she **removed** it from the shopping list.

renew
verb to begin something again » Dawn renewed her subscription to the magazine.
begin again, recommence, re-establish, reopen, resume

renounce
verb (formal) to reject something or give it up » Tina renounced all fast food.
disown, give up, reject, relinquish, eschew (formal)

Tina **renounced** all fast food.

renovate
verb to repair an old building or machine » My aunt bought a rundown house and renovated it.
modernize, overhaul, recondition, refurbish, repair, restore, revamp

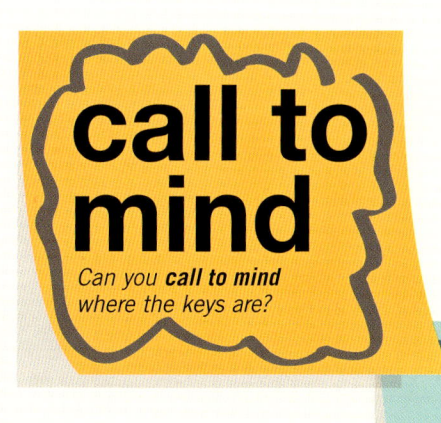

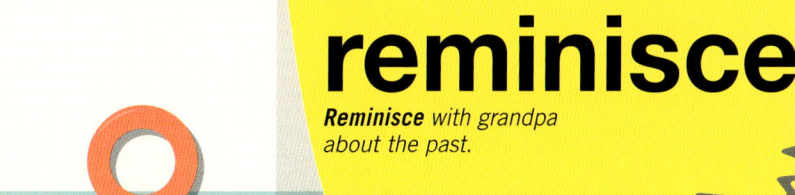

---

call to mind
Can you **call to mind** where the keys are?

reminisce
Reminisce with grandpa about the past.

recollect
Do you **recollect** what we did last Tuesday?

antonym: **forget**
Don't **forget** to do your homework!

repair

*My dad carried out the **repairs** on the car himself.*

repair 1
noun something you do to mend something that is damaged » *My dad carried out the repairs on the car himself.*
darn, mend, patch, rehabilitation, restoration

repair 2
verb to mend something that is damaged » *The money will be used to repair the faulty TV.*
fix, mend, patch, patch up, rehabilitate, renovate, restore

repay
verb to give back money which is owed » *It will take me years to repay the loan.*
pay back, refund, settle up, make restitution, recompense, reimburse, remunerate, square

repeat
verb to say or write something again » *Since you didn't listen, I'll repeat that.*
echo, reiterate, say again, iterate, recapitulate, restate

repel 1
verb to horrify and disgust » *The thought of eating snails repels me.*
disgust, offend, revolt, sicken
antonym: attract

repel 2
verb to fight and drive back enemy forces » *Troops positioned along the border are ready to repel an enemy attack.*
drive off, repulse, resist

replace
verb to take the place of something else » *He replaced his car with a bicycle.*
succeed, supersede, supplant, take over from, take the place of

replacement
noun a person or thing that takes the place of another » *Glen has nominated Adam to be his replacement.*
proxy, stand-in, substitute, successor, surrogate

reply 1
verb to give someone an answer » *She quickly replied to my email.*
answer, counter, respond, retort, return, reciprocate, rejoin, riposte

reply 2
noun an answer given to someone » *He gave a sharp reply to her endless questions.*
answer, response, retort, rejoinder, riposte

report 1
verb to tell about or give an official account of something » *Owen reported the theft to the police.*
cover, describe, inform of, notify, state

report 2
noun an account of an event or situation » *The news report suggested it was a very exciting match.*
account, description, statement

*The news **report** suggested it was a very exciting match.*

represent 1
verb to stand for something else » *In algebra, letters are used to represent numbers.*
mean, stand for, symbolize, betoken, equate with

represent 2
verb to describe something in a particular way » *The newspapers represent him as a hero.*
depict, describe, picture, portray, show

representative 1
noun a person who acts on behalf of another or others » *We elected a school representative.*
agent, delegate, deputy, proxy, spokesman, spokeswoman

representative 2
adjective typical of the group to which it belongs » *This building is representative of Gaudí's style of architecture.*
characteristic, illustrative, typical, archetypal, emblematic, indicative

*This building is **representative** of Gaudí's style of architecture.*

reputation
noun the opinion that people have of a person or thing » *The college has a reputation for getting good grades.*
character, name, renown, repute, standing, stature

request 1
verb to ask for something politely or formally » *Alana requested that the door be left open.*
ask, beg, seek, entreat, solicit

request 2
noun the action of asking for something politely or formally » *The examiner refused the boy's request for more time.*
appeal, application, call, plea, entreaty, petition

require 1
verb to need something » *A plant requires light, water, and nutrients in order to grow.*
demand, depend on, be in need of, need, want (informal)

require 2
verb to say that someone must do something » *The rules require employers to provide safety training.*
compel, demand, direct, instruct, oblige, order

requirement
noun something that you must have or do » *There is a legal requirement for children to attend school.*
demand, essential, necessity, need, specification, prerequisite (formal), stipulation (formal)

research 1
noun the act of studying and finding out about something » *I've been doing some research for my project.*
analysis, examination, exploration, investigation, study

*I've been doing some **research** for my project.*

research 2
verb to study and find out about something » *She researched good places to visit while they were on vacation.*
analyze, examine, explore, google, investigate, study

resemblance
noun a similarity between two things » *I can see a resemblance between you two.*
analogy, correspondence, likeness, parallel, similarity, comparability, parity, semblance, similitude

resemble
verb to be similar to something else » *Limes resemble green lemons, and they both taste sour, too.*
bear a resemblance to, be like, be similar to, look like, parallel, take after

Limes resemble green lemons, and they both taste sour, too.

resent
verb to feel bitter and angry about something » *I resent being treated like an idiot.*
be angry about, be offended by, dislike, object to, take offence at

resentful
adjective bitter about something that has happened » *The boys were resentful that they weren't allowed to go to the park.*
aggrieved, angry, bitter, embittered, huffy, indignant, offended, peeved, piqued

resentment
noun a feeling of anger and bitterness » *Resentment is growing among students at what they claim is unfair treatment by some teachers.*
anger, animosity, bitterness, grudge, huff, indignation, rancour, pique, umbrage

A table has been reserved for us at the restaurant.

reserve 1
verb to keep for a particular person or purpose » *A table has been reserved for us at the restaurant.*
hoard, hold, keep, put by, save, set aside, stockpile, store

reserve 2
noun a supply kept for future use » *We have plenty of food reserves if we get snowed in.*
cache, fund, hoard, stock, stockpile, store, supply

resign 1
verb to leave a job » *Scott resigned from the firm to take another job elsewhere.*
abdicate, hand in your notice, leave, quit, step down (informal)

resign 2: resign oneself
verb to accept an unpleasant situation » *After playing badly, Samantha had resigned herself to losing her place on the team.*
accept, reconcile yourself, bow

resist
verb to refuse to accept something and try to prevent it » *She resisted her mother's attempts to get her to clean her bedroom.*
defy, fight, oppose, refuse, struggle against
antonym: **accept**

resolve 1
verb to decide firmly to do something » *Miguel resolved to do more exercise.*
decide, determine, intend, make up your mind

resolve 2
verb to find a solution to a problem » *We must find a way to resolve this problem.*
clear up, find a solution to, overcome, solve, sort out, work out

resolve 3
noun absolute determination » *Nothing could weaken Laura's resolve to get fit.*
determination, resolution, tenacity, doggedness, single-mindedness, willpower

Nothing could weaken Laura's resolve to get fit.

respect 1
verb to have a good opinion of someone » *The new teacher wanted his pupils to respect him.*
admire, have a good opinion of, have a high opinion of, honour, look up to, think highly of, venerate, esteem, revere, reverence, set store by
antonym: **disrespect**

respect 2
noun a good opinion of someone » *The hockey team had a lot of respect for their old manager.*
admiration, esteem, regard, reverence
antonym: **disrespect**

respectable 1
adjective considered to be acceptable and correct » *Timothy comes from a respectable family.*
decent, good, honourable, proper, reputable, upright, worthy

respectable 2
adjective adequate or reasonable » *His grades were respectable, but not amazing.*
appreciable, considerable, decent, fair, reasonable

responsibility 1
noun the duty to deal with or take care of something » *Mom took care of the house while the garden was my responsibility.*
duty, obligation, onus

responsibility 2
noun the blame for something which has happened » *We must all accept responsibility for our mistakes.*
blame, fault, guilt, liability, accountability, culpability

responsible 1
adjective being the person in charge of something » *I am responsible for making the sandwiches for the picnic.*
in charge, in control

responsible 2
adjective being to blame for something » *I wonder who is responsible for this mess!*
at fault, guilty, to blame

I wonder who is responsible for this mess!

responsible 3
adjective sensible and dependable » *Patrick had to show that he would be a responsible pet owner.*
dependable, level-headed, reliable, sensible, sound, trustworthy
antonym: **irresponsible**

»rest

Greg took one slice of cake and left the rest.

rest [1]
noun the remaining parts of something » *Greg took one slice of cake and left the rest.*
balance, others, remainder, surplus

rest [2]
noun a period when you relax and do nothing » *I could do with a rest from all this work.*
break, holiday, leisure, relaxation, respite

rest [3]
verb to relax and do nothing for a while » *Gary rested on the sofa all night.*
have a break, idle, laze, put your feet up, relax, sit down, take it easy

restless
adjective unable to sit still or relax » *She had been restless and irritable all day.*
edgy, fidgety, fretful, jumpy, on edge, unsettled

restore [1]
verb to cause something to return to its previous state » *The restaurant was anxious to restore its reputation after the poor review.*
re-establish, reinstate, reintroduce, return

restore [2]
verb to clean and repair something » *He specializes in restoring ancient parchments.*
fix up, mend, rebuild, reconstruct, refurbish, renovate, repair, recondition, retouch

restrain
verb to hold someone or something back » *Noah had to be restrained by his friends.*
contain, control, curb, hamper, hinder, hold back, inhibit, constrain, rein

restrict
verb to limit the movement or actions of someone or something » *I restricted the dog to the ground floor of the house.*
confine, contain, hamper, handicap, impede, inhibit, limit, restrain, circumscribe, demarcate

restriction
noun a rule or situation that limits what you can do » *There is a parking restriction outside the hospital entrance.*
constraint, control, curb, limitation, regulation, restraint, stipulation

There is a parking restriction outside the hospital entrance.

result [1]
noun the situation that is caused by something » *He was eager to hear the result of the match.*
consequence, effect, outcome, product, upshot

result [2]
verb to be caused by something » *Sarah's gold medal resulted from a lot of training and hard work.*
arise, derive, develop, ensue, follow, happen, stem

result in
verb to cause something to happen » *Good study habits result in better grades.*
bring about, cause, lead to

retaliate
verb to do something to someone in return for what they did » *Tara retaliated by hiding her sister's favourite book.*
get back at, get even with (informal), hit back, pay someone back, reciprocate, take revenge

retreat [1]
verb to move away from someone or something » *The sunbathers on the beach retreated as the tide came in.*
back away, back off, draw back, pull back, withdraw
antonym: **advance**

retreat [2]
noun the action of moving away from someone or something » *We made a hasty retreat when the hotel fire alarm went off.*
departure, evacuation, flight, withdrawal
antonym: **advance**

retreat [3]
noun a quiet place you can go to » *Ben's favourite retreat was his tree house, where he could relax.*
haven, refuge, sanctuary

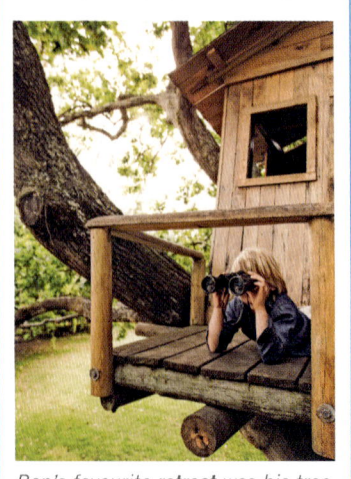

Ben's favourite retreat was his tree house, where he could relax.

Peter called for the dog, and it returned carrying a stick.

return [1]
verb to go back to a place » *Peter called for the dog, and it returned carrying a stick.*
come back, go back, reappear, turn back

return [2]
verb to give something back » *The company guaranteed to return our money if we didn't like the product.*
give back, pay back, refund, repay, recompense, reimburse

reveal [1]
verb to tell people about something » *The article revealed all the details about the celebrity's life.*
announce, disclose, divulge, get off your chest (informal), **let on**

reveal [2]
verb to uncover something that is hidden
▶▶ SEE RIGHT

revenge
noun vengeance for wrongs or injury received » *Chris plotted his revenge for the trick his friends had played on him earlier.*
reprisal, retaliation, retribution, vengeance

reverse [1]
verb to change into something different or contrary » *The store won't reverse their decision to increase prices.*
change, invalidate, overrule, overturn, retract, countermand, negate, rescind, revoke

reveal

[2] *verb* to uncover something that is hidden
» Curtis pulled aside the curtain to **reveal** dazzling treasure.

uncover
He **uncovered** a royal crown.

unveil
He **unveiled** a priceless sculpture.

bring to light
He **brought to light** the lost pearl necklace.

unearth
He **unearthed** a heap of ancient coins.

lay bare
He **laid bare** the glittering necklace.

reverse

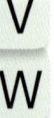

right
3 *noun* what is just and fair
» Jacob's parents taught him to know **right** from wrong.

virtue
equity
justice
legality
honour
fairness
morality
integrity

sin
crime
abuse
injustice
» She did him a **wrong** when she assumed he was lying.

antonym: **wrong**

reverse 2
noun the opposite of what has just been said or done » That's not right—in fact, the reverse is true.
contrary, converse, opposite

review 1
noun a critical assessment of a book or performance » The movie got good reviews in Andy's blog.
commentary, criticism, notice

The movie got good **reviews** in Andy's blog.

review 2
noun a general survey or report » Our class project was to do a review of pupils' opinions on school lunches.
analysis, examination, report, study, survey

revise
verb to alter or correct something » Carlos revised his opinion when he heard Stefan's point of view.
amend, correct, edit, refresh, revamp, update

revive
verb to make or become lively or active again » The concert revived my love of rock music.
rally, resuscitate, invigorate, reanimate, rekindle, revitalize

reward
noun something given in return for a service » My mother bought me a new bike as a reward for good behaviour.
bonus, bounty, payment, prize

rhythm
noun a regular movement or beat » The dancers swayed to the rhythm of the music.
beat, pulse, tempo, time

rich 1
adjective having a lot of money and possessions » He was a rich young man with lots of money.
affluent, loaded (slang)**, opulent, prosperous, wealthy, well off**
antonym: **poor**

He was a **rich** young man with lots of money.

rich 2
adjective abundant in something » Bananas are rich in vitamin A.
abundant, fertile, plentiful, copious, fecund, plenteous

rid: get rid of
verb to remove or destroy something » Arnold got rid of the spider in the bathtub.
dispose of, dump, eject, jettison, remove, weed out

ridiculous
adjective very foolish » Josh made the ridiculous claim of having met the queen.
absurd, laughable, ludicrous, preposterous

right 1
adjective in accordance with the facts » She had all the right answers and got full marks in the test.
accurate, correct, exact, factual, genuine, precise, strict, true, valid, unerring
antonym: **wrong**

right 2
adjective most suitable » The right time to sleep is at night.
acceptable, appropriate, desirable, done, fit, fitting, okay or **OK** (informal)**, proper, seemly, suitable**

right 3
noun what is just and fair
◀◀ SEE LEFT

right-wing
adjective believing in capitalist policies » *Steve agreed with some of the party's right-wing policies, especially lower taxes for the rich.*
conservative, reactionary, Tory

rigid 1
adjective not easy to bend » *The rigid metal of the chair was uncomfortable to sit on.*
firm, hard, solid, stiff
antonym: **flexible**

rigid 2
adjective unchangeable and often considered severe » *The school has a rigid timetable that cannot be altered.*
fixed, inflexible, set, strict, stringent

ring 1
verb to make a loud clear sound » *Skye heard the school bell ring.*
chime, clang, peal, resonate, toll

ring 2
noun an object or group of things in the shape of a circle » *My little brother floated on an inflatable rubber ring.*
band, circle, hoop, loop, round

My little brother floated on an inflatable rubber ring.

ring 3
noun a group of people who help each other, often secretly » *The twist in the movie's plot was that Jimmy was part of a spy ring.*
band, cell, clique, syndicate

riot 1
noun a disturbance made by an unruly mob » *Large numbers of fans were involved in a riot after the game.*
anarchy, disorder, disturbance, mob violence, strife

riot 2
verb to take part in a riot » *Some people rioted in protests against the new laws.*
go on the rampage, rampage, run riot, take to the streets

rise 1
verb to move upwards » *Smoke rose from the campfire.*
ascend, climb, go up, move up

Smoke rose from the campfire.

rise 2
verb to increase » *Customers were warned that the prices would rise next year.*
go up, grow, increase, intensify, mount
antonym: **fall**

rise 3
noun an increase in something » *The glowing review led to a rise in sales of the game.*
improvement, increase, upsurge
antonym: **fall**

risk 1
noun a chance that something unpleasant might happen » *If I go out now, there's a risk I'll miss my parcel being delivered.*
danger, gamble, peril, pitfall

risk 2
verb to do something knowing that something unpleasant might happen » *If he misses this game, he risks losing his place in the team.*
chance, dare, gamble, jeopardize, put in jeopardy

rival 1
noun the person someone is competing with » *The race winner was well ahead of his nearest rival.*
adversary, antagonist, challenger, opponent

rival 2
verb to be the equal or near equal of » *As a vacation destination, South Africa rivals Kenya for weather.*
be a match for, equal, match

river
noun a natural stream of fresh water flowing along a definite course, usually into the sea » *A fast-flowing river runs through the provincial park.*
beck, brook, creek, estuary, rivulet, stream, tributary, watercourse, waterway

A fast-flowing river runs through the provincial park.

There was no traffic at all on the road through the mountains.

road
noun a route used by travellers and vehicles » *There was no traffic at all on the road through the mountains.*
motorway, route, street, track

rob
verb to take something from a person illegally » *He was robbed of his money.*
burgle, con (informal)**, defraud, loot, steal from, swindle**

romantic
adjective connected with love » *Andy was very romantic and often bought Grace flowers.*
amorous, loving, tender

room 1
noun a separate section in a building » *You can stay in my spare room.*
chamber, office

room 2
noun unoccupied space » *There wasn't enough room for all his belongings.*
capacity, elbow room, space

rot 1
verb to become rotten » *The food in the broken fridge started to rot.*
decay, decompose, fester, spoil
related word: adjective **putrid**

rot »

rot ②
noun the condition that affects things when they rot » Dad varnished the timber frame to protect against rot.
decay, deterioration, mould, putrefaction, putrescence

rotten ①
adjective decayed and no longer of use » The strawberries I bought last week are rotten.
bad, decayed, decomposed, mouldy, sour

The strawberries I bought last week are rotten.

rotten ②
adjective (informal) of very poor quality » Whose rotten idea was it to go for a picnic in the rain?
inferior, lousy (slang), poor, unsatisfactory

rough ①
adjective uneven and not smooth » My bicycle bumped along on the rough ground.
bumpy, craggy, rocky, rugged, uneven
antonym: smooth

rough ②
adjective difficult or unpleasant » She had a rough time on the ship, feeling seasick all day.
difficult, hard, tough, unpleasant

rough ③
adjective only approximately correct » At a rough guess, I'd say there were 1000 students in my school.
approximate, estimated, sketchy, vague, imprecise, inexact

round ①
adjective shaped like a ball or a circle » Not all balls are round—rugby balls are oval.
circular, cylindrical, rounded, spherical

round ②
noun one of a series of events » After round three, the red team are in the lead by three points to two.
lap, period, session, stage

Tom couldn't remember the route, so he got out his map.

route
noun a way from one place to another » Tom couldn't remember the route, so he got out his map.
channel, course, itinerary, path, road, way

routine ①
adjective ordinary and done regularly » Dylan underwent a series of routine medical tests.
everyday, normal, ordinary, regular, standard, typical, usual

routine ②
noun the usual way or order someone does things » My morning routine is always to shower before breakfast.
order, pattern, practice, procedure, program, schedule, system

row ①
noun several things arranged in a line » There were rows of empty seats in the theatre.
bank, column, line, queue, rank, series

row ②
noun a serious disagreement » I had a row with my brother about who broke the laptop.
altercation, argument, fight, quarrel, squabble

rowdy
adjective rough and noisy » Nasir complained about being disturbed by his neighbours' rowdy parties.
boisterous, noisy, unruly, wild, obstreperous, uproarious

royal
adjective concerning a king or a queen or their family » We saw the royal yacht moored in the harbour.
imperial, regal, sovereign

rubbish ①
noun unwanted things or waste material » Rubbish was piled up at the side of the road, waiting to be removed.
garbage, litter, refuse, trash, waste

---

gallop The children galloped down the steep hill.

bolt The hound bolted after stealing the pie.

dart The dog darted left and right to avoid capture.

hare The dog hared off down the hill.

pound Tired out, Harry pounded along behind his sister.

jog The children jogged slowly up the steep inclines.

sprint Melissa was faster than Harry at sprinting after the dog.

rubbish [2]
noun foolish words or speech
» *Don't talk rubbish!*
drivel, garbage, hot air (informal), nonsense, rot

rude [1]
adjective not polite
» *Ignoring your friends is rude.*
disrespectful, impertinent, impudent, insolent, churlish, discourteous, peremptory
antonym: **polite**

rude [2]
adjective unexpected and unpleasant » *The campers had a rude awakening when a goat ran into their tent.*
abrupt, unpleasant, violent

ruin [1]
verb to destroy or spoil something » *The crops have been ruined by pests.*
break, damage, destroy, devastate, impair, mar, mess up, spoil, undo, wreck

ruin [2]
noun the state of being destroyed or spoiled » *The castle was falling into ruin.*
decay, destruction, devastation, disrepair, downfall, fall

*Sheep grazed near the **ruins** of the ancient temple.*

ruin [3]
noun the remaining parts of a severely damaged thing » *Sheep grazed near the ruins of the ancient temple.*
remains, shell, wreck

rule [1]
noun a statement of what is allowed » *Coming in late was against the rules.*
decree, guideline, law, order, regulation, dictum, ordinance, precept

rule [2] : as a rule
adverb usually or generally » *As a rule, I eat my meals at the kitchen table.*
generally, mainly, normally, on the whole, usually

rule [3]
verb to govern people » *Queen Elizabeth II has ruled the UK longer than any other monarch.*
administer, be in power, govern, lead, reign

ruler
noun a person who rules or commands » *Augustus was a decisive ruler of ancient Rome.*
commander, governor, head of state, leader, monarch, sovereign

rumour
noun a story which may or may not be true » *I heard a rumour that our trip might be cancelled.*
gossip, hearsay, whisper, word

run [1]
verb to move on foot at a rapid pace, never having both or all the feet on the ground at the same time
▼ SEE BELOW

run [2]
verb to manage » *Sean ran a small hotel.*
administer, be in charge of, control, direct, look after, manage

rush [1]
verb to move fast or do something quickly » *The plumber unblocked the pipe, and the water rushed out.*
dash, fly, gush, hasten, hurry, race, run, scurry, shoot

rush [2]
verb to force into immediate action without sufficient preparation » *I don't want to rush you, but I need to know soon if you're coming tonight.*
hurry, hustle, press, pressurize, push

rush [3]
noun a state of hurrying » *Fred was in a rush to catch the last train.*
bustle, dash, hurry, race, scramble, stampede

*Fred was in a **rush** to catch the last train.*

run
[1] verb to move on foot at a rapid pace, never having both or all the feet on the ground at the same time
» *The children **ran** down the hill after their dog.*

scurry
*The dog **scurried** away when it was chased.*

scamper
*The dog grabbed the pie from the picnic and **scampered** off.*

» sack

Ss

sack [1]
verb (informal) to dismiss from a job » Kevin was sacked from his weekend job because of his constant lateness.
can (informal), **discharge, dismiss, fire** (informal)

sack [2] : the sack
noun (informal) dismissal from a job » He got the sack after three months.
discharge, dismissal, termination of employment

sacrifice [1]
verb to give something up » Betsy sacrificed her lunch hour to distribute leaflets for charity.
forego, forfeit, give up, surrender

Betsy sacrificed her lunch hour to distribute leaflets for charity.

sacrifice [2]
noun the action of giving something up » Louise made many sacrifices in order to save money for her round-the-world trip.
renunciation, self-denial

I'm sad because my best friend's moved away.

sad [1]
adjective feeling unhappy about something » I'm sad because my best friend's moved away.
dejected, depressed, dismal, down, downcast, gloomy, glum, grief-stricken, low, melancholy, mournful, unhappy, wistful, blue, disconsolate, doleful, heavy-hearted, low-spirited, lugubrious, woebegone
antonym: **happy**

sad [2]
adjective making you feel unhappy » She sang a sad song of love and loss.
depressing, dismal, gloomy, harrowing, heart-rending, melancholy, mournful, moving, pathetic, poignant, tragic, upsetting

sadness
noun the feeling of being unhappy » I said goodbye with a mixture of sadness and joy.
dejection, depression, despondency, melancholy, unhappiness, cheerlessness, dolefulness, dolour
antonym: **happiness**

safe [1]
adjective not causing harm or danger » The lifeguard's green flag showed that the water was safe for swimming.
harmless, innocuous, wholesome
antonym: **dangerous**

safe [2]
adjective not in any danger » Everyone was safe from the storm in the shelter.
all right, in safe hands, okay or **OK** (informal), **out of danger, out of harm's way, protected, safe and sound, secure**

safeguard [1]
verb to protect something » A plan was in place to safeguard the park from developers who wanted to build on it.
defend, guard, look after, preserve, protect, save, shield

safeguard [2]
noun something that protects people or things » The charity puts safeguards in place to protect endangered species.
barrier, cover, defence, protection

safety
noun the state of being safe from harm or danger » For everyone's safety, the flight attendant ran through the emergency procedure.
immunity, protection, security
antonym: **danger**

For everyone's safety, the flight attendant ran through the emergency procedure.

Mounds of salt were harvested from the salty water.

salty
adjective tasting of or containing salt » Mounds of salt were harvested from the salty water.
briny, saline, salted

same
adjective exactly like one another
▶▶ SEE RIGHT

sanction [1]
verb to officially approve of or allow something » The school has sanctioned the selling of cupcakes on the premises to raise money for charity.
allow, approve, authorize, back, endorse, permit, support
antonym: **veto**

sanction [2]
noun official approval of something » The teacher required the sanction of each pupil's parent for the school trip to go ahead.
approval, authorization, backing, blessing, permission, support, assent, mandate, ratification (formal)

sanctions
plural noun penalties for countries that break the law » Trade sanctions were imposed for four years.
ban, boycott, embargo, penalties

194

save

sane 1
adjective having a normal healthy mind » *As the dog ran around in circles, Audrey wondered if it was sane.*
lucid, normal, rational, compos mentis, in your right mind, of sound mind
antonym: **insane**

sane 2
adjective showing good sense » *We respected her sane decision to stay at home.*
judicious, level-headed, rational, reasonable, sensible, sound

sarcastic
adjective saying the opposite of what you mean to make fun of someone » *A sarcastic remark about missing the ball was on the tip of her tongue.*
caustic, ironic, sardonic, satirical, derisive, mordacious, mordant

satisfactory
adjective acceptable or adequate » *The restaurant's food was satisfactory, but nothing special.*
acceptable, adequate, all right, good enough, passable, sufficient
antonym: **unsatisfactory**

satisfied
adjective happy because you have got what you want » *The satisfied customers left the sale, loaded with bargains.*
content, contented, happy, pleased
antonym: **disappointed**

satisfy 1
verb to give someone something they want » *By giving each team member a particular task, Liam found a solution to satisfy everyone.*
gratify, indulge, please, assuage, pander to, sate, satiate, slake

satisfy 2
verb to convince of something » *Ethan had to satisfy the coach that he was fit to play.*
convince, persuade, put someone's mind at rest, reassure

satisfy 3
verb to fulfill a requirement » *Pupils must satisfy the grade requirements to get into college.*
fulfill, meet

savage 1
noun a violent and uncivilized person or thing » *My mom was cross and accused us of eating like savages.*
barbarian, beast, brute, lout, monster

savage 2
verb to attack and bite someone or something » *The pup savaged the toy rattle.*
attack, bite, maul

The savage lion let out a sudden roar.

savage 3
adjective cruel and violent » *The savage lion let out a sudden roar.*
barbaric, barbarous, brutal, cruel, ferocious, inhuman, vicious, violent

save 1
verb to rescue someone or something » *Eli saved my life.*
come to someone's rescue, deliver, redeem, rescue, salvage

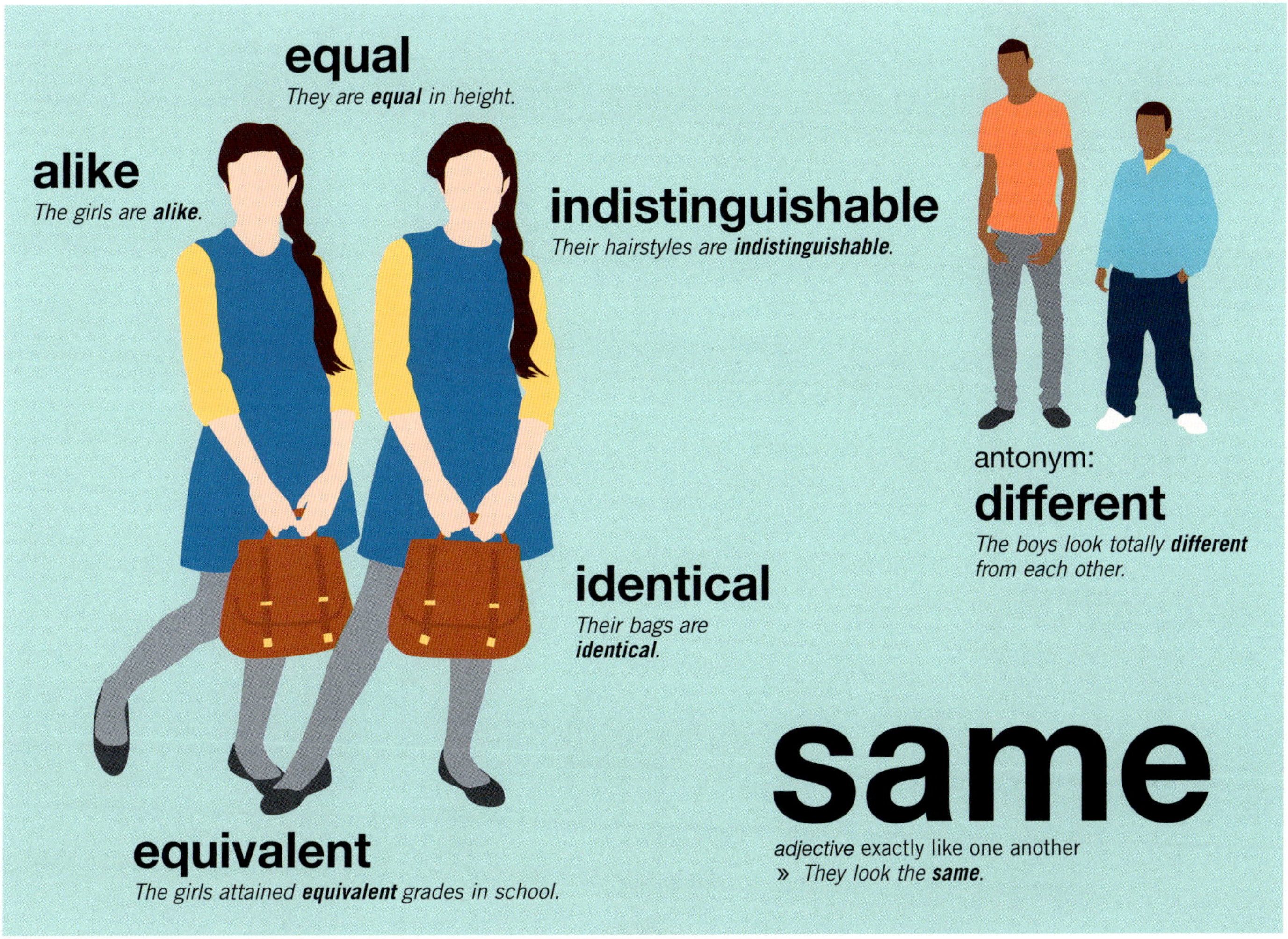

---

same
adjective exactly like one another » *They look the same.*

equal — They are **equal** in height.

alike — The girls are **alike**.

indistinguishable — Their hairstyles are **indistinguishable**.

identical — Their bags are **identical**.

equivalent — The girls attained **equivalent** grades in school.

antonym: **different** — The boys look totally **different** from each other.

save

say
1 *verb* to speak words
» "I love going to the movies," she **said**.

- announce
- comment
- state
- utter
- "I really enjoyed the show," she **remarked**.

- gabble
- chatter
- ramble
- prattle
- "I like cats, dogs, fish... everything!" he **babbled**.

- croak
- gasp
- pant
- rasp
- "I need to do more exercise," he **wheezed**.

- murmur
- mutter
- whisper
- "I hate getting the bus," he **mumbled**.

- converse
- chat
- gossip
- natter
- "It was just like when we were little," she **chattered**.

- growl
- hiss
- retort
- snarl
- "Keep quiet!" she **snapped**.

- interrupt
- mention
- note
- point out
- put in
- "I thought the book was good, too," he **added**.

- articulate
- declare
- express
- speak
- answer
- respond
- "I'm fine, thank you," ...he **replied**.

- inquire
- question
- query
- "How are you today?" she **asked**.

scrounge

save [2]
verb to keep someone or something safe » *Fences around playgrounds save children from running onto busy roads.*
keep safe, preserve, protect, safeguard

save [3]
verb to keep something for later use » *Chen was saving his allowance money to buy a new bike.*
hoard, keep, put by, reserve, set aside, economize, husband, retrench
antonym: **waste**

Chen was saving his allowance money to buy a new bike.

say [1]
verb to speak words
◀◀ SEE LEFT

say [2]
noun a chance to express your opinion » *Our teacher called a meeting so everyone could have a say.*
voice, vote

saying
noun a well-known sentence or phrase » *"Look before you leap" is a well-known saying.*
adage, axiom, maxim, proverb, aphorism, dictum

scarce
adjective rare or uncommon » *As fresh strawberries became scarce, she made her jam with frozen fruit.*
few, rare, uncommon, unusual
antonym: **common**

scare [1]
verb to frighten someone » *Mike jumped out and scared Clare.*
alarm, frighten, give someone a fright, intimidate, startle, terrify, terrorize, unnerve

scare [2]
noun a short period of feeling very frightened » *Caleb gave me a scare when he shrieked.*
fright, shock, start

scare [3]
noun a situation where people worry about something » *The bird flu scare is now over.*
alert, hysteria, panic

scary
adjective (informal) frightening » *We watched a scary film about ghosts.*
alarming, chilling, creepy (informal), eerie, frightening, hair-raising, spooky, terrifying, unnerving

scatter
verb to throw or drop things all over an area » *The wind scattered the dandelion seeds.*
shower, sow, sprinkle, throw about, broadcast, disseminate, strew
antonym: **gather**

The wind scattered the dandelion seeds.

scene [1]
noun a picture or view of something » *The scene in the painting was a house on a hill.*
landscape, panorama, view, outlook, vista

The police were first on the scene.

scene [2]
noun the place where something happens » *The police were first on the scene.*
location, place, setting, site, spot

scene [3]
noun an area of activity » *He is a well-known guitarist on the music scene.*
arena, business, environment, world

scenery
noun the things you see in the countryside » *We drove through the provincial park, admiring the scenery.*
landscape, panorama, surroundings, terrain, view, outlook, vista

scold
verb to tell someone off » *The teacher scolded the class for being too rowdy.*
chide, lecture, rebuke, reprimand, tell off (informal), berate, castigate, reprove, upbraid

scorn [1]
noun great contempt felt for something » *Tom thought his idea was a good one, and ignored the scorn shown by his friends.*
contempt, derision, disdain, mockery

scorn [2]
verb to treat with great contempt » *Eleanor scorned my offer of help.*
disdain, look down on, slight, deride, hold in contempt

scornful
adjective showing contempt » *Peter is scornful of his rivals and sure that he will win.*
contemptuous, disdainful, scathing, sneering, supercilious, withering

scrape [1]
verb to rub a rough or sharp object against something » *We had to scrape the frost from the windshield.*
graze, scour, scratch, scuff, skin

We had to scrape the frost from the windshield.

scrape [2]
verb to make a harsh noise by rubbing » *Sarah scraped her chair across the floor.*
grate, grind, rasp, scratch

scream [1]
verb to shout or cry in a high-pitched voice » *Cameron screamed as his bike sped down the hill.*
cry, howl, screech, shout, shriek, squeal, yell

scream [2]
noun a loud, high-pitched cry » *Hilda let out a scream of joy when she opened her present.*
cry, howl, screech, shriek, squeal, yell

scrounge
verb (informal) to get something by asking rather than working for it » *Harry tried to scrounge a lift.*
beg, bum (informal), **cadge, freeload** (informal), **sponge** (informal)

197

»scruffy

*Sadie and Ryan wore their **scruffy** clothes for painting.*

scruffy
adjective dirty and untidy » *Sadie and Ryan wore their scruffy clothes for painting.*
ragged, seedy, shabby, tatty, unkempt,
disreputable, slovenly, ungroomed
antonym: **neat**

scrutinize
verb to examine something very carefully » *Arianna scrutinized the chess board before she made her move.*
examine, inspect, pore over, scan, search, study

search 1
verb to look for something
▶▶ SEE RIGHT

search 2
noun the action of looking for something » *Kit began a search for a different type of skateboard.*
hunt, quest

secret
adjective known about by only a few people » *The movie stars got married at a secret location on a Pacific island.*
closet (informal),
confidential, covert, furtive, hidden, undercover, underground,
cloak-and-dagger, conspiratorial, undisclosed
related word: *adjective* **cryptic**

secretive
adjective hiding your feelings and intentions » *Skylar was secretive about her longing for a pony in case people laughed.*
cagey (informal), **reserved, reticent,** tight-lipped, uncommunicative, unforthcoming

section
noun one of the parts into which something is divided » *The dog is allowed only in this section of the house.*
division, instalment, part, piece, portion, segment

secure 1
verb (formal) to manage to get something » *Julian's good exam marks helped him to secure a place at university.*
acquire, gain, get, obtain, procure (formal)

secure 2
verb to make something safe » *The mighty stone walls secured the town against attack.*
fortify, make impregnable, make safe, strengthen

secure 3
verb to fasten or attach something firmly » *The train carriages were secured to the engine before it left the station.*
attach, bind, fasten, fix, lock, moor, tie up
antonym: **release**

secure 4
adjective tightly locked or well protected » *The bike was secure after he locked it to the rail.*
fortified, impregnable, protected, safe, shielded

*The bike was **secure** after he locked it to the rail.*

secure 5
adjective firmly fixed in place » *She finally made the child's safety seat secure in the back of the car.*
fastened, firm, fixed, locked, solid, stable, tight

secure 6
adjective feeling safe and happy » *The baby was sound asleep, secure in its mother's arms.*
confident, protected, reassured, relaxed, safe
antonym: **insecure**

*The baby was sound asleep, **secure** in its mother's arms.*

see 1
verb to look at or notice something » *I can see a herd of elephants.*
behold, discern, glimpse, look, notice, observe, perceive, sight, spot,
catch sight of, espy

see 2
verb to realize or understand something » *I see exactly what you mean.*
appreciate, comprehend, follow, get, grasp, realize, understand

see 3
verb to find something out » *I'll see what's happening outside the gates.*
ascertain, determine, discover, find out

seek 1
verb to try to find something » *Becky was seeking a book on bonsai trees from her library.*
be after, hunt, look for, search for

seek 2
verb to try to do something » *I seek to raise as much money as possible for charity.*
aim, aspire to, attempt, endeavour, strive, try

seem
verb to appear to be » *Lucas seemed shy at first because he was very quiet.*
appear, give the impression of, look, look like

seize 1
verb to grab something firmly » *Jim seized the phone from my hand.*
grab, grasp, snatch

seize 2
verb to take control of something » *The knights seized the castle.*
ambush, annex, appropriate, capture, confiscate, hijack, impound, take over,
commandeer, take possession of

select 1
verb to choose something » *The guests each selected a differently decorated cupcake.*
choose, decide on, opt for, pick, settle on, single out, take

*The guests each **selected** a differently decorated cupcake.*

select 2
adjective of good quality » *The team was a select group of the best players.*
choice, exclusive, first-class, first-rate, hand-picked, prime, special, superior

selfish
adjective caring only about yourself » *Ella knew it was selfish not to share her candy.*
egotistic or **egotistical, greedy, self-centred,** self-interested, self-seeking, ungenerous

sell 1
verb to let someone have something in return for money » *I decided to sell my bike.*
deal in, hawk, peddle, trade in
antonym: **buy**

sell 2
verb to have available for people to buy » *The café sells doughnuts.*
deal in, peddle, stock
antonym: **buy**

*The café **sells** doughnuts.*

send 1
verb to arrange for something to be delivered » *We sent Mom flowers for Mother's Day.*
dispatch, forward, remit

send 2
verb to transmit a signal or message » *Satellites send and receive signals to and from Earth.*
broadcast, stream, transmit

senior
adjective the highest and most important in an organization » *The senior officer trained the new recruits.*
best, better, high-ranking, superior
antonym: **junior**

sense 1
noun a feeling you have about something » *Zoe had a sense that everything was going well.*
consciousness, feeling, impression

sense 2
noun the ability to think and behave sensibly » *Oliver had the sense to call me when he got lost.*
brains (informal)**, common sense, intelligence, judgment, reason, wisdom,** sagacity, wit, wits

sense 3
verb to become aware of something » *Chloe sensed that Jayden wasn't telling her the whole story.*
be aware of, feel, get the impression, have a hunch, realize

sensible
adjective showing good sense and judgment » *We panicked when the dog got stuck, but Ted was sensible and calmly freed it.*
down-to-earth, judicious, practical, prudent, rational, sound, wise
antonym: **foolish**

*We panicked when the dog got stuck, but Ted was **sensible** and calmly freed it.*

sensitive
adjective easily upset about something » *The little boy was sensitive about other children playing with his toys.*
easily offended, easily upset, thin-skinned, touchy

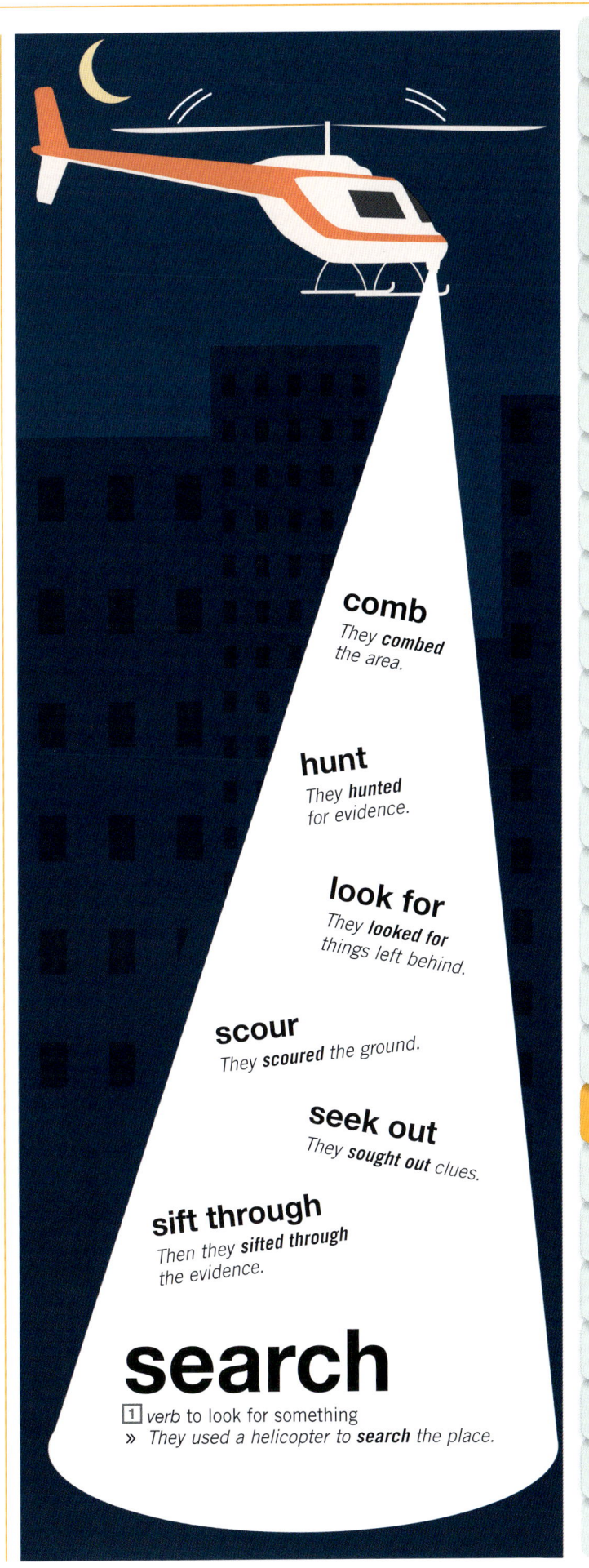

search
1 *verb* to look for something » *They used a helicopter to search the place.*

comb They **combed** the area.

hunt They **hunted** for evidence.

look for They **looked for** things left behind.

scour They **scoured** the ground.

seek out They **sought out** clues.

sift through Then they **sifted through** the evidence.

199

sentimental

*Isabella had a **sentimental** attachment to her old teddy bear.*

sentimental
adjective expressing exaggerated sadness or tenderness » *Isabella had a sentimental attachment to her old teddy bear.*
maudlin, mushy (informal), **nostalgic, sloppy** (informal), **dewy-eyed, mawkish, overemotional**

separate 1
adjective not connected to something else » *The house stood in a field, separate from the other houses.*
detached, disconnected, discrete, divorced, isolated, unconnected
antonym: **connected**

separate 2
verb to end a connection between people or things » *The two train carriages separated, taking the passengers to different destinations.*
detach, disconnect, divide, sunder, uncouple
antonym: **connect**

sequence 1
noun a number of events coming one after another » *The team enjoyed a sequence of wins.*
chain, course, cycle, series, string, succession

sequence 2
noun a particular order in which things are arranged » *The sequence of each day's TV programs is decided in advance.*
arrangement, order, progression, structure

series
noun a number of things coming one after the other » *Logan read a series of books about the same character.*
chain, run, sequence, string, succession

serious 1
adjective very bad and worrying » *Appendicitis is a serious but treatable illness.*
acute, alarming, bad, critical, dangerous, extreme, grave, grievous, grim, intense, precarious, severe, worrying

serious 2
adjective important, deserving careful thought » *Getting a dog is a serious responsibility.*
crucial, deep, difficult, far-reaching, grave, important, momentous, pressing, profound, significant, urgent, weighty
antonym: **funny**

serious 3
adjective sincere about something » *I thought Craig was joking, but he was serious.*
earnest, genuine, heartfelt, honest, in earnest, resolute, resolved, sincere

serious 4
adjective quiet and not laughing » *Keira put on a serious expression for her passport photograph.*
earnest, grave, humourless, pensive, sober, solemn, staid, stern

*Keira put on a **serious** expression for her passport photograph.*

set 1
noun a group of things that belong together » *The set of tools belonged in the shed.*
batch, bunch, bundle, collection, kit, outfit, series, assemblage, compendium, ensemble

set 2
verb to put or place something somewhere » *Eloise set her bag down on the ground.*
deposit, lay, locate, place, position, put, rest, stick

*Eloise **set** her bag down on the ground.*

set 3
adjective fixed and not varying » *We arrived at the set time.*
arranged, established, firm, fixed, predetermined, scheduled

set on
adjective determined to do something » *Josie was set on going to the beach.*
bent on, determined, intent on

settle 1
verb to put an end to an argument or problem » *The dispute was finally settled.*
clear up, decide, dispose of, put an end to, reconcile, resolve, straighten out

settle 2
verb to decide or arrange something » *My friends and I settled on going to the movies.*
agree, arrange, decide on, determine, fix

settle 3
verb to make your home in a place » *We settled in a new part of town.*
make your home, move to, put down roots, take up residence

set up
verb to make arrangements for something » *My sister set up a couple of interviews for part-time jobs.*
arrange, establish, install, institute, organize

sever
verb to cut something off » *The flowers had been severed from their stems during the storm.*
chop off, hack off, lop off

several
adjective more than two, but not many » *Clive won several medals in the competition.*
assorted, some, sundry, various

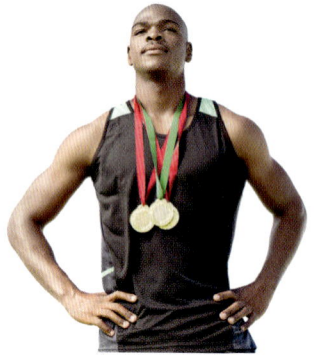

*Clive won **several** medals in the competition.*

severe 1
adjective extremely bad or unpleasant » *The hurricane caused severe damage.*
acute, critical, dire, extreme, grave, intense, serious, terrible
antonym: **mild**

severe 2
adjective stern and harsh » *Janet gave Lee a severe look when he dropped the vase.*
disapproving, grim, hard, harsh, stern, strict

shelter

shabby [1]
adjective ragged and worn in appearance » *Dad's favourite coat was now old and shabby.*
dilapidated, ragged, scruffy, seedy, tatty, threadbare, worn, down at heel, run-down, the worse for wear

shabby [2]
adjective behaving meanly and unfairly » *My aunt complained to the manager about the family's shabby treatment by the waiter.*
contemptible, despicable, dirty, mean, rotten (informal), dishonourable, ignoble

shake [1]
verb to move something from side to side or up and down » *Shake the bottle before opening it.*
agitate, brandish, flourish, wave

shake [2]
verb to move from side to side or up and down » *The earthquake caused the ground to shake.*
jolt, quake, quiver, shiver, shudder, tremble, vibrate, joggle, oscillate

shake [3]
verb to shock and upset someone » *The news shook me and I had to lie down.*
distress, disturb, rattle (informal)**, shock, unnerve, upset,** discompose, traumatize

shaky
adjective weak and unsteady » *The rope bridge was shaky.*
rickety, tottering, trembling, unstable, unsteady, wobbly

The rope bridge was shaky.

shame [1]
noun a feeling of guilt or embarrassment » *The shame Ryan felt over his rushed homework made him determined to do well next time.*
embarrassment, humiliation, ignominy, abashment, loss of face, mortification

shame [2]
noun something that makes people lose respect for you » *Bullies bring shame on a school.*
discredit, disgrace, dishonour, scandal

shame [3]
verb to make someone feel ashamed » *My mom was so upset about the state of my bedroom that she shamed me into tidying it.*
disgrace, embarrass, humiliate, abash, mortify

shameless
adjective behaving badly without showing any shame » *Greg complimented the teacher in a shameless attempt to get better grades.*
barefaced, brazen, flagrant, unabashed, unashamed

shape [1]
noun the outline of something » *The geometric shapes formed a starlike pattern.*
contours, figure, form, lines, outline

The geometric shapes formed a starlike pattern.

shape [2]
verb to make something in a particular form » *Shape the dough into a loaf.*
fashion, form, make, model, mould

The friends shared the pizza.

share [1]
verb to divide something between two or more people » *The friends shared the pizza.*
divide, split

share [2]
noun a portion of something » *I took my share of popcorn.*
allotment, portion, quota, ration

sharp [1]
adjective having a fine cutting edge or point » *Ian used the sharp knife to cut up an apple.*
jagged, keen, pointed, razor-sharp
antonym: **blunt**

sharp [2]
adjective quick to notice or understand things » *The mouse was sharp enough to leave the cheese on the mousetrap.*
alert, astute, bright, observant, perceptive, quick, quick-witted

sharp [3]
adjective sudden and significant » *Josie made a sharp turn into the parking lot.*
abrupt, marked, sudden

sheer [1]
adjective complete and total » *The nursery rhyme was sheer nonsense.*
absolute, complete, pure, total, unqualified, utter, unadulterated, unmitigated (formal)

sheer [2]
adjective vertical » *The climbing wall was on the sheer face of a building.*
perpendicular, steep, vertical

sheer [3]
adjective very light and delicate » *Molly wore a sheer black scarf.*
delicate, fine, lightweight, thin
antonym: **thick**

shelter [1]
noun a place providing protection » *We all met at the bus shelter.*
hostel, refuge, sanctuary

shelter [2]
noun protection from the weather or danger » *The hut provided shelter from the snowy mountainside.*
asylum, cover, harbour, haven, protection, refuge, safety, sanctuary

The hut provided shelter from the snowy mountainside.

shelter [3]
verb to stay somewhere in order to be safe » *Luca sheltered in the doorway until the rain stopped.*
hide, huddle, take cover

shelter [4]
verb to hide or protect someone or something » *The mother bird sheltered the chicks until they could fly.*
harbour, hide, protect, shield

shine
verb to give out a bright light » *The stars shone brightly in the night sky.*
beam, gleam, glow, radiate, shimmer, sparkle

shining
adjective giving out or reflecting light » *Eleanor put sunglasses on to protect her eyes from the shining sunlight.*
bright, brilliant, gleaming, luminous, radiant, shimmering, sparkling, incandescent

shock 1
noun a sudden upsetting experience » *It was a shock to discover that the screen on her phone had shattered.*
blow, bombshell, distress, trauma

shock 2
verb to make you feel upset » *He was shocked when his exam was cancelled at the very last minute.*
numb, paralyze, shake, stagger, stun, traumatize

shock 3
verb to offend because of being rude or immoral » *Nana is easily shocked by my jokes.*
appal, disgust, offend, outrage, nauseate, scandalize

shop
noun a place where things are sold
▼ SEE BELOW

shore
noun land that borders a body of water » *The sandy shore was littered with shells.*
bank, beach, coast, foreshore, front, lakefront, lakeside, sands, seaboard, seashore, shingle, waterside

The sandy shore was littered with shells.

short 1
adjective not lasting very long » *We enjoyed a short break in the countryside.*
brief, fleeting, momentary, short-lived
antonym: long

Naomi arranged the Russian dolls from short to tall.

short 2
adjective small in height » *Naomi arranged the Russian dolls from short to tall.*
little, small, diminutive, tiny, petite, squat
antonym: tall

short 3
adjective not using many words » *Kevin's speech was short and to the point.*
brief, concise, succinct, terse, abridged, laconic, pithy

shortage
noun a lack of something » *There was a shortage of bananas at the store.*
dearth, deficiency, lack, scarcity, shortfall, want, insufficiency, paucity
antonym: abundance

shorten
verb to make something shorter » *Alexander shortened his name to Alex.*
abbreviate, cut, trim, abridge, downsize, truncate
antonym: lengthen

shout 1
noun a loud call or cry » *I heard a distant shout and ran to see what the matter was.*
bellow, cry, roar, scream, yell

shout 2
verb to call or cry loudly » *Paul shouted downstairs to his brother.*
bawl, bellow, call, cry, roar, scream, yell

show 1
noun a public exhibition » *Our class went to see a show at the local theatre.*
display, exhibition, presentation

show 2
noun a display of a feeling or quality » *Granny gave all of us hugs and kisses in a big show of affection.*
air, display, pose, pretense, semblance

---

shop

noun a place where things are sold » *I went to the coffee shop.*

store — *I browsed in the store.*

boutique — *I bought smart clothes in the boutique.*

show 3
verb to prove something » *The experiment showed that oil is less dense than water.*
demonstrate, prove

show 4
verb to display a quality or characteristic » *Savannah's sketches showed real skill.*
demonstrate, display, indicate, manifest, reveal, evince, testify to

show 5 : show how
verb to do something to teach someone else » *Dad showed me how to play the game.*
demonstrate, instruct, teach

Dad showed me how to play the game.

shrewd
adjective showing intelligence and good judgment » *She was shrewd with money and saved most of it.*
astute, canny, crafty, perceptive, sharp, smart, perspicacious, sagacious

shrill
adjective high-pitched and piercing » *The bird's call was shrill and loud.*
penetrating, piercing, sharp

shrink
verb to become smaller » *Paul's sweater had shrunk in the wash.*
contract, diminish, dwindle, get smaller, narrow
antonym: **grow**

Paul's sweater had shrunk in the wash.

shut 1
verb to close something » *Someone had forgotten to shut the door.*
close, fasten, slam
antonym: **open**

shut 2
adjective closed or fastened » *Eva heard a sound coming from behind the shut door.*
closed, fastened, sealed
antonym: **open**

Pete was shy and found it hard to make friends at school.

shy
adjective nervous in the company of other people » *Pete was shy and found it hard to make friends at school.*
bashful, retiring, self-conscious, timid, diffident, self-effacing
antonym: **bold**

sick 1
adjective unwell or ill » *The doctor's waiting room was full of sick people.*
ailing, ill, poorly (informal)**, run down, under par** (informal)**, under the weather, unwell**
antonym: **well**

sick 2
adjective feeling as if you are going to vomit » *The stomach bug made Lily feel sick.*
ill, nauseous, queasy

sick 3 : sick of
adjective (informal) tired of something » *Cora was sick of listening to the same music over and over again.*
bored of, fed up with, tired of, weary of

side 1
noun the edge of something » *Tyler sat up and dangled his legs over the side of the bed.*
border, edge, verge
related word: *adjective* **lateral**

side 2
noun one of two groups involved in a dispute or contest » *Both sides had won the competition before.*
camp, faction, party, team

side with
verb to support someone in an argument » *Louise always sided with her sister when anyone was mean to her.*
agree with, stand up for, support, take the part of

sight 1
noun the ability to see » *My sight is so much better now that I wear glasses.*
eyesight, visibility, vision
related words: *adjectives* **optical, visual**

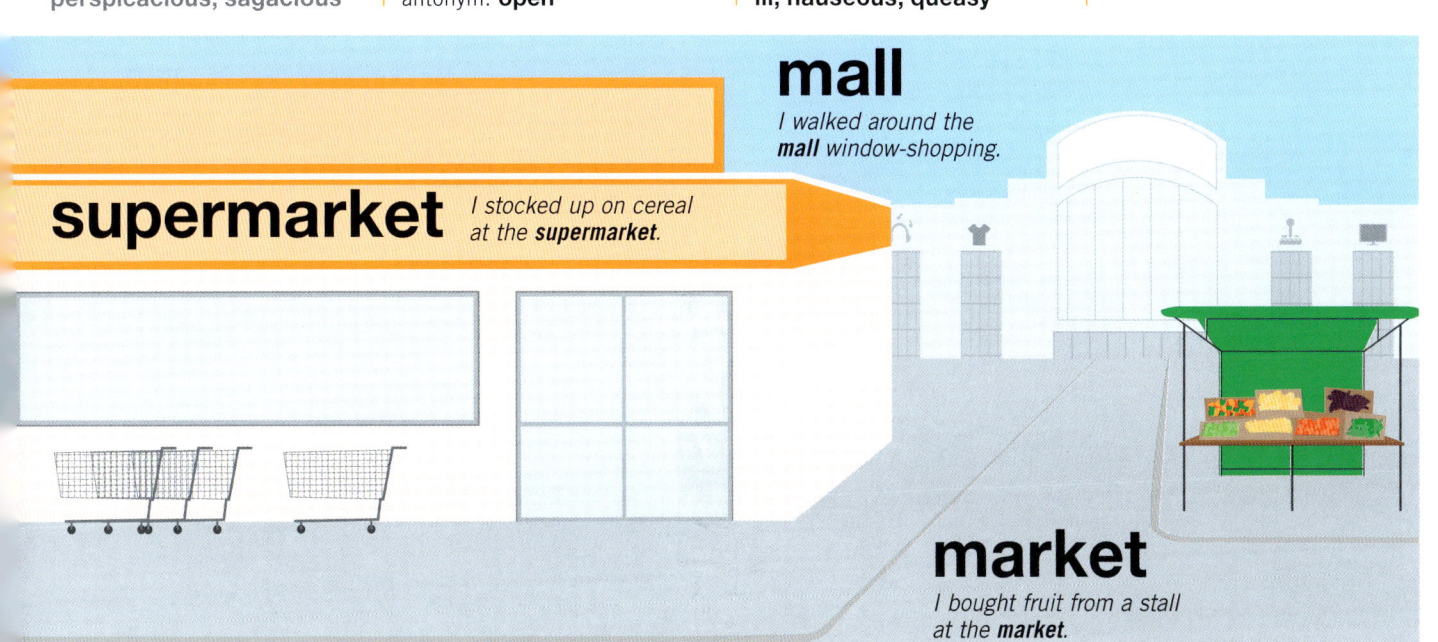

---

sight »

mall
I walked around the mall window-shopping.

supermarket
I stocked up on cereal at the supermarket.

market
I bought fruit from a stall at the market.

203

» sight

sight [2]
noun something you see
» *The fields of wildflowers were a beautiful sight.*
display, scene, spectacle

sight [3]
verb to see something or someone » *We sighted a rare red squirrel on our walk in the woods.*
see, spot

sign [1]
noun a mark or symbol
» *A check mark is a sign to show good work.*
character, emblem, logo, mark, symbol

sign [2]
noun a notice put up to give a warning or information
» *The sign warned that the floor was wet and slippery.*
billboard, notice, placard, poster

The sign warned that the floor was wet and slippery.

sign [3]
noun evidence of something
» *The green shoots of plants and flowers were a sign that spring was on its way.*
clue, evidence, hint, indication, omen, symptom, token, trace

signal [1]
noun something that is intended to give a message
» *The traffic signal turned red, so I stopped the car.*
beacon, cue, gesture, sign

Hayley signalled for a taxi.

signal [2]
verb to make a sign as a message to someone
» *Hayley signalled for a taxi.*
beckon, gesticulate, gesture, motion, nod, sign, wave

significant
adjective large or important
» *The medicine had a significant effect on Evan's stomach bug, and he was feeling better in no time.*
considerable, important, impressive, marked, notable, pronounced, striking
antonym: **insignificant**

silence [1]
noun an absence of sound
» *There was total silence in the room while the class took the exam.*
calm, hush, lull, peace, quiet, stillness
antonym: **noise**

silence [2]
noun an inability or refusal to talk » *Mary maintained a respectful silence, keeping her thoughts to herself.*
dumbness, muteness, reticence, speechlessness, taciturnity, uncommunicativeness, voicelessness

silence [3]
verb to make someone or something quiet » *The crying baby was silenced by the arrival of his mother with some milk.*
deaden, gag, muffle, quiet, quieten, stifle, still, suppress

silent [1]
adjective not saying anything
» *The class fell silent when the teacher entered the room.*
dumb, mute, speechless, taciturn, wordless, tongue-tied, uncommunicative

silent [2]
adjective making no noise
» *The clock was silent because its battery needed replacing.*
hushed, quiet, soundless, still
antonym: **noisy**

silly
adjective foolish or ridiculous
» *The dog wore a silly hat.*
absurd, crazy (informal)**, foolish, frivolous, idiotic, inane, ridiculous, stupid, asinine, fatuous, puerile, witless**

The dog wore a silly hat.

similar
adjective like something else
» *Our red dresses were similar.*
alike, analogous, comparable, like, uniform
antonym: **different**

similarity
noun the quality of being like something else
» *The similarity between the two paintings is striking.*
analogy, likeness, resemblance, sameness, comparability, congruence, similitude
antonym: **difference**

simple [1]
adjective easy to understand or do » *The recipe had only three simple steps.*
easy, elementary, straightforward, uncomplicated, understandable
antonym: **complicated**

simple [2]
adjective plain in style
» *Sarah wore a simple but stylish outfit.*
classic, clean, plain, severe
antonym: **elaborate**

simplify
verb to make something easier to do or understand
» *The teacher had to simplify her instructions as some of the students didn't understand them.*
make simpler, streamline

sin [1]
noun wicked and immoral behaviour » *The man asked for forgiveness for his sins.*
crime, evil, offence, wickedness, wrong, iniquity, misdeed, transgression, trespass

sin [2]
verb to do something wicked and immoral » *I didn't mean to lie—I'm sorry I sinned.*
cheat, do wrong, go astray, misbehave, transgress

sincere
adjective saying things that you really mean
» *Ashley gave her sincere thanks for the thoughtful gifts.*
genuine, heartfelt, real, wholehearted
antonym: **insincere**

single [1]
adjective only one » *Ruby kept the single sock in case the matching one turned up.*
lone, one, only, sole, solitary

Ruby kept the single sock in case the matching one turned up.

sleepy »

single [2]
adjective not married
» *Barry was single and enjoyed living on his own.*
unattached, unmarried

single [3]
adjective for one person only
» *Mom booked a single room at the hotel because Dad couldn't go.*
individual, separate

singular
adjective (formal) unusual and remarkable » *Mary had a singular smile—it lit up her whole face.*
exceptional, extraordinary, rare, remarkable, uncommon, unique, unusual

sinister
adjective seeming harmful or evil » *The bad guy in the book was a sinister character.*
evil, forbidding, menacing, ominous, threatening,
baleful, bodeful, disquieting

situation
noun what is happening
» *Mr. Lee mistaking me for my brother was a funny situation.*
case, circumstances, plight, scenario, state of affairs

The bears came in various sizes.

size [1]
noun how big or small something is » *The bears came in various sizes.*
dimensions, extent, proportions

size [2]
noun the fact of something being very large » *The sheer size of the island meant that it would take weeks to travel its entire coastline.*
bulk, immensity,
magnitude, vastness

skilful
adjective able to do something very well » *Kate had regular tennis coaching and was a skilful player.*
able, accomplished, adept, competent, expert, masterly, proficient, skilled,
adroit, dexterous
antonym: **incompetent**

skill
noun the ability to do something well
» *Completing such a complex task requires skill.*
ability, competence, dexterity, expertise, facility, knack, proficiency

skilled
adjective having the knowledge to do something well
» *The model was made by a highly skilled carpenter.*
able, accomplished, competent, experienced, expert, masterly, professional, proficient, skilful, trained
antonym: **incompetent**

skinny
adjective extremely thin
» *The boy ate like a horse but was naturally skinny.*
bony, emaciated, lean, scrawny, thin, underfed, undernourished
antonym: **plump**

slander [1]
noun something untrue and malicious said about someone
» *It was slander to say that someone else wrote her books.*
libel, scandal, slur, smear,
aspersion, calumny, defamation

slander [2]
verb to say untrue and malicious things about someone
» *She apologized for slandering the Prime Minister.*
libel, malign, smear,
defame, traduce, vilify

sleep [1]
noun the natural state of rest in which you are unconscious
» *Heather woke up feeling rested after a good sleep.*
doze, forty winks (slang), **hibernation, nap, slumber, snooze** (informal),
dormancy, repose, siesta

sleep [2]
verb to rest in a natural state of unconsciousness
▼ SEE BELOW

sleepy [1]
adjective tired and ready to go to sleep » *The cat was sleepy and curled up on the rug.*
drowsy, lethargic, sluggish,
somnolent, torpid

sleepy [2]
adjective not having much activity or excitement » *We live in a sleepy little village.*
dull, peaceful, quiet

---

doze
Orlando **dozed**.

snooze
Smudge **snoozed** on and off.

slumber
Violet **slumbered** peacefully for hours.

take a nap
Kitty regularly **took a nap** on the sofa.

sleep
[2] verb to rest in a natural state of unconsciousness » *The cats slept.*

hibernate
Ferdinand **hibernated** during winter.

205

» slender

smell

[1] *noun* the quality of something that you sense through your nose
» There were so many **smells** in the room.

fragrance — A fruity **fragrance** wafted from the shampoo.

odour — The **odour** from her brother's sports gear was not pleasant.

perfume — The lemon tree released a tangy **perfume**.

aroma — She smelled the strong **aroma** of fresh coffee.

scent — The flowers had been specially chosen for their **scent**.

stink — There was a **stink** from the dog: what had it rolled in?

reek — That **reek** is coming from your running shoes.

funk (informal) — Something in the garbage was giving off a horrible **funk**.

stench — There was a **stench** of burned food.

206

*The woman was tall and **slender**.*

slender [1]
adjective thin and lean, not muscular » *The woman was tall and slender.*
lean, slight, slim, svelte, sylphlike, willowy

slender [2]
adjective small in amount or degree » *The politician won the vote by a slender margin.*
faint, remote, slight, slim, small, inconsiderable, tenuous

slight
adjective small in amount or degree » *Tallulah found a slight dent on her phone.*
insignificant, minor, negligible, small, trivial, inconsiderable, paltry, scanty
antonym: **large**

slip [1]
verb to lose your footing and slide unintentionally » *Gavin slipped on the ice.*
skid, slide, slither, glide, skate

slip [2]
verb to go somewhere quickly and quietly » *Amy slipped away to her room while the others watched TV.*
creep, sneak, steal

slip [3]
noun a small mistake » *Levi worked hard to ensure there were no slips in the calculations.*
blunder, error, mistake, slip-up, faux pas, imprudence, indiscretion

slogan
noun a short, easily remembered phrase » *Justin Trudeau campaigned for Prime Minister with the slogan "Real Change Now."*
jingle, motto

slope [1]
noun a flat surface with one end higher than the other » *The slope was so steep it was for advanced skiers only.*
gradient, incline, ramp, declination, declivity, inclination

*The **slope** was so steep it was for advanced skiers only.*

slope [2]
verb to be at an angle » *The bank sloped sharply down to the river.*
fall, rise, slant

slouch
verb to stand or sit with your shoulders and head drooping forwards » *Dom slouched, so his dad told him to sit straight.*
bow, droop, loaf, loll, lounge, slump, stoop

slow
adjective moving or happening with little speed » *We made slow progress climbing the hill.*
gradual, leisurely, lingering, ponderous, sluggish, unhurried
antonym: **fast**

slow: slow down
verb to go or cause to go more slowly » *The car slowed down and then stopped.*
check, decelerate

slowly
adverb not quickly or hurriedly » *A tortoise walks very slowly.*
by degrees, gradually, unhurriedly
antonym: **quickly**

sly
adjective cunning and deceptive » *The sly fox is known for its crafty hunting techniques.*
crafty, cunning, devious, scheming, underhand, wily

small [1]
adjective not large in size, number, or amount » *Everything in the dollhouse was on a small scale.*
little, miniature, minuscule, minute, restricted, tiny
antonym: **large**

*Everything in the dollhouse was on a **small** scale.*

small [2]
adjective not important or significant » *Mom made small changes to the seating plan.*
inconsequential, insignificant, little, minor, negligible, petty, slight, trifling, trivial, unimportant

smart [1]
adjective clean and neat in appearance » *My brother looked smart in his new school uniform.*
chic, dashing, elegant, neat, spruce, stylish, modish, natty, snappy
antonym: **scruffy**

smart [2]
adjective clever and intelligent » *Eliza was smart and always got good grades at school.*
astute, bright, canny, clever, ingenious, intelligent, shrewd
antonym: **dumb**

smell [1]
noun the quality of something that you sense through your nose
◀◀ SEE LEFT

smell [2]
verb to have an unpleasant smell » *Do my feet smell?*
reek, stink

smell [3]
verb to become aware of the smell of something » *Connie could smell the flowers as soon as she walked into the room.*
get a whiff (informal), **scent, sniff**

smelly
adjective having a strong unpleasant smell » *Something in the garbage was extremely smelly.*
foul, reeking, stinking, fetid, malodorous
antonym: **fragrant**

smile [1]
verb to move the corners of your mouth upwards because you are pleased » *When Jon saw me, he smiled and waved.*
beam, grin, smirk

smile [2]
noun the expression you have when you smile » *Using an emoticon of a smile is a way of flagging up a joke.*
beam, grin, smirk

*Using an emoticon of a **smile** is a way of flagging up a joke.*

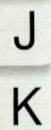

smooth

Pebbles have a smooth surface, worn down by the sea.

smooth
adjective not rough or bumpy
» *Pebbles have a smooth surface, worn down by the sea.*
glassy, glossy, polished, silky, sleek
antonym: **rough**

smug
adjective pleased with yourself
» *Rory felt smug after he scored the winning goal.*
complacent, conceited, self-satisfied, superior

snag
noun a small problem or disadvantage » *The snag was that I had no way to get home.*
catch, difficulty, disadvantage, drawback, glitch, problem, downside, **stumbling block**

sneak 1
verb to go somewhere quietly » *I like to sneak up on my brother and surprise him.*
creep, lurk, sidle, slip, steal, skulk, slink

sneak 2
verb to put or take something somewhere secretly
» *I sometimes sneak an extra banana from the fruit bowl.*
slip, smuggle, spirit

sneaky
adjective doing things secretly or things being done secretly
» *My cat took a sneaky mouthful of our tuna salad.*
crafty, deceitful, devious, dishonest, mean, slippery, sly, underhanded, untrustworthy

snoop 1
noun a person who interferes in other people's business
» *The guy was a snoop and kept asking lots of questions.*
busybody, detective, eavesdropper, meddler, private detective, snooper, busybody, buttinsky (slang), **nosy parker**

snoop 2
verb to interfere in other people's business
» *She snooped into my private locker.*
interfere, intrude, meddle, nose around, peek, peep, pry, spy

soak
verb to make something very wet » *The spray soaked us.*
bathe, permeate, steep, wet, drench, **saturate**

The spray soaked us.

sociable
adjective enjoying the company of other people » *The girl was sociable and liked to spend time with her friends.*
friendly, gregarious, outgoing, companionable, **convivial**

society 1
noun the people in a particular country or region » *She comes from a traditional society.*
civilization, culture

society 2
noun an organization for people with the same interest or aim
» *He signed up to the school debating society to improve his public speaking skills.*
association, circle, club, fellowship, group, guild, institute, league, organization, union

soft 1
adjective not hard, stiff, or firm
» *Eric quickly fell asleep on the soft, comfy bed.*
flexible, pliable, squashy, supple, yielding, bendable, **ductile, gelatinous, malleable, tensile**
antonym: **hard**

soft 2
adjective quiet and not harsh
» *Oscar could barely hear the soft tapping at the door.*
gentle, low, mellow, muted, quiet, subdued, dulcet, **mellifluous**

software
noun computer programs used on a particular system
» *The computer's software needed updating.*
app, application, code, program

soil 1
noun the surface of the earth
» *The soil is full of nutrients that plants use as food.*
clay, dirt, earth, ground

soil 2
verb to make something dirty
» *The towel was soiled after he dried the muddy dog with it.*
dirty, foul, pollute, smear, spatter, stain, befoul, begrime, defile, sully
antonym: **clean**

solemn
adjective not cheerful or humorous » *Angela's speech was solemn and thoughtful.*
grave, serious, sober, sombre, staid

solid 1
adjective hard and firm
» *The sculpture was carved from a block of solid ice.*
firm, hard

solid 2
adjective not likely to fall down
» *The solid tower had stood for hundreds of years.*
stable, strong, sturdy, substantial

solitude
noun the state of being alone
» *Jeff needed solitude so he could finish writing his story.*
isolation, loneliness, privacy, seclusion

solve
verb to find the answer to a problem or question
» *We solved the big mystery.*
clear up, crack, decipher, get to the bottom of, resolve, work out

sometimes
adverb now and then
» *Stefan sometimes felt like bouncing on the trampoline.*
at times, every now and then, every so often, from time to time, now and again, now and then, occasionally, once in a while

soon
adverb in a very short time
» *I'll see you soon.*
any minute now, before long, in a minute, in the near future, presently, shortly
antonym: **later**

sophisticated 1
adjective having refined tastes
» *The new restaurant was fashionable and sophisticated.*
cosmopolitan, cultivated, cultured, refined, urbane

sophisticated 2
adjective advanced and complicated » *The airport had sophisticated eye-scanning security equipment.*
advanced, complex, complicated, elaborate, intricate
antonym: **simple**

sore
adjective causing pain and discomfort » *The cut on Stephanie's finger was sore.*
inflamed, painful, raw, sensitive, smarting, tender

sorrow [1]
noun deep sadness or regret » *The story was about a boy who overcame sorrow and lived happily ever after.*
grief, heartache, melancholy, misery, mourning, pain, regret, sadness, unhappiness, woe (formal)
antonym: **joy**

sorrow [2]
noun things that cause sadness and regret » *Jim remembered with nostalgia both the joys and sorrows of his time at sea.*
hardship, heartache, misfortune, trouble, woe (formal)**, worry, affliction, tribulation** (formal)
antonym: **joy**

sorry [1]
adjective feeling sadness or regret » *I'm sorry to bother you.*
apologetic, penitent, regretful, remorseful, repentant, conscience-stricken, contrite, guilt-ridden, shamefaced

sorry [2]
adjective feeling sympathy for someone » *Renata felt sorry for the injured girl.*
moved, sympathetic

sorry [3]
adjective in a bad condition » *The boat was in a sorry state after the storm.*
deplorable, miserable, pathetic, pitiful, poor, sad, wretched, piteous, pitiable

*The boat was in a **sorry** state after the storm.*

sort [1]
noun one of the different kinds of something » *What sort of ice cream would you like?*
brand, category, class, group, kind, make, species, style, type, variety, ilk, stamp

sort [2]
verb to arrange things into different kinds » *Jay sorted his notes and put them into three folders.*
arrange, categorize, classify, divide, grade, group, separate

sound [1]
noun something that can be heard » *The sound of thunder rumbled in the distance.*
din, hubbub, noise, racket, tone
antonym: **silence**
related words: *adjectives* **acoustic, sonic**

sound [2]
verb to produce or cause to produce a noise » *The teacher sounded the bell to mark the end of lunch.*
blow, chime, clang, peal, ring, set off, toll

sound [3]
adjective healthy, or in good condition » *Everyone is safe and sound, thank goodness.*
all right, fine, fit, healthy, in good condition, intact, robust

sound [4]
adjective reliable and sensible » *The teacher gave Alice sound advice about entering the poetry competition.*
down-to-earth, good, reasonable, reliable, sensible, solid, valid

sour [1]
adjective having a sharp taste
▶▶ SEE RIGHT

sour
[1] *adjective* having a sharp taste » *The lemon tasted **sour**.*

acidic — *I'm acidic.*
bitter — *I'm a bitter lemon.*
pungent — *I give off a pungent smell.*
sharp — *I have a sharp flavour.*
tart — *I have a tart taste.*
acerbic — *I'm acerbic on the tongue.*
acetic — *I'm as acetic as vinegar.*

antonym: **sweet**
*The strawberry tasted **sweet**.*

sour

sour [2]
adjective unpleasant in taste because no longer fresh » *Yuck, the milk's gone sour.*
curdled, off, rancid

sour [3]
adjective bad-tempered and unfriendly » *The teacher wore a sour expression, which meant we were in trouble.*
disagreeable, embittered, jaundiced, tart, churlish, peevish, waspish

source
noun the place where something comes from » *The source of the river is in the mountains.*
beginning, cause, derivation, origin, originator, fount, fountainhead, wellspring

souvenir
noun something you keep as a reminder » *I bought a snow globe from the market as a souvenir.*
keepsake, memento, relic, reminder, token

*I bought a snow globe from the market as a **souvenir**.*

space [1]
noun an area that is empty or available » *The yard has plenty of space for a slide and swings.*
accommodation, capacity, room
related word: *adjective* **spatial**

space [2]
noun the gap between two things » *Fay squeezed into the small space between the table and chair.*
blank, distance, gap, interval

space [3]
noun a period of time » *Max and Josh received two pieces of good news in the space of a week.*
interval, period, span, time, while

spacious
adjective having or providing a lot of space » *The car was spacious enough to fit seven people.*
ample, broad, expansive, extensive, huge, large, vast, capacious, commodious, roomy, sizable

spare [1]
adjective in addition to what is needed » *Liz kept a spare pair of glasses in her bag.*
extra, free, superfluous, surplus, leftover, supernumerary

spare [2]
verb to make something available » *Please could you spare us some bread?*
afford, give, let someone have

spare [3]
verb to save someone from an unpleasant experience » *The teacher told us off but spared us the full lecture.*
let off (informal)**, pardon, relieve of, save from**

sparkle
verb to shine with small bright points of light » *The water sparkled in the sunshine.*
gleam, glisten, glitter, shimmer, twinkle, coruscate, scintillate

*The water **sparkled** in the sunshine.*

*Jim wanted to **speak** to his best friend so he could tell her all about the trip.*

speak
verb to use your voice to say words » *Jim wanted to speak to his best friend so he could tell her all about the trip.*
articulate, comment, converse, declare, explain, observe, pronounce, state, tell, affirm, assert, utter

special [1]
adjective more important or better than others of its kind » *They were celebrating a special occasion—it was his sister's 16th birthday.*
exceptional, important, significant, unique
antonym: **ordinary**

special [2]
adjective relating to one person or group in particular » *You will have to wear special gloves when you work with chemicals in the laboratory.*
characteristic, distinctive, individual, particular, peculiar, specific
antonym: **general**

specify
verb to state or describe something precisely » *To avoid disappointment, please specify which size and colour you would like the coat to be.*
be specific about, indicate, name, spell out, state, stipulate

spectator
noun a person who watches something » *Spectators lined the route of the parade.*
bystander, eyewitness, observer, onlooker, witness, fan, viewer, watcher

speech
noun a formal talk given to an audience » *He delivered his speech in three languages.*
address, discourse, lecture, talk, disquisition, harangue, homily, oration

speed [1]
noun the rate at which something moves or happens » *The Formula One drivers increased their speed.*
haste, momentum, pace, rapidity, swiftness, velocity

*The Formula One drivers increased their **speed**.*

speed [2]
verb to move quickly » *The motorbike sped along the road.*
career, flash, fly, gallop, hasten, hurry, race, run, rush, tear

spin
verb to turn quickly around a central point » *The wheels spun around as the bicycle gathered speed.*
pirouette, revolve, rotate, turn, whirl

spirit [1]
noun the part of you that is not physical » *Leo had a strong spirit and was determined to complete the race.*
essence, life force, soul

squabble

spirit [2]
noun a ghost or supernatural being » *In the movie, a spirit haunted the house.*
apparition, ghost, phantom, spectre, sprite

spirit [3]
noun liveliness and energy » *The young dog had so much spirit.*
animation, energy, enthusiasm, fire, force, vigour, zest, brio, mettle

*The young dog had so much **spirit**.*

spite [1] : in spite of
preposition even though something is the case » *In spite of the power outage, Fi completed her homework.*
despite, even though, notwithstanding, regardless of, though

spite [2]
noun a desire to hurt someone » *Liam broke his sister's toy out of spite.*
ill will, malevolence, malice, spitefulness, venom, malignity, rancour

spiteful
adjective saying or doing nasty things to hurt people » *It was spiteful to laugh at them.*
catty (informal)**, cruel, malevolent, malicious, nasty, snide, venomous, vindictive**

splendid [1]
adjective very good indeed » *I've had a splendid time.*
excellent, exceptional, fantastic (informal)**, fine, glorious, great** (informal)**, marvellous, superb, wonderful**

*The Taj Mahal looks **splendid**.*

splendid [2]
adjective beautiful and impressive » *The Taj Mahal looks splendid.*
gorgeous, grand, imposing, impressive, magnificent, superb

split [1]
verb to divide into two or more parts » *The team decided to split the prize money equally among all its members.*
diverge, fork, part, separate, bifurcate, cleave, disunite

split [2]
verb to have a crack or tear » *Oh no, my pants have split and there's a gaping hole.*
burst, come apart, crack, rip, slit, tear

split [3]
noun a crack or tear in something » *I can see through the split in the curtain.*
crack, fissure, rip, slit, tear

split [4]
noun a division between two things » *There's a split between those who want to go outdoors and those who want to stay in and draw.*
breach, breakup, divergence, division, rift, schism

spoil [1]
verb to damage or destroy something » *She tried to keep the party a secret so as not to spoil the surprise.*
damage, destroy, harm, impair, mar, mess up, ruin, wreck

spoil [2]
verb to give someone everything they want » *Grandpa spoils us with more candy than we can eat.*
cosset, indulge, pamper, coddle, mollycoddle, overindulge

spoilsport
noun a person who spoils other people's fun » *I felt like a spoilsport for not joining in the game.*
downer, drag, killjoy, sourpuss (slang)

spooky
adjective eerie and frightening » *The old ruin had a spooky atmosphere.*
creepy (informal)**, eerie, frightening, ghostly, haunted, scary, supernatural, uncanny**

spot [1]
noun a small round mark on something » *Dalmatians have a white coat with black spots.*
blemish, blot, blotch, mark, smudge, speck

*Dalmatians have a white coat with black **spots**.*

spot [2]
noun a location or place » *It was the perfect spot for a picnic.*
location, place, point, position, scene, site

spot [3]
verb to see or notice something » *Belinda spotted an owl in the tree.*
catch sight of, detect, discern, observe, see, sight, descry, espy

spread [1]
verb to open out or extend over an area » *He spread the picnic blanket on the grass for everyone to sit on.*
extend, fan out, open, sprawl, unfold, unfurl, unroll

spread [2]
verb to put a thin layer on a surface » *Melissa spread icing on the cake.*
apply, coat, cover, overlay, plaster, smear

*Melissa **spread** icing on the cake.*

spread [3]
verb to reach or affect more people gradually » *Excitement is spreading through the school as the holidays draw near.*
circulate, grow, expand, increase, proliferate, travel

spread [4]
noun the extent or growth of something » *The spread of interest in the zoo brought new visitors each week.*
diffusion, expansion, extent, growth, increase, progression, proliferation, upsurge

squabble [1]
verb to quarrel about something trivial » *My brother and sister squabble about who gets to sit in the front seat of the car.*
argue, bicker, fall out, feud, fight, quarrel, row, wrangle

squabble

squabble [2]
noun a minor quarrel » We keep having squabbles about whose turn it is to wash the dishes after dinner.
altercation, argument, disagreement, dispute, fight, quarrel, row, spat, tiff

staff
noun the people who work for an organization » The company's senior staff went to a meeting about new research.
employees, personnel, team, workers, workforce

The company's senior staff went to a meeting about new research.

stage [1]
noun a part of a process » Cycling is the second stage of a triathlon race.
lap, period, phase, point, step

stage [2]
verb to organize something » School pupils have staged a fun run to help raise money for a new sports centre.
arrange, engineer, mount, orchestrate, organize

stain [1]
noun a mark on something » His T-shirt was covered in grass stains.
blot, mark, spot

stain [2]
verb to make a mark on something » The spilled drink stained the carpet.
dirty, mark, soil, spot, discolour, besmirch

stale
adjective no longer fresh » We fed the stale bread to the ducks and ate the fresh bread ourselves.
flat, old, sour, stagnant, fusty, musty
antonym: fresh

standard [1]
noun a particular level of quality or achievement » To join the club you had to play tennis to a high standard.
calibre, criterion, guideline, level, norm, quality, requirement

standard [2]
adjective usual, normal, and correct » It is standard practice for schools to hold a teacher-parent evening every year.
accepted, correct, customary, normal, orthodox, regular, usual

standards
plural noun principles of behaviour » The principal has high standards.
ethics, ideals, morals, principles, rules, scruples, values

star
noun a famous person » The movie stars walked down the red carpet.
celebrity, idol, luminary (literary)

The movie stars walked down the red carpet.

stare
verb to look at something for a long time » Ed stared out of the window at the rain.
gawk, gaze, look, gawp, goggle, ogle

start [1]
verb to begin to take place » School starts again next week.
arise, begin, come into being, come into existence, commence, get under way, originate
antonym: finish

start [2]
verb to begin to do something » Susie started to read the book Judy had recommended.
begin, commence, embark upon, proceed, set about
antonym: stop

start [3]
verb to cause something to begin » The official started the race by firing the pistol.
begin, create, establish, get going, inaugurate (formal), initiate, instigate, institute, introduce, launch, open, pioneer, set in motion, set up
antonym: stop

The official started the race by firing the pistol.

start [4]
noun the beginning of something » It was the start of a new era in the country's history.
beginning, birth, commencement, dawn, foundation, inauguration, inception (formal), initiation, onset, opening, outset
antonym: finish

state [1]
noun the condition or circumstances of something » The garden was in a better state now that all the building work was finished.
circumstances, condition, plight, position, predicament, shape, situation

state [2]
noun a country, especially in political terms » The European Union is made up of a number of European states.
country, kingdom, land, nation, republic, body politic, commonwealth, federation

state [3]
verb to say something, especially in a formal way » Please state your name and age.
affirm, articulate, assert, declare, express, say, specify, aver, expound, propound

statement
noun a short written or spoken piece giving information » The school released a statement expressing delight over its pupils' achievements.
account, announcement, bulletin, declaration, explanation, proclamation, report, testimony

status
noun a person's social position » Felix was congratulated on his new status as captain.
position, prestige, rank, standing

Felix was congratulated on his new status as captain.

stick »

stay
verb to remain somewhere
» *Would you like to stay for dinner?*
hang around (informal), **linger, loiter, remain, tarry, wait**

steadfast
adjective refusing to change or give up » *Jill was a steadfast supporter of animal rights and went on every march.*
constant, faithful, firm, immovable, resolute, staunch, steady, unshakeable

steady 1
adjective continuing without interruptions » *There was a steady rise in temperature throughout the morning.*
consistent, constant, continuous, even, nonstop, regular, uninterrupted

steady 2
adjective not shaky or wobbling » *Tom has a steady hand and can draw very neatly.*
firm, secure, stable

The surfers steadied themselves on the surf boards.

steady 3
verb to prevent something from shaking or wobbling » *The surfers steadied themselves on the surf boards.*
brace, secure, stabilize, support

steal 1
verb to take something without permission » *Did Elsa steal that apple from the fruit bowl, or did she ask permission?*
appropriate, lift (informal), **loot** (informal), **pilfer, pinch** (informal), **swipe** (slang), **take, embezzle, filch, misappropriate, purloin, thieve**

steal 2
verb to move somewhere quietly and secretly
» *Greg stole out of the class without the teacher noticing.*
creep, slip, sneak, tiptoe

steep 1
adjective rising sharply and abruptly » *The steep hill was difficult to climb.*
sheer, vertical
antonym: **gradual**

steep 2
adjective larger than is reasonable » *We noticed a steep rise in the price of bananas.*
excessive, extortionate, high, unreasonable, exorbitant, overpriced

steep 3
verb to soak something in a liquid » *Steep the vegetables in water to keep them fresh.*
immerse, soak, marinate

sterile
adjective free from germs » *Ted bandaged the cut with a sterile dressing.*
antiseptic, germ-free, sterilized

stick 1
noun a long, thin piece of wood
» *William threw a stick for the dog to fetch.*
bat, cane, mace, pole, rod, truncheon, twig, wand

stick 2
verb to thrust something somewhere » *Christine stuck her arm through the fence to pick flowers from the other side.*
insert, jab, poke, push, put, ram, shove, stuff, thrust

Christine stuck her arm through the fence to pick flowers from the other side.

stick 3
verb to attach
▼ SEE BELOW

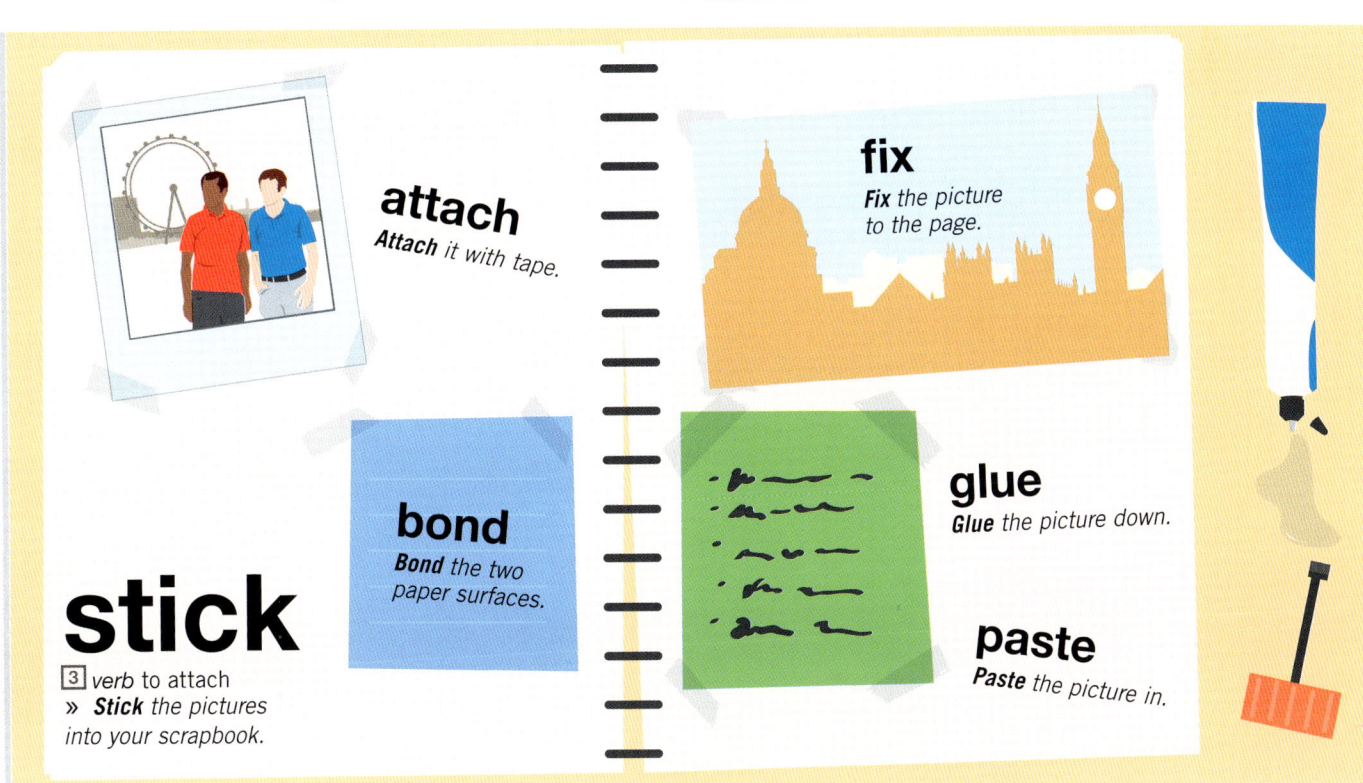

---

stick
3 **verb** to attach
» *Stick the pictures into your scrapbook.*

attach
Attach it with tape.

bond
Bond the two paper surfaces.

fix
Fix the picture to the page.

glue
Glue the picture down.

paste
Paste the picture in.

213

stick

stick 4
verb to become attached » *Mud was stuck to the bottom of my boots.*
adhere, bond, cling, fuse

stick 5
verb to jam or become jammed » *The cat was stuck in her cat flap, but we finally got her out.*
catch, jam, lodge, snag

sticky
adjective covered with a substance that sticks to other things » *Vi stepped accidentally on the sticky blob of gum.*
adhesive, tacky, glutinous, viscid, viscous

*Vi stepped accidentally on the **sticky** blob of gum.*

stiff 1
adjective firm and not easily bent » *The cardboard was stiff.*
firm, hard, rigid, solid, taut
antonym: **limp**

stiff 2
adjective not friendly or relaxed » *The lady was stiff and uncomfortable.*
cold, forced, formal, stilted, unnatural, wooden, constrained, prim, standoffish

stiff 3
adjective difficult or severe » *There were stiff penalties for breaking the rules.*
arduous, difficult, exacting, formidable, hard, rigorous, tough

*The water on the lake was **still**.*

still
adjective not moving » *The water on the lake was still.*
calm, inert, motionless, stationary, tranquil

stink 1
verb to smell very bad » *My breath stinks of garlic.*
reek, smell

stink 2
noun a very bad smell » *The stink of smelly cheese filled the house.*
reek, stench, fetor, malodour

stock 1
noun the total amount of goods for sale in a store » *The store counted how much stock it had in its storeroom.*
goods, merchandise (formal)

stock 2
noun a supply of something » *The store had a large stock of electrical equipment.*
reserve, reservoir, stockpile, store, supply

stock 3
noun shares bought in an investment company » *The reporter said stocks in the company were increasing.*
bonds, investments, shares

stock 4
noun an animal or person's ancestors » *Many people in Newfoundland come from Irish stock.*
ancestry, descent, extraction, lineage, origin, parentage

stock 5
verb to keep a supply of goods to sell » *The store stocks a wide range of paint and other artists' materials.*
deal in, sell, supply, trade in

stock 6
adjective commonly used » *Dad's stock answer to every question was "Ask your mother."*
hackneyed, overused, routine, standard, typical, usual

stockpile 1
verb to store large quantities » *My neighbour stockpiled cans of food when he heard there was a blizzard on the way.*
accumulate, amass, collect, gather, hoard, save, stash (informal), **store up**

stockpile 2
noun a large store of something » *Chris and Bill used the planks from the stockpile outside to make the new shed.*
cache, hoard, reserve, stash (informal), **stock, store**

*Chris and Bill used the planks from the **stockpile** outside to make the new shed.*

stocky
adjective short but solid-looking » *The pygmy hippo is small but stocky.*
chunky, solid, sturdy, stubby, thickset

stomach
noun the front part of the body around the waist » *David's T-shirt was too short and showed his stomach.*
abdomen, belly, gut, paunch, tummy (informal)

stop 1
verb to cease doing something
▶▶ **SEE RIGHT**

stop 2
verb to prevent something » *The sudden downpour stopped the barbecue.*
arrest, check, prevent, forestall, nip something in the bud

stop 3
verb to come to an end » *Elsie hoped that the rain would stop so she could ride her new bike outside.*
cease, come to an end, conclude, end, finish, halt
antonym: **start**

store 1
noun a supply kept for future use » *The chipmunk added to its store of nuts.*
cache, fund, hoard, reserve, reservoir, stock, stockpile, supply

*The chipmunk added to its **store** of nuts.*

store 2
noun a place where things or services are available for sale » *We went to the clothing store to shop for new outfits.*
boutique, mall, market, outlet, shop

214

stop

1 *verb* to cease doing something
» He **stopped** playing the piano when the doorbell rang.

cease
The baby **ceased** crying when she was fed.

cut out (informal)
Cut out that racket!

desist
Kindly **desist** from giggling when the teacher is talking.

discontinue
They **discontinued** selling his favourite pens.

end
The conductor **ended** with a flourish.

quit
She **quit** playing the flute.

antonym: start
Turn the key to **start** the car.

story

noun a tale told or written to entertain people
» We read a funny **story** together.

account The book included a true **account** of Scott's expedition to the Antarctic.

anecdote The actor had a store of entertaining **anecdotes** about his life in the theatre.

legend The teacher told us the **legend** of King Arthur.

narrative The **narrative** moved swiftly from one event to the next in the heroine's life.

tale My favourite fairy **tale** is Hansel and Gretel.

yarn My uncle told us an extraordinary **yarn** about his days as a student.

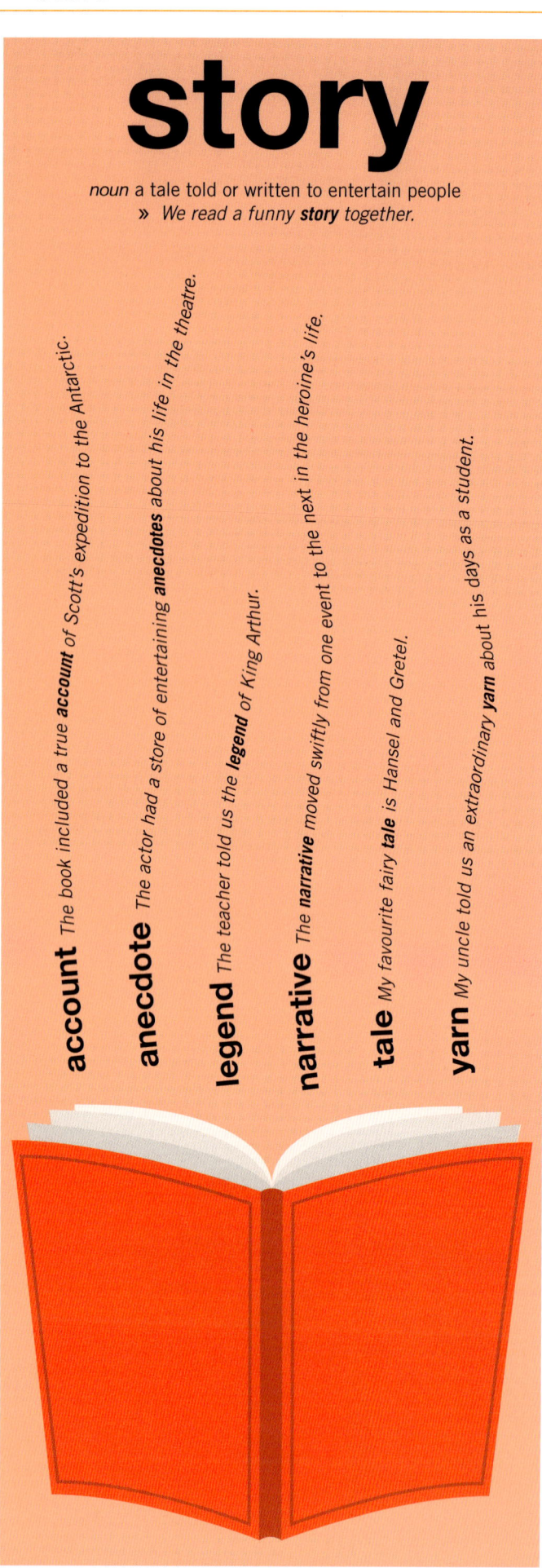

store 3

verb to keep something for future use » The photos are stored on your computer.
hoard, keep, save, stash (informal)**, stockpile**

story

noun a tale told or written to entertain people
◄◄ SEE LEFT

straight 1

adjective upright or level, not curved » Hold your arms straight out to the side.
erect, even, level, perpendicular, upright
antonym: **crooked**

Hold your arms straight out to the side.

straight 2

adjective honest, frank, and direct » Andy's answer was straight and to the point.
blunt, candid, forthright, frank, honest, outright, plain, point-blank

straightforward 1

adjective easy and involving no problems » The question seemed straightforward.
basic, easy, elementary, routine, simple, uncomplicated
antonym: **complicated**

straightforward 2

adjective honest, open, and frank » I liked his straightforward manner.
candid, direct, forthright, frank, honest, open, plain, straight
antonym: **devious**

strain 1

noun worry and nervous tension » The strain that Nadine had felt during her exams was now gone.
anxiety, pressure, stress, tension

strain 2

verb to make something do more than it is able to do » The men strained to lift the bench.
overwork, tax, overexert, overtax, push to the limit

The men strained to lift the bench.

strange 1

adjective unusual or unexpected » It was strange to bump into my old classmate.
abnormal, bizarre, curious, extraordinary, funny, odd, peculiar, uncommon, weird, out-of-the-way, outré, unaccountable

strange 2

adjective new or unfamiliar » We found it exciting to be on vacation in a strange country.
alien, exotic, foreign, new, novel, unfamiliar

strength 1

noun physical energy and power » The bear pushed over a tree in an astonishing display of strength.
brawn, might, muscle, stamina, brawniness, lustiness, sinew
antonym: **weakness**

strength 2

noun the degree of intensity » The cheering and loud applause revealed the strength of feeling in the room.
force, intensity, potency, power, vehemence, vigour
antonym: **weakness**

strengthen [1]
verb to give something more power » *The lateness of the trains strengthens the case for an improved railway system.*
encourage, fortify, harden, toughen, hearten, invigorate
antonym: **weaken**

strengthen [2]
verb to support the structure of something » *Dad strengthened the treehouse with some timber beams.*
bolster, brace, fortify, reinforce, support
antonym: **weaken**

stress [1]
noun worry and nervous tension » *Louis didn't like the stress that came with taking tests every semester.*
anxiety, hassle (informal)**, pressure, strain, tension, worry**

stress [2]
verb to emphasize something » *The teacher stressed the importance of doing your best.*
accentuate, emphasize, repeat, underline, belabour, dwell on, point up, underscore

stretch [1]
verb to extend over an area or time » *The boy stretched the slingshot and aimed at the target.*
continue, cover, extend, go on, last, reach, spread

The boy stretched the slingshot and aimed at the target.

stretch [2]
verb to reach out with part of your body » *Megan stretched out her hand.*
extend, reach, straighten
antonym: **bend**

stretch [3]
noun an area of land or water » *We travelled along a smooth stretch of road.*
area, expanse, extent, sweep, tract

We travelled along a smooth stretch of road.

stretch [4]
noun a period of time » *My father often worked for eight-hour stretches.*
period, run, space, spell, stint, term, time

strict [1]
adjective very firm in demanding obedience » *The teacher was strict, and we didn't dare talk in class.*
authoritarian, firm, rigid, rigorous, stern, stringent

strict [2]
adjective precise and accurate » *The referee had a strict interpretation of the rules.*
accurate, exact, meticulous, particular, precise, true

strive
verb to make a great effort to achieve something » *Mason strives to keep himself fit by running every day.*
attempt, do your best, do your utmost, endeavour (formal)**, make an effort, seek, try**

strong [1]
adjective having powerful muscles » *Gorillas are incredibly strong.*
athletic, brawny, burly, muscular, powerful, strapping, well-built
antonym: **weak**

strong [2]
adjective able to withstand rough treatment » *Strong armour kept the knight safe during battle.*
durable, hard-wearing, heavy-duty, reinforced, sturdy, substantial, tough, well-built
antonym: **fragile**

Strong armour kept the knight safe during battle.

strong [3]
adjective great in degree or intensity » *Caroline had a strong feeling that something exciting was about to happen.*
acute, ardent, deep, fervent, fierce, intense, keen, passionate, profound, vehement, violent, zealous
antonym: **faint**

structure [1]
noun the way something is made or organized » *The science class learned all about the structure of a plant.*
arrangement, construction, design, makeup, organization, configuration, conformation

The museum building is an imposing structure.

structure [2]
noun something that has been built » *The museum building is an imposing structure.*
building, construction, edifice

struggle [1]
verb to try hard to do something » *We struggled up to the top of the mountain.*
strain, strive, toil, work

struggle [2]
noun something that is hard to achieve » *The marathon was a struggle, but Josh felt proud when he crossed the finish line.*
effort, labour, toil, work

stubborn
adjective determined not to change or give in » *Helen's stubborn refusal to give up is an inspiration.*
dogged, inflexible, obstinate, tenacious, wilful, intractable, obdurate, recalcitrant, refractory

stuck-up
adjective (informal) arrogant and conceited » *She was famous but not stuck-up.*
arrogant, conceited, disdainful, haughty, proud, snobbish

study [1]
verb to spend time learning about something » *Billy enjoyed studying history.*
hit the books (informal)**, learn, read up**

study

The tourists studied the map to work out their best route.

study [2]
verb to look at something carefully » *The tourists studied the map to work out their best route.*
contemplate, examine, pore over, peruse, scrutinize

study [3]
noun the activity of learning about a subject » *Mary threw herself into the study of ancient Egypt as she was going to see the pyramids.*
application, course, lessons, research, school work

stuff [1]
noun a substance or group of things » *"That's my stuff," Luke said, pointing to a bag.*
apparatus, belongings, equipment, gear, material, substance, tackle, things, paraphernalia, trappings

stuff [2]
verb to push something somewhere quickly and roughly » *Martin stuffed the paper into the recycling bin.*
cram, force, jam, push, ram, shove, squeeze, thrust

stuff [3]
verb to fill something with a substance or objects » *The jar was stuffed with candies.*
cram, fill, load, pack

The jar was stuffed with candies.

stuffy [1]
adjective formal and old-fashioned » *At first I found Aunt Jane rather stuffy, but we soon became great friends.*
dull, formal, old-fashioned, staid, strait-laced, fusty, old-fogeyish, priggish, stodgy

stuffy [2]
adjective not containing enough fresh air » *It was hot and stuffy in the classroom because the windows wouldn't open.*
close, heavy, muggy, oppressive, stale, stifling, fetid, unventilated

stupid
adjective lacking intelligence or good judgment » *Mom told me off for making stupid jokes while she was talking to the new neighbours.*
absurd, dim, foolish, idiotic, inane, obtuse, silly, asinine, crass, fatuous
antonym: clever

stupidity
noun lack of intelligence or good judgment » *Robert wondered at the bird's stupidity as it flew into the window for the third time.*
absurdity, folly, foolishness, inanity, silliness, asininity, fatuity, imbecility, obtuseness

sturdy
adjective strong and unlikely to be damaged » *My sturdy boots protect my feet during long hiking trips.*
durable, hardy, robust, solid, substantial, stout, strong, well-built
antonym: fragile

My sturdy boots protect my feet during long hiking trips.

success
[2] noun a person or thing achieving popularity or greatness » *You're a school success!*

sensation

Rory read about the latest sporting sensation in the newspaper.

celebrity

The children were hailed as celebrities after appearing on TV.

hit

Stanley was an online hit with his blog.

218

success

style 1
noun the way in which something is done » *Mr. Preston's style of teaching made every subject seem interesting.*
approach, manner, method, mode, technique, way

style 2
noun smartness and elegance » *Leonie has such style, especially when she wears that evening dress.*
chic, elegance, flair, sophistication, taste, élan, panache, savoir-faire

subdue
verb to bring under control by force » *Police were called in to subdue the protesters.*
crush, defeat, overcome, overpower, quell, vanquish

subject 1
noun the thing or person being discussed » *Maryam was able to talk about a range of subjects, from pet care to philosophy and painting.*
issue, matter, object, point, question, theme, topic

subject 2
verb to make someone experience something » *Chris was subjected to continual questions from his classmates, who were eager to hear more details.*
expose, put through, submit

submit 1
verb to accept or agree to something unwillingly » *I eventually submitted to my sister's nagging to borrow my dress, even though I knew she'd get it dirty.*
bow, capitulate, comply, give in, surrender, yield
antonym: resist

submit 2
verb to formally present a document or proposal » *Jeff submitted his short story for publication in the school magazine.*
hand in, present, propose, put forward, send in, table, tender
antonym: withdraw

Poisonous substances are labelled with a warning sticker.

substance
noun a solid, powder, liquid, or gas » *Poisonous substances are labelled with a warning sticker.*
element, material, stuff

substitute 1
verb to use one thing in place of another » *You can substitute honey for sugar.*
exchange, interchange, replace, swap, switch

substitute 2
noun someone or something used in place of another » *Nylon is sometimes used as a substitute for silk.*
deputy, proxy, replacement, representative, surrogate, makeshift, stopgap

subtract
verb to take one number away from another » *Subtracting 3 from 5 leaves 2.*
deduct, take away, take from
antonym: add

succeed
verb to achieve the result you intend » *Lina succeeded as a professional musician.*
be successful, do well, flourish, make it (informal), prosper, thrive, triumph, work
antonym: fail

success 1
noun the achievement of a goal, fame, or wealth » *Liv's success was unparalleled: no one had more awards than her.*
celebrity, eminence, fame, prosperity, triumph, victory, wealth, ascendancy (formal)
antonym: failure

success 2
noun a person or thing achieving popularity or greatness
▼ SEE BELOW

star
She's a *star!*

triumph
The posters declared the movie a triumph.

winner
Nathan was a real winner, excelling in every sport he tried.

successful

successful
adjective having achieved what you intended to do
» Carol was a highly successful artist.
flourishing, lucrative, profitable, rewarding, thriving, top

sudden
adjective happening quickly and unexpectedly » The sudden opening of the jack-in-the-box gave us all a shock.
abrupt, hasty, quick, swift, unexpected
antonym: **gradual**

*The **sudden** opening of the jack-in-the-box gave us all a shock.*

suffer
verb to be affected by pain or something unpleasant
» Milo suffered an injury while playing hockey.
bear, endure, experience, go through, sustain, undergo

sufficient
adjective being enough for a purpose » Rick had sufficient time to write a good essay.
adequate, ample, enough
antonym: **insufficient**

suggest 1
verb to mention something as a possibility or recommendation
» Clive suggested going out for ice cream.
advise, advocate, propose, recommend

suggest 2
verb to hint that something is the case » The girls' smiling faces suggested they had done well in the test.
hint, imply, indicate, insinuate, intimate

suggestion 1
noun an idea mentioned as a possibility » May I offer a suggestion for what to do next?
plan, proposal, proposition, recommendation

suggestion 2
noun a slight indication of something » There was a suggestion of a smile on Carl's face as they waited for the winner to be announced.
hint, indication, insinuation, intimation, trace

suit
verb to be acceptable » The house suits our needs.
be acceptable to, please, satisfy

suitable
adjective right or acceptable for a particular purpose
» Rita's slip-on sandals were not suitable for running in.
acceptable, appropriate, apt, fit, fitting, proper, right, apposite, befitting, pertinent, seemly
antonym: **unsuitable**

sulky
adjective showing annoyance by being silent and moody » Kim was sulky because she hadn't been invited to the party.
huffy, moody, petulant, resentful, sullen

*Kim was **sulky** because she hadn't been invited to the party.*

summary
noun a short account of something's main points
» Peter ended his essay with a three-point summary.
outline, review, rundown, summing-up, synopsis, abridgment, digest, précis, recapitulation

sum up
verb to describe briefly
» Rudi summed up his week in one word: "Fantastic!"
recapitulate, summarize

superb
adjective very good indeed
» The pilot had a superb flight with a perfect landing.
breathtaking, excellent, exquisite, magnificent, marvellous, outstanding, splendid, superior, unrivalled, wonderful, superlative

superior 1
adjective better than other similar things » The new software is superior to the old—much faster and with more functions.
better, choice, deluxe, exceptional, first-rate, surpassing, unrivalled
antonym: **inferior**

superior 2
adjective showing pride and self-importance » The wealthy people in the mansion felt superior to their neighbours.
condescending, disdainful, haughty, lofty, patronizing, snobbish, stuck-up (informal), **supercilious**

superior 3
noun a person in a higher position than you
» The trainee had to report to his superior.
big cheese (informal), **boss** (informal), **chief, controller, director, employer, head, leader, manager, senior, supervisor**
antonym: **inferior**

*The trainee had to report to his **superior**.*

supervise
verb to oversee a person or activity » Wendy supervised more than 400 volunteers.
be in charge of, direct, handle, keep an eye on, look after, manage, oversee, run, preside over, superintend

supplement 1
verb to add to something to improve it » Mom supplemented the main course with a salad.
add to, augment, complement, reinforce, top up

*Mom **supplemented** the main course with a salad.*

supplement 2
noun something added to something else
» The magazine was a free supplement with the newspaper.
addition, appendix, complement, extra

supplies
plural noun food or equipment for a particular purpose
» Leila carried her supplies for the hike in a backpack.
equipment, provisions, rations, stores

supply 1
verb to provide someone with something » The company will supply all the equipment for the scuba dive.
equip, furnish, give, provide, endow, purvey

supply 2
noun an amount of something available for use » *Our fridge contained a plentiful supply of food for the week.*
cache, fund, hoard, reserve, stock, stockpile, store

support 1
verb to agree with someone's ideas or aims » *I support your idea for creating more bicycle lanes.*
back, champion, defend, promote, second, side with, uphold
antonym: **oppose**

support 2
verb to help someone in difficulties » *You should support your friends when they are feeling down.*
assist, encourage, help

support 3
verb to hold something up from underneath » *The pillars support the cathedral roof.*
bolster, brace, hold up, prop up, reinforce, buttress, shore up

The pillars support the cathedral roof.

support 4
noun an object that holds something up » *The metal supports will hold up the tent.*
brace, foundation, pillar, post, prop, abutment, stanchion

The supporters wore team colours to cheer on their team.

supporter
noun a person who agrees with or helps someone » *The supporters wore team colours to cheer on their team.*
adherent, advocate, ally, champion, fan, follower, sponsor, patron, protagonist

suppose
verb to think that something is probably the case » *I suppose Jon will have an apple as usual.*
assume, believe, expect, guess, imagine, presume, think, conjecture, surmise (formal)

supposed 1
adjective planned, expected, or required to do something » *You're supposed to ride your bike in the bicycle lane rather than on the sidewalk.*
expected, meant, obliged, required

supposed 2
adjective generally believed or thought to be the case » *His supposed date of birth was in 1952.*
alleged, assumed, believed, meant, presumed, reputed, rumoured

suppress 1
verb to prevent people from doing something » *The teachers aimed to suppress bullying among the students.*
crack down on (informal)**, crush, quash, quell, stamp out, stop**

suppress 2
verb to stop yourself from expressing a feeling or reaction » *Vikram suppressed a cry by turning it into a cough.*
conceal, contain, curb, repress, restrain, smother, stifle

supreme
adjective of the highest degree or rank » *The principal has supreme authority over the school.*
chief, foremost, greatest, highest, leading, paramount, pre-eminent, principal, top, ultimate

sure 1
adjective having no doubts » *Jonathan was sure that he was right.*
certain, clear, convinced, definite, positive, satisfied
antonym: **unsure**

sure 2
adjective reliable or definite » *The dark clouds were a sure sign that it was going to rain.*
definite, dependable, foolproof, infallible, reliable, trustworthy, undeniable

surprise 1
noun something unexpected » *Danny's gift to the teacher came as a delightful surprise.*
bombshell, revelation, shock, start

Danny's gift to the teacher came as a delightful surprise.

surprise 2
noun the feeling caused by something unexpected » *He let out a gasp of surprise.*
amazement, astonishment, incredulity, wonder

surprise 3
verb to give someone a feeling of surprise » *I was surprised by how many people came to the party.*
amaze, astonish, astound, jolt, stagger, stun, take aback, flabbergast, nonplus

surrender 1
verb to agree that the other side has won » *I surrender! You have won the game.*
capitulate, give in, submit, succumb, yield

surrender 2
verb to give something up to someone else » *Marcus surrendered the ball to the puppy.*
cede, give up, relinquish, renounce, yield

surrender 3
noun a situation in which one side gives in to the other » *The blue team waved a white flag in surrender.*
capitulation, submission

The blue team waved a white flag in surrender.

surround
verb to be all around a person or thing » *The calf was surrounded by cows.*
encircle, enclose, encompass, envelop, hem in

surroundings

*The farm's **surroundings** were stunning.*

surroundings
plural noun the area and environment around a person or place » *The farm's surroundings were stunning.*
background, environment, location, neighbourhood, setting, environs, milieu

survive
verb to live or exist in spite of difficulties » *We survived the intense heat by sitting in an air-conditioned café.*
endure, last, live, outlive, pull through

suspect 1
verb to think something is likely » *I suspect we'll have more to do after lunch.*
believe, feel, guess, suppose

suspect 2
verb to have doubts about something » *Troy suspected something was wrong when he saw Dylan had walked away.*
distrust, doubt, mistrust

suspect 3
adjective not to be trusted » *Peter's claims to be related to royalty were highly suspect.*
doubtful, dubious, fishy (informal)**, questionable, suspicious**

suspicion 1
noun a feeling of mistrust » *Having been bitten before, Cara regarded the parrot with suspicion.*
distrust, doubt, misgiving, mistrust, scepticism, qualm

suspicion 2
noun a feeling something is true » *I have a suspicion this route is the long way around.*
hunch, idea, impression

suspicious 1
adjective feeling distrustful of someone or something » *Jez was highly suspicious as the fox approached the chicken coop.*
apprehensive, distrustful, doubtful, sceptical, wary

*Jez was highly **suspicious** as the fox approached the chicken coop.*

suspicious 2
adjective causing feelings of distrust » *Brenda wondered why the lights were off—there was something suspicious going on.*
doubtful, dubious, fishy (informal)**, funny, questionable, shady** (informal)**, suspect**

swap
verb to replace one thing for another » *The girls decided to swap coats for the day.*
barter, exchange, interchange, switch, trade

*After her dinner, Kate loves to eat something **sweet**.*

sweet 1
adjective containing a lot of sugar » *After her dinner, Kate loves to eat something sweet.*
cloying, sugary, sweetened
antonym: **sour**

sweet 2
adjective having a pleasant smell » *The air was filled with the sweet smell of roses.*
aromatic, fragrant, perfumed, sweet-smelling

sweet 3
adjective pleasant-sounding and tuneful » *The audience listened to the sweet sound of the children singing.*
harmonious, mellow, melodious, musical, tuneful, dulcet

sweet 4
noun a sweet-tasting thing such as a toffee » *We were each allowed some sweets as a treat.*
bonbon, candy, confectionery

*We were each allowed some **sweets** as a treat.*

swerve
verb to change direction suddenly to avoid hitting something » *The girl on the bike swerved around the trees.*
swing, turn, veer

swift
adjective happening or moving very quickly » *The bird was swift in flight.*
brisk, express, fast, hurried, prompt, quick, rapid, speedy
antonym: **slow**

*The bird was **swift** in flight.*

symbol
noun a design or idea used to represent something
▶▶ SEE RIGHT

sympathy
noun kindness and understanding towards someone in trouble » *When Alan's friend broke his leg, he looked after him with great sympathy.*
compassion, empathy, pity, understanding

system
noun an organized way of doing or arranging something » *The new system is much more efficient than the old way of doing things.*
arrangement, method, procedure, routine, structure, technique, methodology, modus operandi

222

sy**stem** »

mark
A name badge is a **mark** of identification.

HELLO MY NAME IS Andrew

sign
2×4=8

2 × 4 = 8 uses **signs** for multiplication and equals.

token
A ring is a **token** of love and marriage.

figure
The **figure** of a dove with an olive branch in its beak stands for peace.

logo
Companies use **logos** to make them instantly recognizable.

DK

emblem
A bald eagle is the American national **emblem**.

symbol
noun a design or idea used to represent something
» The chemical **symbol** for the element oxygen is O.

emoticon
He signed off with a happy-face **emoticon**.

representation
In Egyptian hieroglyphics, a lion is the **representation** for the letter "L."

223

» tact

Tt

tact
noun the ability not to offend people » *The teacher corrected Ed's mistakes with great tact.*
delicacy, diplomacy, discretion, sensitivity

tactful
adjective careful not to offend » *Jon asked a few tactful questions.*
diplomatic, discreet, sensitive
antonym: **tactless**

take 1
verb to require something » *My sister takes three hours to get ready.*
demand, need, require

take 2
verb to carry something » *I'll take your bag for you.*
bear (formal), **bring, carry, convey** (formal), **ferry, fetch, transport**

I'll take your bag for you.

take 3
verb to lead someone somewhere » *She took John to the bus stop to make sure he didn't get lost.*
bring, conduct (formal), **escort, guide, lead, usher**

take care of 1
verb to look after someone or something » *Abigail was asked to take care of the baby for the day.*
care for, look after, mind, nurse, protect, tend, watch
antonym: **neglect**

Abigail was asked to take care of the baby for the day.

take care of 2
verb to deal with a problem, task, or situation » *Darcy took care of tidying the house.*
attend to, cope with, deal with, handle, manage, see to

take in 1
verb to deceive someone » *I was taken in by the girl at the market; the apples she sold me were old and nasty.*
con (informal), **deceive, dupe, fool, mislead, trick**

take in 2
verb to understand something » *Tara took in everything the coach said, and her technique soon improved.*
absorb, appreciate, assimilate, comprehend, digest, get, grasp, understand

talent
noun a natural ability » *Jess had a talent for ballet.*
ability, aptitude, capacity, flair, genius, gift, knack

talk 1
verb to say things » *My parents talked about the vacation they were planning.*
chat, converse, natter, ramble, gossip, say, state, mention

talk 2
noun a conversation » *The students had a long talk about the new teacher.*
chat, chatter, conversation

talk 3
noun an informal speech » *The visitor gave a talk about volunteering for charity.*
address, discourse, lecture, sermon, speech, disquisition, oration

talkative
adjective talking a lot » *The boy was so talkative; he never stopped!*
chatty, communicative, long-winded

tall
adjective higher than average
▶▶ SEE RIGHT

tangle 1
noun a mass of long things knotted together » *There was a tangle of wires behind the television.*
jumble, knot, mass, mat, muddle, web

There was a tangle of wires behind the television.

tangle 2
verb to twist together or catch someone or something » *The kite became tangled in the tree's branches.*
catch, jumble, knot, twist

task
noun a job that you have to do » *Emily had the task of walking the dog.*
assignment, chore, duty, job, mission, undertaking

taste 1
noun the flavour of something » *I like the taste of fresh strawberries.*
flavour, tang

taste 2
noun a small amount of food or drink » *The chef had a taste of the sauce before it was served.*
bite, mouthful, sip

The chef had a taste of the sauce before it was served.

taste 3
noun a liking for something » *My Aunt Jean has a real taste for adventure.*
appetite, fondness, liking, penchant (formal), **partiality, predilection**

tasteless 1
adjective having little flavour » *The vegetables were overcooked and tasteless.*
bland, flavourless, insipid
antonym: **tasty**

tasteless 2
adjective vulgar and unattractive » *Decorating your bathroom gold is rather tasteless.*
garish, gaudy, tacky (informal), **tawdry, vulgar**
antonym: **tasteful**

tasty
adjective having a pleasant flavour » *The soup was extremely **tasty**.*
appetizing, delicious, luscious, palatable, yummy (informal), **flavourful, flavoursome, delectable, scrumptious**
antonym: **tasteless**

tax 1
noun money paid to the government » *The amount of tax paid by each person was reduced this year.*
duty, excise, levy (formal), **tariff**

tax 2
verb to make heavy demands on someone » *The difficult jigsaw puzzle **taxed** Norah's patience.*
drain, exhaust, sap, strain, stretch

*The difficult jigsaw puzzle **taxed** Norah's patience.*

teach
verb to instruct someone how to do something » *Emma decided to teach the class the rules of the game.*
coach, drill, educate, instruct, school, train, tutor

teacher
noun someone who teaches something » *My English teacher inspired me to become a writer.*
coach, don, guru, instructor, lecturer, professor, schoolteacher, tutor, educator, pedagogue

*The girls' basketball **team** won the championship again last year.*

team 1
noun a group of people » *The girls' basketball team won the championship again last year.*
band, crew, gang, group, side, squad, troupe

team 2 or team up
verb to work together » *The teacher said we could team up with a classmate to work on the project.*
collaborate, co-operate, join forces, link up, pair up, unite, work together

tear 1
noun a hole or rip in something » *I found a tear in my jeans.*
cut, gash, hole, rip, rupture, scratch, split

tear 2
verb to make a hole or rip in something » *The cat tore a hole in the curtains.*
cut, gash, rip, rupture, scratch, shred, split, rend

tear 3
verb to go somewhere in a hurry » *Mike tore along the road on his bike.*
charge, dart, dash, fly, race, run, shoot, speed, zoom, bolt, career

tease
verb to make fun of someone » *I teased my elder sister about her new boyfriend.*
make fun of, mock, needle (informal), **taunt**

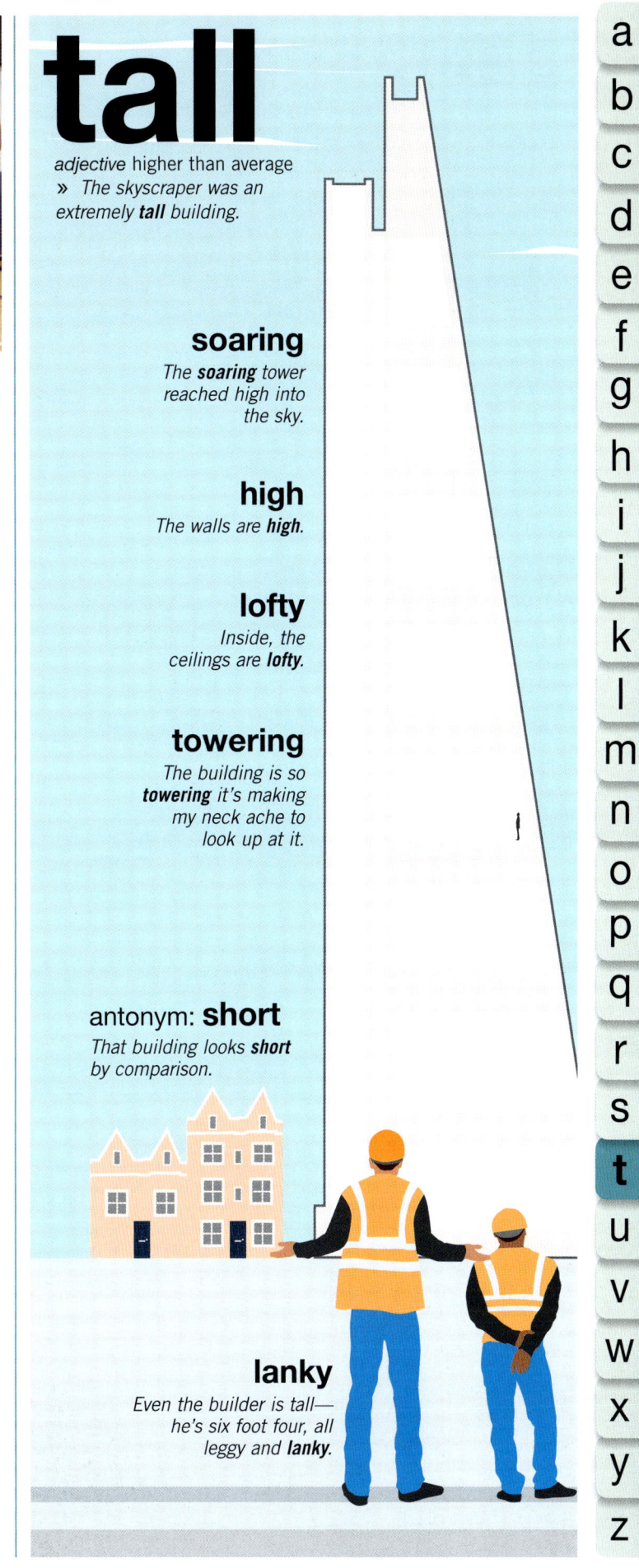

tall
adjective higher than average » *The skyscraper was an extremely **tall** building.*

soaring
The **soaring** tower reached high into the sky.

high
The walls are **high**.

lofty
Inside, the ceilings are **lofty**.

towering
The building is so **towering** it's making my neck ache to look up at it.

antonym: **short**
That building looks **short** by comparison.

lanky
Even the builder is tall—he's six foot four, all leggy and **lanky**.

telephone

thin
[2] *adjective* not carrying a lot of fat » *The **thin** cat crept through the fence.*

- emaciated
- underweight
- bony
- spare
- lanky
- scrawny
- scraggy
- slight
- skinny
- lean
- slender
- slim
- light

telephone [1]
noun a device that allows you to speak to someone in another place » *Will you please answer the telephone?*
cell, cellphone, mobile, mobile phone, phone

telephone [2]
verb to contact a person by telephone » *Telephone me when you get home.*
buzz (slang), **call, contact, phone, ring**

tell [1]
verb to let someone know something » *Vanessa told us she was expecting twins.*
inform, notify, acquaint, apprise

tell [2]
verb to give someone an order » *The police officer told Jan to stop driving so fast in the town centre.*
command, direct (formal), **instruct, order, call upon, enjoin**

*The police officer **told** Jan to stop driving so fast in the town centre.*

tell [3]
verb to judge something correctly » *I could tell by her smile that my aunt was pleased to see me.*
discern, see

temporary
adjective lasting a short time » *Fred took a temporary job for the summer.*
ephemeral, fleeting, interim, momentary, passing, provisional, transient, transitory, impermanent, short-lived
antonym: **permanent**

*Joe was **tempted** to eat all of the cookies.*

tempt
verb to persuade someone to do something » *Joe was tempted to eat all of the cookies.*
entice, lure, seduce

tend [1]
verb to happen usually or often » *I tend to dress in jeans during the weekend.*
be apt, be inclined, be liable, be prone, have a tendency

tend [2]
verb to look after someone or something » *The farmer tended the lambs.*
care for, look after, nurse, take care of

tendency
noun behaviour that happens often » *Dad has a tendency to talk too fast.*
inclination, leaning, propensity, predisposition, proclivity, proneness

tender [1]
adjective showing gentle and caring feelings » *My niece is a naturally tender and loving person.*
affectionate, caring, compassionate, gentle, kind, loving, sensitive, warm
antonym: **tough**

tender [2]
adjective painful and sore » *My ribs felt tender for days after the fall.*
aching, bruised, inflamed, painful, raw, sensitive, sore

thin »

*Al **tendered** his resignation after being offered a new job.*

tender [3]
verb to offer something such as an apology or resignation » *Al tendered his resignation after being offered a new job.*
hand in, offer

tender [4]
noun a proposal to provide something at a price » *The builders submitted a tender for building a garden wall.*
bid, estimate, package, submission

tense [1]
adjective nervous and unable to relax » *Anthony felt tense as he entered the hall to take his exam.*
anxious, edgy, jittery (informal), **jumpy, nervous, uptight** (informal)
antonym: **calm**

tense [2]
adjective causing anxiety » *There was a tense silence as the judges prepared to reveal the winner.*
anxious, nerve-racking, stressful

tense [3]
adjective having tight muscles » *The doctor recommended a massage to help relax Fleur's tense shoulders.*
rigid, strained, taut, tight
antonym: **relaxed**

term [1]
noun a fixed period of time » *Sebastian took the job for a term of six weeks.*
period, session, spell, stretch, time, duration, incumbency

term [2]
noun a name or word for a particular thing » *The scientific term for birds is aves.*
designation, expression, name, word

terms
plural noun conditions that have been agreed » *The terms of the deal were clear.*
conditions, provisions, proviso, stipulations

terrible [1]
adjective serious and unpleasant » *Dan suffered from terrible headaches.*
appalling, awful, desperate, dreadful, frightful (old-fashioned), **horrendous, horrible, horrid** (old-fashioned), **rotten**

terrible [2]
adjective of very poor quality » *Pat liked his haircut, but his mom thought it was terrible.*
abysmal, appalling, awful, dire, dreadful, horrible, rotten
antonym: **excellent**

territory
noun the land that a person or country controls » *The map showed the territory belonging to each country.*
area, country, district, domain, dominion, land, province, state

*The map showed the **territory** belonging to each country.*

test [1]
verb to find out what something is like » *Stu went for a ride across the lake to test the boat.*
assess, check, try, try out

test [2]
noun an attempt to check or assess something » *He had routine eye tests.*
assessment, check, trial

texture
noun the way that something feels » *The rabbit's fur has a soft, smooth texture.*
consistency, feel

*The rabbit's fur has a soft, smooth **texture**.*

theft
noun the crime of stealing » *The squirrel's theft of the nuts meant there was none left for the birds.*
robbery, stealing, thieving, larceny, pilfering

theory
noun an idea that explains something » *The class performed an experiment to test the theory.*
conjecture, hypothesis, supposition, surmise (formal)

therefore
adverb as a result » *Candy contains sugar and is therefore bad for your teeth.*
as a result, consequently, for that reason, hence (formal), **so, thus**

thick [1]
adjective measuring a large distance from side to side » *It took Clarissa a couple of months to finish reading the thick book.*
fat, wide
antonym: **thin**

thick [2]
adjective containing little water » *The thick vegetable soup was delicious and filling.*
concentrated, condensed, viscous
antonym: **watery**

thick [3]
adjective grouped closely together » *The thick undergrowth in the forest was difficult to walk through.*
bristling, crowded, dense, close, impenetrable
antonym: **sparse**

thicken
verb to become thicker » *The fog thickened, making it hard to see.*
condense, congeal, set, coagulate, jell
antonym: **thin**

thief
noun someone who steals something » *The security cameras in the store were there to deter thieves.*
burglar, crook (informal), **mugger** (informal), **pickpocket, robber, shoplifter, housebreaker, pilferer**

thin [1]
adjective measuring a small distance from side to side » *My dad cut the bread into thin slices.*
fine, narrow, slim
antonym: **thick**

*My dad cut the bread into **thin** slices.*

thin [2]
adjective not carrying a lot of fat
◀◀ SEE LEFT

» thin

*Mary added more water to the gravy and now it was too **thin**.*

thin 3
adjective containing a lot of water » *Mary added more water to the gravy and now it was too thin.*
dilute or diluted, runny, watery, weak
antonym: **thick**

thing
noun a physical object » *What do you call that thing on the shelf?*
article, object

things
plural noun someone's clothes or belongings » *Mom looked in despair at Peter's things lying on the bedroom floor.*
belongings, effects, gear, possessions, stuff, chattels, gear, wares

think 1
verb to consider something » *Chris sat down to think about what he should do.*
consider, contemplate, deliberate, meditate, mull over, muse (literary)**, ponder, reflect,** cogitate, ruminate

think 2
verb to believe something » *I think he goes to the same school as me.*
believe, consider, deem (formal)**, hold, imagine, judge, understand**

thorough
adjective careful and complete » *The vet gave the guinea pig a thorough examination.*
complete, comprehensive, exhaustive, full, intensive, meticulous, painstaking, scrupulous, all-embracing, in-depth

thought 1
noun an idea or opinion » *What are your thoughts on the subject?*
idea, notion, opinion, view

thought 2
noun the activity of thinking » *The girl was lost in thought and didn't hear the phone ring.*
consideration, contemplation, deliberation, meditation, reflection, thinking, cogitation, introspection, rumination

thoughtful 1
adjective quiet and serious » *Sam looked thoughtful as he tried to answer the question.*
contemplative, pensive, reflective, introspective, meditative, ruminative

*Sam looked **thoughtful** as he tried to answer the question.*

thoughtful 2
adjective showing consideration for others » *Liam was a thoughtful and caring man.*
attentive, caring, considerate, kind, solicitous, unselfish
antonym: **thoughtless**

thoughtless
adjective showing a lack of consideration » *Ava was thoughtless and always phoned very early in the morning.*
insensitive, tactless, inconsiderate, undiplomatic
antonym: **thoughtful**

threat 1
noun a statement that someone will harm you » *David said he was going to tell the teacher, but it was just an empty threat.*
menace, threatening remark

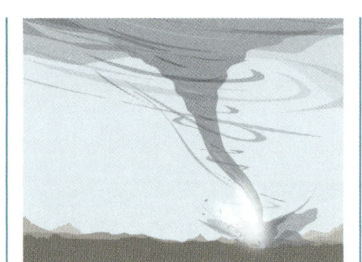

*The approaching tornado posed a **threat** to the crops.*

threat 2
noun something that seems likely to harm you » *The approaching tornado posed a threat to the crops.*
hazard, menace, risk

threaten 1
verb to promise to do something bad » *The teacher threatened to give a detention if the class didn't settle down.*
make threats to, menace

threaten 2
verb to be likely to cause harm » *The new supermarket threatened to bring more traffic to the area.*
endanger, jeopardize, put at risk, put in jeopardy

thrifty
adjective careful not to waste money or resources » *Kirsty was thrifty with money and always found the best bargains.*
careful, economical, frugal, prudent

thrill 1
noun a feeling of excitement » *The children enjoyed the thrill of waking up on Christmas morning.*
high (informal)**, kick** (informal)

thrill 2
verb to cause a feeling of excitement » *I was thrilled to see everyone at the party.*
excite, give a kick (informal)

thrive
verb to be successful » *The children are thriving at their new school and getting top marks.*
do well, flourish, prosper

throw
verb to make something move through the air
▶▶ SEE RIGHT

thug
noun a very violent person » *Joe may look a bit like a thug, but he is very gentle.*
bully, hooligan, tough

tidy 1
adjective arranged in an orderly way » *The teacher's desk was always extremely tidy.*
neat, orderly, shipshape, spick-and-span
antonym: **untidy**

tidy 2
verb to make something neat » *Krishnan tidied his room.*
spruce up, straighten
antonym: **mess up**

tie 1
verb to fasten something » *Mel tied her shoelaces.*
bind, fasten, knot, lash, rope, secure, tether, truss
antonym: **untie**

*Mel **tied** her shoelaces.*

tie 2
verb to have the same score » *The two teams tied in the semi-final.*
be even, be level, draw

tie 3
noun a connection with something » *My family has close ties to the village.*
affiliation, affinity, bond, connection, relationship

228

tired

tight 1
adjective fitting closely » *My shoes are too tight and squash my toes.*
constricted, cramped, snug
antonym: **loose**

tight 2
adjective firmly fastened » *There was a tight knot in the rope.*
firm, secure

There was a tight knot in the rope.

tight 3
adjective not slack or relaxed » *Pull the string tight.*
rigid, taut, tense
antonym: **slack**

tilt 1
verb to raise one end of something » *Leonard tilted his chair back on two legs.*
incline, lean, slant, slope, tip

tilt 2
noun a raised position » *The tilt of the boat on the choppy sea made Max feel nauseous.*
angle, gradient, incline, slant, slope, camber, list, pitch

time 1
noun a particular period » *We enjoyed our time on vacation.*
interval, period, spell, stretch

time 2
verb to plan when something will happen » *We timed our visit to coincide with the school holidays.*
schedule, set

The timid kitten hid from us.

timid
adjective lacking courage or confidence » *The timid kitten hid from us.*
bashful, cowardly, nervous, shy, faint-hearted
antonym: **bold**

tiny
adjective very small » *We found a tiny frog in the garden.*
diminutive, microscopic, miniature, minute, negligible, puny, infinitesimal, Lilliputian
antonym: **huge**

tire
verb to use a lot of energy » *You'll tire yourself out in no time if you keep bouncing on the trampoline.*
drain, exhaust, fatigue, enervate, wear out, weary

tired
adjective having little energy » *I feel tired after my long day.*
beat (informal), **drained, drowsy, exhausted, fatigued, sleepy, weary, worn out**

I feel tired after my long day.

throw
verb to make something move through the air » *He went to throw the ball.*

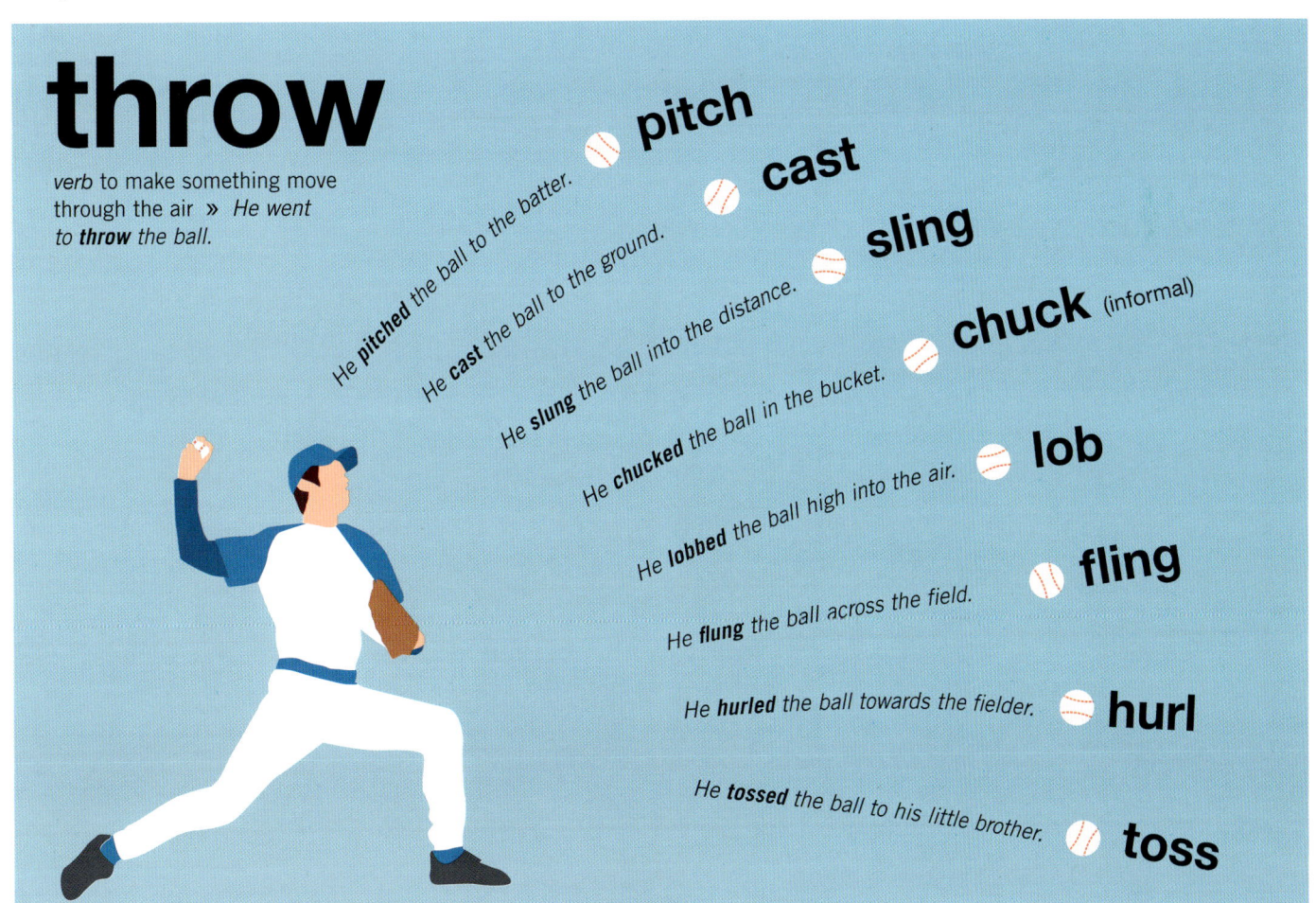

- **pitch** — *He pitched the ball to the batter.*
- **cast** — *He cast the ball to the ground.*
- **sling** — *He slung the ball into the distance.*
- **chuck** (informal) — *He chucked the ball in the bucket.*
- **lob** — *He lobbed the ball high into the air.*
- **fling** — *He flung the ball across the field.*
- **hurl** — *He hurled the ball towards the fielder.*
- **toss** — *He tossed the ball to his little brother.*

together

*We went on long bicycle rides **together**.*

together 1
adverb with other people » *We went on long bicycle rides together.*
collectively, en masse, in unison, jointly, shoulder to shoulder, side by side

together 2
adverb at the same time » *Three horses crossed the finish line together.*
as one, at once, concurrently, simultaneously, with one accord

tolerable 1
adjective able to be put up with » *The accommodation was simple but tolerable.*
acceptable, bearable
antonym: **unbearable**

tolerable 2
adjective fairly satisfactory » *Mo is making tolerable headway with his essay and will finish it before the deadline.*
acceptable, adequate, okay or **OK** (informal), passable, reasonable, so-so (informal)

tolerant
adjective accepting of different views and behaviour » *Our teacher is tolerant of unruly behaviour in the playground, but not in the classroom.*
liberal, broad-minded, open-minded, understanding, easygoing, forbearing, forgiving, lenient, permissive
antonym: **narrow-minded**

tolerate 1
verb to accept something you disagree with » *Jen tolerates her children's laziness as long as they get their chores done.*
accept, put up with

tolerate 2
verb to accept something unpleasant » *Henry tolerated his brother's messiness in the room they shared.*
bear, endure, stand

tomb
noun a burial chamber » *The pyramids in Egypt are ancient tombs.*
grave, mausoleum, sarcophagus, sepulchre (literary), vault

too 1
adverb also or as well » *It wasn't just me. You were there, too.*
as well, besides, in addition, likewise, moreover, to boot (informal)

too 2
adverb more than a desirable or acceptable amount » *Ben had a tummy ache after eating too much candy.*
excessively, over-, overly, unduly, unreasonably

tool
noun a hand-held instrument for doing a job » *They had a shed full of gardening tools.*
implement, instrument, utensil

*They had a shed full of gardening **tools**.*

*I waited at the **top** of the cliff.*

top 1
noun the highest part of something » *I waited at the top of the cliff.*
apex, brow, crest, crown, culmination, head, height, high point, peak, pinnacle, ridge, summit, zenith (literary), acme, apex, apogee
antonym: **bottom**

top 2
noun the lid of a container » *Marie put the top back on the bottle.*
cap, lid, stopper

top 3
adjective being the best of its kind » *Ivan was the team's top goal scorer.*
best, chief, elite, foremost, head, highest, lead, leading, pre-eminent, premier, prime, principal

top 4
verb to be greater than something » *The temperature topped 35 degrees celsius.*
cap, exceed, go beyond, outstrip, surpass

top 5
verb to be better than someone or something » *The world record was going to be quite difficult to top.*
beat, better, eclipse, improve on, outdo, surpass

total 1
noun several things added together » *The school has a total of 1776 pupils.*
aggregate, sum, whole

total 2
adjective complete in all its parts » *There was total mayhem after the animals escaped from the zoo.*
absolute, complete, outright, unconditional, undivided, unmitigated, unqualified, all-out, utter

total 3
verb to reach the sum of » *The money they raised for charity totalled $3000.*
add up to, amount to, come to

touch 1
verb to put your hand on something » *Please do not touch anything in the museum.*
feel, finger, handle

touch 2
verb to come into contact with » *Annie lowered herself down until her feet touched the floor.*
brush, graze, meet
related word:
adjective **tactile**

touch 3
verb to emotionally affect someone » *I was touched by the stranger's kindness.*
affect, move, stir

touching
adjective causing sadness or sympathy » *The touching tale moved Anika to tears.*
affecting (literary), moving, poignant

*The **touching** tale moved Anika to tears.*

travel

touchy
adjective easily upset » *Elle was always touchy after an argument with her parents.*
easily offended, sensitive, oversensitive, thin-skinned

tough 1
adjective able to put up with hardship » *Marian is a tough and ambitious woman.*
hardened, hardy, resilient, robust, rugged, strong

tough 2
adjective difficult to break or damage » *The lid was too tough for Mark to unscrew.*
durable, hard-wearing, leathery, resilient, robust, rugged, solid, strong, sturdy
antonym: **fragile**

The lid was too tough for Mark to unscrew.

tough 3
adjective full of hardship » *The obstacle course was tough but fun.*
arduous, difficult, exacting, hard
antonym: **easy**

trace 1
verb to look for and find something » *Chloe was trying to trace her family tree.*
locate, track down

trace 2
noun a sign of something » *Derek's keys had disappeared without a trace.*
evidence, hint, indication, record, sign, suggestion, whiff

trace 3
noun a small amount of something » *There was a trace of cinnamon in the muffin.*
dash, drop, remnant, suspicion, tinge, touch, vestige, iota, jot, soupçon

trade 1
noun the buying and selling of goods » *The country relies heavily on foreign trade.*
business, commerce

trade 2
noun the kind of work someone does » *Ed learned his trade while working as an apprentice.*
business, line of work, occupation, profession, skill

trade 3
verb to buy and sell goods » *My parents have years of experience in trading clothes.*
deal, do business, traffic

trader
noun someone who trades in goods » *Many fur traders worked for the Hudson's Bay Company.*
broker, dealer, merchant

tradition
noun a long-standing custom » *The town's tradition was to hold a Christmas concert.*
convention, custom, practice

traditional
adjective existing for a long time » *The family wore traditional Indian dress.*
conventional, established
antonym: **unconventional**

The family wore traditional Indian dress.

tragic
adjective very sad » *The book had a tragic ending; the hero dies.*
distressing, heartbreaking, heart-rending

train
verb to teach someone how to do something » *We train our volunteers in first aid.*
coach, drill, educate, instruct, school, teach, tutor

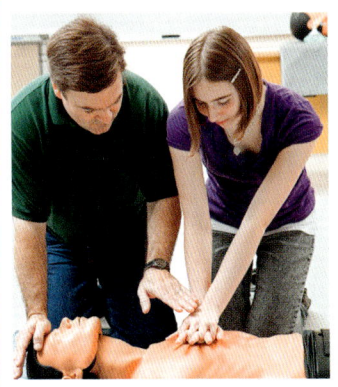

We train our volunteers in first aid.

transfer
verb to move something from one place to another » *It was easy to transfer the photos from the camera to the computer.*
carry, download, move, upload

transform
verb to change something completely » *The run-down building was transformed into a trendy café.*
alter, change, convert, reform, revolutionize

transparent
adjective able to be seen through » *Glass is transparent.*
clear, crystalline (literary), **sheer, translucent, diaphanous, see-through**
antonym: **opaque**

transport
verb to move people or goods somewhere » *A bus transported passengers from the terminal to the plane.*
carry, convey (formal), **ship, transfer**

transportation
noun the moving of goods and people » *Danny booked a vacation that included transportation to the hotel.*
removal, shipment, transportation

trap 1
noun a device for catching animals » *The net acted as a trap for catching fish.*
net, snare

trap 2
verb to catch animals » *Clara tried to trap the butterfly.*
catch, corner, snare

Clara tried to trap the butterfly.

trap 3
verb to trick someone » *She knew Kelly was trying to trap her into agreeing to swap shoes, but she kept refusing.*
dupe, trick, ensnare, entrap

trash 1
noun waste material » *The trash was collected every Monday.*
garbage, refuse, rubbish, waste

trash 2
noun something of poor quality » *The magazine was trash, but Jo still liked reading it.*
garbage (informal), **rubbish**

travel
verb to make a journey somewhere » *Ben travelled to Edmonton by train.*
go, journey (formal), **make your way, take a trip, proceed, voyage**

» treacherous

trip

[1] *noun* a journey to a place
» Guy was saving up for his **trip** around the world.

excursion
We're going on an **excursion** to the old town.

jaunt
We're off on a **jaunt** to the seaside.

journey
It's a long car **journey** across the country.

outing
We're having a class **outing** to the castle.

voyage
We're going on a **voyage** across the sea.

tour
The best way to see everything is to take a **tour**.

expedition
I'm excited about our **expedition** to the countryside.

day trip
We're taking a **day trip** to the cottage.

trek
He's going on a **trek** in the Rockies.

treacherous [1]
adjective likely to betray someone » *He was a treacherous character, betraying the hero's hideout to the enemy.*
disloyal, faithless, unfaithful, untrustworthy, traitorous
antonym: **loyal**

treacherous [2]
adjective dangerous or unreliable » *The vehicle travelled slowly along the treacherous mountain roads.*
dangerous, hazardous, perilous (literary)

*The vehicle travelled slowly along the **treacherous** mountain roads.*

treasure
verb to consider something very precious » *Friendship is something to treasure.*
cherish, hold dear, prize, value, revere, venerate

treat [1]
verb to behave towards someone in a certain way » *The manager treated all the players fairly.*
act towards, behave towards, deal with, handle

treat [2]
verb to give someone medical care » *The doctor who treated me was kind and caring.*
care for, nurse

trendy
adjective (informal) fashionable » *I took my friend for smoothies at a trendy café.*
fashionable, in (slang)**, in fashion, in vogue, latest, stylish**

tribute
noun something that shows admiration » *The statue was a tribute to the former president.*
accolade (formal)**, compliment, honour, praise, testimony**

trick [1]
noun something that deceives someone » *Joshua liked to play tricks on his family.*
con (informal)**, deception, hoax, ploy, ruse,** stratagem, subterfuge

trick [2]
verb to deceive someone » *A magician tricks the audience into believing the unbelievable.*
con (informal)**, deceive, dupe, fool, take in** (informal)**,** hoax, hoodwink

*A magician **tricks** the audience into believing the unbelievable.*

tricky
adjective difficult to do or to deal with » *The family sat down to figure out the tricky problem together.*
complex, complicated, delicate, difficult, hard, problematic, puzzling, sensitive

trip [1]
noun a journey to a place
◀◀ SEE LEFT

trip [2]
verb to fall over » *I tripped on the stairs.*
fall over, lose your footing, stumble

triumph [1]
noun a great success » *The band's final concert was a triumph, delighting their fans.*
success, victory, accomplishment, achievement, coup, hit, tour de force
antonym: **failure**

triumph [2]
verb to be successful » *The host country won the most medals and triumphed at the Olympics.*
come out on top (informal)**, prevail, succeed, win**
antonym: **fail**

trivial
adjective not important » *The problem was trivial and could wait to be dealt with.*
insignificant, minor, negligible, paltry, petty, slight, trifling, unimportant, frivolous, inconsequential
antonym: **important**

trouble [1]
noun a difficulty or problem » *Finn was having some trouble understanding his math homework.*
bother, difficulty, hassle (informal)**, problem**

trouble [2]
verb to make someone feel worried » *The missing bag troubled Janet, as her keys were in there.*
agitate, bother, disturb, worry

trouble [3]
verb to cause someone inconvenience » *Can I trouble you for some milk?*
bother, disturb, impose upon, inconvenience, put out

true [1]
adjective not invented » *The new action movie is based on a true story.*
accurate, correct, factual
antonym: **inaccurate**

true [2]
adjective real or genuine » *Alicia is a true friend—she's always there for me.*
authentic, bona fide, genuine, real
antonym: **false**

trust
verb to believe that someone will do something » *My parents trust me to do the right thing.*
count on, depend on, have confidence in, have faith in, place your trust in, rely upon

trusty
adjective considered to be reliable » *I bought my trusty old bike years ago, but it's still going strong.*
dependable, faithful, firm, reliable, solid, staunch, true, trustworthy

truth
noun the facts about something » *The documents revealed the truth about the mystery.*
fact, reality
related words: *adjectives*
veritable, veracious

try [1]
verb to make an effort to do something » *I tried my best in the test and received a satisfactory grade.*
attempt, endeavour (formal)**, make an attempt, make an effort, seek, strive**

try [2]
verb to test the quality of something » *Howard tried the soup to see how hot it was.*
check out, sample, test, try out

*Howard **tried** the soup to see how hot it was.*

try

try [3]
noun an attempt to do something » *After only a few tries, Mario played the piece of music perfectly.*
attempt, **effort**, **endeavour** (formal), **go** (informal), **shot** (informal)

tug [1]
verb to give something a quick, hard pull » *The climber tugged hard on the rope to test it was secure.*
drag, **draw**, **haul**, **heave**, **jerk**, **pluck**, **pull**, **wrench**, **yank**

The climber tugged hard on the rope to test it was secure.

tug [2]
noun a quick, hard pull » *Sam felt a tug at his arm.*
heave, **jerk**, **pull**, **wrench**, **yank**

tune
noun a series of musical notes » *Betty hummed a tune that had been stuck in her head for days.*
melody, **strains**, air, theme

turn [1]
verb to change the direction or position of something » *Dan turned the car around so that they were facing the right direction.*
rotate, **spin**, **swivel**, **twirl**, **twist**

turn [2]
verb to become or make something different » *Your body turns food into energy.*
change, **convert**, **mutate**, **transform**, metamorphose, transfigure, transmute

turn [3]
noun someone's right or duty to do something » *Tonight, it's my turn to cook.*
chance, **go**, **opportunity**

twist [1]
verb to turn something around » *Dad twisted the strands of dough to make a loaf.*
bend, **curl**, **twine**, **weave**, **wring**, entwine, wreathe

Dad twisted the strands of dough to make a loaf.

twist [2]
verb to bend into a new shape » *The bike was twisted out of shape in the accident.*
distort, **mangle**, **screw up**, contort, warp

twist [3]
verb to injure a part of your body » *I've twisted my ankle.*
sprain, **wrench**, turn

two-faced
adjective not honest in dealing with other people » *Bev is so two-faced. She talks about her friends behind their backs.*
deceitful, **dishonest**, **disloyal**, **false**, **hypocritical**, **insincere**, **treacherous**

type
noun a group of things that have features in common
▶▶ SEE RIGHT

typical
adjective having the usual characteristics of something » *Today was just another typical day at school.*
average, **characteristic**, **normal**, **regular**, **representative**, **standard**, **stock**, **usual**, archetypal, archetypical, stereotypical
antonym: **uncharacteristic**

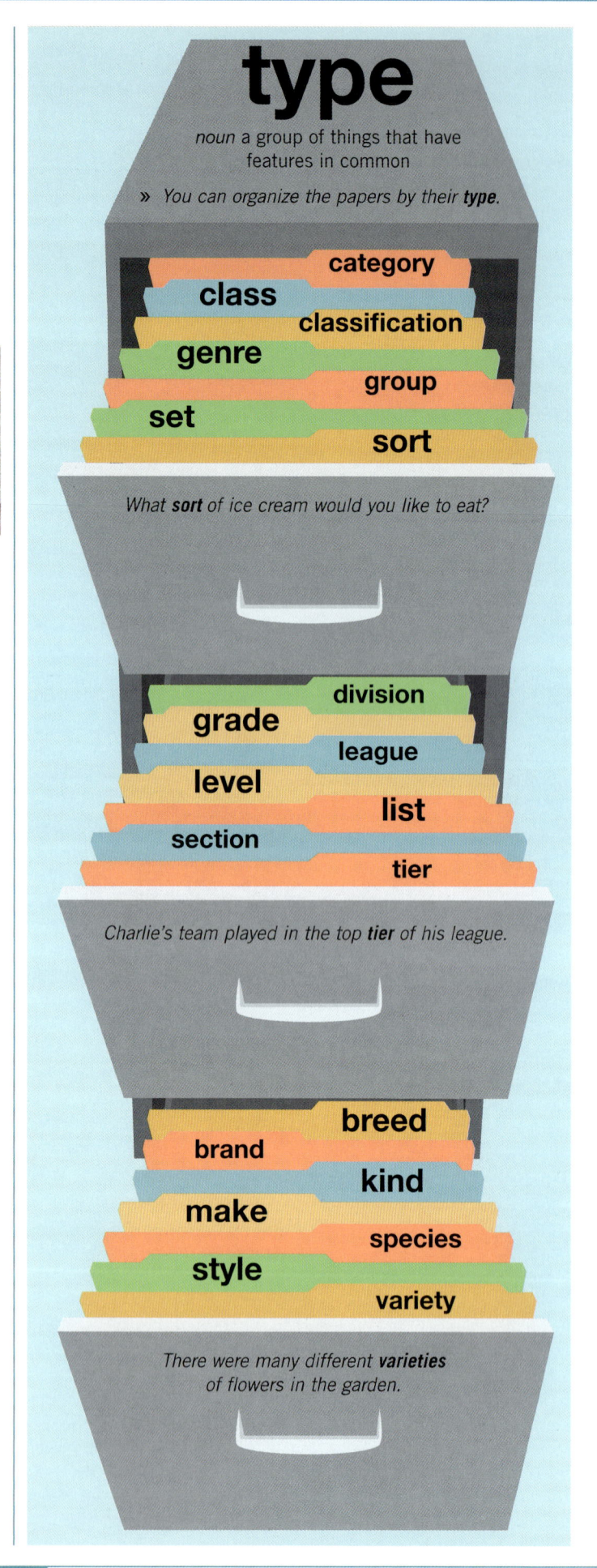

type
noun a group of things that have features in common
» *You can organize the papers by their type.*

category, **class**, **classification**, **genre**, **group**, **set**, **sort**

What sort of ice cream would you like to eat?

division, **grade**, **league**, **level**, **list**, **section**, **tier**

Charlie's team played in the top tier of his league.

brand, **breed**, **kind**, **make**, **species**, **style**, **variety**

There were many different varieties of flowers in the garden.

Uu

ugly
adjective having a very unattractive appearance » *The fish was very ugly, with bulging eyes.*
plain, unattractive, unsightly, unlovely, unprepossessing
antonym: **beautiful**

ultimate 1
adjective being the final one of a series » *It is not possible to predict the ultimate winner of the talent show.*
eventual, final, last

ultimate 2
adjective the most important or powerful » *The ultimate goal of any tennis professional is to win a Grand Slam.*
greatest, paramount, supreme, utmost

ultimate 3
noun the finest example of something » *The fancy hotel is the ultimate in luxury.*
epitome, extreme, height, peak

unaware
adjective not knowing about something » *She was unaware of the large spider dangling beside her.*
ignorant, oblivious, unconscious, unsuspecting
antonym: **aware**

unbearable
adjective too unpleasant to be tolerated » *The midday heat was unbearable.*
intolerable, oppressive, unacceptable, insufferable, unendurable
antonym: **tolerable**

unbelievable 1
adjective extremely great or surprising » *Hugh showed unbelievable courage.*
colossal, incredible, stupendous

unbelievable 2
adjective so unlikely it cannot be believed
▼ SEE BELOW

uncertain 1
adjective not knowing what to do » *Jim looked uncertain after hearing Sal's insane plan.*
doubtful, dubious, unclear, undecided, irresolute, vacillating
antonym: **certain**

uncertain 2
adjective not definite » *The injured player was facing an uncertain future.*
ambiguous, doubtful, indefinite, indeterminate, conjectural, undetermined
antonym: **certain**

unclear
adjective confusing and not obvious » *It is unclear exactly how much support Tia has for the new design.*
ambiguous, confused, vague
antonym: **clear**

uncomfortable 1
adjective feeling or causing discomfort » *Sarah slept badly because her bed was uncomfortable.*
awkward, cramped, disagreeable, ill-fitting, painful
antonym: **comfortable**

uncomfortable 2
adjective not relaxed or confident » *Talking about money made Mick uncomfortable.*
awkward, embarrassed, ill at ease, self-conscious, uneasy
antonym: **comfortable**

uncommon 1
adjective not happening or seen often » *A lynx is an uncommon sight round here.*
abnormal, exceptional, extraordinary, infrequent, out of the ordinary, rare, scarce, sparse, unusual, unprecedented
antonym: **common**

---

implausible — *That's an implausible claim.*

incredible — *It's incredible you think that.*

improbable — *It's an improbable outcome.*

preposterous — *It's a preposterous statement.*

inconceivable — *It's inconceivable that'll happen.*

unconvincing — *It's an unconvincing argument.*

unbelievable
2 adjective so unlikely it cannot be believed » *"Maybe we'll live on Mars." "And maybe pigs will fly," snorted Dad. "Unbelievable!"*

»uncommon

uncommon [2]
adjective unusually great » *Sue read Cecilia's letter with uncommon interest.*
acute, exceptional, extraordinary, extreme, great, intense, remarkable, unparalleled

unconscious [1]
adjective in a state similar to sleep » *Frank banged his head and knocked himself unconscious.*
asleep, out cold (informal), **senseless, comatose, insensible**
antonym: **conscious**

unconscious [2]
adjective not aware of what is happening » *The fox was quite unconscious of their presence.*
oblivious, unaware, unknowing, unsuspecting
antonym: **aware**

uncover [1]
verb to find something out » *The journalist uncovered the truth behind the scandal.*
bring to light, expose, reveal, show up, unearth

uncover [2]
verb to remove the lid or cover from something » *When the seedlings sprout, lift the plastic to uncover the tray.*
expose, lay bare, open, reveal, unveil, unwrap

*When the seedlings sprout, lift the plastic to **uncover** the tray.*

*The young children played with their toys **under** the table.*

under
preposition at a lower level than something » *The young children played with their toys under the table.*
below, beneath, underneath
antonym: **above**

undergo
verb to have something happen to you » *My uncle had to undergo major surgery.*
be subjected to, endure, experience, go through, suffer

undermine
verb to secretly weaken or sabotage something » *I won't let you undermine me—I know I'm right.*
impair, sabotage, sap, subvert, torpedo (informal), **undercut, weaken**
antonym: **strengthen**

understand [1]
verb to know what someone means » *Do you understand what I'm saying?*
catch on (informal), **comprehend, follow, get, grasp, see**

understand [2]
verb to know why or how something is happening » *Ria was too young to understand what was happening.*
appreciate, comprehend, fathom, grasp, realize, conceive, discern

understand [3]
verb to hear of something » *I understand your cousin hasn't been well.*
believe, gather, hear, learn

understanding [1]
noun a knowledge of something » *Kai has a good understanding of computers.*
appreciation, comprehension, grasp, knowledge, perception

understanding [2]
noun an informal agreement » *They came to an understanding that worked for both of them.*
accord, agreement, pact

*They came to an **understanding** that worked for both of them.*

understanding [3]
adjective having a sympathetic nature » *My parents are very understanding.*
compassionate, considerate, sensitive, sympathetic

undertaking
noun a task which you have agreed to do » *Organizing the show has been a massive undertaking.*
affair, business, endeavour, enterprise, job, operation, project, task, venture

uneasy
adjective worried that something may be wrong » *I was very uneasy about the plans to close the library.*
agitated, anxious, nervous, perturbed, worried, apprehensive, discomposed, restive
antonym: **comfortable**

unemployed
adjective not having a job » *Henry is unemployed and looking for work.*
idle, jobless, laid off, redundant
antonym: **employed**

uneven [1]
adjective not the same or consistent » *Brooke drew six lines of uneven length.*
fluctuating, inconsistent, irregular, patchy, variable
antonym: **even**

uneven [2]
adjective having an unlevel or rough surface » *The bikers raced over the uneven terrain.*
bumpy, not level, not smooth, rough
antonym: **level**

*The bikers raced over the **uneven** terrain.*

unexpected
adjective not considered likely to happen » *Raj's win was completely unexpected—he was last in the semi-finals.*
astonishing, chance, surprising, unforeseen, fortuitous, unanticipated

unfailing
adjective continuous and not weakening as time passes » *I admire Jan's unfailing cheerfulness, even in the most stressful times.*
constant, endless, unremitting

unhappy »

unfair
adjective without right or justice » *Joe said it was unfair that he wasn't allowed to go to the party.*
unjust, wrong, wrongful, inequitable, iniquitous
antonym: **fair**

unfamiliar
adjective not having been seen or heard of before » *Amber grew many plants that were unfamiliar to me.*
alien, exotic, foreign, new, novel, strange, unknown

unfriendly
adjective not showing any warmth or kindness » *The cats were unfriendly and hissed at each other.*
aloof, antagonistic, cold, disagreeable, hostile, unkind, ill-disposed, uncongenial
antonym: **friendly**

*The cats were **unfriendly** and hissed at each other.*

ungrateful
adjective not appreciating the things you have » *The guests were ungrateful and didn't thank us when they left.*
unappreciative, unthankful
antonym: **grateful**

unhappy
adjective feeling sad or depressed
▶▶ SEE RIGHT

---

crestfallen **gloomy**

down **despondent**

sad **miserable**

sorrowful **depressed**

disconsolate antonym: **happy**

| **unhappy** *adjective* feeling sad or depressed » *He was **unhappy** that the holiday was coming to an end.*

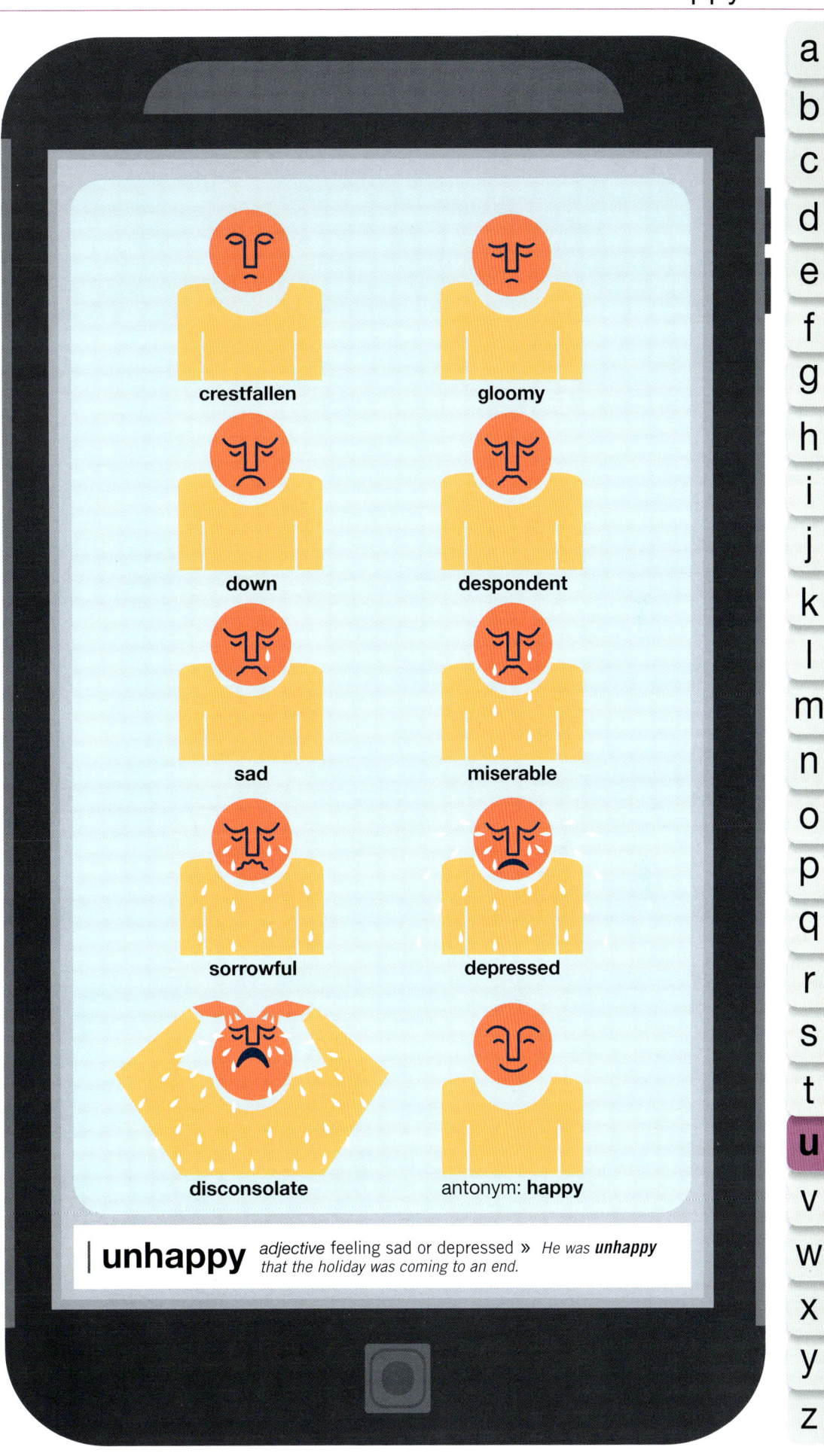

237

unhealthy

*Dennis eats too much **unhealthy** food.*

unhealthy [1]
adjective likely to cause illness » *Dennis eats too much unhealthy food.*
bad for you, harmful, noxious, unsanitary, unwholesome
antonym: **healthy**

unhealthy [2]
adjective not well » *Ross looks rather pale and unhealthy.*
ailing, ill, not well, poorly (informal), **sick, unwell, wretched**
antonym: **healthy**

unimportant
adjective having little significance or importance » *The difference in their ages is unimportant and doesn't affect their friendship.*
insignificant, minor, paltry, slight, trivial
antonym: **important**

uninterested
adjective not interested in something » *I'm completely uninterested in politics.*
apathetic, bored, impassive, indifferent, nonchalant, passive, unconcerned
antonym: **interested**

union [1]
noun an organization of people or groups with mutual interests » *Julie belongs to several different unions.*
association, coalition, confederation, federation, league

union [2]
noun the joining together of two or more things » *We formed a union with another dance troupe.*
amalgamation, blend, combination, fusion, mixture, amalgam, conjunction, synthesis

*We formed a **union** with another dance troupe.*

unite
verb to join together and act as a group » *The rival bands united to perform a charity concert.*
collaborate, combine, join, join forces, link up, merge, pull together, work together
antonym: **divide**

universal
adjective relating to everyone or to the whole universe » *The programs have a universal appeal and are suitable for the whole family.*
common, general, unlimited, widespread, worldwide, omnipresent, overarching

unkind
adjective lacking in kindness and consideration » *It's very unkind to call anyone names.*
cruel, malicious, mean, nasty, spiteful, thoughtless
antonym: **kind**

unknown
adjective not familiar or famous » *Tim was an unknown writer before he won the book prize.*
humble, obscure, unfamiliar, unsung
antonym: **famous**

*The two butterflies looked completely **unlike** one another.*

unlike
preposition different from » *The two butterflies looked completely unlike one another.*
different from, dissimilar to, distinct from, divergent from (formal), **far from**
antonym: **like**

unlikely
adjective probably not true or likely to happen » *Sofia blamed her lateness on the unlikely excuse that there were no buses.*
implausible, incredible, unbelievable, unconvincing
antonym: **likely**

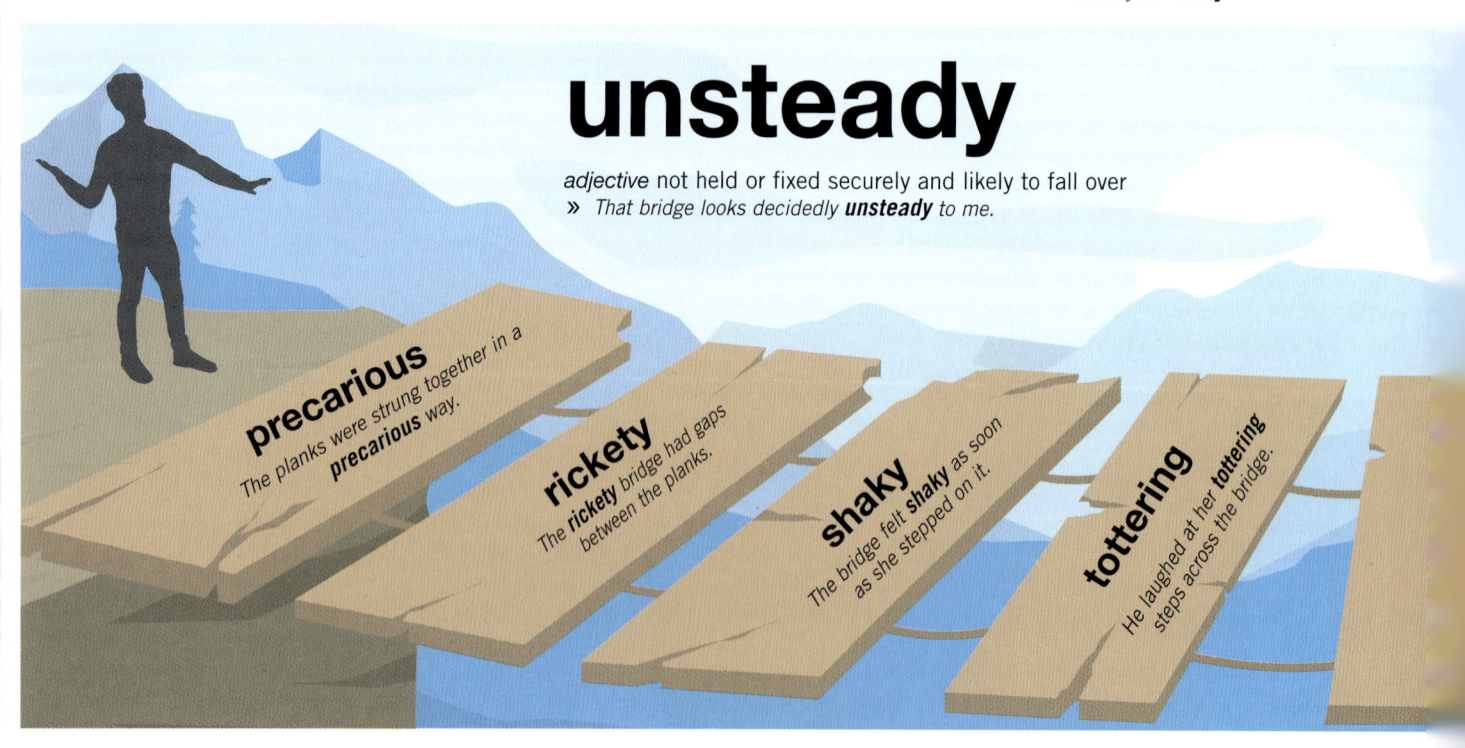

unsteady

adjective not held or fixed securely and likely to fall over » *That bridge looks decidedly **unsteady** to me.*

precarious — *The planks were strung together in a precarious way.*

rickety — *The rickety bridge had gaps between the planks.*

shaky — *The bridge felt shaky as soon as she stepped on it.*

tottering — *He laughed at her tottering steps across the bridge.*

untrue »

unlucky
adjective having bad luck
» Elias was unlucky not to score in the first half.
cursed, hapless, luckless, unfortunate
antonym: **lucky**

unnecessary
adjective completely needless
» My father considers taxis to be an unnecessary expense, so we always take the bus.
needless, pointless, uncalled-for
antonym: **necessary**

unpleasant 1
adjective causing feelings of discomfort or dislike
» Dirty socks have a very unpleasant smell!
bad, disagreeable, distasteful, nasty, repulsive, unpalatable
antonym: **pleasant**

unpleasant 2
adjective rude or unfriendly
» He was thoroughly unpleasant to me earlier.
disagreeable, horrid, objectionable, obnoxious, rude, unfriendly
antonym: **pleasant**

*The ginger cookies were **unpopular**, and everyone wanted the chocolate ones.*

unpopular
adjective disliked by most people » The ginger cookies were unpopular, and everyone wanted the chocolate ones.
detested, disliked, shunned, undesirable
antonym: **popular**

unpredictable
adjective unable to be foreseen
» The weather in the mountains is unpredictable—one minute it's sunny and the next it's raining.
chance, doubtful, hit-or-miss (informal)**, unforeseeable**
antonym: **predictable**

unsatisfactory
adjective not good enough
» Emma's work was judged unsatisfactory by the teacher.
disappointing, inadequate, mediocre, poor, unacceptable
antonym: **satisfactory**

unsteady
adjective not held or fixed securely and likely to fall over
▼ SEE BELOW

unsuitable
adjective not appropriate for a purpose » Tom's attire was unsuitable for running.
improper, inappropriate, unacceptable, unfit, inapposite, unseemly
antonym: **suitable**

*Tom's attire was **unsuitable** for running.*

*My bedroom is very **untidy**.*

untidy
adjective not neatly arranged
» My bedroom is very untidy.
bedraggled, chaotic, cluttered, jumbled, messy, unkempt, disordered, shambolic
antonym: **tidy**

untrue
adjective not true
» The allegations that he lied were completely untrue.
erroneous, false, fictitious, inaccurate, incorrect, misleading, mistaken
antonym: **true**

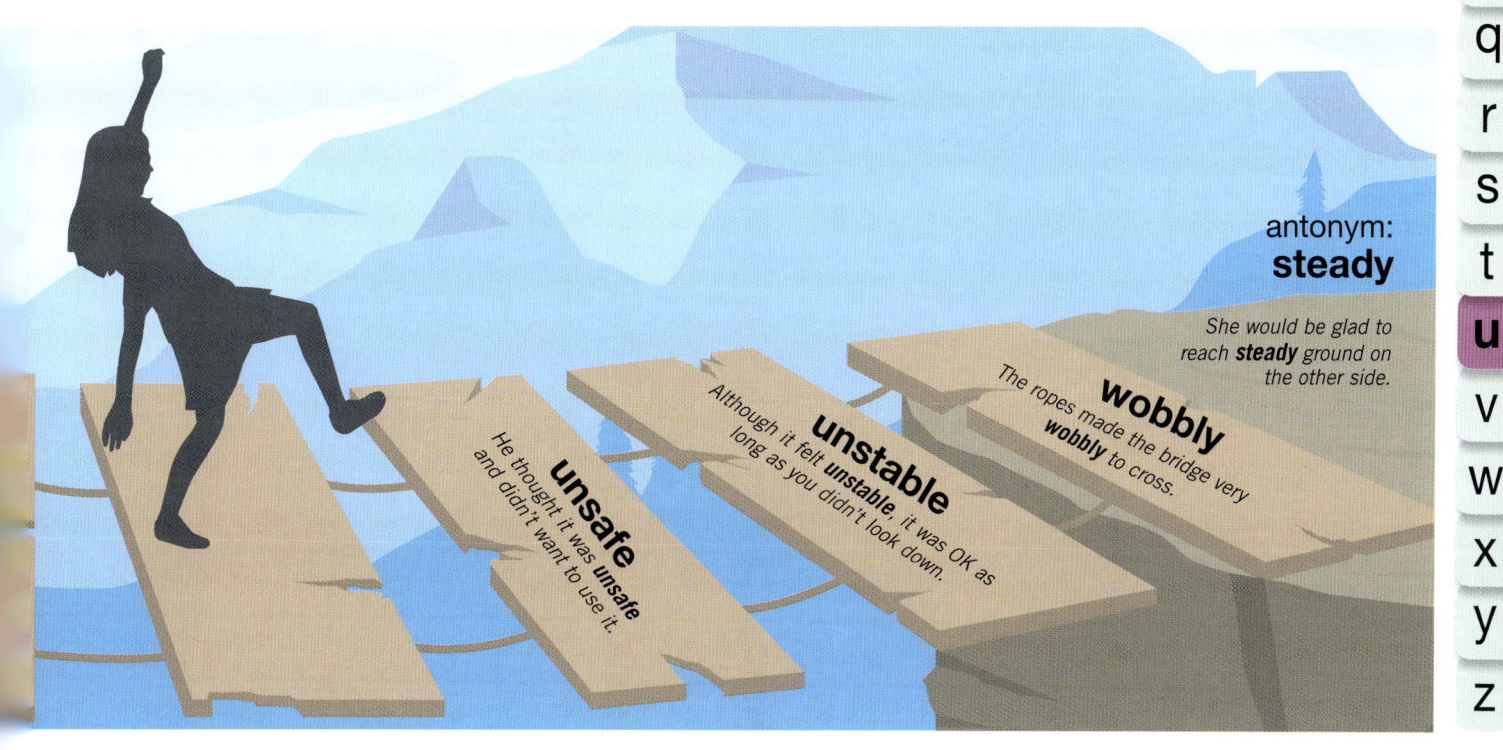

He thought it was **unsafe** and didn't want to use it.

Although it felt **unstable**, it was OK as long as you didn't look down.

The ropes made the bridge very **wobbly** to cross.

antonym: **steady**
She would be glad to reach **steady** ground on the other side.

239

» unusual

*Baobabs are **unusual** trees with thick trunks and few leaves.*

unusual
adjective not occurring very often » *Baobabs are unusual trees with thick trunks and few leaves.*
curious, exceptional, extraordinary, rare, uncommon, unconventional, atypical, unwonted
antonym: **common**

unwell
adjective ill or sick » *Noah felt unwell and had to go home early.*
ailing, ill, poorly (informal), **queasy, sick, wretched,** indisposed, under the weather
antonym: **well**

unwilling
adjective not wanting to do something » *Amelia was unwilling to get too involved in school politics.*
averse, grudging, loath, reluctant
antonym: **willing**

unwise
adjective foolish or not sensible » *It's very unwise to go out in the sunshine without wearing sunscreen.*
foolish, idiotic, irresponsible, rash, senseless, silly, stupid, imprudent, injudicious
antonym: **wise**

upkeep
noun the process and cost of maintaining something » *The school is raising money for the upkeep of the grounds.*
keep, maintenance, preservation, running

upset 1
adjective feeling unhappy about something » *Chloe was very upset when she heard the bad news.*
agitated, distressed, frantic, hurt, troubled, unhappy

*Chloe was very **upset** when she heard the bad news.*

upset 2
verb to make someone worried or unhappy » *The news about the missing dog upset me terribly.*
agitate, bother, distress, disturb, grieve, ruffle, discompose, faze, perturb

upset 3
verb to turn something over accidentally » *Aiden upset the coffee cup.*
capsize, knock over, overturn, spill

*Aiden **upset** the coffee cup.*

urge 1
noun a strong wish to do something » *Evelyn stifled the urge to laugh at her friend's singing.*
compulsion, desire, drive, impulse, longing, wish

urge 2
verb to try hard to persuade someone » *Michel left early, despite being urged to stay.*
beg, beseech, implore, plead, press, entreat, exhort, solicit

urgent
adjective needing to be dealt with quickly » *The rescued sailors had an urgent need for food and water.*
compelling, immediate, imperative, pressing

use 1
verb to perform a task with something » *Use a sharp knife to cut into the lemon.*
apply, employ, operate, utilize, avail oneself of, ply

***Use** a sharp knife to cut into the lemon.*

use 2
noun the act of using something » *There is rarely any need for the use of force.*
application, employment, operation, usage

useful
adjective something that helps or makes things easier » *This booklet contains a great deal of useful information.*
beneficial, effective, helpful, practical, valuable, worthwhile
antonym: **useless**

useless
adjective not suitable or useful » *My jacket was useless in the rain because it wasn't waterproof.*
futile, impractical, unproductive, unsuitable, worthless, disadvantageous, ineffectual, unavailing
antonym: **useful**

*My jacket was **useless** in the rain because it wasn't waterproof.*

usual
adjective done or happening most often » *You'll find Enzo sitting at his usual table—he's always there.*
accustomed, common, customary, habitual, normal, regular, standard

utter
adjective complete or total » *The teacher walked into the classroom to find a scene of utter chaos, with children running riot.*
absolute, complete, consummate, out-and-out, outright, perfect, pure, sheer, thorough, total, unconditional, unmitigated, unqualified

Vv

vague
adjective not clearly expressed or clearly visible » *Uncle Bill was very vague about his job, so we didn't know what he did.*
hazy, indefinite, indistinct, loose, uncertain, unclear, ill-defined, indeterminate, nebulous
antonym: **definite**

vain [1]
adjective very proud of your looks or qualities » *Sarah is so vain—she's always looking at herself in the mirror.*
conceited, egotistical, ostentatious, proud, stuck-up (informal), **narcissistic, swaggering**

vain [2]
adjective not successful in achieving what was intended » *Danny made a vain attempt to stop the baby crying.*
abortive, fruitless, futile, unproductive, useless
antonym: **successful**

vain [3]: in vain
adjective unsuccessful in achieving what was intended » *Sally tried in vain to open the locked door.*
fruitless, to no avail, unsuccessful, wasted

valley
noun an area of low-lying land between hills, often with a river or stream flowing through it » *On the floor of the valley lay a beautiful lake.*
dale, glen, hollow, vale

*On the floor of the **valley** lay a beautiful lake.*

valuable [1]
adjective having great importance or usefulness » *Tim's experience as a mechanic was very valuable when the car wouldn't start.*
beneficial, helpful, important, prized, useful, worthwhile, cherished, esteemed, treasured
antonym: **useless**

valuable [2]
adjective worth a lot of money » *Diamonds are valuable gems.*
costly, expensive, precious
antonym: **worthless**

valuables
plural noun the things you own that cost a lot of money » *Keep your valuables in a safe place.*
heirlooms, treasures

value [1]
noun the importance or usefulness of something » *The fact that Maria spoke Spanish was of great value.*
advantage, benefit, effectiveness, importance, merit, use, usefulness, virtue, worth

value [2]
noun the amount of money that something is worth » *The value of my stamp collection has risen by 50 percent.*
cost, market price, price, selling price, worth

value [3]
verb to appreciate something and think it is important » *I really value all the help that Ashley gave me.*
appreciate, cherish, have a high opinion of, prize, rate highly, respect, treasure

value [4]
verb to decide how much money something is worth » *Grandma had her jewellery valued for insurance purposes.*
appraise, assess, cost, estimate, evaluate, price

vanish [1]
verb to disappear » *The Moon vanished behind a cloud.*
become invisible, be lost to view, disappear, fade, recede
antonym: **appear**

vanish [2]
verb to cease to exist
▼ SEE BELOW

vanquish
verb to defeat someone completely » *I read a gripping story about a knight who vanquished his enemies.*
beat, conquer, crush, defeat, overcome, trounce

---

become extinct · cease to exist · dissolve · fade away · melt away · pass · go away · evaporate · die out · cease

vanish
[2] *verb* to cease to exist » *Dinosaurs vanished from Earth millions of years ago.*

241

variation

view
[2] noun the things you can see from a particular place
» What a beautiful **view**!

landscape
The **landscape** is stunning.

perspective
I've got a good **perspective** from here.

aspect
Such a sunny **aspect**!

spectacle
Yes, all that sparkling water is quite a **spectacle**.

variation
noun a change from the normal or usual pattern » There was no variation in Jim's mood from one day to the next—he was always grumpy.
alteration, change, departure, deviation, difference, diversion

variety [1]
noun a number of different kinds of things » An encyclopedia contains a wide variety of subjects.
array, assortment, collection, medley, mixture, range, cross section, miscellany, multiplicity

variety [2]
noun a particular type of something » The café owner asked Carlos which variety of coffee he wanted.
category, class, kind, sort, strain, type

Various sorts of trees grow in the local park.

various
adjective of several different types » Various sorts of trees grow in the local park.
assorted, different, disparate, diverse, miscellaneous, sundry, manifold

vary [1]
verb to change to something different » The weather here varies greatly from day to day.
alter, alternate, change, fluctuate

vary [2]
verb to introduce changes in something » I try to vary my diet as much as possible.
alternate, diversify, modify, permutate, reorder

vast
adjective extremely large » We gazed at the Milky Way, one small part of our vast Universe.
colossal, enormous, giant, gigantic, great, huge, immense, massive
antonym: **tiny**

*We gazed at the Milky Way, one small part of our **vast** Universe.*

*The jury delivered their **verdict**: he was innocent.*

verdict
noun a decision or opinion on something » The jury delivered their verdict: he was innocent.
conclusion, decision, finding, judgment, opinion

very
adverb to a great degree » I know Chloe very well.
deeply, extremely, greatly, highly, really, exceedingly, profoundly, remarkably

veto [1]
verb to forbid something » The government authorities vetoed the building plans.
ban, forbid, prohibit

242

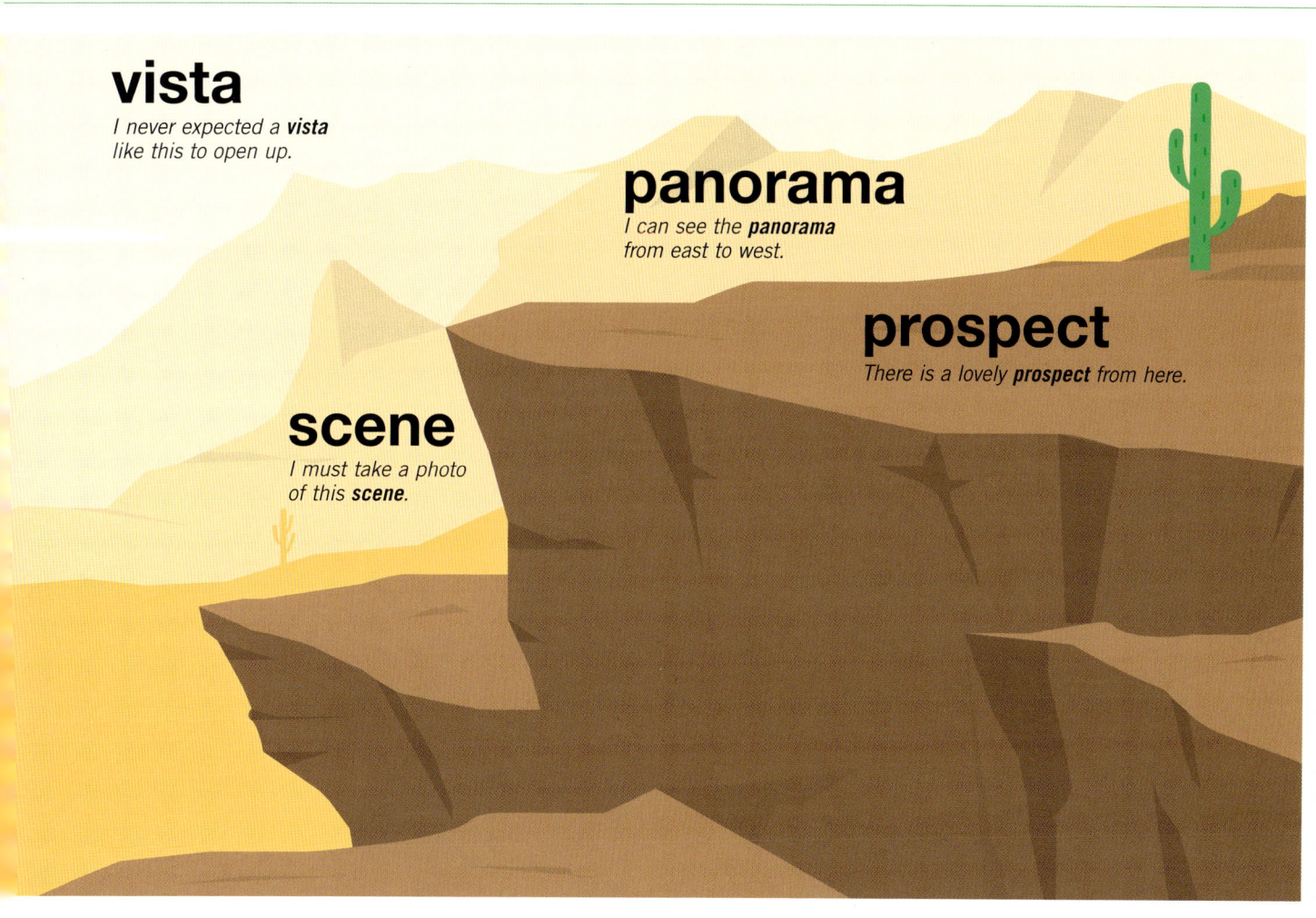

violent

vista
I never expected a vista like this to open up.

panorama
I can see the panorama from east to west.

prospect
There is a lovely prospect from here.

scene
I must take a photo of this scene.

---

veto [2]
noun the act of forbidding or power to forbid something » *The principal issued a veto on the school board's proposal to stop homework.*
ban, prohibition

victory
noun a success in a battle or competition » *The team celebrated its fifth consecutive victory in the tournament.*
laurels, success, superiority, triumph, win
antonym: **defeat**

The team celebrated its fifth consecutive victory in the tournament.

Ian told me his views on sports and I could hardly get a word in.

view [1]
noun a personal opinion » *Ian told me his views on sports and I could hardly get a word in.*
attitude, belief, conviction, feeling, opinion, point of view

view [2]
noun the things you can see from a particular place
▲ SEE ABOVE

view [3]
verb to think of something in a particular way » *Tina viewed the noisy kids as troublemakers.*
consider, deem (formal), **judge, regard**

viewpoint
noun an attitude towards something » *The parents had differing viewpoints on the new teacher.*
attitude, belief, conviction, feeling, opinion, point of view

violence [1]
noun behaviour which is intended to do damage » *Nina absolutely hates seeing violence on television.*
bloodshed, brutality, cruelty, force, savagery

violence [2]
noun force and energy » *Amy was furious and slammed the door with great violence.*
fervour, force, harshness, intensity, severity, vehemence

violent [1]
adjective intending to hurt or kill » *The violent criminals were sent to prison.*
bloodthirsty, brutal, cruel, murderous, savage, vicious
antonym: **gentle**

violent [2]
adjective happening with great force » *Violent waves crashed against the rocks.*
powerful, raging, rough, strong, turbulent, wild, tempestuous, tumultuous

Violent waves crashed against the rocks.

violent

violent 3
adjective said, felt, or done with great force » *Jake was not expecting his chemistry experiment to give such a violent reaction.*
acute, furious, intense, powerful, severe, strong, forcible, passionate, vehement

virtue 1
noun the quality of doing what is morally right » *My grandmother reminded me that patience is a virtue.*
goodness, integrity, morality, probity, rectitude, righteousness

virtue 2
noun an advantage something has » *The players discussed the virtues of various hockey teams.*
advantage, asset, attribute, merit, plus, strength

virtue 3 : **by virtue of**
preposition because of » *Ben succeeds at school by virtue of hard work.*
as a result of, because of, by dint of, on account of, thanks to

visible 1
adjective able to be seen » *Wait until the signal becomes visible before crossing the road.*
clear, conspicuous, distinguishable, in sight, observable, perceptible
antonym: **invisible**

Jude ate the popsicle with visible enjoyment.

visible 2
adjective noticeable or evident » *Jude ate the popsicle with visible enjoyment.*
apparent, evident, manifest, noticeable, obvious, plain, conspicuous, discernible, patent

vision 1
noun a mental picture in which you imagine things » *My vision of the future includes flying cars.*
conception, daydream, dream, fantasy, ideal, image

My vision of the future includes flying cars.

vision 2
noun the ability to imagine future developments » *Lisa had a vision for her science project—it was going to be amazing!*
foresight, imagination, insight, intuition

Wait until the signal becomes visible before crossing the road.

vision 3
noun an experience in which you see things others cannot » *Lily was convinced her visions of fairies were real.*
apparition, hallucination, illusion, mirage, phantom, spectre, phantasm, wraith

visit 1
verb to go to see and spend time with someone » *Simon visited his brother in North Bay.*
call on, go to see, look up

visit 2
noun a trip to see a person or place » *Helen had recently paid her aunt a visit.*
call, stay, stop

vital 1
adjective necessary or very important » *As the goal-scorer, Sam played a vital role in winning the game.*
central, critical, crucial, essential, important, indispensable, necessary, pivotal

vital 2
adjective energetic and full of life » *The dog was old, but it was vital and full of energy.*
active, dynamic, energetic, lively, spirited, sprightly, vivacious
antonym: **dull**

The dog was old, but it was vital and full of energy.

vomit
verb to have food and drink come back up through the mouth » *Any product made from milk made Andrea vomit.*
be sick, heave, hurl (informal), **regurgitate**

The staff took a vote on whether to move offices.

vote 1
noun a decision made by allowing people to state their preference » *The staff took a vote on whether to move offices.*
ballot, plebiscite (formal), **polls, referendum**

vote 2
verb to indicate a choice or opinion » *Many people voted for the new candidate in this year's election.*
cast a vote, choose, elect, go to the polls, opt, return

vote 3
verb to suggest that something should happen » *I vote that we go to the theme park.*
propose, recommend, suggest

vulgar 1
adjective socially unacceptable or offensive » *Adam was told off for using vulgar language in front of his little brother.*
coarse, rude, uncouth, improper, unrefined
antonym: **refined**

vulgar 2
adjective showing a lack of taste or quality » *My mom says it's vulgar to boast about how much money you have.*
common, gaudy, tasteless, tawdry
antonym: **sophisticated**

vulnerable
adjective weak and without protection » *In the wild, newborn animals are especially vulnerable to predators.*
exposed, sensitive, susceptible, weak, assailable, defenceless, unprotected

244

Ww

wait 1
verb to spend time before something happens » We waited all evening for Elizabeth to arrive.
linger, pause, remain, stand by, stay

wait 2
noun a period of time before something happens » The passengers faced a three-hour wait for the next train.
delay, interval, pause

wake
verb to make or become conscious again after sleep » It was still dark when Fred woke early that morning.
awake, come to, rouse, stir, waken

walk 1
verb to go on foot
▼ SEE BELOW

Let's take a quick walk before it rains.

walk 2
noun a journey made by walking » Let's take a quick walk before it rains.
hike, march, ramble, stroll, trek, constitutional, perambulation, saunter

walk 3
noun the way someone moves when walking » Although Sid was far away, I recognized him from his walk.
carriage, gait, pace, stride

wander
verb to move about in a casual way » The tourists wandered aimlessly around the village.
cruise, drift, ramble, range, roam, stroll

want 1
verb to feel a desire for something » I want a red car, for a change.
covet, crave, desire, wish

want 2
noun a lack of something » Phil started to feel weak from want of food.
absence, deficiency, lack, scarcity, shortage, dearth, insufficiency, paucity
antonym: **abundance**

war 1
noun a period of armed conflict between countries » The war dragged on for five years.
combat, conflict, fighting, hostilities, strife, warfare
antonym: **peace**
related words: *adjectives* **belligerent, martial**

war 2
verb to fight against something » The two countries had been warring with each other for years.
battle, clash, combat, fight

warm 1
adjective having some heat but not hot » It was a warm spring day.
balmy, heated, lukewarm, mild, pleasant, tepid
antonym: **cold**

warm 2
adjective friendly and affectionate » Jane has a warm and likable personality.
affectionate, amiable, cordial, friendly, genial, loving
antonym: **unfriendly**

warm 3
verb to heat something gently » The sun came out and warmed his back.
heat, heat up, melt, thaw, warm up
antonym: **cool**

warn
verb to give advance notice of something unpleasant » I warned Sam that he might slip on the wet floor.
alert, caution, forewarn, notify, admonish, apprise

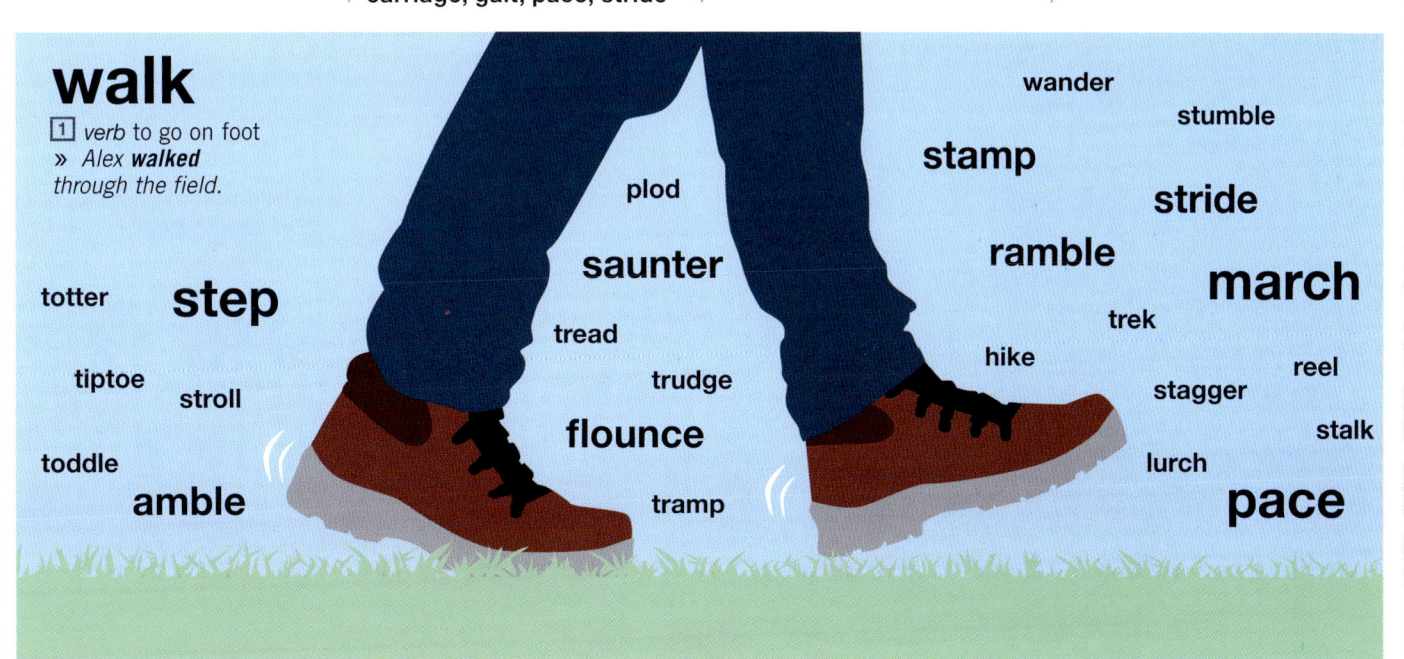

---

walk
1 *verb* to go on foot » Alex walked through the field.

totter, step, tiptoe, stroll, toddle, amble, plod, saunter, tread, trudge, flounce, tramp, stamp, ramble, hike, wander, stumble, stride, trek, march, stagger, reel, lurch, stalk, pace

watch

2 *verb* to look at something for some time » *He liked to watch distant objects through his binoculars.*

gaze at
A clear night is the best time to gaze at the stars.

observe
Scientists observed the experiment.

look at
Come and look at what's going on in the garden!

pay attention to
The teacher told her class to pay attention to the board.

view
He viewed the latest videos online.

see
We went to see his latest movie.

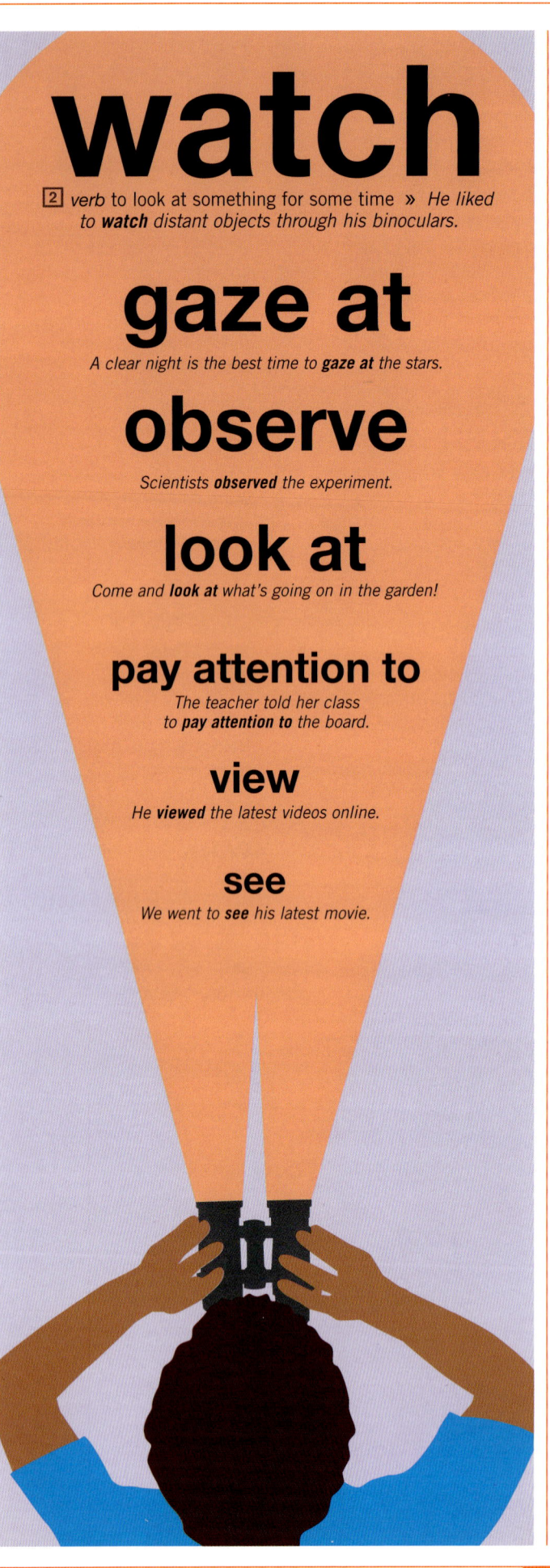

---

warning
noun something that tells people of possible danger » *We had warning of the flood, so were able to protect our house.*
alarm, alert, caution, notice, premonition, augury, caveat, presage

wary
adjective showing lack of trust in something » *Deer are usually wary of people.*
cautious, distrustful, guarded, suspicious, vigilant, chary, circumspect, heedful

Deer are usually wary of people.

wash 1
verb to clean something with water » *Pete got a job washing dishes.*
bathe, cleanse, launder, rinse, scrub, shampoo

wash 2
verb to carry something by the force of water » *Large clumps of seaweed were washed ashore by the waves.*
carry off, erode, sweep away

waste 1
verb to use too much of something unnecessarily » *I wouldn't waste my money on junk like that.*
blow (informal), **fritter away, squander, throw away**
antonym: **save**

waste 2
noun using something excessively or unnecessarily » *What a complete waste of money!*
extravagance, misuse, squandering, dissipation, misapplication

waste 3
adjective not needed or wanted » *The floor was covered in waste paper by the time she finally decided what to write.*
leftover, scrap, superfluous, unused, dross

wasteful
adjective using something in a careless or extravagant way » *He has a wasteful habit of leaving all the lights on.*
extravagant, uneconomical, improvident, profligate, spendthrift
antonym: **thrifty**

watch 1
noun a period of time when a guard is kept on something » *Keep a close watch on the cake so the dog doesn't eat it.*
observation, supervision, surveillance, vigilance, **watchfulness**

watch 2
verb to look at something for some time
◀◀ SEE LEFT

watch 3
verb to look after something » *You must watch the baby carefully.*
guard, look after, mind, take care of, tend to

You must watch the baby carefully.

246

wear out

Watch out for the lamp post!

watch out
verb to be careful or alert for something » *Watch out for the lamp post!*
be alert, be watchful, keep your eyes open, look out

waterfall
noun a place where a river falls over a steep cliff » *The noise of the waterfall was deafening.*
cascade, cataract, chute, fall

wave 1
verb to move or flap to and fro » *The supporters waved their scarves in the air.*
brandish, flap, flourish, flutter, shake, oscillate, undulate

wave 2
noun a ridge of water on the surface of the sea » *The surfer paddled frantically to catch the wave.*
breaker, ripple, swell

wave 3
noun an increase in a type of activity » *He felt a sudden wave of panic at the thought of the exam the next day that he had not prepared for.*
flood, movement, outbreak, rush, surge, trend, upsurge

way 1
noun a manner of doing something » *Freezing is an excellent way to preserve food.*
approach, manner, means, method, practice, procedure, technique

way 2
noun the customs or behaviour of a person or group » *I'll never get used to the way young people communicate.*
conduct, custom, manner, practice, style, idiosyncrasy, wont

way 3
noun a route taken to a particular place » *I can't remember the way.*
channel, course, lane, path, road, route

weak 1
adjective lacking in strength » *Carol felt weak after her illness.*
anemic, delicate, faint, feeble, frail, sickly, wasted, debilitated, decrepit, enervated, infirm
antonym: **strong**

Carol felt weak after her illness.

weak 2
adjective likely to break or fail » *The loft had a weak floor, so we had to tread carefully.*
deficient, faulty, fragile, inadequate

weak 3
adjective easily influenced by other people » *He is a weak man who can't say no to those around him.*
powerless, spineless, indecisive, irresolute
antonym: **resolute**

weaken
verb to make or become less strong » *Dad's difficulty in keeping a straight face weakened his authority.*
diminish, fail, flag, lessen, reduce, sap, undermine, wane, debilitate, enervate, mitigate
antonym: **strengthen**

weakness 1
noun a lack of physical or moral strength » *His main weakness is his bad temper.*
defect, flaw, fragility, frailty, imperfection, vulnerability, Achilles' heel, debility, infirmity
antonym: **strength**

weakness 2
noun a great liking for something » *Jess has a weakness for chocolate.*
fondness, liking, passion, penchant, partiality, predilection
antonym: **dislike**

wealth 1
noun a large amount of money » *Mr. Brown used his wealth to build several new schools.*
affluence, fortune, means, money, prosperity, riches, substance

wealth 2
noun a lot of something » *She found a wealth of information about the artist.*
abundance, bounty, plenty, store, copiousness, cornucopia, plenitude, profusion
antonym: **shortage**

wealthy
adjective having plenty of money » *Isabella came from a very wealthy background.*
affluent, comfortable, opulent, prosperous, rich, well-to-do, well-off
antonym: **poor**

The guard was wearing a blue uniform.

wear 1
verb to be dressed in something » *The guard was wearing a blue uniform.*
be clothed in, be dressed in, don, have on, put on, sport (informal)

wear 2
verb to become worse in condition with use or age » *The walls of the old building were worn in places.*
corrode, erode, fray, rub, wash away, abrade, deteriorate

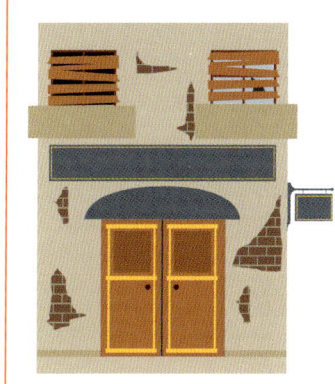

The walls of the old building were worn in places.

wear 3
noun the type of use which causes something to be damaged » *The old tires showed signs of wear.*
corrosion, deterioration, erosion, use, abrasion, attrition

wear out
verb to make someone tired » *The past few days have really worn me out.*
exhaust, tire, weary

weary
adjective very tired » *She sank to the ground, too weary to walk another step.*
beat (informal), **drained, exhausted, fatigued, pooped** (informal), **tired, tuckered out** (informal), **worn out**

weather
noun the condition of the atmosphere at a certain place and time » *What's the weather like today?*
climate, conditions
▶▶ SEE RIGHT

weird
adjective strange or odd » *I had a weird dream I could fly.*
bizarre, curious, extraordinary, funny, odd, peculiar, singular (formal), **strange**
antonym: **ordinary**

well 1
adverb in a satisfactory way » *The interview went well, so I hope I get in.*
satisfactorily, smoothly, splendidly, successfully

well 2
adverb with skill and ability » *She draws well—I wish I had her talent and dedication.*
ably, adequately, admirably, competently, effectively, efficiently, expertly, professionally, skilfully, adeptly, proficiently
antonym: **badly**

*She draws **well**—I wish I had her talent and dedication.*

well 3
adverb fully and with thoroughness » *She washed her hands well to get rid of the paint.*
amply, closely, completely, fully, highly, meticulously, rigorously, thoroughly

well 4
adverb in a kind way » *My boss is a good man and treats his employees well.*
compassionately, considerately, favourably, humanely, kindly, with consideration

well 5
adjective having good health » *I'm feeling very well today.*
fit, healthy, in good condition, in good health, robust, sound, strong, able-bodied, hale, in fine fettle
antonym: **sick**

wet 1
adjective in rainy weather conditions » *It was a miserable wet day.*
humid, misty, rainy, showery
antonym: **dry**

*It was a miserable **wet** day.*

wet 2
adjective covered in liquid » *Keep that wet dog away!*
damp, drenched, moist, saturated, soaked, sodden, soggy, waterlogged
antonym: **dry**

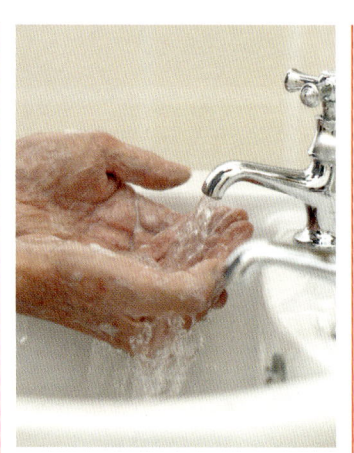

Wet your hands before applying soap.

wet 3
verb to put liquid on to something » *Wet your hands before applying soap.*
dampen, irrigate, moisten, soak, spray, water, drench, humidify, saturate
antonym: **dry**

whim
noun a sudden desire for something » *At the very last minute, we decided on a whim to go to the zoo.*
craze, fad (informal), **fancy, impulse, urge, caprice, vagary, whimsy**

white
noun or *adjective*
Shades of white:
alabaster, bleached, chalky, ivory, milky, pearly, snowy

whole 1
adjective indicating all of something » *We spent the whole summer abroad.*
complete, entire, full, total, uncut, undivided

whole 2
noun the full amount of something » *I would love to explore the whole of Canada.*
aggregate, all, everything, lot, sum total, total

wicked 1
adjective very bad or evil » *Stealing that watch was a wicked thing to do.*
atrocious, bad, depraved, evil, sinful, vicious, egregious, iniquitous, nefarious

wicked 2
adjective mischievous in an amusing or attractive way » *She always felt wicked when eating chocolate in bed.*
impish, mischievous, naughty

wide 1
adjective measuring a large distance from side to side » *The river was too wide to cross.*
ample, broad, expansive, extensive, full, immense, large, roomy, spacious, sweeping, vast, voluminous
antonym: **narrow**

wide 2
adjective extensive in scope » *The pencils came in a wide range of colours.*
ample, broad, comprehensive, encyclopedic, exhaustive, extensive, far-ranging, immense, inclusive, large, vast, wide-ranging
antonym: **narrow**

*The pencils came in a **wide** range of colours.*

weather
types of weather

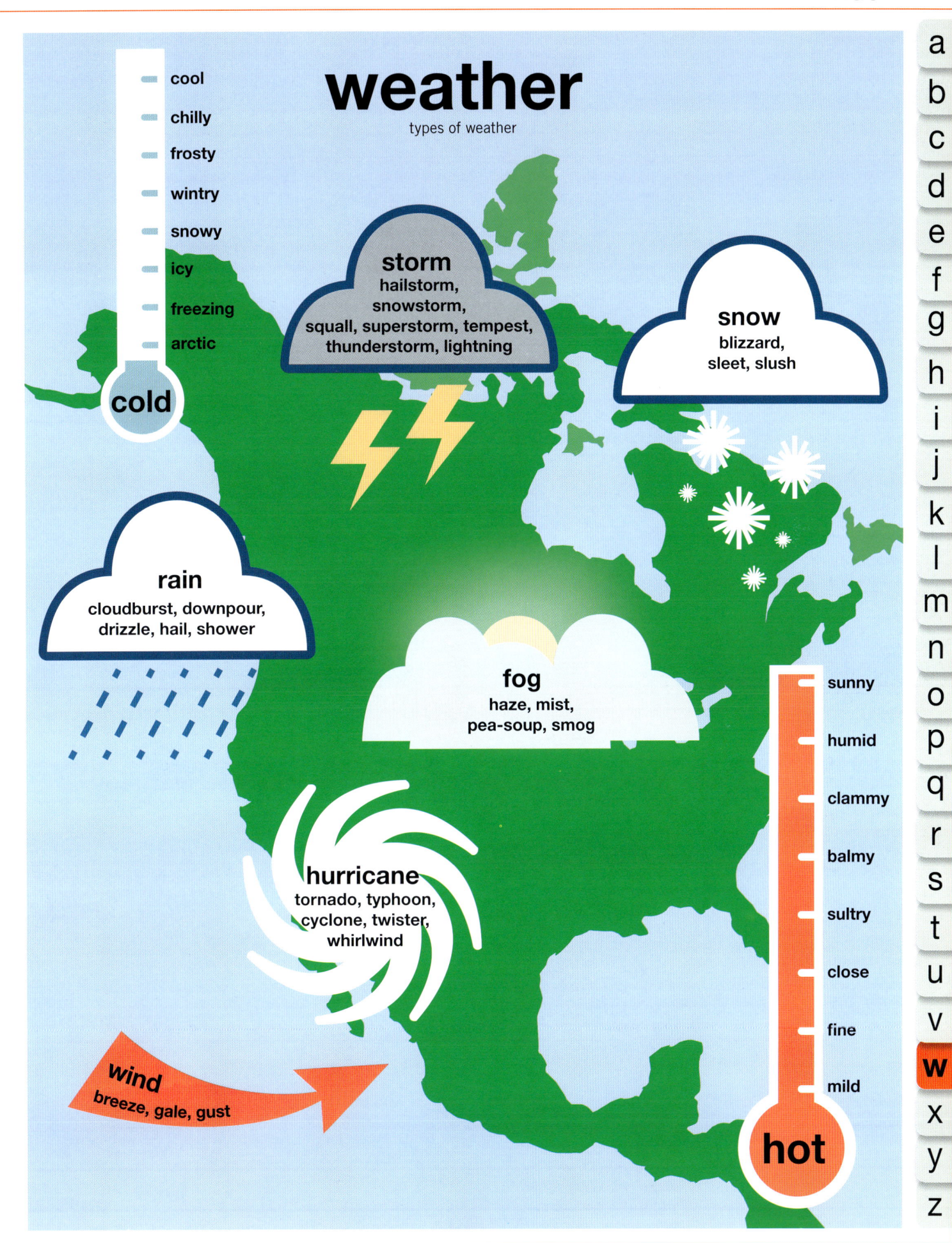

cold
- cool
- chilly
- frosty
- wintry
- snowy
- icy
- freezing
- arctic

storm
hailstorm, snowstorm, squall, superstorm, tempest, thunderstorm, lightning

snow
blizzard, sleet, slush

rain
cloudburst, downpour, drizzle, hail, shower

fog
haze, mist, pea-soup, smog

hurricane
tornado, typhoon, cyclone, twister, whirlwind

wind
breeze, gale, gust

hot
- sunny
- humid
- clammy
- balmy
- sultry
- close
- fine
- mild

» **wi**de

wonderful
[2] adjective very impressive
» The sunset was a truly **wonderful** sight.

incredible
The colours had **incredible** intensity.

remarkable
It was a **remarkable** achievement to capture the whole sunset in a photo.

amazing
It was **amazing** to be there at the exact moment the sun disappeared.

phenomenal
They would remember the **phenomenal** scene for years to come.

magnificent
There were **magnificent** views across the valley.

astounding
The view was **astounding**.

wondrous
The sky was decorated in **wondrous** colours.

wide [3]
adverb as far as possible
» The dentist asked Sal to open her mouth wide.
completely, fully

widespread
adjective existing over a large area » Food shortages were widespread during the war.
broad, common, extensive, pervasive, prevalent, rife

wild [1]
adjective not cultivated or domesticated » We went on a safari to see the wild animals.
free, free-range, natural, uncultivated, undomesticated, untamed

*The boat held its course despite the **wild** weather.*

wild [2]
adjective in stormy conditions » The boat held its course despite the wild weather.
howling, raging, rough, stormy, violent

wild [3]
adjective without control or restraint » The birthday girl was wild with excitement.
boisterous, rowdy, turbulent, uncontrolled, wayward, disorderly, riotous, uproarious

will [1]
noun the strong determination to achieve something » His will to win was stronger than the pain in his leg.
determination, purpose, resolution, resolve, willpower

will [2]
noun what someone wants » Against her mother's will, she went out.
choice, inclination, mind, volition, wish
related word:
adjective **voluntary**

will [3]
verb to leave something to someone when you die » He had willed his fortune to his daughter.
bequeath, leave, pass on

willing
adjective ready and eager to do something » The children were willing to learn.
agreeable, eager, game (informal)**, happy, prepared, ready,** amenable, compliant, desirous
antonym: **unwilling**

*The children were **willing** to learn.*

250

word »

She won the tournament after defeating her closest rival.

win 1
verb to defeat your opponents » *She won the tournament after defeating her closest rival.*
be victorious, come first, prevail, succeed, triumph
antonym: **lose**

win 2
verb to succeed in obtaining something » *Her wonderful cooking won her a prize.*
achieve, attain, gain, get, secure

win 3
noun a victory in a contest » *He has now suffered a run of seven games without a win.*
success, triumph, victory
antonym: **defeat**

winner
noun a person who wins something » *The competition winners all received prizes.*
champion, conqueror, victor
antonym: **loser**

wisdom
noun judgment used to make sensible decisions » *Grandparents have wisdom that comes from experience.*
discernment, insight, judgment, knowledge, reason, astuteness, erudition, sagacity
antonym: **foolishness**

wise
adjective able to make use of experience and judgment » *The professor is a wise old man.*
informed, judicious, perceptive, rational, sensible, shrewd
antonym: **foolish**

wish 1
noun a desire for something » *Val's wish was to become an actress.*
desire, hankering, hunger, longing, urge, want

wish 2
verb to want something » *Colin was bored and wished he could go home.*
desire, hanker for, hunger, long, pine for, thirst, want, yearn

withdraw 1
verb to take something out » *Si withdrew some money from the bank.*
extract, remove, take out

Si withdrew some money from the bank.

withdraw 2
verb to back out of an activity » *He withdrew from the team.*
back out, leave, pull out, retire, retreat, disengage, secede

wither 1
verb to become weaker and fade away » *Support for the government has withered since they shut the libraries.*
decline, fade

The sunflower withered from lack of water.

wither 2
verb to shrivel up and die » *The sunflower withered from lack of water.*
droop, shrivel, waste away, wilt

witness 1
noun someone who has seen something happen » *The police appealed for witnesses to come forward.*
bystander, eyewitness, observer, onlooker, spectator

witness 2
verb to see something happening » *Anyone who witnessed the incident should call the police.*
be present at, observe, see, watch

witty
adjective amusing in a clever way » *He's so witty, I could listen to him for hours.*
amusing, brilliant, clever, funny, humorous, sparkling

woman
noun an adult female human being » *The audience was made up mostly of women.*
dame (slang), female, girl, lady, lass
antonym: **man**

wonder 1
verb to think about something with curiosity » *I wondered what the strange noise was.*
ask yourself, ponder, puzzle, speculate

wonder 2
verb to be surprised and amazed » *He wondered at her great confidence on stage.*
be amazed, be astonished, boggle, marvel

wonder 3
noun something that amazes people » *The migration of monarch butterflies is one of the wonders of nature.*
marvel, miracle, phenomenon, spectacle

wonderful 1
adjective extremely good » *It's wonderful to see you.*
excellent, great (informal), marvellous, superb, tremendous

wonderful 2
adjective very impressive
◀◀ SEE LEFT

word 1
noun a remark » *I'd like to say a word of thanks to everyone who helped me.*
comment, remark, statement, utterance

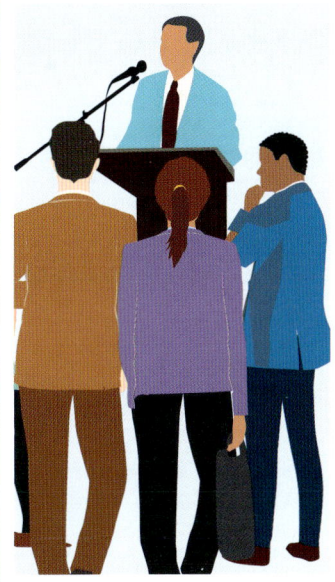

I'd like to say a word of thanks to everyone who helped me.

word 2
noun a brief conversation » *James, could I have a quick word with you?*
chat, conversation, discussion, talk

word

word [3]
noun a message » *We've had no word from our neighbours since they went abroad.*
announcement, bulletin, communication, information, intelligence, message, news

word [4]
noun a promise or guarantee » *Phil gave me his word that he would be there.*
assurance, oath, pledge, promise, word of honour

work [1]
verb to do the tasks required of you » *I work 12 hours a day.*
labour, slave, slog away, toil
antonym: **laze**

work [2]
noun someone's job » *Vicky's work involves travelling abroad each week.*
business, craft, employment, job, livelihood, occupation, profession, calling, métier, pursuit

work [3]
noun the tasks that have to be done » *Sometimes George had to take work home.*
assignment, chore, duty, job, task

Sometimes George had to take work home.

worker
noun a person who works
▼ SEE BELOW

work out [1]
verb to find the solution to something » *It took us some time to work out the answer to the puzzle.*
calculate, figure out, resolve, solve

work out [2]
verb to happen in a certain way » *It worked out that we could get to the theatre after all.*
develop, go, happen, turn out

worn-out [1]
adjective no longer usable because of extreme wear » *The marathon runner threw away her worn-out running shoes.*
broken-down, tattered, threadbare, worn

worn out [2]
adjective extremely tired » *You must be worn out after the long journey.*
exhausted, fatigued, prostrate, tired, weary

*Rebecca was **worried** about her presentation the next day.*

worried
adjective being anxious about something » *Rebecca was worried about her presentation the next day.*
anxious, bothered, concerned, nervous, troubled, uneasy, overwrought, perturbed, unquiet
antonym: **unconcerned**

---

worker
noun a person who works » *He got a job as a farm worker for the summer.*

businesswoman
*The **businesswoman** ran a successful company.*

employee
*The store's **employees** had a competition to see who could serve the most customers.*

artisan
*Local **artisans** displayed their handmade goods, from bread to pots.*

craftswoman
*The **craftswoman** created kitchen cabinets and furniture.*

wrong

worry 1
verb to feel anxious about something » *Don't worry, I'll help you with your work.*
be anxious, brood, feel uneasy, fret

worry 2
verb to disturb someone with a problem » *I didn't want to worry you with my homework.*
bother, hassle (informal), pester, plague, trouble, harry, importune, perturb

worry 3
noun a feeling of anxiety » *Lack of money was a worry.*
anxiety, apprehension, concern, fear, misgiving, unease

worsen
verb to become more difficult » *My dog's behaviour has worsened—now he's chewing the furniture.*
decline, degenerate, deteriorate, go downhill (informal)
antonym: **improve**

worship 1
verb to praise and revere something » *The ancient Egyptians worshipped many gods.*
glorify, honour, praise, pray to, venerate, deify, exalt, revere
antonym: **dishonour**

worship 2
verb to love and admire someone » *Your little sister worships you.*
adore, idolize, love
antonym: **despise**

worship 3
noun a feeling of love and admiration for something » *The emperor was used to the worship of his subjects.*
admiration, adoration, adulation, devotion, homage, praise, deification, exaltation

worthless
adjective having no real value or worth » *Why did you buy that worthless piece of junk?*
meaningless, paltry, poor, trifling, trivial, useless, valueless, negligible
antonym: **valuable**

write
verb to record something in writing » *Write your answers in pencil on the page.*
inscribe, record, take down

Write your answers in pencil on the page.

wrong 1
adjective not correct or truthful » *The girl on the game show gave the wrong answer and was knocked out of the competition.*
false, faulty, incorrect, mistaken, unsound, untrue, erroneous, fallacious
antonym: **right**

wrong 2
adjective morally unacceptable » *It's wrong to hurt people.*
bad, evil, illegal, immoral, unfair, unjust, felonious, iniquitous, reprehensible, unethical
antonym: **right**

wrong 3
noun an unjust action » *A great wrong has been done to him in the past.*
abuse, crime, grievance, injustice, sin

---

labourer
There were at least 10 **labourers** on the building site.

operative
The production line would break down without good machine **operatives**.

hand
The farm employed extra **hands** when it was time to harvest the vegetables.

workman
The **workman** came to fix the pipe.

Yy

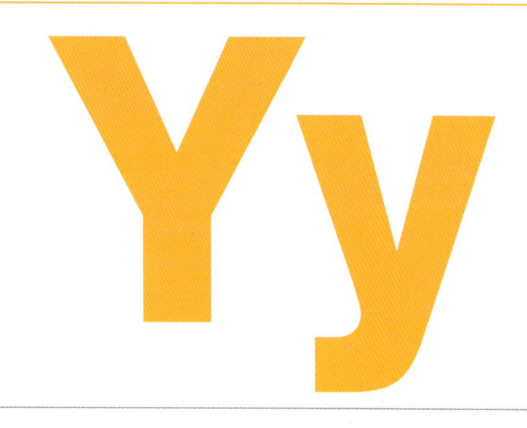

yell ①
verb to shout loudly, usually because you are excited, angry, or in pain » *Tom yelled in delight on winning the handpainting competition.*
bellow, cheer, cry, cry out, roar, shout, scream, yell out

Tom yelled in delight on winning the handpainting competition.

yell ②
noun a loud, piercing cry of fear, anger, or pain » *She let out a yell as something brushed past her in the haunted house.*
cry, howl, scream, screech, shriek, whoop

yellow
noun or *adjective*
Shades of yellow:
amber, canary yellow, citrus yellow, daffodil, gold, lemon, mustard, primrose, saffron, sand, straw, topaz

yes
interjection an expression used to agree with something or say it is true
▼ SEE BELOW

young ①
adjective not yet mature » *The campsite was full of young people.*
adolescent, immature, infant, junior, juvenile, little, youthful
antonym: **old**

The campsite was full of young people.

young ②
plural noun the babies an animal has » *Cats carry their young by the scruff of their necks.*
babies, brood, family, litter, little ones, offspring

Cats carry their young by the scruff of their necks.

Do you want to go to the swimming pool?

Yes, I want to go to the pool!

Sure, I'd love to come.

Yeah, I love swimming.

All right, count me in.

Of course, let's go!

Okay, thanks. I really like the slides there.

antonym: **No.** I hate getting my hair wet.

interjection an expression used to agree with something or say it is true

254

Zz

The added orange gave zest to the sauce.

zoo
noun a large place where different types of wild animals are kept, usually enclosed, for people to see them
▼ SEE BELOW

zoom
verb to move very fast
» *The car zoomed past before I could see who was driving it.*
bolt, dart, dash, flash, hurry, race, rocket, rush, sail, scoot, soar, speed, streak, zip

zero
noun nothing or the number 0
» *The temperature showing on the thermometer was zero.*
nada, nil, nothing, nought

The temperature showing on the thermometer was zero.

zest [1]
noun enthusiasm and energy
» *Grandma had great zest for life.*
appetite, eagerness, enjoyment, enthusiasm, excitement, gusto, joy, passion, relish

zest [2]
noun flavour » *The added orange gave zest to the sauce.*
flavour, piquancy, pungency, spice, tang, taste

zone
noun an area separated off for a purpose » *If you park in the free-parking zone you don't have to pay.*
area, district, locality, neighbourhood, region

The car zoomed past before I could see who was driving it.

---

safari park

wildlife park

aviary

menagerie

zoological gardens

aquarium

petting zoo

ZOO
noun a large place where different types of wild animals are kept, usually enclosed, for people to see them
» *We went to the zoo to see all the animals.*

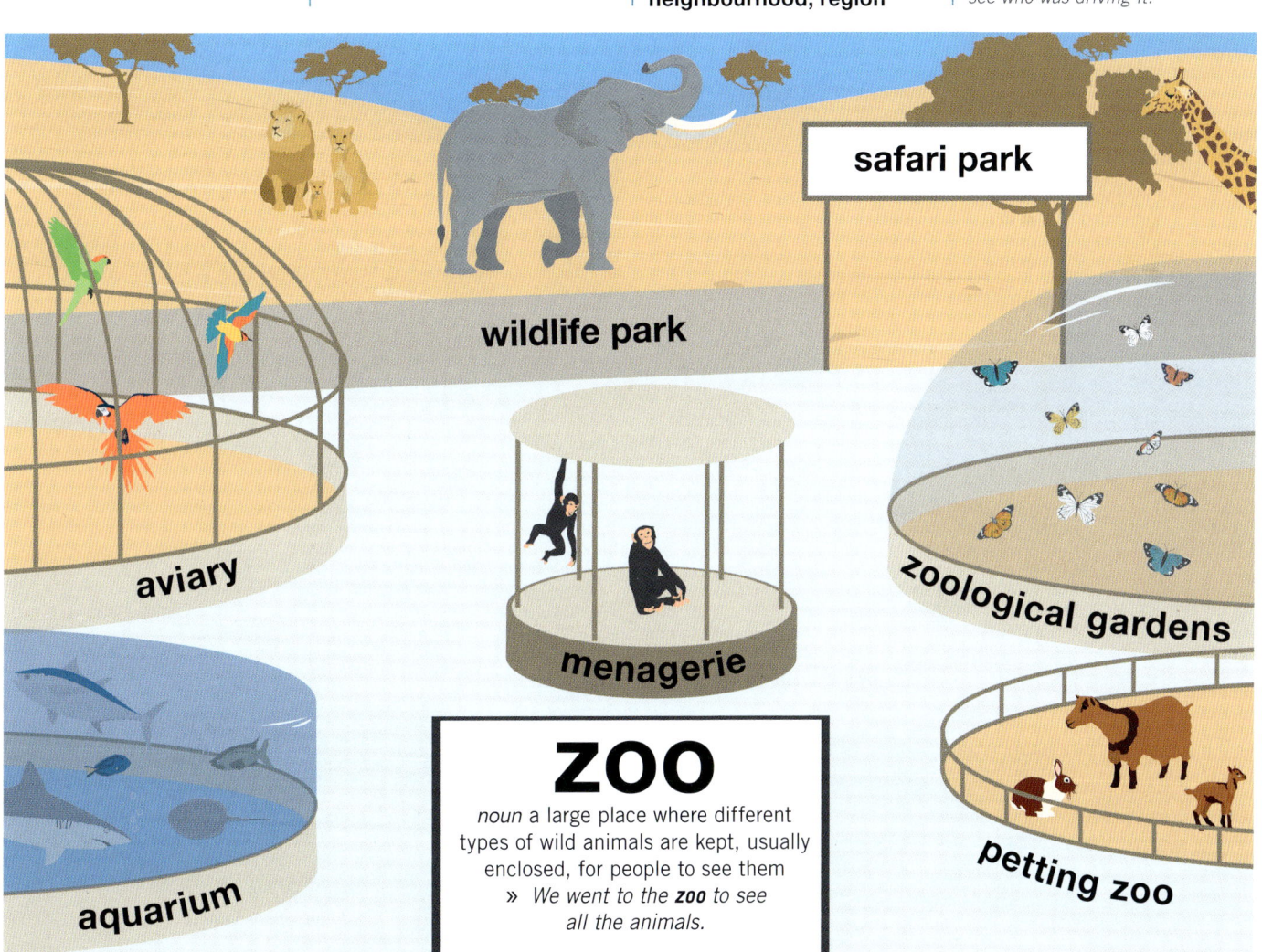

Acknowledgements

Dorling Kindersley would like to thank the following people for their help in the production of this book:

Additional editorial assistance
Sugandha Agarwal, Nandini Gupta, and Sonia Yooshing

Additional technical assistance
Ruchi Bansal and Rachana Kishore

Picture agency credits
KEY: a-above; b-below/bottom; c-centre; f-far; l-left; r-right; t-top.
The publisher would like to thank the following for their kind permission to reproduce their photographs:

2 **123RF.com:** Kanvag (bl). 6 **123RF.com:** Sergey Novikov (cra). 7 **123RF.com:** jahmaica (ca); Ksenia Raykova (cr); Luiscarceller (cla); Shao-Chun Wang (cb). **Dreamstime.com:** Justin Skinner (clb). 10 **Dreamstime.com:** Lasse Kristensen (bl). 11 **Dreamstime.com:** Ana Blazic Pavlovic (cla). 15 **Dreamstime.com:** Michal Bednarek (cla). 16 **Dreamstime.com:** Edward J Bock 111 (tr); Katrina Brown (tl). 18 **Dreamstime.com:** Photographerlondon (cb). 20 **Dorling Kindersley:** Anthony Posner. Hendon Way Motors (c). 21 **123RF.com:** Stephen Coburn (cl). **Alamy Stock Photo:** Fabian Bimmer (tr). **iStockphoto.com:** Eugenio Marongiu (br). 23 **Dreamstime.com:** Valentin Armianu (tc). **iStockphoto.com:** kirstypargeter (br). 24 **123RF.com:** Federico Rostagno / ilfede (tr). 25 **123RF.com:** Maryna Pleshkun (cb). 26 **123RF.com:** gabe123 (bl). 27 **123RF.com:** Olga Chirkova (crb). **Dreamstime.com:** Mallivan (bc). 28 **123RF.com:** xalanx (clb). **Dreamstime.com:** Epicstock (tc). 29 **123RF.com:** auremar (c). 30 **Alamy Stock Photo:** Horizon (cb/dog). **Dreamstime.com:** Nexus7 (ca); Stef22 (cb). **iStockphoto.com:** urbancow (tl). 32 **Dreamstime.com:** Gordon Miller (bc); Photographerlondon (cl). 33 **123RF.com:** besjunior (bc). **Alamy Stock Photo:** Martyn Williams (cra). **Dreamstime.com:** Brett Critchley (bc). 34 **123RF.com:** ptnphoto (cla). 37 **Alamy Stock Photo:** Bob Elsdale (br). **Dorling Kindersley:** Christopher Pillitz (cb). 38 **Dreamstime.com:** Nilanjan Bhattacharya (cr). 39 **123RF.com:** Anna Bizon / gpointstudio (ca). **Dreamstime.com:** Tyler Olson (cb). 40 **123RF.com:** Ivan Kuznetsov (clb). **Dreamstime.com:** Jens Tobiska (cb). 41 **iStockphoto.com:** wakila (clb). 43 **123RF.com:** Comaniciu Dan (tr). **Dreamstime.com:** Branislav Ostojic (ca). **Getty Images:** Vasiliki Varvaki (cb). 44 **Dreamstime.com:** Breadmaker (cb). **iStockphoto.com:** wdstock (cr). 46 **Dreamstime.com:** Waihs (cr). **iStockphoto.com:** apCincy (bc). 47 **123RF.com:** Alexey Filatov (tc); Andriy Popov (c). **Alamy Stock Photo:** moodboard (clb). 48 **123RF.com:** Cathy Yeulet (cra). **Dreamstime.com:** Razvan Ionut Dragomirescu (cb). 49 **123RF.com:** luchschen (tr). **Dreamstime.com:** Manfredxy (cb). 50 **123RF.com:** maridav (clb). 52 **Dreamstime:** Piksel (crb). 53 **123RF.com:** Thomas Fikar (bc). 54 **Dreamstime.com:** Nagy-bagoly Ilona (cb). 55 **123RF.com:** Karel Joseph Noppe Brooks (ca). **Alamy Stock Photo:** Ben Cranke (tr). 56 **Dorling Kindersley:** University of Pennsylvania Museum of Archaeology and Anthropology (cb). **Dreamstime.com:** Gustavo Andrade (tr). 57 **Dreamstime.com:** Eric Gevaert (tc); Ryan Stevenson (clb). 58 **Dreamstime.com:** Feverpitched (cb). 59 **Alamy Stock Photo:** Jamie Grill (cl). 60 **Dreamstime.com:** Jose Manuel Gelpi Diaz (bc); Redbaron (tc). 62 **123RF.com:** blueone (cb). **Dreamstime.com:** Isselee (crb); Michal Kaco (cb). 64 **Dreamstime.com:** Stefano Armaroli (cr); Paulus Rusyanto (cla). 65 **Dreamstime.com:** Thandra (cl). 67 **Alamy Stock Photo:** D Core / Ocean (c/sand castle). **Dreamstime.com:** Cristian Borod (c). 69 **Dreamstime.com:** Derektenhue (cra). 71 **123RF.com:** Zoran Orcik (tc). 73 **Dreamstime.com:** Jorg Hackemann (tc). 74 **123RF.com:** Stanislav Bokser (br). 76 **Alamy Stock Photo:** Chris Robbins (c). 77 **123RF.com:** rawpixel (tc). **iStockphoto.com:** michaeljung (c). 78 **123RF.com:** Anthony Totah (cl). **Dreamstime.com:** Katarzyna Bialasiewicz (cb). 80 **123RF.com:** awrangler (cb). 81 **Dreamstime.com:** Gvictoria (ca). 82 **123RF.com:** Elena Moiseeva (c); Theartofphoto (cr). **Dreamstime.com:** Sean Nel (tc). 83 **123RF.com:** Taras Kushnir (cb); Quangpraha (b). 84 **123RF.com:** Oleksii Sidorov (tr); Yarruta (clb); Tinna2727 (tc). 85 **123RF.com:** Cathy Yeulet (cb). **Dreamstime.com:** Gsphotography (clb). 86 **123RF.com:** Ian Allenden (tr); Tatsiana Yatsevich (ca). **iStockphoto.com:** Blackwaterimages (cb). 87 **Dreamstime.com:** Pixattitude (cr). 88 **Dreamstime.com:** Marianne Campolongo (c); Olga Vasilkova (cb). 89 **123RF.com:** Payphoto (tl). 90 **Dreamstime.com:** Sonya Etchison (c). 91 **Dreamstime.com:** Liubirong (ca). 93 **Dreamstime.com:** Olesia Bilkei (tc); Haveseen (cla); Photographerlondon (cb). 94 **123RF.com:** Dean Drobot (br). **Dreamstime.com:** Brett Critchley (cb). **Getty Images:** Robert Daly (bc). 95 **123RF.com:** Antonio Guillem (crb); Rubisco (clb). 96 **123RF.com:** Serezniy (ca). 98 **Alamy Stock Photo:** Duncan Usher (ca). **Dreamstime.com:** Marcel De Grijs (cr); Martin Novak (bl). 99 **Alamy Stock Photo:** Mandygodbehear (ca). 100 **Dreamstime.com:** Shae Cardenas (c). 101 **Dreamstime.com:** Jose Manuel Gelpi Diaz (cl); Denis Raev (tc). **iStockphoto.com:** Serge-Kazakov (bc). 102 **Dreamstime.com:** Pablo Caridad (bc); Jonathan Ross (bl). 103 **123RF.com:** Graham Oliver (br). **Dreamstime.com:** Andreeacoman (cb). 104 **Dreamstime.com:** Jean Paul Chassenet (cla); Dmitry Kalinovsky (bc). 105 **iStockphoto.com:** Kaarsten (c). 106 **Dreamstime.com:** Katarzyna Bialasiewicz (crb). 109 **iStockphoto.com:** PeopleImages (cla). 110 **123RF.com:** Inspirestock International (Exclusive Contributor&#x (tc). **iStockphoto.com:** Tagstock1 (cb). 112 **Alamy Stock Photo:** Capt.digby (c). **Dreamstime.com:** Piksel (tr). 114 **123RF.com:** Otnaydur (br); Pahham (tc). 117 **Getty Images:** Morsa Images (ca). **iStockphoto.com:** Betty4240 (c). 119 **Dreamstime.com:** Thierry Vialard (tc). 120 **Dreamstime.com:** Mato750 (cl); Paulus Rusyanto (cb). 122 **123RF.com:** Langstrup (tc). **Alamy Stock Photo:** Nik Taylor (clb). 126 **Dreamstime.com:** Robert Crum (c). 127 **Getty Images:** Dave King (tr). 128 **Dreamstime.com:** Voyagerix (cb). 133 **Dreamstime.com:** Mathew Hayward (tc). 134 **Dreamstime.com:** Tamara Bauer (br). 136 **Dreamstime.com:** Monkey Business Images (cla). 137 **Alamy Stock Photo:** Ian Allenden (cra). 138 **Dreamstime.com:** Monkey Business Images (tl); Wavebreakmedia Ltd (c). 139 **123RF.com:** Monika Wisniewska (crb). **Alamy Stock Photo:** IS-200703 (tc). **Dreamstime.com:** Wavebreakmedia Ltd (cr). 140 **iStockphoto.com:** FatCamera (cb). 143 **123RF.com:** Nagy-Bagoly Ilona (br). **Dreamstime.com:** Lamai Prasitsuwan (cb). 144 **Dreamstime.com:** Dean Drobot (tc); Darrin Henry (cr). **iStockphoto.com:** Ljupco (fcr). 146 **123RF.com:** Hongqi Zhang (ca). **Dreamstime.com:** Lio2012 (bc). 148 **Dreamstime.com:** Sophiejames (cra). 149 **123RF.com:** Tiago Fernandez (crb). **Dreamstime.com:** Cheryl Casey (tc). 150 **Alamy Stock Photo:** Peter Bennett (crb). 151 **iStockphoto.com:** Jashlock (c). 152 **123RF.com:** Roman Samokhin (crb). 153 **123RF.com:** Liorpt (br). **iStockphoto.com:** Xavierarnau (bl). 154 **Alamy Stock Photo:** SJH Photography (cra). 155 **Dreamstime.com:** Dastin50 (tr); Monkey Business Images (cb). 156 **Dreamstime.com:** Kiosea39 (clb); Kim Reinick (cr). 157 **123RF.com:** Nebojsa Markovic (cr). **Alamy Stock Photo:** Randy Green (c). 158 **123RF.com:** Anelina (bl). **Alamy Stock Photo:** Tim Gainey (cb). 159 **Dreamstime.com:** Gale Verhague (c). 161 **Alamy Stock Photo:** ImageGB (cb); Vast Photography (tl). **Dreamstime.com:** Wavebreakmedia Ltd (c). 163 **123RF.com:** thamkc (crb). **iStockphoto.com:** deepblue4you (bl). 165 **Dreamstime.com:** Davidmartyn (cb). 166 **iStockphoto.com:** Kali9 (tl). 168 **Dreamstime.com:** Evemilla (tl). 170 **123RF.com:** Wavebreak Media Ltd (c). **Dreamstime.com:** Steve Allen (clb). 171 **Dreamstime.com:** Ldprod (cb); Vladimir Mudrovcic (tr). 173 **Alamy Stock Photo:** Alexander Caminada (clb). **Dreamstime.com:** Błażej Łyjak (crb); Peanutroaster (c); Vadymvdrobot (tc). 174 **Dreamstime.com:** Djem82 (br). 175 **Alamy Stock Photo:** Simon Belcher (c). 176 **iStockphoto.com:** PeopleImages (c). 177 **123RF.com:** Dean Drobot (c). **Dreamstime.com:** Monkey Business Images Ltd (tc). 178 **Alamy Stock Photo:** Finnbarr Webster (c). 179 **123RF.com:** Viacheslav Nikolaienko (cr). **Dreamstime.com:** Mystock88photo (ca); Eva Vargyasi (bc). **iStockphoto.com:** PeopleImages (bl). 181 **123RF.com:** Wichan Sumalee (cr). **iStockphoto.com:** JackF (bc). 183 **123RF.com:** Leung Cho Pan (tl). **Dreamstime.com:** Monkey Business Images (crb). 185 **Dreamstime.com:** Helen Hotson (ca). **iStockphoto.com:** Eugenesergeev (cra). 186 **Dreamstime.com:** Steve AllenUK (cb). 187 **Dreamstime.com:** Aleksandar Mijatovic (tc). **Dreamstime.com:** Jaromír Chalabala (crb); Joseph Golby (ca). 188 **Alamy Stock Photo:** Kim Karpeles (cb). **Dreamstime.com:** Wundervisuals (bc). 191 **123RF.com:** Vesilvio (tr); Anastasy Yarmolovich (bl). **Dorling Kindersley:** Fleur Star (bc). **Dreamstime.com:** Tsomka (cb). 192 **Dreamstime.com:** Thanthima Limsakul (cla). 193 **Dreamstime.com:** Pawel Kowalczyk (tc). 194 **Dreamstime.com:** Abdone (ca); Kungverylucky (tr). 195 **Dorling Kindersley:** Jerry Young (tr). 197 **123RF.com:** wckiw (cla). **Dreamstime.com:** Michael Courtney (tc); Mario Kelichhaus (cra). 198 **Dreamstime.com:** dolgachov (bc). **Dreamstime.com:** Corepics Vof (tc). 199 **123RF.com:** Iakov Filimonov (cr). 200 **123RF.com:** Jose Manuel Gelpi Diaz (bc); Wavebreak Media Ltd (crb). **Dreamstime.com:** Tatiana Dyuvbanova (tl). 201 **123RF.com:** (crb). **Dreamstime.com:** Puhhha (tc). **iStockphoto.com:** fstop123 (bl). 202 **123RF.com:** Kanvag (tc). **Dorling Kindersley:** Bethany Dawn Collection (c). 203 **123RF.com:** Volodymyr Nikulin (cr). **Alamy Stock Photo:** Hero Images (cl); Mike Kemp (c). 204 **123RF.com:** paleka (br); tobkatrina (cl). **Alamy Stock Photo:** Steve Hamblin (tc). **Dreamstime.com:** Nikita Rogul (cl). 207 **Alamy Stock Photo:** Adrian Sherratt (c). **Dreamstime.com:** Monkey Business Images (ca). 208 **Alamy Stock Photo:** moodboard (tl); Ellie Reed (c). 209 **123RF.com:** siraphat thanyaphuriwat (bl). 210 **123RF.com:** gopixa (cb). **Dreamstime.com:** Elena Elisseeva (cb). 211 **Dorling Kindersley:** Peter Cook Photography (tc). 212 **Alamy Stock Photo:** Richard Green (cb). 214 **123RF.com:** belchonock (cl); Iakov Filimonov (br). **Dreamstime.com:** Chris Lorenz (crb). 217 **Dreamstime.com:** Ampack (clb). 218 **Dorling Kindersley:** Stephen Oliver (c). **Dreamstime.com:** Tatonka (cr). 219 **Dorling Kindersley:** Pablo H. Caridad (tc). 220 **Dreamstime.com:** Glenda Powers (cb). 221 **123RF.com:** Kaleryna Levchenko (clb). **Dreamstime.com:** Luis Carlos Torres (tc); Lisa F. Young (cb). 222 **Dreamstime.com:** Grosescu Alberto (tl). **Alamy Stock Photo:** Corina Marie Howell (tc). 224 **Dreamstime.com:** Mykola Komarovskyy (bc). **Dreamstime.com:** Simone Van Den Berg (cr). 225 **Dreamstime.com:** Cathy Yeulet (tc). 226 **Dreamstime.com:** Diego Vito Cervo (tr). 228 **123RF.com:** Vladyslav Starozhylov (crb). 230 **123RF.com:** warrengoldswain (tl). **Dreamstime.com:** Alxcrs (tl). 231 **Dreamstime.com:** Lisa F. Young (tl). **iStockphoto.com:** subodhsathe (tl). 236 **Alamy Stock Photo:** Geoffrey Robinson (cr). 237 **Alamy Stock Photo:** Juniors Bildarchiv / F279 (cl). 239 **Alamy Stock Photo:** Jeremy Pembrey (c). 240 **Dreamstime.com:** Gstrange (ca); Zuzana Randlova (tl). 242 **Alamy Stock Photo:** Christophe Lehenaff (bc); Chris Ryan (cr). 243 **iStockphoto.com:** Delpixart (br). 244 **123RF.com:** Ksenia Raykova (crb). **Alamy Stock Photo:** IE131 (tc). 246 **123RF.com:** pat kullberg (ca). **iStockphoto.com:** SolStock (br). 250 **Dreamstime.com:** Ed Francissen (cb). 251 **123RF.com:** Weerachat Chatroopamai (tc). 254 **123RF.com:** Cathy Yeulet (ca). **Dreamstime.com:** Vallorie Francis (tr). 255 **123RF.com:** klotz (cla). **Dreamstime.com:** Rotarepok (cra)

All other images © Dorling Kindersley
For further information see: www.dkimages.com